HEALTH AND SOCIAL CARE

Published by Pearson Education Limited, Edinburgh Gate, Harlow, Essex, CM20 2JE.

www.pearsonschoolsandfecolleges.co.uk

Units 1, 2 and 8 © Pearson Education Limited 2012, Unit 11 © Pearson Education Limited 2013;
Units 3, 4, 5 and 7 © Liz Haworth 2012, Unit 9 © Liz Haworth 2013; Unit 6 © Siân Lavers 2012,
Units 10 and 12 © Siân Lavers 2013.
Typeset by Phoenix Photosetting, Chatham, Kent, UK
Original illustrations © Pearson Education Limited 2012, 2013
Illustrated by Vicky Woodgate and Phoenix Photosetting
Cover design by Pearson Education Limited and Andrew Magee Design
Front cover photo: Getty Images: Digital Vision
Indexing by Sophia Clapham.

The rights of Penelope Garnham, Liz Haworth, Heather Higgins and Siân Lavers to be identified as
authors of this work have been asserted by them in accordance with the Copyright, Designs and
Patents Act 1988.

Units 1-8 first published 2012.
This full edition published 2013.

16 15 14 13
10 9 8 7 6 5 4 3 2

British Library Cataloguing in Publication Data
A catalogue record for this book is available from the British Library

ISBN 978 1 446901 35 9

Printed and bound in Slovakia by Neografia

Websites
There are links to relevant websites in this book. In order to ensure that the links are up to date,
that the links works, and that the sites aren't inadvertently links to sites that could be considered
offensive, we have made the links available on our website at www.pearsonhotlinks.co.uk. Search for
the title BTEC First Health and Social Care Student Book or ISBN 978 1 446901 35 9.

Copies of official specifications for all Edexcel qualifications may be found on the Edexcel website:
www.edexcel.com

A note from the publisher
In order to ensure that this resource offers high-quality support for the associated BTEC qualification,
it has been through a review process by the awarding organisation to confirm that it fully covers the
teaching and learning content of the specification or part of a specification at which it is aimed, and
demonstrates an appropriate balance between the development of subject skills, knowledge and
understanding, in addition to preparation for assessment.
While the publishers have made every attempt to ensure that advice on the qualification and its
assessment is accurate, the official specification and associated assessment guidance materials are
the only authoritative source of information and should always be referred to for definitive guidance.
No material from an endorsed book will be used verbatim in any assessment set by BTEC.
Endorsement of a book does not mean that the book is required to achieve this BTEC qualification,
nor does it mean that it is the only suitable material available to support the qualification, and
any resource lists produced by the awarding organisation shall include this and other appropriate
resources.

Contents

Acknowledgements

I'd like to dedicate the five units of this book which I have written to my father, Trevor John Davis, who sadly died at the age of 90 in January 2012. His diverse experiences of health and social care in the last three years of his life, until when he had always been fit and active, and his courageous fight for life at the end, have given me much insight and inspiration. He and Mum have always been very supportive and proud of me and I miss him so much.

Liz Haworth.

Credits

The publisher would like to thank the following for their kind permission to reproduce their photographs:

(Key: b-bottom; c-centre; l-left; r-right; t-top)

Alamy Images: Beaconstox 145b, Blend Images 32, 127, BRT Food 144, BSIP SA 323, Corbis Bridge 171, Cultura Creative 268b, Fancy 139, 160, Fancy 139, 160, FogStock 33tr, Food Ingredients 145t, fStop 106, Glow Wellness 38, 39, Gordon Scammell 292b, INSADCO Photography 42, Janine Wiedel Photolibrary 276b, Jeff Gilbert 138, Carolyn Jenkins 108, Jonny Abbas 291, Medical-on-line 143tr, Paul Doyle 339, RubberBall 187, Science Photo Library 67, Yuri Arcurs 45t; **Corbis:** Lynnette Astaire 126, Pascal Deloche / Godong 179, Lester V. Bergman 269t; **Fotolia.com:** auremar 328b, Chad McDermott 213, dalaprod 274b, eurobanks 209, godfer 281, Jasmin Merdan 306b, Lisa F. Young 352b, Lsantilli 313, michaeljung 232, Monkey Business 284tl, 284br, picsfive 267, Sabphoto 280; **Getty Images:** altrendo images 347, Chris Whitehead 299, Jeffrey Coolidge 134t, Cultura / Frank and Helena 334b, Peter Dazeley 47, Douglas Menuez 329l, Huntstock 355, Barnabas Kindersley 177b, kristian sekulic 324b, PBNJ Productions 289b, Popperfoto 83, Monty Rakusen 183, Sam Diephuis 216b, tomprout 296b; **MindStudio:** 71; **Pearson Education Ltd:** Gareth Boden 29, Lord & Leverett 48, Jules Selmes 33tl, 33c, 52, 111, 288c, 321, 342b, Unit 2 (Banner), Unit 3 (Banner); **Pearson Education Ltd:** Stuart Cox 345, Studio 8 206; **Rex Features:** Rex Features 117; **Science Photo Library Ltd:** 289t, BIOPHOTO ASSOCIATES 143, Ian Boddy 148, LEA PATERSON 268c, POWER AND SYRED 233; **Shutterstock.com:** AISPIX by Image Source 40, Aletia 202, Alexander Raths 35, 203, Aliaksei Lasevich 6, Alsu 60, Andrey Sratilatov 20, Anetta 36, 149, Anetta 36, 149, Apollofoto 182, Yuri Arcurs 63, 188, 195, Yuri Arcurs 63, 188, 195, Auremar 45c, 215, AVAVA 33br, Blaj Gabriel 44, Bogdan Wankowicz Unit 6 (Banner), CREATISTA 157, Daria Filimonova 165, Dmitriy Shironosov 95, Sukharevskyy Dmytro 135b, Elena Kouptsova-Vasic 86, Fotokostic 18, Gelpi 121, Goodluz 100, Gyuszkofoto 177t, Helder Almeida 45b, Darrin Henry 28, 156, Darrin Henry 28, 156, Hinochika Unit 5 (Banner), Jason Stitt 261, Ken Hurst 285, Kevin Eaves 175, Lana K 56, Lisa F. Young 193, Littleny 123, Lofoto Unit 4 (Banner), Mangostock 114, Marcel Jancovic 41, Martin Novak 10, 85, Mary Hathaway 65, maska 140, Maxim Ibragimov 316b, Michael Higginson 189, Michaeljung 53, Michaelpuche 101, Mikhail Tchkheidze 72, Monkey Business Images 11, 12, 50, 77, 88, 109, 113, 119, 150, 153, 167, 225, Unit 1 (Banner), Unit 7 (Banner), Unit 8 (Banner), Monkey Business Images 11, 12, 50, 77, 88, 109, 113, 119, 150, 153, 167, 225, Unit 1 (Banner), Unit 7 (Banner), Unit 8 (Banner), monticello 135t, Morgan Lane Photography 130, muszy 46, Martin Novak 10, 85, oliveromg 62, originalpunkt 146, Peter Polak 2, Robert Kneschke 173, Robert O. Brown Photography 96, Rohit Seth 3, Sergign 120, Maksim Shmeljov 134b, StockLite 14, 191, szefei 80, Tracy Whiteside 303t, Tyler Olson 73, v.s.anandhakrishna 93, 169, v.s.anandhakrishna 93, 169, vgstudio 76, Valentyn Volkov 135c, Wavebreakmedia 304b, wavebreakmedia ltd 8, 118, 152, Yuri Arcurs 63, 188, 195, Zurijeta 177c; **Stroke Association:** www.stroke.org.uk 105; **Veer/Corbis:** Andresr 207, 311, Andy Dean 300b, avava 272c, Brenda Carson 247, CandyBoxImages 287, 337, Corepics 290b, David Castillo Dominici 284tr, David Davis 273b, Digitalpress 269b, Dmitry Kalinovsky 273t, Gabriel Blaj 278b, goldenKB 284bl, 319, iodrakon 308, iofoto 309, Jeffwqc 225b, Leaf 325, Marco Lensi 318b, Mehmet Can 279, Monkey Business Images 208, 272b, 275, 286b, 288b, 315, 322b, 326b, 330b, Moodboard Photography 16, Nruboc 303b, onescu Bogdan Cristian 211, Petr Malyshev 314b, redcrayola 346b, Robert Marmion 340b, salpics32 214b, Sorymur 219, Stuart Jenner 295, Take A Pix Media 332b, Terry Schmidbauer 322c, totalpics 263, Wavebreakmediamicro 265, Wavebreakmediamicrro 235, 331t, 333, Yuri Arcurs 223

Cover image: Getty Images: Digital Vision

All other images © Pearson Education

In some instances we have been unable to trace the owners of copyright material, and we would appreciate any information that would enable us to do so.

About this book

This qualification will help to prepare you for virtually any career in any sector by equipping you with communication skills, organisational ability, and the ability to present your ideas clearly. Awareness of the stages of human lifespan development and an understanding of health and social care values underpin every role in the wide-ranging health and social care sector, meaning that you will have skills and knowledge that will be valued by employers. In addition, a BTEC First Health and Social Care qualification can help you to progress to the next level of study.

About the authors

Andy Ashton is the Assistant Vice Principal, Curriculum and Academic Standards at Trinity Academy, Doncaster, where he leads the health and social care teaching. He is an author of several books on health and social care, and road safety, and he is actively involved in the coaching of young athletes.

Penelope Garnham has worked as a nurse and midwife for many years prior to entering the field of education. She has taught, lectured, written, verified and trained in schools, FE, HE and the private sector in a great many health-related subjects.

Elizabeth Haworth has taught GCSE Health and Social Care at Lowton High School for over 15 years and has taken a prominent role in LA Steering Groups for developing GCSE and the Diploma. She is the author of several books on Health and Social Care for GCSE, Diploma and BTEC.

Heather Higgins has worked in adults' and children's social services and is a qualified nurse. She taught health and social care in the FE sector for 15 years and is the author of several books on health and social care. Heather was also involved for several years as a volunteer, working with young offenders and latterly with adults who have learning disabilities.

Siân Lavers has 16 years' experience in teaching health and social care in both colleges and universities and is a specialist in health and nutrition education. She is the author of several books on health and social care and is a qualified nurse.

How to use this book

This book contains many features that will help you use your skills and knowledge in work-related situations, and assist you in getting the most from your course.

These introductions give you a snapshot of what to expect from each unit – and what you should be aiming for by the time you finish it.

How this unit is assessed

Learning aims describe what you will be doing in the unit.

A learner shares their experience in relation to the unit.

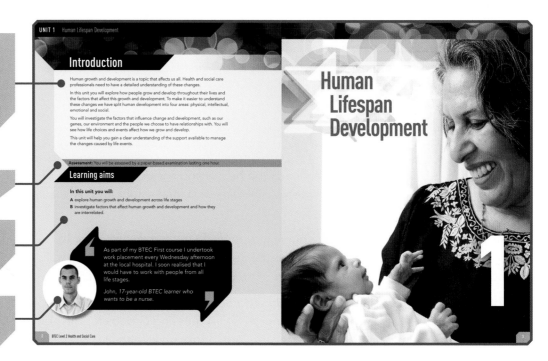

Features of this book

There are lots of features in this book to help you learn about the topics in each unit, and to have fun while learning! These pages show some of the features that you will come across when using the book.

Topic references show which parts of the BTEC you are covering on these pages.

Getting started with a short activity or discussion about the topic.

Key terms appear in blue bold text and are defined either within the text or in a key term box on the page.

Also see the glossary for definitions of important words and phrases.

Someone who works in the Health and Social Care industry explains how this unit of the BTEC First applies to the day-to-day work they do as part of their job.

WorkSpace

▶ April Forrester

School Nurse

I am a school nurse based in a small town. I work in a team that includes three early years workers, other health professionals and various support staff. We have a base, but I spend most of my time in the various secondary schools to which I am allocated.

My main task is to provide preventative health services to help the learners grow and develop in the best way possible. I identify problems and provide services, such as health education, and referral to other services and care, in order to prevent more serious problems developing later, which would be more difficult to deal with and more costly to address. I work with groups of, and individual, learners. I sometimes speak to a whole year group about an issue, and hold drop-in clinics at schools for any learners to come along and have a private chat with me. Issues they talk to me about are very varied, from unwanted pregnancies to personal hygiene or problems with parents and friends. I have a full range of printed health-promotion materials available, so I can give learners leaflets, which tell them where to find more help if needed. I can also refer them to more specialist agencies that can help them with their specific problems.

I help at school events, such as learning days, when a health input is required, and work with other nurses to carry out year group vaccinations, such as HPV. It is a very satisfying job, because although I speak to many learners when they are upset or worried, it is good to feel that I am helping them, and as no two problems are exactly the same it is a very varied job, so never boring. Sometimes it is very sad, such as when a relative, friend, learner or teacher has died, and learners need to talk through their feelings, but it is often fun, as I really enjoy working with young people.

Think about it

1. Why are communication skills so important to April's job?
2. How does April promote health among young people?
3. How can you make use of health-promotion materials to make sure you keep yourself fit and healthy?

121

This section also gives you the chance to think more about the role that this person does, and whether you would want to follow in their footsteps once you've completed your BTEC.

BTEC Assessment Zone

You will be assessed in two different ways for your BTEC First in Health and Social Care. For most units, your teacher/tutor will set assignments for you to complete. These may take the form of projects where you research, plan, prepare, and evaluate a piece of work or activity. The table in this BTEC Assessment Zone explains what you must do in order to achieve each of the assessment criteria. Each unit of this book contains a number of assessment activities to help you with these assessment criteria.

The table in the BTEC Assessment Zone explains what you must do in order to achieve each of the assessment criteria, and signposts assessment activities in this book to help you to prepare for your assignments

Assessment criteria		
Level 1	**Level 2 Pass**	**Level 2 Merit**
Learning aim A: Explore the core values that underpin current practice in health and social care		
1A.1 English	**2A.P1** English	**2A.M1** English
Identify how care values are used to support users of services.	Describe how care values support users of services, using relevant examples. **Assessment activity 2.1 See page 41.**	Discuss the importance of the values that underpin current practice in health and social care, with reference to selected examples. **Assessment activity 2.1 See page 41.**

Activities in this book will show you the kinds of task you might be asked to do to meet these criteria when your tutor sets an assignment.

Background information

John is 31 years of age and a care assistant in a day centre for older people. He works closely with Betty and Ray, who are both 83 years of age.

Betty and Ray both have problems with walking and mobility. They find completing everyday tasks quite difficult. They have two children and a number of close friends who live very near their home.

'Identify the current life stages of John and Betty'. (2 marks)

This is a very straightforward question. You will need to have learned off by heart the life stages and the ages attached to them to answer this question.

In answering the question you just need to state the life stage for each person and do not need to write in full sentences.

'Give two examples of physical changes which occur in middle adulthood'. (2 marks)

'Explain how two different types of informal support could help Betty and Ray with their everyday living'. (4 marks)

In this sort of question hints are often given in the background information which help you in your answers. It is important to go back and look at the information given. Make sure that you look at two different types of informal support and try to make sure you do not repeat yourself in your answer.

You will need to write in full sentences and make sure you link the types of support to how they could help Betty and Ray with everyday living.

'Assess the possible impact attending the day centre may have for Betty and Ray's development'. (8 marks)

There will usually be at least one longer question on the paper where you will be required to write at length about a particular topic or issue.

This type of question will be worth the most marks on the paper and you will need to do a lot of thinking before you write. You are likely to be asked to look at something from a number of different points of view and asked to 'assess' or 'evaluate' the effect of something.

For Unit 1 and 9 of your BTEC, you will be assessed by a paper-based exam. The BTEC Assessment Zone in Unit 1 and 9 helps you to prepare for your exam by showing you some of the different types of questions you will need to answer.

Planning and getting organised

The first step in managing your time is to plan ahead and be well organised. Some people are naturally good at this. They think ahead, write down commitments in a diary or planner, and store their notes and handouts neatly and carefully so they can find them quickly.

How good are your working habits?

Improving your planning and organisational skills

1 Use a diary to schedule working times into your weekdays and weekends.

2 Also use the diary to write down exactly what work you have to do. You could use this as a 'to do' list and tick off each task as you go.

3 Divide up long or complex tasks into manageable chunks and put each 'chunk' in your diary with a deadline of its own.

4 Always allow more time than you think you need for a task.

Sources of information

You will need to use research to complete your BTEC First assignments, so it's important to know what sources of information are available to you. These are likely to include the following:

Textbooks
These cover the units of your qualification and provide activities and ideas for further research.

Internet
A vast source of information, but not all sites are accurate and information and opinions can often be **biased** – you should always double-check facts you find online.

Sources of information

Newspapers and magazines
These often contain articles about health and social care issues, from healthy living to how people using services are treated.

People
People you know can be a great source of opinion and experience – particularly if you want feedback on an idea.

Television
Programmes such as *Panorama* or other documentaries often cover health and social care topics. The news often covers aspects of health and social care such as the NHS.

Take it further

If you become distracted by social networking sites or texts when you're working, set yourself a time limit of 10 minutes or so to indulge yourself. You could even use this as a reward for completing a certain amount of work.

Key terms

Bias – People often have strong opinions about certain topics. This is called 'bias'. Newspaper or magazine articles, or information found on the internet, may be biased to present a specific point of view.

Remember!

Store relevant information when you find it – keep a folder on your computer specifically for research – so you don't have to worry about finding it again at a later date.

Organising and selecting information

Organising your information

Once you have used a range of sources of information for research, you will need to organise the information so it's easy to use.

- Make sure your written notes are neat and have a clear heading – it's often useful to date them, too.
- Always keep a note of where the information came from (the title of a book, the title and date of a newspaper or magazine and the web address of a website) and, if relevant, which pages.
- Work out the results of any questionnaires you've used.

Selecting your information

Once you have completed your research, re-read the assignment brief or instructions you were given to remind yourself of the exact wording of the question(s) and divide your information into three groups:

1 Information that is totally relevant.

2 Information that is not as good, but which could come in useful.

3 Information that doesn't match the questions or assignment brief very much, but that you kept because you couldn't find anything better!

Check that there are no obvious gaps in your information against the questions or assignment brief. If there are, make a note of them so that you know exactly what you still have to find.

Presenting your work

Before handing in any assignments, make sure:

- you have addressed each part of the question and that your work is as complete as possible
- all spelling and grammar is correct
- you have referenced all sources of information you used for your research
- all work is your own – otherwise you could be committing **plagiarism**
- you have saved a copy of your work.

Key terms

Plagiarism – If you are including other people's views, comments or opinions, or copying a diagram or table from another publication, you must state the source by including the name of the author or publication, or the web address. Failure to do this (when you are really pretending other people's work is your own) is known as plagiarism. Check your school's policy on plagiarism and copying.

Introduction

Human growth and development is a topic that affects us all. Health and social care professionals need to have a detailed understanding of these changes.

In this unit you will explore how people grow and develop throughout their lives and the factors that affect this growth and development. To make it easier to understand these changes we have split human development into four areas: physical, intellectual, emotional and social.

You will investigate the factors that influence change and development, such as our genes, our environment and the people we choose to have relationships with. You will see how life choices and events affect how we grow and develop.

This unit will help you gain a clear understanding of the support available to manage the changes caused by life events.

Assessment: You will be assessed by a paper-based examination lasting one hour.

Learning aims

In this unit you will:

A explore human growth and development across life stages

B investigate factors that affect human growth and development and how they are interrelated.

> As part of my BTEC First course I undertook work placement every Wednesday afternoon at the local hospital. I soon realised that I would have to work with people from all life stages.
>
> John, *would-be nurse, aged 17 years.*

Human Lifespan Development

1

Marching on through life?

Key terms

Life stages – a number of distinct phases people pass through during their lives.

Infancy (0–2 years)
▼
Early childhood (3–8 years)
▼
Adolescence (9–18 years)
▼
Early adulthood (19–45 years)
▼
Middle adulthood (46–65 years)
▼
Late adulthood (65+ years)

Figure 1.1 Life stages

Introduction

During their life course people can pass through six different life stages. Some people may die in infancy and others can live until they are over 100. Many more people now live into their eighties and nineties as a result of better diet and hygiene and medical advances.

The ages attached to each life stage are really only a rough guide to human growth and development. Each individual grows and develops in unique ways. Some girls, for instance, can start adolescence at nine or ten, whereas others may not experience some of the physical changes until they are 14 or 15. Also, some people in later adulthood can be physically fitter than people who are much younger.

Growth and development

As we pass through the different life stages, we all grow and develop in different ways.

Growth is a change in size or weight and is easy to measure.

Development is different as it involves acquiring new skills and capabilities. Being able to count, write and handle our own feelings and emotions are all important aspects of human development.

When we study human growth and development in each of the life stages, we split the different aspects into four groups: physical, intellectual, emotional and social (**PIES**).

Physical change happens to the human body throughout each of the life stages. When we are young our physical skills improve and develop; however, as we age and enter the later stages of life physical growth may be negative. For example, some older people may lose their hearing and not see as well as they did when they were younger.

Intellectual development involves changes in the brain and the acquisition of thinking and reasoning skills. From birth, our memory develops and improves and we can start to solve problems and make sense of the world we live in.

Understanding and managing our feelings is an important part of our emotional development. As people pass through adolescence into the different stages of adulthood, most usually become better at handling their feelings as they have had more experience of life.

Self-image and self-esteem

Who we are and how we see ourselves are influenced by the people in our lives, the things that happen to us, and how we respond to these events.

Self-image

Self-image is the mental picture we have of ourselves. Some people see themselves in a positive light – for instance, intelligent, attractive and talented, whereas others may see only negatives.

A person's positive or negative self-image is influenced by such things as:

- personal appearance
- the media – television and magazine images of what is attractive and expected
- comparison with other people
- the comments of other people.

Self-esteem

Self-esteem is about how much you like, accept and respect yourself – this is often talked about in terms of how much you value yourself.

High self-esteem leads to confidence and is useful in work and in maintaining personal relationships. People with low self-esteem may believe they are worthless and that no one will like them.

Self-esteem can change on a daily basis. Things that can affect self-esteem include:

- the attitudes of parents, carers and families
- success or lack of it at school or work
- the comments of friends.

Social development includes the ability to interact with others in society and build relationships. Human beings are social animals and as such need to be able to build relationships with others.

Activity My family

For some people family means those who live within their house, which might be a small unit of two, three or four people. For others, family includes relatives from a number of different generations who may or may not live together. This broader category is often called the 'extended family'.

Renée is 15 years old and lives in an extended family in Nottingham. The family members are:

Marcie (Mother, age 36)	Ben (Grandfather, age 74)	Tanesa (Cousin, age 18 months)	Larron (Father, age 47)
Renée (15)	Ramone (Twin sister, age 15)	Florence (Aunt, age 24)	Mikey (Brother, age 6)

1 Design a table that identifies and shows all the people in Renée's family and their current life stage.
2 Suggest three social activities that Renée and Ben might take part in on a regular basis.
3 Explain why Renée and Ben may be involved in very different social activities.

Starting out

Infancy (0–2)

From being born weighing just a few kilos to reaching the age of two, an infant grows and develops in many ways. In fact, infancy is the time when growth and development are at their most rapid.

Physical development

The physical changes that happen in infancy can be split into **gross motor skill** and **fine motor skill** development. Gross motor skills mean that the infant can start to control the larger muscles of the body; fine motor skills mean that it can control the smaller muscles. Examples of each would be starting to walk and holding a spoon. These skills improve and develop greatly in early childhood.

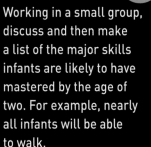

Key terms

Gross motor skill – the ability to control and coordinate the movement of the large limbs of the body, e.g. crawling, walking and running.

Fine motor skill – the ability to control and coordinate the movements of the hands and fingers, e.g. writing, painting, tying shoelaces and holding a spoon.

Language development – the process which children go through as they learn to communicate with others using words and speech.

Egocentric – seeing things from only your own perspective or viewpoint.

Bond – to form an attachment with a parent/carer.

Table 1.1 Muscle control

Muscle control	Approximate age
Can grasp objects with whole hand	4 months
Can start to crawl	8 months
Can climb stairs and run – but often falls	18 months
Can control big muscles, which allows for toilet training	2 years

Infancy is a major developmental stage.

Intellectual development

Intellectual development is about thinking and the way the mind works. At birth babies respond to the world through their senses and communicate mainly through sound. Smiles and noises become the main way of communicating with carers. If infants are hungry they cry. Words do not usually form part of communication until around the age of one year. Before learning to use words, infants babble a lot to express their feelings. By 18 months most infants will know about six words and by two years most will be able to put two to three words together into a simple sentence. **Language development** is a major intellectual change during infancy. During infancy a baby experiences the world through its senses and can only see the world from their own viewpoint. This is known as being **egocentric**.

Emotional development

During the first two years of life infants **bond** with those who care for them. Up to about six months babies do not mind who holds them, though they may not like being put down. Between 7 and 12 months infants form a strong bond with their main carers and will be very wary of strangers and often cry if held by others. From about 12 months infants are able to start to form bonds with other people. This is known as the attachment process. It is important that infants receive love and affection during the attachment process as this influences emotional development throughout future life stages.

Social development

Early relationship development in infancy is based on interaction with others and this shapes social development. These relationships also act as a model for future relationships. The main relationships in infancy are those with parents, carers and brothers and sisters.

A great deal of social learning comes through play. In early infancy children play alone but as they grow older they begin to play first alongside others, and eventually with others, and start to learn about the process of sharing.

Activity　　Learning to share

The process of learning to share with others continues during childhood and adolescence, although some people still find it hard to share even when they are adults.

It is important that parents and carers encourage sharing during infancy and childhood.

1　Identify three play activities that would be ideal for a group of infants or young children that would encourage them to share.

2　Select one of these activities and plan and carry it out with two or three infants.

3　Write up your observations and conclusions.

Bigger and better?

Getting started

In a small group, think back to when you were six or seven. What sort of games did you play?

How did these games help promote the development of the PIES stages?

In what ways are the games girls play different from those that boys play?

Introduction

All children love to play, and in early childhood play is important for development.

Early childhood (3–8)

Early childhood is an exciting time for growth and development as infants become more independent from their carers and begin to make more sense of the world and their place in it. Children love to learn and develop new skills at this age.

Physical development

The development of gross and fine motor skills improves greatly during childhood. From only being able to do a limited range of activities with support in early infancy, by the age of eight most children can do many activities independently. At five, children can walk upstairs unaided and hold a crayon or pencil to draw and write. By eight, children can usually catch and throw quite well and will have a good sense of balance. Many top-class tennis players, for example, were already very good at the game by this age, having already developed good hand–eye coordination.

Intellectual development

By the end of early childhood children have progressed greatly in their intellectual development. Most children are able to speak in full sentences and have quite a good vocabulary. Children also start school during this stage of their life, and this helps with development of language and understanding of numbers.

In infancy, the world is experienced through the senses alone. In childhood this changes as children have the ability to be able to think about things that happen to them. However, they still tend to be egocentric, seeing the world from only their own viewpoint.

Children learn how to act and behave in particular situations by watching others and asking questions. For example, children have to be taught how to behave and eat at the dining table. As children see how their carers respond in particular situations, they begin to copy this behaviour. This is why it is important that children have positive role models in their lives.

Children can learn both how to behave at the dining table and about healthy eating from role models such as their parents.

Emotional development

Between the ages of three and eight children will begin to learn how to handle their feelings. They learn how to share and cooperate with other people. Children can tell others when they feel happy or sad and begin to explain their feelings. It is also during this period that children begin to develop their own self-concept, which will be further developed throughout life.

Social development

Between three and eight years of age children begin to widen their social group and form friendships with others. In the early part of this life stage children often have temper tantrums if they cannot have their own way. Gradually they begin to realise that they have to cooperate with others. By the age of eight, children will usually have a number of friends and often have what they call a 'best friend'.

There are different stages that children go through as they learn to play.

Table 1.2 Children's play stages

Type of play	Age	Description of play
Solitary play (Infancy)	0–2 years	Children play alone using their imagination and do not interact with other children.
Parallel play	2–3 years	Children play alongside each other, but not together. Toys are not shared cooperatively.
Social play	3–8 years	Children play together, sharing their toys. By the age of eight they will engage in quite complex games, often requiring the use of imagination.

Assessment practice 1.1

Kian is 6 years old. He lives with his mother, baby sister, Ella (9 months old), his grandfather and grandmother.

1 Identify three fine motor skills Kian will have developed by the age of six. (3 marks)

2 Identify three physical skills Kian has mastered that Ella couldn't do in infancy. (3 marks)

3 Explain, using examples, the difference between fine and gross motor skills. (6 marks)

4 Explain why having positive 'role models' is important for children. (4 marks)

It is really important to make sure that you answer the questions set. For questions that ask you to 'identify' a list will be good enough to get the marks.

For 'Explain' questions you will need to write in more depth, using sentences and paragraphs, for these answers.

Always make sure you do exactly what the question asks. If you are asked to give examples, for instance, these are required to get the marks, so don't miss them out.

Teenage years

Introduction

Adolescence is a time of great physical and emotional change.

Adolescence (9–18)

Adolescence is a stage of great physical, intellectual, emotional and social change. Children entering adolescence pass through puberty and become adults. One of the key physical features of puberty is the reaching of sexual maturity. People enter adolescence at different ages, with girls on average entering adolescence slightly earlier than boys. But everyone is different and the normal age range for entering puberty is quite wide. For instance, although on average most girls start menstruation between the ages of 12 and 13, the normal range is anything from eight to 16.

Physical development

In adolescence there is a rapid process of physical change caused as a result of hormonal change. The physical changes in girls are caused by **oestrogen**, and those in boys are caused by **testosterone**.

Intellectual development

One of the biggest intellectual changes that happens in adolescence is the development of **abstract thinking**. This is the ability to think using concepts and ideas rather than through using objects and doing tasks. A seven-year-old child may be able to calculate how long it takes to travel to a destination by train through pushing the fingers of a clock round its face, whereas teenagers can usually do this calculation in their heads.

Adolescents also begin to think in a more logical way to solve problems and can **empathise** – see things from other people's perspective and realise that the world is not centred totally round them. This period is also a time when teenagers develop their own set of morals and ideas about what is right and wrong.

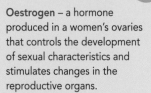

Key terms

Oestrogen – a hormone produced in a women's ovaries that controls the development of sexual characteristics and stimulates changes in the reproductive organs.

Testosterone – a hormone produced by the testes that controls the development of male sexual characteristics.

Abstract thinking – the ability to think about something that might not be there or even exist.

Peer group – the social group a person belongs to which influences beliefs and behaviour.

Have you had to comfort a friend?

Emotional development

The large hormonal changes in the body mean that adolescence can be a difficult time for teenagers. Mood swings, frustrations, insecurities and confusions are all common and most teenagers experience them. It is at this time that young people begin to form their own personality and identity.

Feelings of physical attraction towards others also begin to develop during adolescence. Young people start to explore their own sexuality, usually with the opposite sex, but sometimes with the same sex. It is during adolescence that many young people have their first close and intimate relationship with another person. Relationships are formed and sometimes maintained for quite long periods of time. However, many are short-lived and the teenager has to handle a whole new range of feelings and emotions to do with loss and grief.

Social development

Social development in teenagers is closely linked to their emotional development. It is during adolescence that young people tend to socialise more and have more independence and freedom. Young people are also influenced greatly by the views, opinions and behaviour of their close friends. This is known as **peer group** pressure.

Peer group pressure is a challenge for all teenagers and their families. It often causes conflict, as the views of teenagers may be very different from the views of their parents. The close friendships formed in adolescence may well last well into adulthood and many people maintain these friendships throughout their whole life.

Discussion point

Many teenagers feel that they can make their own decisions. This independence can cause conflict with parents/carers. In pairs, discuss the following statements. Do you agree?

- 17 is old enough for someone to decide what time they come home.

- It is acceptable for teenagers to receive family planning advice and treatment without their parents'/carers' knowledge or consent.

Why is it difficult to remain unaffected by peer pressure?

Being independent

Getting started ▶▶

Working in a small group, discuss how and why the social life of a person who is 22 may be very different from a person who is 42. Be prepared to share your views with the group.

Introduction

Early adulthood is the time when many young people have an active social life and a wide network of friends.

◤ Early adulthood (19–45)

Early adulthood is a time when people reach their physical peak and become mature. Common features of this period include starting work, meeting a partner, settling down and starting a family. It is an exciting time for most people as they grow and develop in different ways.

Physical development

Most people reach their physical peak in the first part of early adulthood. This is when they are physically at their strongest. Top sprinters, for example, are usually at their best when they are in their mid-twenties. However, with training and good levels of motivation, athletes can continue to perform at the top level well into their thirties.

Early adulthood is the time when many people find partners, marry and have children.

Towards the end of this life stage physical capabilities start to diminish and fertility levels also begin to fall. Some women will to go through the **menopause** in early adulthood and the live sperm count of men also begins to fall. As people's metabolic rates slow down they also begin to burn fewer calories and as a result some people will put on weight. However, gaining weight can be countered through a careful diet and regular exercise. People who exercise regularly and take care of their diet often look much younger than their biological age.

Intellectual development

Nearly all people have the capability for intellectual development throughout adulthood. Many people who did not focus fully on learning at school often decide to carry on their education in their twenties or thirties. Many people develop in their careers and need to gain new skills and better qualifications to improve their career prospects. 'Lifelong learning' is now accepted as being important for all people and intellectual capability is often improved in early adulthood.

Emotional development

Early adulthood is the time that many people develop close and intimate relationships with others. Some people cohabit, some choose to marry or, if a same-sex couple, have a civil partnership ceremony. Intimate relationships create feelings of security and allow people to give and receive love. Some people may choose to live alone and others live alone as a result of relationship breakdown.

Early adulthood is also the time when most people choose to start a family. Having children often gives people a sense of direction in life and they enjoy forming close emotional bonds with their children. Time spent with children also gives parents a lot of pleasure as they watch their children take their first steps and speak their first words. But parenthood comes with responsibilities and not all couples choose to have children.

Social development

During the early years of young adulthood, people are generally free to have a very active social life, making new friends and building new relationships. As people move through early adulthood they usually gain more responsibilities. By 45, for instance, many people will be married, and have children, a responsible job and a mortgage to pay. Balancing work life, family life and a social life can be very difficult for people as their responsibilities increase.

Key terms

Menopause – the natural and permanent stopping of menstruation (periods), occurring usually between the ages of 45 and 55.

Discussion point

John and Mike have been together for four years and have recently been through a civil ceremony and consider themselves married. They want to start a family and Mike's friend from college has agreed to be a surrogate mother.

1 Explain how starting a family may affect John and Mike's social life.

2 Discuss the benefits of having children for John and Mike's emotional development.

3 How might John and Mike's relationship be affected by having a family of their own?

4 Do you think John and Mike's life as parents would be any different from a heterosexual couple starting a family?

Halfway through?

Getting started

Working with a partner, draw up two lists for:

- the benefits of being in middle adulthood
- the possible negatives of being in middle adulthood.

Be prepared to share your ideas with the group.

Key terms

Mid-life crisis – a dramatic period of self-doubt caused by the passing of youth and the move into later adulthood.

Introduction

As people enter middle adulthood they begin to realise that they are no longer young.

Middle adulthood (46–65)

Middle adulthood is a time when many major physical and emotional changes take place in people's lives. As they reach the age of 50 or 60 people begin to realise that they are getting older but still feel young inside. This can lead to some people having a **mid-life crisis**.

Physical development

As people move through middle adulthood the ageing process begins to take effect in the human body. Physical capabilities start to decline and muscle tone isn't as good as it was. People often feel they have lower energy levels than in early adulthood, and sight and hearing may start to decline. As the skin begins to lose its elasticity wrinkles often become more noticeable. Hair becomes greyer and some men lose more of their hair and may become bald.

It is during this life stage that most women go through the menopause. This usually happens between the ages of 45 and 55. Women produce less oestrogen and the menstrual cycle eventually stops for most women by the end of this life stage. Men also produce less testosterone and live sperm production decreases.

Intellectual development

Intellectual development continues throughout middle adulthood and many people choose to return to education and study. This sometimes happens by choice as some people want a new direction in life, but for others it may be sparked through the need to get new qualifications. Most people will have a variety of jobs throughout their working lives and therefore need retraining.

As we age, our memories might not be as quick as they once were, but older people have a lot of life experience.

Getting older doesn't have to slow you down.

Emotional development

During middle adulthood hormone changes take place in the body which can be linked to changing feelings and emotions.

This leads many people to review their lives at this stage. Some try to recapture their youth through behaving in ways similar to those in early adulthood. They may dress younger than their years and start going out more. They may wish to try things they have never done before. This sort of behaviour has led to the use of the phrase 'mid-life crisis'.

These sorts of feelings are quite normal and may last for a number of years until people come to terms with who they are.

Activity   Empty nest syndrome

With a partner explore what is meant by the term 'empty nest syndrome'.

Social development

As children may have left the family home and become independent, middle-aged people often have more time on their hands and have more money to spend than ever before. This provides an opportunity for some people to extend their social lives. Middle-aged people may start to build new relationships, travel more and just have more quality time to spend with their family. However, in more difficult financial times, with high unemployment and limited job opportunities, many middle-aged people may find themselves out of work or having to support their adult children financially and help with child support for grandchildren.

Assessment practice 1.2

Jozef (59) and Kamilla (55) have been married for 30 years. Their youngest child Beata (21) left home last year and lives nearby with her boyfriend and their baby.

1 Identify three features that indicate that people are ageing. (3 marks)
2 Explain what is meant by the term 'mid-life crisis'. (4 marks)
3 Explain why middle adulthood may be a time of opportunity for Jozef and Kamilla. (4 marks)
4 In what ways are the social lives of Jozef and Kamilla different from Beata's social life? (6 marks)

Remember to work on your examination technique in your practice answers.

You will be asked to remember key facts that you have learned – questions for this will normally have 1 mark for each answer.

Questions may ask, for example, 'identify', 'give', 'define' or 'select' (from a list).

'Explain' means the examiner needs some depth in the answer.

Remember you need to do what the question asks.

Ensure answers are written in full sentences and make sure the answer makes sense.

Re-read your answers at the end of the examination to make sure that you have not misunderstood the question and that you have completed all parts of the question.

Times of change

Getting started

Working with a partner, draw up a list of reasons why older people find these types of puzzles interesting and how they might help promote intellectual development.

Introduction

Puzzles, quizzes, crosswords and sudoku are all popular with some people in later adulthood.

Later adulthood (65+)

In later adulthood people often find they have more time on their hands. Improvements in diet and medical treatment mean many people can expect to live 20 to 30 more years after they retire from work at 65. In fact more people are now choosing to work until they are 70 and some even beyond this age. Older people can be some of the most productive members of society, with skills younger people often wish they had.

Physical development

The ageing process in later adulthood is very clear to see. The skin is thinner, joints are stiffer, muscles weaker and bones often more brittle. Older people are frequently less mobile than younger people and some begin to stoop and lose height. Physical development in this life stage can involve the loss of skills and physical capacities.

Although these changes may seem negative, people in later adulthood can still be very active. Many older people take regular exercise as they have more time than when they were working. This might be through joining gyms, taking exercise classes, walking, running or jogging. Older people appreciate the benefits of regular exercise in keeping mobile and supple.

Fauja Singh is believed to have set the world record for a 100-year-old in the London Marathon in October 2011. He completed the course in 8 hours, 25 minutes and 16 seconds. Most people of any age would find it hard to match this time if they ran a marathon.

Keeping fit in later life is just as important as when we are younger.

Intellectual development

Although speed of thinking and short-term memory might decline in later adulthood, it is thought that intelligence does not change with age. Many older people are keen to learn new things, develop their knowledge and keep their minds active. As older people have more leisure time they may take up new interests, such as learning a different language, gaining new experiences through travel and learning new skills.

Some older people may experience **dementia** as they age and it is more common now as more people live longer on average.

Emotional development

Later adulthood offers the opportunity to spend more quality time with family and friends. Older people often enjoy seeing their children and grandchildren and spending time with them. Instead of rushing and fitting people in around work commitments, retired people can take things at a steadier pace. More time can be spent with people and closer friendships and relationships developed. This often leads to feelings of contentment and happiness.

However, later adulthood can also be a challenge for many people. It is during this stage that people often lose their life partner and friends as they die. Some of these relationships will have existed throughout the person's whole life. This can be distressing and hard to cope with. The support of family, other friends and neighbours can be really important at this stage to make sure the person does not feel isolated and lonely.

Social development

Later adulthood is often split into two parts. The first stage is 65 to 75 and the second stage 75 plus. During the first stage people still tend to be very active and often have a busy social life. They are often 'on the go' and say they don't know how they managed to fit work in when they were younger. As people age beyond 75 they tend to slow down, but this doesn't mean they socialise any less. It just means the type of social life they have may be different.

Key terms

Dementia – an illness that affects the brain and memory, and makes you gradually lose the ability to think and behave normally.

Case study

Liz is 75 years old and is coming to terms with the death of her husband six months ago. They had been happily married for 54 years.

1 Describe two ways in which Liz's children could support her at this difficult time.

2 How might a doctor or counsellor help Liz?

3 Suggest some possible activities Liz could take up to help her meet new people.

Born this way?

 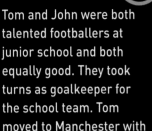
How does ability in childhood translate into success in adulthood?

The influences on human growth and development

How people grow and develop depends on the genes they inherit from their parents and the events and factors that influence them as they age.

The influence of physical factors

With the exception of identical twins, we each have a unique set of genes. Children inherit physical features from their parents. If both parents are tall, for example, there is a much greater chance that their children will also be tall.

Skills and talents can also be passed from parents to children through genes. Talented athletes and sportspeople who marry other top athletes are much more likely to have children who have the same natural talents as well. Some people also argue that other aspects of human nature such as intelligence, personality and sexuality are also linked to our genes.

Some people inherit adverse genetic conditions, which they live with throughout their lives. Down's syndrome is one example. As we age, degenerative diseases also develop as our bodies cope with everyday life. These factors will certainly affect how a person grows and develops across the different life stages.

The choices we make in life regarding diet, exercise, alcohol, smoking and drug use will also affect growth and development. If, for example, a person is heavily overweight this can affect their joints as they become older, and increase the risk of diabetes and heart disease. Type 2 diabetes and high blood pressure are often caused through the type of lifestyle choices we make.

Many people make really positive choices in life, which have a big impact on growth and development. Developing a wide network of friends can have a positive effect on a person's emotional and social wellbeing. Having people to turn to and share problems with is really important when we face unexpected life events such as serious illness, stress or coping with the death of a close family member.

Working in pairs, look at the possible negative effects of one of the following on growth and development:

- binge drinking
- smoking
- regular eating of fast foods
- running five miles every day
- taking recreational drugs at weekends.

The influence of environmental factors

Although inherited genes do influence growth and development, a whole range of other factors, often known as 'environmental' factors, influence how we grow and develop. For example, a person who has a serious car accident and has to be off school for six months is unlikely to do as well at school as someone who is fully healthy.

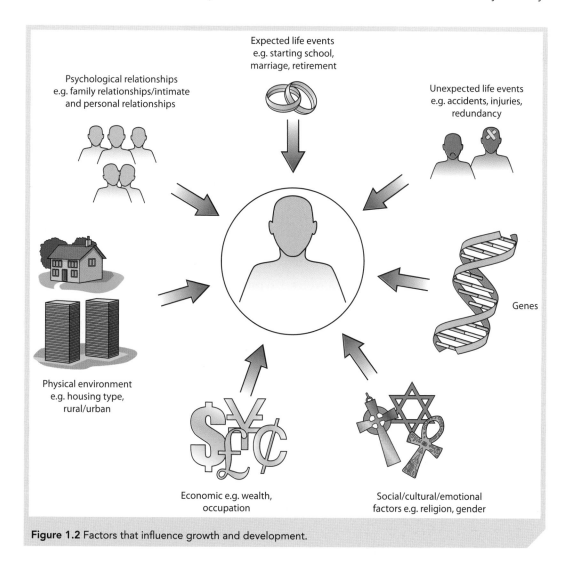

Figure 1.2 Factors that influence growth and development.

Social, cultural and emotional factors

Introduction

Growth and development are influenced throughout the life course by many different social, cultural and emotional factors. Some factors are more important in particular life stages than they are in others.

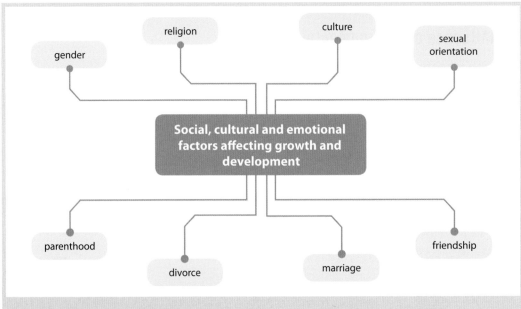

Figure 1.3 Social, cultural and emotional factors affecting growth and development.

Play in infancy and childhood

During the first year of life the infant will begin to play alone. This is known as solitary play.

By the age of two most children are involved in parallel play alongside other children, and they later move on to social play, which involves playing with others. This is sometimes called cooperative play, as children learn to share, use their imagination and get involved in role play. Children love to dress up and learn about the different jobs people have in the world. At this time children are learning the important skills of how to build relationships with others and how to behave as a friend.

What type of play can you identify in this photo?

Activity   Play! Play! Play!

Working in small groups, select four games which children often play together.

For each game identify the skills which the children are likely to be developing.

Remember to use all aspects of the PIES stages in your thinking.

Role models

As people grow and develop they are influenced by the people they interact with in their everyday lives. These people act as **role models** to children and adolescents, who look up to them and often copy their behaviour patterns. Many boys, for example, look up to sports stars such as footballers or rugby players, and many girls want to be like pop stars and models. Children as young as eight will copy the behaviour shown by others.

It is important that young people have good role models in their lives who demonstrate behaviour which has a positive effect on others and society as a whole.

Key terms

Role model – someone whose behaviour and/or attitudes people try to copy because they admire them.

Gender role – a role that is determined by a person's gender.

Activity	Role models

Working with a partner, identify two positive and two negative ways in which the following may be role models to young people:

- celebrities
- parents
- school teachers.

A person's **gender role** is also learned from the people they interact with. In the past there were very separate gender roles for men and women. Men went out to work and women stayed at home and were involved in looking after and raising the children. This has now changed hugely and both men and women go out to work and share the caring roles for their children. This means that men are said to have become more in touch with their nurturing side and it is much more acceptable for women to want to follow and develop a career. As a result, we now have much more social equality between men and women and more equality of opportunity in the world of work.

Culture

How people develop is influenced by the community they live in and the values and beliefs which their family and friends hold. Religion can influence how people choose to lead their lives, the food they eat and how they choose to dress. Some people live in communities which hold traditional values about marriage and family roles, while others may live in communities with very different beliefs and values. For example, a Muslim woman may find being examined by a male doctor or nurse traumatic because strict Muslims forbid any physical contact between males and females unless they are married.

It is important that people feel accepted as part of their family and community. Being involved with others makes people feel wanted and valued. This helps people have good self-esteem and promotes growth and development. Unfortunately, some people feel socially isolated from their families and have few friends. This can have a negative impact on growth and development.

Link

This topic links to Unit 7: Equality and Diversity in Health and Social Care.

Activity	Taking part

In later adulthood many people live by themselves because of the death of their life partner.

Working with a partner, research the types of social groups and activities which are available in your local community which may offer opportunities for older people to meet others and socialise.

Influences on life

Key terms

Manual work – work that requires the use of physical skills.

Non-manual work – work that depends primarily on mental skills.

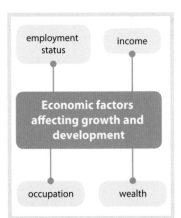

Figure 1.4 Economic factors that affect human growth and development.

Introduction

Getting their first full-time job with regular pay will affect a young person's physical, intellectual, emotional and social development.

Economic factors

How people grow and develop is also influenced greatly by the work they do and how much money they earn. People whose jobs involve **manual work** are often more affected physically by their work than people who do a **non-manual** job such as a desk job. Non-manual and professional jobs also tend to be more highly paid than manual jobs.

Being employed provides workers with an income, allowing them to buy the things they need for themselves and for their families. Work can lead to feelings of contentment and worth and raise self-esteem. Conversely, being unemployed and living on a limited income can lead to feelings of stress and anxiety and a lowering of self-esteem. Some people inherit wealth, which gives them the possibility of a lifestyle very different from that of people who have limited income.

Assessment practice 1.3

Anthony is 22 and works as a manual labourer for a local building company. He works outside all day moving heavy loads and helping the skilled trades people. He earns the minimum wage and lives at home with his parents and two younger brothers.

1 Explain two effects on health and wellbeing of living on a limited income. (4 marks)

2 Explain two possible effects of being employed in manual work on physical health. (4 marks)

You will need to think hard before you write and also make sure you answer the question.

Always write in full sentences and remember to use capital letters and full stops.

Remember to work on your examination technique in your practice answers.

You may be asked to apply your knowledge to a particular situation. Remember that 'explain' means the examiner needs some depth in the answer. Re-read your answers at the end of the examination to make sure you have not misunderstood the question and have completed all parts of the question.

Physical environment factors

Where you live and work can have a major effect on your development, health and wellbeing. City centres can be noisy and crowded with many more health risks. Crime rates tend to be higher and there is often more air and noise pollution. Air pollution has been linked to increases in illnesses, such as asthma. Having space, warmth and a clean home environment all have a positive effect on growth and development. Living in rural areas often provides families with more green space so children can play outside more and have more freedom. Housing can often be cheaper in rural areas, but a disadvantage is that there is often less work available. Rural occupations are often low-paid.

Young people can be attracted to the social opportunities that city life provides, but many people choose to move out of the city when they decide to start a family.

Psychological factors

People have a whole range of different relationships in their lives. These can be split into three main types:

- those with family members
- friendships
- personal and intimate relationships with partners.

Having positive relationships with other people is really important. There are times in life when we will all need the support of our family and friends to help us deal with the problems we face.

If a person is having difficulties with members of their family or friends this might have an effect on how they grow and develop. For example, some children grow up in care and this can sometimes have a negative effect on their self-esteem as they think they are different from other children.

As people progress through different stages in life they may experience stress from life events and this can affect all aspects of growth and development. High levels of stress at work can lead to high blood pressure and increase the risk of heart attacks and strokes.

In the early life stages the family is crucially important as infants and children depend on their parents to meet nearly all their needs. Parents give their children security and accept them as they are. This is known as unconditional acceptance.

As children move into adolescence they begin to be influenced more by their friends and the views and opinions they have. It is also in adolescence that many young people develop their first close and intimate relationships with other people.

Relationships are important for growth and development, and having positive relationships with others leads to the development of a good self-image and high self-esteem. Having a good network of close friends can lead to a sense of happiness and contentment. Most people also enjoy spending time with others and taking part in social activities. However, on some occasions friends can cause distress to others through their actions.

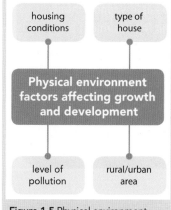

Figure 1.5 Physical environment factors that affect human growth and development.

Discussion point

In small groups, discuss the possible help and support friends might be able to offer a young person who has just had an argument with their best friend.

23

Life events

Getting started

Discuss with a partner the possible support family and friends might be able to offer a teenager who is about to sit GCSE examinations.

Be prepared to feed back to a whole class discussion.

Introduction

Having a supportive family and friends is important for everyone.

As we pass through life we face a whole range of events that will affect aspects of our growth and development. For example, moving to a new house in a different part of the country will be a challenge for all members of a family. Children will have to make new friends and will probably miss the friends they used to see every day. Starting a new school could affect a young person's intellectual development as well. A teenager who moves to a new school part of the way through Year 10 might not be able to complete the course they were doing in their previous school, which could affect their examination results at 16 and influence them for the rest of their life.

Expected life events

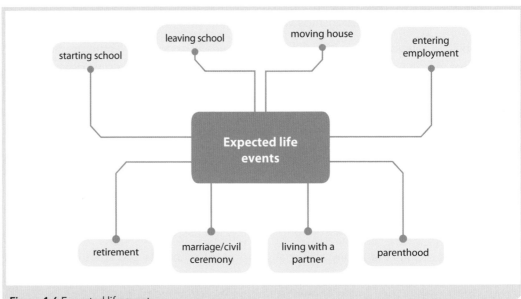

Figure 1.6 Expected life events.

It is important to remember that some life events are expected and predictable, and can therefore be planned for and managed.

Activity   The effect of expected life events

In small groups, consider how the physical, intellectual, emotional and social development of a person might be affected by each of the following expected life events:

- starting or leaving school
- getting a full-time job

- moving in with a partner
- retiring from work.

Unexpected life events

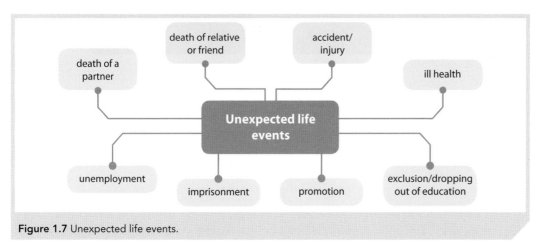

Figure 1.7 Unexpected life events.

Unfortunately, life does not always go to plan and unexpected life events will happen. For example, if a close relative dies in a car accident this will have both short and long-term effects on other people's growth and development.

Managing changes

Managing the challenges and changes we face in life can be difficult. It is important to seek the help of others when it is needed. The support people can access can be split into two main types:

- formal support
- informal support.

Most people can access a whole range of professional support to help them deal with difficult life events, such as serious illness or accidents.

Professional carers, such as doctors, nurses and counsellors are all examples of people who can provide formal support. Formal support comes from people who are trained and skilled in their work and they are paid for what they do. The specialist training formal carers have also means they have the knowledge and experience to help others handle the life events they may never have experienced before. Dealing with the death of a loved one can make some people depressed, and counsellors can be a great support in helping people deal with their grief.

Family and friends are also able to offer support to others in difficult times, helping with everyday physical tasks such as shopping, housework and washing and bathing. These people offer informal support. Informal supporters are not trained for what they do and don't get paid for their work. However, the work they do is really important. Many people in later adulthood rely on the informal support they receive from their families and friends to be able to remain independent and continue to live in their own homes.

In the UK there are thousands of people who act as informal supporters every day, working in different ways to improve the lives of others. Many of these informal supporters are under the age of 16. Spending time with family and friends who are housebound or going through a difficult time in life can be a great source of emotional and social help.

Assessment Zone

How you will be assessed

What you need to know about the examination

There are a number of key things you need to be aware of:

- The examination is 60 minutes long and there is a maximum mark of 50.
- Examiners work on the principle of a mark a minute, so you have some extra time here to think and plan your answers. Remember to read the questions, think about them, plan your answers, write your answers and review what you have written.
- There will be a range of questions on the paper – short multiple-choice-type questions, short answer questions and some longer questions.
- There will be a range of different command words used in the questions – make sure you know what they are asking you to do!

How to approach answering the examination paper

You need to revise everything in this unit, including the areas where you have been set tasks to do some research, as not all the information you need would fit in this book. Your teacher/tutor is likely to give you some practice questions to complete and a mock/practice paper to complete. This is a good way to practise your examination technique and how to use your time well. This will mean that you are well prepared to sit the question paper.

When you open the paper it is a good idea to remember the following:

- Quickly look through the whole paper to see what it looks like. Be careful not to turn over two pages together and miss a whole question, and check the last page so you don't miss any questions. This will calm you down, as you will know what is coming. It will also help you plan how to use the 60 minutes you have to get the best results. Some people rush their answers and sit for 30 minutes doing very little, thinking they have finished, when they could have written better answers. Some people spend too long on the first part of the paper and never reach the end, losing out on many marks. Plan what time you want to start the second half of the paper and space your time evenly.
- There will be one long question at the end of the paper. Even if it looks hard, you will need to attempt it, especially if you are hoping to do well in the exam.

How to approach answering questions

You will be given some background information on which the questions are based. Look at the sample and the practice questions for the unit. After each question are some tips on how to answer them well.

Background information

John is 31 years of age and a care assistant in a day centre for older people. He works closely with Betty and Ray, who are both 83 years of age.

Betty and Ray both have problems with walking and mobility. They find completing everyday tasks quite difficult. They have two children and a number of close friends who live very near their home.

'Identify the current life stages of John and Betty'. (2 marks)

This is a very straightforward question. You will need to have learned off by heart the life stages and the ages attached to them to answer this question.

In answering the question you just need to state the life stage for each person and do not need to write in full sentences.

'Give two examples of physical changes which occur in middle adulthood'. (2 marks)

In order to answer this type of question you will need to have learned the types of physical changes which happen at each life stage. These are identified for you in this unit. It would be a good idea to create a mind map diagram showing the main changes which happen physically, intellectually, emotionally and socially in each life stage.

As this is a question worth only two marks, a list will do and you will not need to write in full sentences.

'Explain how two different types of informal support could help Betty and Ray with their everyday living'. (4 marks)

In this sort of question hints are often given in the background information which help you in your answers. It is important to go back and look at the information given. Make sure that you look at two different types of informal support and try to make sure you do not repeat yourself in your answer.

You will need to write in full sentences and make sure you link the types of support to how they could help Betty and Ray with everyday living.

'Assess the possible impact attending the day centre may have for Betty and Ray's development'. (8 marks)

There will usually be at least one longer question on the paper where you will be required to write at length about a particular topic or issue.

This type of question will be worth the most marks on the paper and you will need to do a lot of thinking before you write. You are likely to be asked to look at something from a number of different points of view and asked to 'assess' or 'evaluate' the effect of something.

In this particular question you are asked to look at how attending the day centre may affect Betty and Ray's development. Most learners will think that attending the day centre will have a positive effect for Betty and Ray, but you will also need to consider that it might have a negative impact on them as well. For example, being at the day centre may make them feel upset that they can no longer do the things they have always done for themselves.

To gain really good marks you will need to be able to consider things from different points of view. You will need to write in full sentences and use paragraphs to structure your written answer.

Disclaimer: These practice questions and sample answers are not actual exam questions and have been provided as a practice aide only. They should be used as practice material only and should not be assumed to reflect the format or coverage of the Edexcel external test. Answers can be found on page 366.

Introduction

How do you recognise good practice in health and social care? This unit will help you to find out about the values that underpin good health and social care practice. These values include confidentiality, treating individuals with dignity and respect, and safeguarding individuals to ensure their physical and emotional safety while they are in your care.

Good practice in health and social care should always aim to empower individuals, enabling them to be involved in decisions and to do as much for themselves as possible. This can include adapting activities: for example, providing playing cards with larger print for an individual with visual impairment or adapting cutlery so that people with physical needs are able to feed themselves.

The values that underpin good health and social care practice are also important to everyday life. We all prefer to be treated with respect, to feel safe and to have our needs considered, and we should all understand how distressing life can be if any of this does not happen. This unit will help you to recognise where the values we all appreciate can be applied to health and social care.

Assessment: You will be assessed by a series of assignments set by your teacher/tutor.

Learning aims

In this unit you will:

A explore the care values that underpin current practice in health and social care

B investigate ways of empowering individuals who use health and social care services.

When I went on placement to a day centre for young adults with learning disabilities, I learned that I should not gossip about the users of the service to my friends when I call them on my mobile phone.

Deena Williams, *would-be care assistant, aged 16 years*

Health and Social Care Values

2

BTEC

Assessment Zone

This table shows you what you must do in order to achieve a **Pass**, **Merit** or **Distinction** grade, and where you can find activities in this book to help you.

Assessment criteria			
Level 1	**Level 2 Pass**	**Level 2 Merit**	**Level 2 Distinction**
Learning aim A: Explore the core values that underpin current practice in health and social care			
1A.1 English Identify how care values are used to support users of services.	**2A.P1** English Describe how care values support users of services, using relevant examples. **Assessment activity 2.1** **See page 41.**	**2A.M1** English Discuss the importance of the values that underpin current practice in health and social care, with reference to selected examples. **Assessment activity 2.1** **See page 41.**	**2A.D1** Assess the potential impact on the individual of effective and ineffective application of the care values in health and social care practice, with reference to selected examples. **Assessment activity 2.1** **See page 41.**
1A.2 Demonstrate the use of care values in a selected health and social care context.	**2A.P2** Demonstrate the use of care values in selected health and social care contexts. **Assessment activity 2.1** **See page 41.**		
Learning aim B: Investigate ways of empowering individuals who use health and social care services			
1B.3 Identify ways in which care workers can empower individuals.	**2B.P3** Describe ways in which care workers can empower individuals, using relevant examples from health and social care. **Assessment activity 2.2** **See page 51.**	**2B.M2** Discuss the extent to which individual circumstances can be taken into account when planning care that will empower them, using relevant examples from health and social care. **Assessment activity 2.2** **See page 51.**	**2B.D2** Assess the potential difficulties in taking individual circumstances into account when planning care that will empower an individual, making suggestions for improvement. **Assessment activity 2.2** **See page 51.**
1B.4 Describe how an individual's circumstances can be used to create a care plan that empowers the individual.	**2B.P4** Explain why it is important to take individual circumstances into account when planning care that will empower an individual, using relevant examples from health and social care. **Assessment activity 2.2** **See page 51.**		

English   English signposting

How you will be assessed

The unit will be assessed by a series of internally assessed tasks. You will be expected to show an understanding of values and how these should be applied in the context of the health and social care sector. The tasks will be based on a scenario where you work in a local health or social care organisation.

Your assessment could be in the form of:

- an induction pack for volunteers in health and social care settings
- training materials, such as leaflets, booklets and PowerPoint® presentations
- a training DVD that demonstrates the application of values to the delivery of health and social care
- an article or set of articles for a magazine.

Values in health and social care

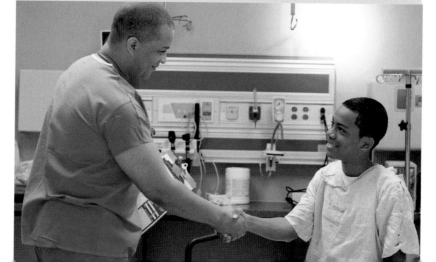

Introduction

In this topic you will learn what is meant by 'health and social care values' and how these are applied to the way in which care is delivered.

Values are the ideas or concepts that ensure health and social care is delivered in the best possible way. They help to ensure that care improves life for individuals, rather than making it worse. This is known as **beneficence**, which means doing good and not harm to someone.

You will often hear the word **underpinning** when values in health and social care are being discussed. We use this word to show how the values support the way care is delivered, in the same way that foundations support the bricks, mortar and wood of a house. Without the values, health and social care would fall down. You can see evidence of this from cases in the media where individuals in residential settings have been mistreated. This mistreatment was, in fact, care delivery that was not underpinned by health and social care values.

Key terms

Values – the ideas that lie behind and inform good health and social care practice.

Beneficence – doing good and not harm to an individual.

Underpin – to provide a supporting framework.

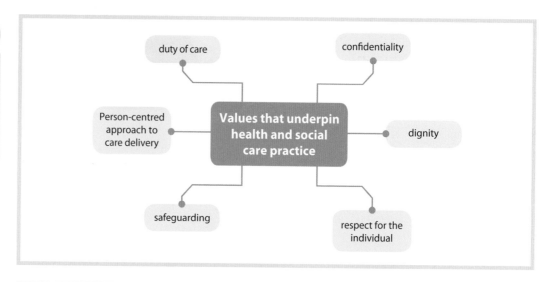

- duty of care
- confidentiality
- Person-centred approach to care delivery
- **Values that underpin health and social care practice**
- dignity
- safeguarding
- respect for the individual

How is this doctor ensuring that the patient feels respected?

Case study

Five years ago, Miss Jane da Silva was diagnosed with a condition that affected her muscles and nerves and she decided she needed to enter residential care. She moved into the Elms Nursing Home, hoping for a more comfortable life with good care.

The Elms Nursing Home is a busy place; the ratio of staff to service users meets the legal requirements, but there are never any extra staff to deal immediately with incidents, such as someone spilling their food or soiling their bed sheets. This means that individuals are sometimes left in uncomfortable situations until a member of staff can help them.

All of the service users are woken up at the same time each morning and placed on the toilet before dressing. None of the service users are ever asked if they need to use the toilet. One morning Miss da Silva decided to object to this routine and was told crossly that she should be glad that someone was looking after her.

Some of the staff were kind, but were just too busy and they would insist on calling Jane by her first name, even though she would have preferred to be called Miss da Silva, but when she mentioned this to the manager, he laughed and said, 'We're all one big family and don't use titles.'

1 How do you think care delivery at the Elms Nursing Home would affect the service users?

2 What changes would you make if you were the manager?

3 How do you think the ratio of staff to service users at the Elms Nursing Home affects the quality of care delivered?

4 Who are the most important people at the Elms Nursing Home?

5 Why is it important that individuals who use services are able to make complaints about the quality of care?

Activity   Values

Look at the photographs. The staff are all busy supporting the users of the service.

What three care values are these care workers exhibiting?

Exploring care values (1)

Confidentiality

We all assume that we understand what confidentiality is and know how to apply it to everyday situations. However, in health and social care the rules are rather different. For example, you might tell your best friend everything, but you cannot tell them everything about the users of the service where you work. This would be breaking the rules of confidentiality.

In health and social care confidentiality means that we do not share *without permission* information that has been entrusted to us. This includes not sharing personal information about users of the services with friends, family or other individuals outside the setting, or chatting about work in public places.

The rules of confidentiality are:

- not discussing one individual with another
- not sharing written information without permission
- secure storage of records, including those stored electronically.

Key terms

Confidential – Information that is secret. It has been entrusted to only the person to whom it has been communicated. It is private and not open for general discussion or publication.

Breaching confidentiality

There are occasions when **confidential** information must be shared: for example, if an individual was at risk of being harmed or of harming another person.

All health and social care settings have procedures that must be followed with regard to the breaching of confidentiality. There is a clear difference between following a procedure that would mean informing the manager or senior member of staff on duty, and telling a friend. Do you know the difference?

Case study

Sarah Smith has just completed a busy night shift at the Countess of Newbury Nursing Home. The home provides residential and nursing care for 12 females who have dementia.

It has been a difficult shift for Sarah, as several of the residents woke up at least three times in the night and became confused and noisy.

When the shift finishes, Sarah and a colleague go to catch the bus and begin chatting about the events of the night. There are several people at the bus stop, including a relative of one of the residents in the nursing home.

Sarah and the nurse are laughing about an incident that involves this relative and mention the resident's name.

When Sarah returns to work the next night, she finds that the relative has made a complaint about their behaviour at the bus stop. The manager said that Sarah and her colleague's behaviour had broken the rules that accompany one of the health and social care values.

1 Can you name the underpinning value that Sarah should have applied to her behaviour?

2 If the relative had not been at the bus stop, would Sarah's behaviour still have been unacceptable?

Dignity

We all want our dignity to be protected, for example by being allowed to dress in private. Individuals who use health and social care services are often vulnerable in some way. Health and social care workers must protect the dignity of each individual by being aware of situations and actions that could cause embarrassment and make the individual feel silly or exposed.

For example, it is important to ensure that when we are supporting individuals to perform personal care tasks, such as dressing, using the toilet and bathing, we close doors, screens and curtains. We should never stare at an individual or expose parts of their body any more than is really necessary.

It is also important to *offer* support to individuals rather than *insisting* on giving support. Allowing individuals to be as independent as possible protects their dignity because it shows that you are recognising them as a person with abilities. Making fun of someone because they have an accident, or take a long time to complete personal tasks, is not only unkind, it also reduces an individual's sense of dignity by embarrassing them.

Sometimes individuals cannot feed themselves; this may be due to illness, injury or age. Care workers can protect the dignity of individuals by speaking politely to the individual, not rushing them and allowing them to finish the first mouthful before offering another. It is also important to allow individuals to leave the food unfinished if they are no longer hungry. Never try to force someone to complete their meal as this will make them feel undignified. All concerns should be reported to the manager or supervisor.

On work placement or in employment, always remember that everyone needs support at some time in their life; deliver care to service users in the way you would wish to be cared for.

How can this care worker protect the dignity of the service user?

Activity	Helping someone to eat

Resources:

- breakfast cereal
- spoons
- milk
- cereal bowls.

In pairs, take turns to feed each other with the breakfast cereal and then answer the following questions:

1 How did being fed make you feel?

2 Did you feel dignified?

3 If you had to be fed by someone else, what points would you like them to consider?

4 What have you learned from this activity?

Exploring care values (2)

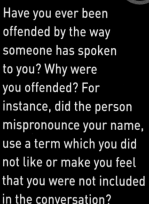

Key terms

Respect – showing recognition of the value of an individual.

Discriminate – to treat a person or group differently from others.

Appropriate terms – ways of addressing individuals that do not offend them.

Offence – words that cause offence can include racist terms or terms that insult an individual's gender, disability or sexuality.

Respect for the individual

We all prefer to be treated with **respect**, for instance being addressed by our name rather than being addressed as 'you' or 'love'. The use of our name shows that we are being fully recognised as an individual, which is important. In order to show respect to the individuals we give care to, it is important for workers in health and social care to remember the following rules:

- Do not **discriminate** against an individual, in other words do not treat one individual differently from another.
- Do not judge individuals for what they may have done.
- Use the **appropriate terms** when addressing an individual, for example Dr, Mrs, Mr, Miss, Begum.
- Do not use words that could cause **offence**.
- Show interest in each individual, which includes learning how to pronounce names that are unfamiliar to you.
- Do not make fun of individuals, for instance if they make a mistake, can't do something, forget something or have an accident.

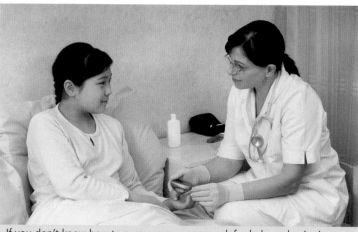

If you don't know how to pronounce a name, ask for help and write it down so you can remember it later.

Activity   Respect and discrimination

Ask your teacher's permission to conduct an internet search:

1 Find out the correct ways of addressing people from three ethnic groups that are different from your own.
2 Find out the correct names of two medical conditions that may cause an individual to be disabled.
3 Investigate two organisations that support individuals who have experienced discrimination.
4 Create a short presentation for your class on your findings.
5 Produce a handout to accompany your presentation to be given to your class colleagues.

Safeguarding

This means that we must ensure the physical and emotional safety of all individuals in our care. For example, signing in and out of a work placement tells the manager who is on the premises and helps to prevent unauthorised people, who could potentially cause harm, coming in. Safeguarding also means that we do not behave in a way that causes the users of the service to feel threatened or afraid. This can include things like not shouting or waving your arms around, as this sort of behaviour can be frightening to a vulnerable person. You must also be careful to take reasonable health and safety precautions, such as replacing disinfectant in the correct cupboard, and reporting trailing flexes and frayed edges of carpets to the manager or senior professional on duty.

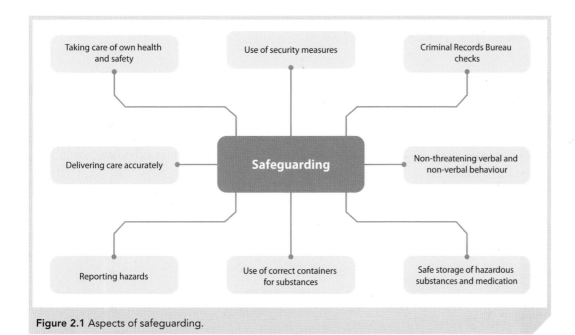

Figure 2.1 Aspects of safeguarding.

Remember

- Everyone who works or is on placement in health and social care has a responsibility to safeguard the users of the service.
- Never assume that safeguarding is only the responsibility of senior staff or, if you are on placement, only of the employed staff.
- The procedures that support safeguarding must be observed at all times.
- Not following safeguarding procedures could mean that you are breaking the law.
- Service users are often vulnerable and are relying on carers to ensure their physical and emotional safety.
- Taking care of your own health and safety helps to safeguard others.
- Everyone needs care at some time in their life; be as careful of the safety of others as you would like others to be of yours.

Exploring care values (3)

Person-centred care

Person-centred care is a way of delivering health and social care that places the individual at the centre of the activity. Rather than professionals deciding what is best for an individual, producing a plan and delivering the care, the individual is involved in every stage of the process. The individual's needs and preferences, likes and dislikes are considered. For example, they may prefer the physiotherapist to attend on a day other than Friday so that they can attend the mosque for prayers. Another example may be that an individual may need crèche facilities in order to attend counselling for depression. This approach to care considers the whole person, rather than just one or two needs. This is why it is called 'person-centred'.

Case study

Mrs Karen Smith is a 42-year-old woman with longstanding mental health problems who has recently suffered a stroke, which has reduced the movement in her left arm and affected her speech.

Following her stroke, Mrs Smith was assessed by the mental health team, the physiotherapist and the speech and language therapist.

The professionals then met to discuss what would be the best way to support Mrs Smith and enable her to live as normal a life as possible.

Mrs Smith was invited to a discussion with the professionals and asked what her needs and wishes were. Mrs Smith wanted to remain at home and continue with her life. She attended a mental health drop-in centre where she had been involved in various activities.

The professionals involved Mrs Smith in the planning of her care and took into account her wishes, likes, dislikes and preferences as much as possible. It was agreed that:

- the physiotherapy appointments could be on Monday mornings, which would enable Mrs Smith to attend the drop-in centre on Monday afternoons; transport was arranged as Mrs Smith has found bus travel difficult since her stroke
- the speech and language therapist would call on Wednesday mornings to enable Mrs Smith to attend the drop-in centre on Wednesday afternoons; again, transport would be arranged
- a community care assistant would call twice daily to assist Mrs Smith with personal care
- the mobile meals service would provide a main meal.

1 How would the care arrangements support Mrs Smith to carry on with her life?

2 Why was it important for Mrs Smith to be involved in planning her own care?

3 How would Mrs Smith have been affected, if she had not been involved in planning her own care?

WorkSpace

▶ **PHIL PETERS**

Healthcare Assistant

I am a healthcare assistant working for a busy NHS Trust. I usually work on one of the general surgical wards, but I may be asked to help out in other areas of the hospital. I really enjoy my work, making patients feel more comfortable and working with the nurses to deliver high-quality care and support. I worked on the hospital main reception at first, but prefer working on the ward as I can follow my patients' progress.

I work 37.5 hours a week on a rota basis, including working some evenings, nights and weekends. You have to be flexible, but that's OK – I prefer shift work to nine to five because it means that I see my patients at different stages of their recovery.

These are some of the tasks I have to do:

- Washing, dressing and feeding patients who cannot do this for themselves and providing support for those who need extra help.
- Helping people to regain their mobility after surgery.
- Bed making.
- Generally assisting with the overall comfort of patients; for example, by smoothing pillows, adjusting bed tables, placing articles such as spectacles and newspapers within easy reach.
- Monitoring the condition of patients by taking temperature, pulse and respiration and accurately recording these details on the patients' medical charts.
- Helping patients to use the toilet or providing bedpans for those who cannot get out of bed.

I found that my BTEC Level 2 qualification in Health and Social Care was really useful in my job, particularly the unit about values. I was able to see how the staff on the ward applied these values in their patient care. I didn't need any particular qualifications to get the job, but having the BTEC Level 2 Certificate really helped.

Think about it

1 Why are the health and social care values important to Phil's role as a healthcare assistant?

2 Which values do you think would apply when helping patients to perform personal care tasks, such as washing or dressing?

Exploring care values (4)

Duty of care

There is a **legal requirement** for all health and social care workers to provide a **duty of care**. This means that while a member of staff is on the premises, even if they are on their break, they have a responsibility to ensure the safety of the individuals who use the service. This can include things like waiting to go for lunch until there are enough staff available to ensure the safety of the individuals using the service. It also means completing tasks to the highest possible standard so that individuals receive the care they need. A duty of care applies to all areas of professional practice, underpinning the delivery of health and social care. Without this, just like the house without foundations, health and social care falls down and individuals are placed at risk.

Key terms

Legal requirement – something that has to be done by law.

Duty of care – responsibility to keep people in our care safe from harm.

Code of practice – list of rules which state how health and social care must be delivered.

Activity — Codes of practice and legislation

A **code of practice** is a list of rules that should be followed by all staff when providing health or social care for individuals.

Ask your teacher's permission to use the internet to find the codes of practice that relate to the following professions:

- Nursing and midwifery
- Social care
- Social work
- Speech and language therapy
- Physiotherapy.

Produce a poster of your findings to display in the classroom.

Why is it important to protect the patient's dignity at all times?

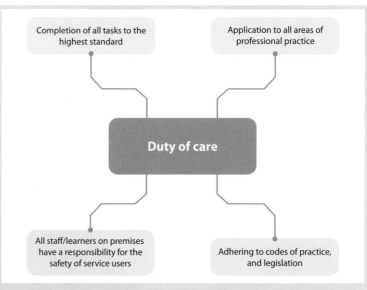

Completion of all tasks to the highest standard

Application to all areas of professional practice

Duty of care

All staff/learners on premises have a responsibility for the safety of service users

Adhering to codes of practice, and legislation

Figure 2.2 What does duty of care mean?

Miss Jennifer van der Pays is 23 and has Down's syndrome. She works at a local supermarket and lives with her parents in the suburb of Welmsley. Jennifer recently had a fall and had to attend the accident and emergency department of her local hospital. The receptionist in the department addressed Jennifer as 'Miss van der Pays' and used a polite tone when speaking to her. The nurse asked Jennifer to come into a cubicle and remove her shoes and tights so that the doctor could examine the injury. The nurse asked if she needed any help to get onto the couch and closed the cubicle curtains.

1 Name two values which underpinned the care received by Jennifer.

2 Name any part of the event where the values you have named could have been used to support Jennifer more.

3 For the values you have named, discuss their importance in providing high-quality care for Jennifer.

4 For the values you have named, assess the impact on Jennifer's care, and say if they were applied effectively or ineffectively.

Tips

You must discuss each value in turn, relating it to the delivery of health and social care and referring to your chosen examples. You should demonstrate in your discussion how each value interrelates to support the delivery of health and social care.

You should extend your work to assess the potential impact on individuals when the values are applied to care delivery. You should give careful consideration of the differences in impact when the values are applied effectively or ineffectively. You should refer to examples; check with your teacher before using examples from the internet.

Take it further

Read the scenario about Jennifer again and answer the following questions:

1 Which code of practice would the nurse be following when she was supporting Jennifer?

2 How can this code of practice ensure that Jennifer receives a high standard of care?

3 What factors could prevent Jennifer receiving a high standard of care?

Empowering individuals

Getting started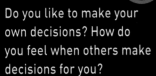

Do you like to make your own decisions? How do you feel when others make decisions for you?

How do you think service users feel when health or social care workers make decisions *for* them rather than *with* them?

Key terms

Empower – to give service users control of their own lives.

Introduction

When we apply values to health and social care practice, we empower individuals who use the services. Health and social care professionals do this by delivering care in a way that enables individuals to take control of their own lives as much as possible. These are some of the ways in which this can happen.

Adapting activities and environments

Activities can include leisure pursuits, such as a game of skittles or a quiz, or everyday tasks, such as feeding or dressing. Adaptations, such as bright-coloured bowling balls, which can be seen more easily by an individual with a visual impairment, or a quiz set at a level that enables individuals with learning disabilities to join in the fun, can mean full participation and an enhanced quality of life.

In the same way, providing an individual who has arthritis with a shoe horn attached to a long handle can enable them to put on their own shoes rather than waiting for assistance.

Environments can also be adapted. For example, improving the lighting in the day centre to enable individuals with a hearing impairment to lip-read will support them in joining in with a conversation rather than feeling like an outsider.

Braille playing cards could enable people with visual impairments to join in.

Taking account of the individual

Recognising an individual's rights is a legal requirement in the United Kingdom and in many other countries. Individuals have a right to health and social care support if they need it. They also have a right to support that is underpinned by values such as respect, dignity and confidentiality. Health and social care professionals agree with these values and work hard to deliver appropriate care and support, meeting the needs of individuals.

In a busy setting, it can be much harder to take account of preferences, likes and dislikes. For example, an individual may prefer to have breakfast after hanging the washing out on the line, but the care worker may find it more convenient to serve breakfast first. It is important to remember that the care worker is there to support the individual and not the other way around. In the same way, it is important to recognise that attending to likes and dislikes is a way of empowering individuals by recognising their individuality. For example, requiring halal meat does not mean that the individual only likes eating food prepared to one recipe; requiring a vegetarian diet does not mean including lentils in every meal. Allowing individuals to state their likes, dislikes and preferences enables them to have some control over their everyday lives. We all like to have this, but it is particularly important for vulnerable individuals who are unable to perform for themselves tasks that others take for granted, such as those involved with personal care.

This is particularly important when supporting individuals who cannot speak for themselves. For example, someone who has a speech and language impairment or who has dementia will receive better care if the care workers have an understanding of the person's likes and dislikes. When caring for a person who cannot express themselves, it is important to involve family and friends who can provide the important details that can make such a difference to care delivery. Just imagine how you would feel if you were constantly having to listen to music you did not like or presented with food that you would not choose to eat and couldn't express your feelings or preferences.

Activity   Considering an individual's preferences

In small groups, discuss how important it is to each of you to have your likes and dislikes considered:

- at meal times
- in deciding which film to see
- when being bought new clothes by relatives
- in choosing what music is played.

Discuss why these things are important to you.

Working in partnership with other people

Introduction

Working in health and social care involves working with others, which may include relatives and friends of an individual, in addition to health and social care professionals. It is important to be willing to work with different people, showing respect for their opinions and accepting their help when you need it. In this way, mistakes can be avoided and you will progress in your career.

Health and social care professionals work cooperatively with fellow professionals, relatives and the individual users of the service to provide a standard of care that meets the needs of the individuals in the setting.

When you show a willingness to work with others, you are contributing to a pleasant working environment. And remember, health and social care teams are more efficient when individuals work together, sharing tasks and supporting each other.

Just checking

1 Describe three ways of adapting activities to meet particular needs.
2 Why does providing care that takes account of an individual's likes, dislikes and preferences empower them?
3 Why is it important to be willing to work with other people in health and social care?

Case study 1

Ramón Suarez is admitted to Ward 17 complaining of severe abdominal pain. He is examined by the surgeon, who decides that Ramón's appendix has perforated and he must have his appendix removed.

Ramón becomes very distressed because having the operation means that he will have to stay in hospital. Ramón has been living with his disabled 82-year-old mother since the death of his father a year ago. The old lady would now be alone at home and unable to care for herself.

The surgeon refers the matter to the ward manager, who contacts social services. A social worker calls to see Ramón's mother and arranges for her to be taken into a local care home until Ramón has fully recovered. He also arranges for someone from the care home to bring Ramón's mother to visit him while he is in hospital.

1 Why do you think the surgeon refers the matter to the ward manager?
2 What partnerships can you find in this case study?

Why is it important to work together to solve problems?

Case study 2

Rebecca and Nigel James live with their three-year-old daughter, Helen, in a pleasant suburb at the edge of a large city.

Helen has autism and attends a special nursery in the city four times a week. As Helen's speech is not progressing at the rate expected for her age, the GP has referred her to Teresa, a speech and language therapist. Teresa has worked with Rebecca and Nigel, showing them how to encourage Rebecca. She has asked them for information about Helen, calling them 'the experts'.

Rebecca and Nigel feel that Teresa shared the support and planning for Helen with them and this has encouraged them to work with her as partners.

1 Why was it important that Teresa worked with Rebecca and Nigel?

2 Why did Teresa call Rebecca and Nigel the experts?

Case study 3

Simon King has just been released from prison where he has served a three-year sentence for burglary. Simon has been referred to the Probation Service and has to meet with his probation officer three times a week.

Simon's wife divorced him while he was in prison, so he needs a new home and the prison service has referred Simon to the local housing officer.

1 Why is it important for the professionals to work in partnership when supporting Simon?

2 What could happen to Simon if the professionals do not communicate with each other?

Discussion point

In small groups, discuss:

* why it is important for each of the groups to work in partnership
* why it is important to include the individuals receiving care in the partnerships.

Promoting choice

Introduction

Do you like to have choices? Do you like to decide what, when and where to eat, what to wear, whether to stay in or go out? Of course you do, and most of the time you can make those choices for yourself without even thinking about it.

Did you know?

There is a clear link between giving an individual the right to make informed choices and their overall wellbeing.

In groups, discuss why you think this could be.

Link

This topic links to Unit 5: Promoting Health and Wellbeing and Unit 8: Individual Rights in Health and Social Care.

Individuals who use health and social care services also like to make choices; they have a right to make choices, but are not always allowed to exercise that right. Health and social care professionals speak about 'informed choices', this means that individuals should be given all of the information they need in order to decide about, for example, accepting treatment or entering residential care.

Here are some of the reasons why this may not happen:

- The member of staff does not realise that there are choices available.
- The individual may have difficulty in expressing choices.
- The member of staff may be in a hurry and decides that it would be quicker to decide for the individual.

None of these is an acceptable reason not to offer the available choices. Individuals have a right to choose what they will eat, what they will wear and whether or not they will take part in an activity. They also have a right to choose whether or not to accept treatment. It is part of the professional's role in health and social care to promote choice and enable individuals to exercise their rights.

Think about the choices you make every day:

- what to wear
- what to eat
- what music to listen to
- which friends you will meet after school or college
- who you will call or text on your mobile phone.

How different would your life be if those choices were removed? Try to imagine what life would be like without those choices. Would you like this restricted life? Would anyone?

How would you feel if you had to play football or were not allowed to?

Why do we support individuals?

Do you ever need support? Of course you do, everyone needs support sometimes. How individuals are supported makes a huge difference to their self-esteem, confidence and self-image. The right type of support is empowering; in other words, it enables people to stay or become independent, allowing them to do as much for themselves as possible. Ways of providing empowering support could include:

- adapting environments – for example, widening access so that individuals who use wheelchairs can go in and out of rooms and buildings without additional help

- offering people a choice of activities that reflect their individual interests and personalities

- providing **advocates** for individuals who cannot speak for themselves, perhaps due to speech and language difficulties or mental health issues

- providing opportunities for individuals to give feedback on the level of service they have received

- providing interpreters and translators for individuals for whom English is an additional language

- promoting **autonomy**; this means encouraging individuals to make their own decisions.

Some people may choose to live at home rather than a care home. What support do you think they may require?

Activity   Adapting activities

Produce a fun activity adapted for one of the following groups:

- visually impaired
- hearing impaired
- users of wheelchairs.

Use the activity yourself and give yourself a score from 1 to 5 on how user-friendly it is. (1 is excellent and 5 means that improvements are needed.)

Write a short report on how this activity could be adapted for use by individuals from one of the other groups in the list.

 Key terms

Advocate – a person responsible for acting and speaking on behalf of someone who is unable to do so.

Autonomy – freedom to make your own decisions.

Communication

Preferred ways of communicating

Effective communication is an important skill in health and social care. Using the appropriate form of communication is particularly important. In supporting service users it is best to use the form of communication that the individual prefers. This shows that we are interested in the individual and recognise them as a person.

Sometimes an individual's preferred way of communicating may be related to disability; for instance, a hearing impaired person might want you to facilitate their lip-reading. Whatever the reason, using an individual's preferred way of communication shows respect, protects dignity and demonstrates that we are delivering care and support that is underpinned by health and social care values.

Communication should be clear, understandable and fitted to the situation; using an individual's preferred way of communicating supports the development of trust between staff and service users, and should be regarded as part of the duty of care.

How is this care assistant adapting their behaviour to put the service user at ease?

Activity   Speaking the same language

- Find out how many different language groups there are in your home area.
- Find out how to say 'hello' in at least four of the different languages.
- Find out how to write 'hello' in as many of the languages as you can.
- Produce a poster for the classroom illustrating your findings.

Alternative methods of communication

Alternative methods of communication that individuals may wish to use could include British Sign Language, preferred by some individuals with a hearing impairment or who are without hearing, and Makaton, used by those with learning difficulties. Remember, individuals who use English as their additional language may be more comfortable using their first language. It is important that users of services are able to communicate in their preferred way; this will mean that they can express their needs and wants in a way that enables them to take part in decisions about their care and support.

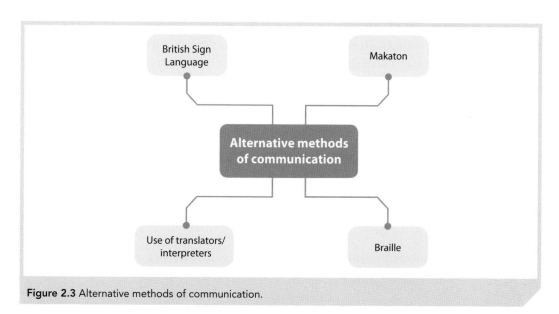

Figure 2.3 Alternative methods of communication.

Activity   Speech is not the only method

1 In groups, use the internet to find out how many different methods of communication exist that do not use speech.

2 Produce a poster for your classroom that shows the different methods of communication.

3 In groups, use the internet to find out about one organisation that supports individuals who use an alternative form of communication.

4 Discuss with your tutor/teacher the possibility of a fundraising event to support your chosen organisation.

Positive working practices

Getting started

How do you like to be supported in class? Choose the item from the list below that is the closest to your choice of support:

- Have the work taken away and finished for you.
- Have someone explain the task in a way that you understand and then allow you to complete it.
- Be offered more support than you really need, which makes you feel useless.

Key terms

Enablement – ways and means to act independently.

There are ways of working with individuals that promote empowerment and **enablement** and recognise each one as a person in their own right. Here are some examples:

- Needs-led assessment, which bases care planning on what an individual actually needs rather than following a general formula.
- Valuing diversity by appreciating the differences between individuals and planning care to fit these differences.
- Recognising that individuals have a right to care that meets their needs and is underpinned by health and social care values.
- Care planning that includes assessment of acceptable risks, rather than restricting individuals.
- Listening to individuals and discussing each stage of the care plan with them.

Just checking

1 What are the values that underpin current health and social care practice?
2 Name three ways of preserving an individual's dignity when delivering health or social care.
3 Explain what is meant by non-discriminatory practice and give an example.
4 Explain what is meant by a person-centred approach to care delivery.
5 Describe three examples of adapting activities.
6 Explain why a hearing-impaired individual would benefit from improved lighting in their setting.
7 Describe how using their preferred method of communication empowers an individual.
8 Give one example of how the provision of an advocate can support an individual.
9 Describe three positive working practices.

Why is it important to discuss a care plan with a patient or service user?

Assessment activity 2.2

The Greenings Day Centre provides life skills training for young adults who have learning disabilities. The centre aims to prepare young adults for independent living by offering the following opportunities:

- money management
- travelling on public transport
- care of clothes
- shopping for clothes
- shopping for food
- working with others.

You are on work experience at the day centre, and are involved in supporting two of the young adults who are learning how to travel on public transport.

1 Name three ways in which you could empower these two young adults when working with them.

2 Explain why it would be important to consider the personal circumstances of both young adults when producing a plan that would empower them to use public transport.

3 Discuss how much you could consider the personal circumstances of these young adults when producing a transport plan. Are their personal circumstances the only factors to be considered, or are there others?

4 What are the potential difficulties in taking the young adults' personal circumstances into account?

5 Suggest ways of overcoming or managing three potential difficulties.

Tips

Question 3 asks you to discuss how much you can take individual circumstances into account when planning empowering care, or whether there are other factors to be considered. You should refer to such issues as:

- levels of resources, including staff
- the needs of other users of the service
- level of risk to the individual (acceptable/unacceptable).

You will need to refer to relevant examples, which could be those referred to in your work for this unit.

You must assess, or give careful consideration to, any potential difficulties that could arise when planning empowering care. For each potential difficulty that you suggest, you must make a suggestion to resolve the difficulty or improve the situation.

Introduction

How can you make sure you communicate with others of all ages and abilities effectively? Health and social care professionals need good communication skills to develop positive relationships and share information with people using services. Clear communication is important to enable service users to understand and agree to the care they are receiving. They also need to be able to communicate well with people's families and/or carers and their own colleagues and other professionals. Good communication between care professionals allows them to perform their roles effectively, work cooperatively with colleagues and build supportive relationships with service users. It is important, therefore, if you are considering a career in health and social care, to gain the knowledge, understanding and practical skills needed to develop effective interpersonal skills.

There are several different forms of communication used in a health and social care environment. This unit looks at verbal and non-verbal communication methods, and you will learn how they are used effectively in health and social care. You will also learn to recognise a range of factors which may create barriers to communication, preventing people accessing health and social care effectively. You will then consider ways in which these barriers may be overcome, including the use of alternative forms of communication.

Assessment: You will be assessed by a series of assignments set by your teacher/tutor.

Learning aims

In this unit you will:

A investigate different forms of communication

B investigate barriers to communication in health and social care

C communicate effectively in health and social care.

> The way you talk to people is really important. When I went on placement to a residential care home for older people I was told to crouch down to the level at which they were sitting so I wouldn't tower over them and intimidate them. I was also told to speak clearly but not patronisingly.
>
> Kirsten, *would-be care assistant, aged 16 years*

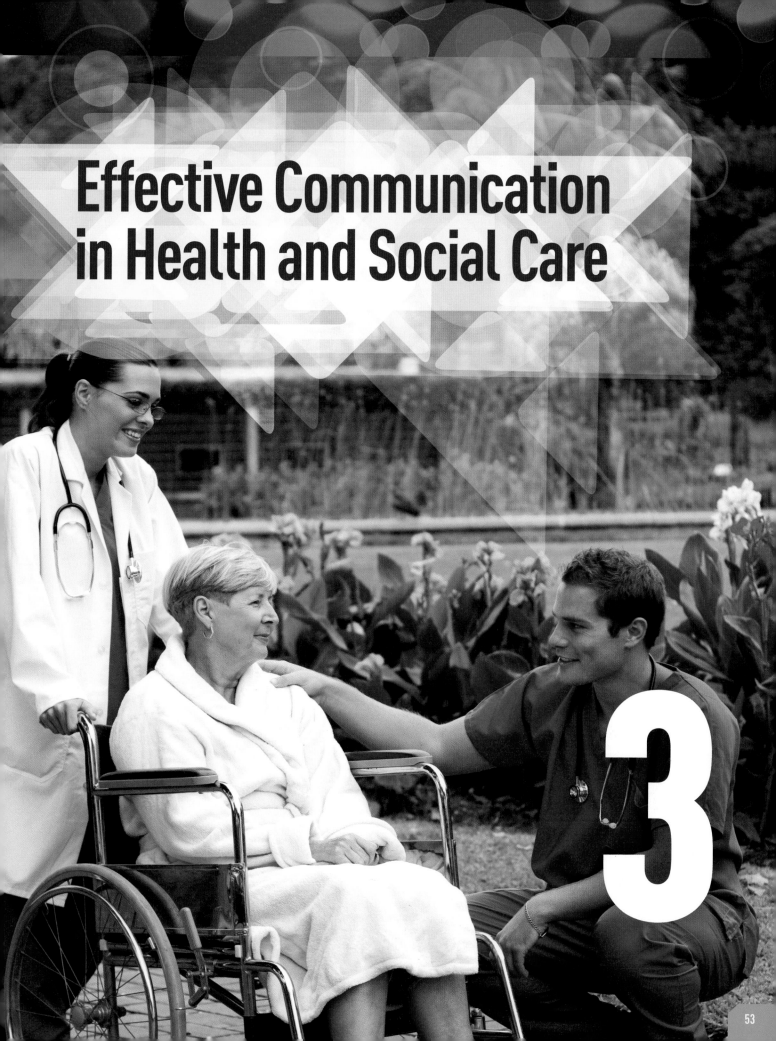

Effective Communication in Health and Social Care

3

Assessment Zone

This table shows what you must do in order to achieve a **Pass**, **Merit** or **Distinction** grade, and where you can find activities in this book to help you.

Assessment criteria			
Level 1	**Level 2 Pass**	**Level 2 Merit**	**Level 2 Distinction**
Learning aim A: Investigate different forms of communication			
1A.1 Identify different forms of verbal and non-verbal communication.	**2A.P1** Describe different forms of verbal and non-verbal communication. **Assessment activity 3.1 See page 62.**	**2A.M1** Explain the advantages and disadvantages of different forms of communication used, with reference to a one-to-one and a group interaction. **Assessment activity 3.1 See page 62.**	**2A.D1** Assess the effectiveness of different forms of communication for service users with different needs. **Assessment activity 3.1 See page 62.**
1A.2 Identify different forms of alternative communication for different needs, using examples from health and social care.	**2A.P2** Describe different forms of alternative communication for different needs, using examples from health and social care. **Assessment activity 3.1 See page 62.**		
Learning aim B: Investigate barriers to communication in health and social care			
1B.3 Outline the barriers to communication in health and social care.	**2B.P3** Describe the barriers to communication in health and social care and their effects on service users. **Assessment activity 3.2 See page 69.**	**2B.M2** Explain how measures have been implemented to overcome barriers to communication, with reference to a selected case. **Assessment activity 3.2 See page 69.**	**2B.D2** Evaluate the effectiveness of measures taken to remove barriers to communication, with reference to a selected case. **Assessment activity 3.2 See page 69.**
1B.4 Identify ways in which barriers to communication may be overcome for individuals with sensory loss.	**2B.P4** Using examples, explain ways in which barriers to communication may be overcome and the benefits to service users of overcoming these barriers. **Assessment activity 3.2 See page 69.**		
Learning aim C: Communicate effectively in health and social care			
1C.5 English Demonstrate communication skills through one interaction in health and social care, identifying the forms of communication used.	**2C.P5** English Demonstrate communication skills through interactions in health and social care, describing their effects. **Assessment activity 3.3 See page 75.**	**2C.M3** English Select and demonstrate communication skills through interactions in health and social care, explaining their effectiveness. **Assessment activity 3.3 See page 75.**	**2C.D3** English Select and demonstrate communication skills through one-to-one and group interactions in health and social care, evaluating their effectiveness and making recommendations for improvement. **Assessment activity 3.3 See page 75.**

English English signposting

How you will be assessed

The unit will be assessed by a series of internally assessed tasks. You will be expected to show an understanding of communication skills in the context of health and social care sectors. The tasks will be based on a scenario where you work in a local health or social care organisation.

Your assessment could be in the form of:

- producing training materials based on a case study and/or DVD based in a health and social care setting, such as a nursery, which:

  - identify, describe and evaluate the effectiveness of different forms of communication used

  - identify and describe a range of barriers to communication, explaining and evaluating ways to overcome them

- a training DVD demonstrating good practice in one-to-one and group interaction.

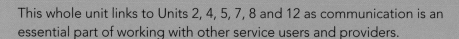

LINK

This whole unit links to Units 2, 4, 5, 7, 8 and 12 as communication is an essential part of working with other service users and providers.

Why do we communicate? (1)

Introduction

In this topic you will learn about why we communicate, why good **communication** skills are so important within a health and social care environment and the different **contexts** for communication. We communicate with others all the time, wherever we may be, often without even realising it and sometimes not intending to.

Communication skills

Interpersonal skills are those that enable us to interact with others, so allowing us to communicate successfully. Good communication skills are vital for those working in health and social care as they help them to:

- develop positive relationships with people using services and their families and friends, so that they can understand and meet their needs
- develop positive relationships with work colleagues and other professionals
- share information with people using the services
- report on the work they do with people.

Why is communication so important between colleagues?

Activity   Portrayal of hospitals on TV

Sit in a circle. Discuss the statement 'TV programmes, such as *Casualty* or *Holby City* create the wrong impression of working life in a large hospital'. One person starts the discussion holding a ball or bean bag. When they have made their point, they throw the ball to someone else in the group and that person responds to what they have said. The ball has to go to each person in the group before anyone who has already spoken can speak again. When the discussion has finished, discuss the following points in your group:

1 Did everyone join in properly? If not, why not?
2 How did sitting in a circle help?
3 How could you tell that someone was about to finish talking?
4 Did you find the task easier or harder with the ball? Why?
5 Look at Figure 3.1. Who in the group used these skills best? How could you tell?

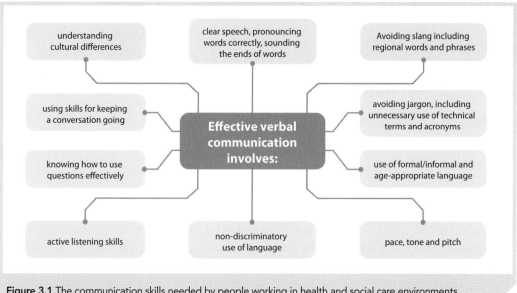

Figure 3.1 The communication skills needed by people working in health and social care environments.

Contexts

One-to-one communication

One-to-one means one person communicating with another person with no other people joining in. The conversation needs a start, for instance a greeting, such as 'Hi', a middle section when you both discuss what you need to talk about, and an ending, such as 'See you later'.

Group communication

Group communication is harder because it only works properly if everyone is able to be involved. Groups work best if there is a team leader who encourages everyone to have a say in turn, rather than several people trying to speak at once and others not joining in.

Formal and informal communication

Formal communication tends to start with a greeting, such as 'Good afternoon. How are you feeling today?' It can be used to show respect for others. Formal conversation is often used when a professional person, such as a health or social care worker, speaks to someone using a service. It is clear, correct and avoids misunderstanding.

Informal communication is more likely to start with 'Hi. How are you?' and allows for a more casual approach and more varied expression, for instance appropriate to the area someone lives. Informal communication is warm and friendly. People usually communicate more informally with friends, including those they work closely with on a day-to-day basis.

Effective verbal communication

Verbal communication uses words to present ideas, thoughts and feelings. Good verbal communication is the ability to both present and explain your ideas clearly through the spoken word, and to listen carefully to other people. This involves using a variety of approaches and styles appropriate to the audience or person you are addressing.

Key terms

Formal – polite, respectful or conventional.

Informal – casual.

Why do we communicate? (2)

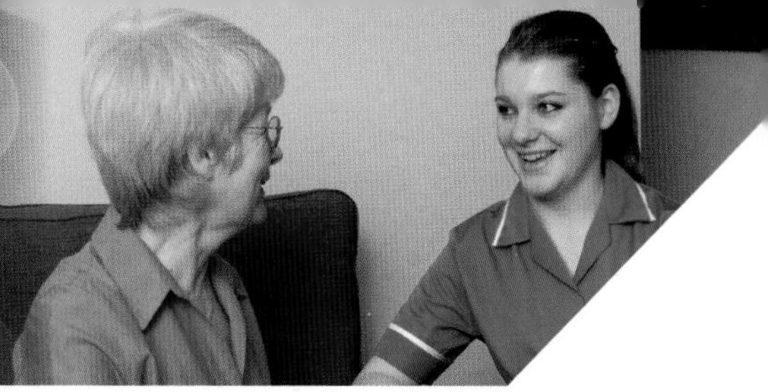

Getting started

Ways to communicate

Think about the different people you identified as communicating with in the last activity. Sketch a quick spider diagram showing all the different ways you communicate with others in a typical day.

Effective non-verbal communication

This topic looks at different forms of non-verbal communication.

Non-verbal communication

This refers to the messages we send out to express ideas and opinions without talking, the main elements of which are shown in Figure 3.2. Understanding body language is very important as it often gives care workers a better idea of how someone is feeling than what they say. It is also important that as a carer you understand what messages your own body language is giving to the person you are trying to help.

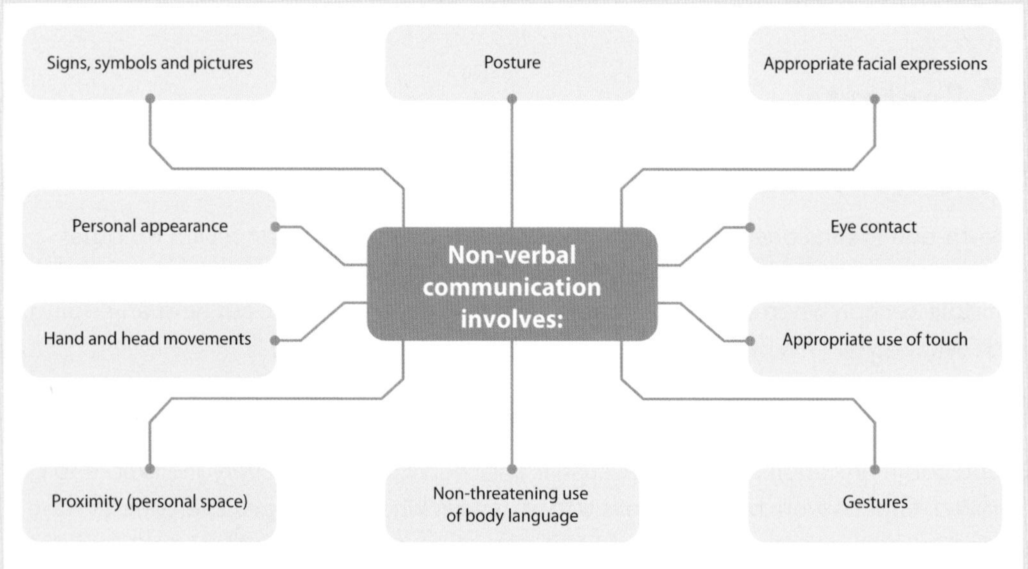

Figure 3.2 The main elements involved in non-verbal communication.

Link

This topic links to Unit 7: Equality and Diversity in Health and Social Care.

Activity Showing emotions

1 Draw a set of cartoon faces showing the following emotions: (i) worried (ii) bored (iii) surprised (iv) sad (v) aggressive.

2 Cut pictures out of magazines with people showing different emotions. Put them into groups according to the emotion and then test your work with a partner to see if they can work out which emotion is being portrayed by each.

Body language includes:

- **Posture**: the way you sit or stand or even move can send messages. For example, shaking your head while someone else is talking might indicate that you disagree with them, or waving your arms around can show you are excited. Sitting facing the person you are talking to, with your arms unfolded and a smile on your face, shows a positive and warm response.

- **Facial expression**: the human face is very expressive, able to convey countless emotions without saying a word. The facial expressions for happiness, sadness, anger, surprise, fear and disgust are the same across cultures. It is important to match your facial expressions to the conversation, for example, not smiling when someone is talking about something sad.

- **Eye contact**: most people find that the visual sense affects them most, so eye contact is especially important. We can often tell what someone is feeling by their eyes. Our eyes become wider when we have positive feelings, for example when we are excited or happy, attracted to, or interested in someone. Eye contact is also important in keeping a conversation going and for judging the other person's response.

- **Appropriate use of touch and personal space**: touching another person or moving into their **personal space** can send messages of care and affection, but it can also indicate threat or power over that person. It is important to think about the health and social care environment you are in and what you are trying to convey before touching a person or getting too close to them.

- **Gestures**: there are certain common signs or gestures that most people automatically recognise, but it is important to understand cultural norms so as not to unintentionally cause offence. For example, thumbs-up can mean that all is well and is perfectly acceptable in Western culture, but in the Middle East it is not only unacceptable but also one of the biggest insults possible. It also causes offence in countries such as Greece and Russia.

- **Non-threatening use of body language**: it is important not to give out negative messages through your body language. Turning away slightly with your arms folded portrays negative feelings of boredom, coldness and lack of interest.

- **Personal space**: getting too close to, or far away from, someone can create unease. Getting too close for instance, and so invading their personal space, can cause discomfort, intimidation or distress. The size of a person's personal space often depends on their culture. Americans tend to require more personal space than people from many other cultures. Also, getting too close to someone with a mental illness can be very distressing for them. If a person backs away a little when you are speaking to them don't try to close the gap, as this will make them feel uncomfortable. How close you can move into a person's personal space is very much an individual preference.

> ### Key terms
>
> **Personal space** – the area immediately surrounding a person that they consider to be their own personal territory. People generally feel uncomfortable if others 'invade' this personal space. Everyone's idea of personal space is different.

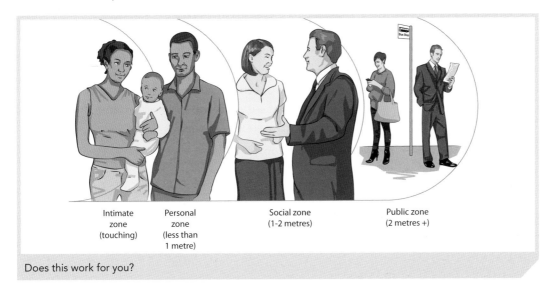

| Intimate zone (touching) | Personal zone (less than 1 metre) | Social zone (1-2 metres) | Public zone (2 metres +) |

Does this work for you?

Alternative forms of communication

Introduction

Sometimes it is necessary to find an alternative form of communication to meet people's particular needs, such as communication challenges caused by visual and hearing impairments and learning difficulties. This topic covers some of the wide range of options available.

The Braille system.

Visual impairment

- **Braille**: the Braille system is widely used by blind people to read and write. It was devised in 1821 by Frenchman, Louis Braille. Each Braille character is made up of six dot positions, arranged in a rectangle. A dot may be raised in any of the six positions to form sixty-four possible combinations and these raised dots are read by touch.
- **Braille software**: this creates Braille and comes in a wide range of packages, including those to create mathematical and musical notation as well as text and to translate different languages.

Hearing impairment

- **British Sign Language**: this system uses visual signs made up of shapes, positions and movements of the hands, arms or body and facial expressions. Sign language is commonly used by the families and friends of deaf people as well as by those who are deaf or hard of hearing themselves.
- **Finger spelling**: this is the representation of letters and sometimes numbers by tracing the shapes of letters in the air or on a hand. American, French and Irish Sign Language are all examples of one-handed finger spelling as compared with British Sign Language, which is two-handed.
- **Text messaging**: the vibration function on mobile phones alerts the hearing-impaired when messages and emails arrive.

Learning or speech difficulties

- **Communication passports**: these were invented in 1991 and are a way of documenting and presenting information about children and adults with disabilities who are unable to speak for themselves. They make sense of formal assessment and record the important things about the individual, in an easy to read, portable and person-centred way. Communication passports are now widely used in home, care, social work and health and education settings and are a way of making and of supporting an individual's transitions between services.
- **Bliss symbols**: these are used to provide a written language for people with severe speech disabilities. The system is based on concepts rather than words. It was developed by the Austrian Charles Bliss who wanted to create a universal written language that people speaking any language could learn and communicate in.

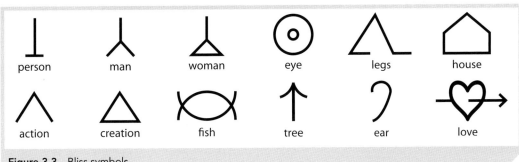

Figure 3.3 Bliss symbols.

- **Makaton**: this is a method of communication using signs and symbols. Unlike British Sign Language, it uses speech as well as actions and symbols, using picture cards. Makaton ties in facial expressions with a word to make the word more easily recognised by those with learning difficulties.
- **Technological aids**: technology provides many electronic aids to help us communicate. For example, computers record, store and communicate information very quickly and efficiently over long distances. Electronic aids can turn small movements into written words and then into speech, such as the voice box most famously used by the scientist, Professor Stephen Hawking.
- **Use of pictures to aid communication**: pictures can be used to communicate with people who have no ability to speak or use a language. For example, many people with autism use picture cards as they tend to learn visually and can communicate better with images and pictures. These have the advantage of being a universal means of communication understandable by people of all ages, abilities and languages.

People who can aid communication

Sometimes it is helpful to involve a specialist to aid communication in health and social care. If someone using a service needs help to communicate because, for example, they use sign language or because they speak a different language, they could use an interpreter. For help with written documents they could use a translator. Some people with speech or learning difficulties could benefit from having an advocate present to help them to communicate.

Activity   Signs, interpreters, translators and advocates

1 Do some research to find out the symbol for at least ten common signs, such as wet floor, used in any health and social care setting, which most people will recognise. Produce an information leaflet for people with learning difficulties to teach them these signs.

2 Find out what the following people do and research how health and social care settings use them:

   (i)   an interpreter for speech

   (ii)   a translator for written word/documents

   (iii)   an advocate.

? Did you know?

We all regularly use non-verbal communication without realising it, for example using symbols in universal chemical formulae. Almost all of us know that water is H_2O. Similarly we recognise road signs and hazard signs, which are often entirely visual.

Investigate different forms of communication

Here are some questions to test what you have learned so far. You will also find a practice assessment assignment to try.

Assessment activity 3.1

2A.P1 | 2A.P2 | 2A.M1 | 2A.D1

You are a trainee early years worker at a nursery in a big town. The children have a wide range of abilities, and a few have learning difficulties. The nursery manager is trying to get some funding from the local council and needs to provide evidence of work she and her staff have done with different children. You have been asked to produce an information pack about the different communication methods that can be used in the nursery by staff and volunteers.

Your pack should include a report on the advantages, disadvantages and effectiveness of each method of communication.

Tip

You could start the activity by producing a mind map of the basic facts about different communication methods. The pack should contain material in a number of formats such as leaflets, booklets and posters.

Just checking

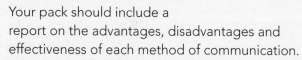

1 What are three features of one-to-one communication?

2 What are three things that help group communication?

3 What is the difference between informal and formal communication? Which would you use with (i) a friend, (ii) someone you have not met before but are trying to help in your job as a doctor's receptionist (iii) your manager?

4 Explain what is meant by verbal communication.

5 Give three examples of non-verbal communication.

6 Describe three examples of when signs, symbols and pictures are useful forms of communication.

7 Describe two alternative methods of communication for someone who (i) is visually impaired, (ii) is hearing impaired, and (iii) has learning difficulties.

WorkSpace

Emily Burgess

Early years worker

I am an early years worker in a busy small town nursery. I work in a team that includes six other early years workers, a manager and a cleaner. We have three separate rooms so children of different age groups can have their own room, although they do mix together for certain activities. There is also a room where staff can keep their personal belongings.

My main task is to help to look after the eight children aged between one and three. I love this age group, as they change so quickly. I organise activities for them, such as big-book reading, playing in the dressing-up corner and creative activities, such as finger painting and making cards for special occasions like Mother's Day. We sing songs every day and play simple musical instruments once a week. I also have to make sure the children are fed and changed. Another task is to keep records of what we do each day, the progress made by individual children and details of any concerns I may have about any of them, which I then discuss with the manager.

Each day the children play in the small enclosed area outside for a short time if the weather is good enough. Although the emphasis is on fun, all the activities are designed to deliver the early learning goals, so helping the children develop their skills and knowledge.

I speak to the parents on a daily basis when they drop off and collect their children. I enjoy the fact that I am helping both the children and their parents. I love my job because I enjoy meeting lots of different people and feeling that I am making a difference to them.

Think about it

1 Why are communication skills so important to Emily's job?
2 What are your strengths when it comes to communication? What are the areas that you would like to improve?
3 How can you make sure you communicate with others of all ages and abilities effectively?

Barriers to communication

Woman found in jungle after 20 years

Rochom P'ngieng was today found alive in the Cambodian jungle where it is believed she has been living for 20 years after getting lost at the age of eight. She is unable to communicate except by using animal noises, hates to wear clothes and crawls rather than walks.

How would being isolated from civilisation affect how well you communicate?

What other forms of isolation could make it difficult to communicate?

Introduction

In this topic you will learn about factors that affect communication, called barriers to communication, and their effects, starting with environmental, physical and language barriers.

Factors that affect communication

It is important to be able to communicate effectively in a health or social care setting because a service user will not be able to take part in a discussion about their care or planning their future if they do not understand what is being said.

There are many barriers to communication.

Environmental barriers, e.g.:

- **Lighting** – someone who doesn't see very well will struggle to read written information in a dimly lit room.
- **Seating** – a person in a wheelchair or with dwarfism will be unable to communicate with a receptionist in a health and social care setting if the desk is too high for them to see over.
- **External noise** – someone with a hearing or speech impairment will not be able to communicate if they cannot receive or pass on information because there is too much noise.
- **Lack of space** – a person in a wheelchair will find it impossible to access a service if they cannot get into a room or across a room to a reception desk to communicate with a service provider.
- **Uneven surface or stairs** – wheelchair users or people with impaired mobility may not be able to access areas that have an uneven surface or stairs.

Physical barriers, e.g.:

- **Sensory deprivation** – when someone cannot receive or pass on information because they have an impairment to one or more of their senses, most commonly a visual or a hearing disability.
- **Physical and mental illness** – when someone is ill they may not be able to communicate as effectively as when they are well. Some long-term (chronic) illnesses such as Parkinson's disease or mental illness also affect an individual's ability to communicate.

Activity   Environmental and physical barriers

Think about your own experience of health and social care settings, such as visits to the doctor, dentist or optician. Can you identify any barriers to communication? Discuss these with a partner and think about how they would make you feel if you were unwell or had a disability.

More factors

Language barriers, e.g.:

- **Foreign language** – someone speaking a different language or using sign language may not be able to make any sense of information they are being given by someone trying to help them.

- **Slang** – when a service user uses language that only a certain group of people use, misunderstanding or lack of understanding can occur. For instance someone saying they have a problem with their waterworks could mean their plumbing system, but also means a problem going to the toilet.

- **Jargon** – when a service provider uses technical language the service user may not understand. For example, the doctor may say that a patient needs bloods and an MRI scan. That can sound very frightening. It is better if the doctor explains that they need to take some blood to do some simple tests and then explains what a MRI scan is.

Social isolation, e.g.:

- **Lack of confidence** – a person may not have the confidence to ask a health or social care professional questions.

- **Intimidation** – when someone is intimidated by someone else, they won't be able to concentrate so will not be able to hear or understand what people are saying to them. They will also be reluctant to ask questions.

- **Following abuse** – abuse can cause someone to become withdrawn and unable to concentrate or communicate.

- **Trauma** – can cause distress and an inability to listen properly and so a person may misinterpret or not understand what is said.

> **Key terms**
>
> **Jargon** – technical words used by a professional person as a short way of saying things. These can be hard for non-professionals to understand.
>
> **Slang** – the use of informal words and expressions that are not considered standard in the speaker's dialect or language.
>
> **Social isolation** – when people live without regular contact with other people, especially family and friends.

Activity   Role play

1. Other barriers to communication include differing humour, sarcasm, inappropriate behaviour and aggression. In a group, discuss how each of these in turn would cause problems in a health and social care setting of your choice.

2. Pick one of these and role-play a situation in which it would be a barrier to communication if the person behaving like this was (i) a physiotherapist helping someone become more mobile after injuries in a road traffic accident, and (ii) a male patient being treated by a female nurse.

Standing over someone makes them feel uncomfortable and so less able to concentrate on what is being said.

Overcoming barriers to communication (1)

Introduction

In this topic you will learn about the effects of barriers to communication and why it is vital to overcome these barriers if people are to receive the care they need. You will also explore some of the ways to overcome these barriers.

Effects of barriers

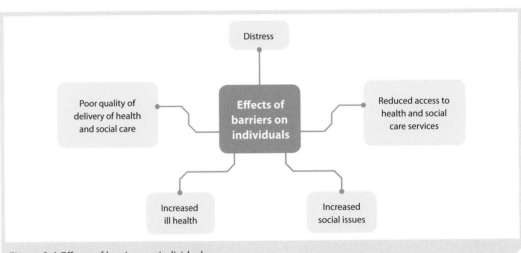

Figure 3.4 Effects of barriers on individuals.

1 Craig is a16-year-old young man who has Down's Syndrome. He lives at home with his parents who love him very much and has just left school to go to college. Do some research into how this change will affect his life and write a case study to describe the young man and his life.

2 Decide which barriers to communication are likely to apply to Craig.

3 Look at the effects of barriers to communication on individuals shown in Figure 3.4 above. Explain what the effects are likely to be on Craig.

4 How do you think this will change as Craig gets older and wants to become more independent?

5 How do you think these barriers could be reduced and maybe overcome?

Overcoming barriers

Preferred method of communication

Service providers need to understand the preferences of the people they are supporting. For example, someone who is hearing-impaired may prefer to use Makaton rather than British Sign Language because that is what they are most familiar with.

Preferred language

It is important to find out what a service user's preferred language is for written and verbal communication. Most leaflets produced by public bodies, such as the NHS, are now written in a variety of languages so that people who do not speak English can access the information. If there is a member of staff who speaks the preferred language of a service user they can be asked to help translate or interpret, or a professional translator or interpreter can be employed.

Adaptations to the physical environment

- Changes to seating – chairs that enable the service user to be at the same level as the service provider, or vice versa, can help the service user feel less intimidated and more able to access the information needed.

- Changes to lighting – improving lighting can help those with sight impairments read information, such as directions.

- Soundproofing of rooms/windows – reducing background noise can help those with hearing impairments.

- Other changes – these might be installing lifts with a voice giving information, such as when the doors are opening and closing and which floor the lift is currently on. Other vital adaptations are adding ramps, lowering reception desks and putting signs lower down on walls for people with physical disabilities, so that they can access the people and information they need.

What potential barriers to communication can you identify in this waiting room and how can they be overcome?

Activity	Effective non-verbal communication

Look back at the two pages on effective non-verbal communication earlier in this unit. Explain how using positive posture, facial expressions and appropriate gestures can help overcome barriers to communication for a service user who (i) has learning difficulties, (ii) has recently arrived in the UK and can't speak English very well, and (iii) is annoyed.

Overcoming barriers to communication (2)

Benefits to individuals when barriers are removed

Raised levels of self-esteem

If people can understand what is being said by service providers they will be able to take part in planning their own care or future, which will make them feel valued and in control. This will result in increased **self-esteem**.

Reducing frustration

When a service user cannot access the information they need they become frustrated and distressed and less likely to understand what is being said to them. This is likely to cause stress symptoms, such as raised blood pressure and irritability. Reducing frustration by reducing or removing barriers to communication will enable service users to be calmer and more capable of accessing the information they need.

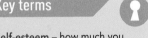

Key terms

Self-esteem – how much you like, accept and respect yourself as a person, how you value yourself.

Activity   Removing barriers to communication

Draw up a mind map to show the benefits to individuals when barriers are removed. Each branch should show one benefit. Create further branches from each benefit to show key words which sum up how this benefit helps the service user. You could use the spider diagram in Figure 3.4 and the information above to help you.

Case study

Communication barriers can also frustrate care givers. Verinda works for a charity that supports victims of road accidents. She works from home and becomes very frustrated on a regular basis by having to fill in a huge online form every time she deals with a client. The charity is only small so cannot afford to pay someone to update its systems but Verinda feels that the work done by the charity could be even more valuable if done more efficiently. Verinda doesn't feel she can ring up her boss and tell her how she feels because her boss lives in Canada, so she doesn't see her often and doesn't know her very well. She also doesn't trust herself not to lose her temper. Verinda has to hide this frustration when she is answering the phone to clients.

1 How do you think Verinda's frustration might affect her work?

2 How do you think Verinda can deal with this problem?

3 Role-play the conversation she could have with her boss on the phone about this, firstly where she lets her frustration show and loses her temper, and secondly where she is polite and manages to hide her frustration. What might be the possible consequences of each of these phone calls?

Using the tasks and questions on this page you will check what you have learned so far.

Assessment activity 3.2

2B.P3 | 2B.P4 | 2B.M2 | 2B.D2

In your role as a trainee early years worker at a nursery in a big town, you are producing information to help the nursery manager get some funding from the local council. She has now asked you to design a PowerPoint presentation with accompanying handout notes on the possible barriers to communication at the nursery and how the staff have worked to overcome them. She tells you that when she first took over as manager the nursery had:

- cluttered corridors so parents couldn't get close to notices pinned on walls
- noticeboards with cracked and dirty plastic covering them
- posters and notices that were old and fading
- no double glazing, curtains or carpets
- single light bulbs hanging from the centre of each ceiling covered with a cloth lampshade
- grubby windows
- very few signs in the corridor to show where different rooms were, how to find her office or where the toilets were
- a high old-fashioned reception desk
- no one who spoke any language other than English and no one had done any research into where to contact an interpreter or translator if needed
- older staff who had had very little additional training in issues such as communication skills since joining the staff many years before.

All these issues have now been addressed and the barriers they caused greatly reduced.

Your pack should include a case study about how effectively the nursery has managed to overcome barriers to communication with one of the children with learning difficulties.

Just checking

1 What do we mean by the expression 'barriers to communication'?
2 Why is it important for people who work in health and social care to understand barriers to communication?
3 Identify three physical barriers to communication and explain how they could be overcome.
4 Describe how an electronic device, such as a mobile phone, can help overcome barriers to communication.
5 How might emotional issues affect communications between a service user and a service provider?
6 Why is social isolation a barrier to communication? Explain your answer.
7 Describe three effects of barriers to communications on service users and explain how these can be reduced.

Developing communication skills (1)

Getting started

Working with a partner, tell each other about something you are proud of. Talk for about two minutes each. The person listening needs to listen carefully without making any notes and then repeat back what they have heard. How can you tell the person listening was concentrating?

Introduction

In this topic you will start to learn more skills for effective communication. These include body language, facial expression and eye contact. You have already looked at these briefly earlier in this unit.

Communicating with groups and individuals

Active listening

Listening to people involves more than just hearing what they say. To listen well you need to be able to hear the words being spoken, think what they mean and then think what to say in reply. You can also show that you are listening and what you think about what is being said by your body language, facial expressions and eye contact. Effective listening also means questioning anything you don't understand.

Yawning or looking at your notes or watch or looking round when someone is speaking will give the impression that you are bored by what is being said. This is not only very rude, but will also cause the person distress and negatively affect their self-esteem.

The process of active listening involves:

- allowing the person talking time to explain
- not interrupting
- giving encouragement by smiling, nodding and making remarks such as 'Really?' and 'Oh, yes?'
- asking questions for **clarification**, such as 'Can you explain that again, please?'
- showing **empathy** by making comments such as 'That must be so difficult for you.'
- looking interested by maintaining eye contact and not looking at anything else
- not being distracted by anything else – switch your mobile off
- summarising to check you have understood by repeating what has been said, saying for example, 'So what you mean is . . .'

Use of appropriate language

It is important to adjust your language to match the situation you are in and who you are talking to. People usually do this without even realising it, unconsciously changing their speech depending on who they are speaking to. For example, when speaking to a family member, they will be less formal than if they are ringing up the doctor for an appointment.

Key terms

Clarification – making something clear and understandable.

Empathy – imagining yourself in someone else's position in order to share and understand their emotions.

How can you tell that the people in the photo are interested and listening very carefully to each other?

Tone of voice

It is not just what you say but the way you say it that is important. If you talk to someone in a loud voice, with a fixed tone, the person will think that you are either angry with them or treating them as though they are less intelligent than you. It is important to speak calmly and quietly with a varying tone so the other person perceives that you are being friendly and kind and are interested in what they are saying.

Activity	Improving communication skills

Work with another member of your group and each sketch a few simple pictures, such as a house drawn as a child would draw it, or a Union flag, without the other one seeing what is being drawn.

Sit back to back, each with a pencil and piece of paper. Take it in turns to describe one of your sketches to the other person while they try to draw it as accurately as possible. You cannot use words that describe shapes, and must just talk about straight or curved lines at certain angles and starting at certain points on the page.

If the person drawing the picture draws it quite accurately, it means that one person has communicated well verbally while the other has listened carefully.

If the drawing is nothing like what it should be, discuss why you think this is.

Do this several times to practise and improve your communication skills.

Pace of speech

If you speak really quickly and excitedly, the person listening to you will not be able to make out everything you say. Similarly, if you speak very slowly, with lots of hesitation umms and errs, it makes it harder for people to concentrate on what you are saying. If you speak at a steady pace, however, you will be able to deliver your message more clearly and the other person will be able to hear every word you say.

Developing communication skills (2)

Proximity

The space around a person is called their personal space. In a formal situation, such as a doctor talking to a patient, the doctor does not sit close enough to the patient to invade their personal space, unless the doctor is going to examine the patient, in which case the doctor should explain in advance what they are planning to do so the patient is prepared. In an informal situation, people who are family, friends or intimate with each other will often sit closer to each other. You tend to stand or sit so you are eye-to-eye with someone if you are in a formal or aggressive situation, but sit at an angle in a more relaxed, friendly and less formal situation.

Other useful verbal skills

- Paraphrasing means repeating something a person has just said in a different way to make sure you have understood. For example, if someone says to you 'I have been feeling achy all over since Friday', you could paraphrase this by saying 'So you have had flu-like symptoms for five days now.'

- Closed questions are questions that can be answered with either a single word or short phrases, for example, 'Have you been sick today?' is likely to be answered by either 'yes' or 'no.' They are useful as an opening or closing question in a discussion, are easy and quick to answer and provide some facts quickly. A doctor might ask, 'So you want to see about having a knee replacement?' at the start of a consultation and finish by saying 'So is that your final decision?'

- Open questions are those that require a longer answer and give control of the conversation to the person you are asking, for example, 'Can you tell me where the pain is exactly and how it affects you?' An open question asks the person to think and reflect, and give opinions and feelings. They are useful to follow up a closed question, to find out more information, to help someone face their problems and to show concern for them.

How can this nurse use communication effectively to make the patient feel comfortable?

Case study

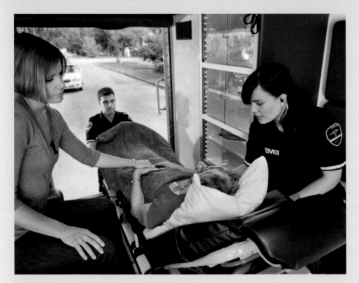

An adventure in France

Liz and Mike were enjoying their stay in France with Mike's daughter Sarah, a fluent French speaker. On their last day Liz was taken ill and passed out. Sarah called an ambulance but the paramedics only spoke very limited English so Sarah had to translate. Liz and Mike struggled to follow any of the conversation. The paramedics said Liz needed to be taken to the hospital, so Mike and Sarah followed the ambulance in Sarah's car.

In the ambulance Liz found herself lying flat on her back on a stretcher with a male paramedic sitting beside her, who kept trying to speak to her in French. During the journey she tried to communicate that she was going to be sick, using gestures and miming actions in order to communicate. At the hospital she was left on a trolley for over six hours in a long narrow corridor, lined with other sick people on trolleys, with no notices up explaining the system and no natural light. Sarah and Mike had to stand by her trolley. She was finally seen by three doctors, who didn't speak any English. Sarah spoke to them

but was then asked to leave the room while tests were carried out. Liz struggled to tell the doctors about her other medication and that she was allergic to penicillin. She was then left in the corridor again to wait for the test results. At 3 am Liz was admitted to the hospital so Sarah and Mike were sent home.

The next day another doctor with a little English came to examine Liz and decided that she was not to eat for at least two more days so she could have a full body scan. The nurses were all very kind, putting together the few English words they knew.

Sarah and Mike visited her for two hours each afternoon but otherwise Liz was on her own in a room.

Liz was finally diagnosed as having a swollen pancreas and told that her blood tests were returning to normal due to the fasting. She was finally allowed to eat again after three days but only dairy products. The next day, after breakfast of yoghurt and milk, she was finally discharged and allowed to fly home.

1 How do you think Liz felt when the paramedics couldn't speak any English?

2 How do you think the paramedics felt when they realised they had a patient who spoke very little French?

3 What were the barriers to communication during the long wait in the hospital corridor?

4 How could these have been minimised? How will they have affected Liz?

5 What were the barriers to communication once Liz had been admitted to a hospital bed?

6 How could these have been minimised? How will they have affected Liz?

7 How did the staff try to improve their communication with Liz?

Effectiveness of communication

Introduction

In this topic you will learn that it is important for health and social care workers to reflect on how effective their communication is as well as the importance of being able to communicate well using the written word. You will then have a chance to check your understanding of the work you have done recently.

Reflecting on skills

It is important to be able to select and demonstrate appropriate communication skills to use in different health and social care settings and for different service users. You should reflect on your communication skills so you know what skills you already have and use effectively. You can then work on improving those you use less well. It is also important to be able to make constructive recommendations for improvement to your friends.

This is also true of health and social care workers as it improves the effectiveness of communication. Remember that by communicating effectively, service users understand and agree to the care they are receiving, and service providers can perform their roles effectively, work cooperatively with each other and build supportive relationships with service users.

Can you read that?

Written communication is central to the work of any person providing a service in a health and social care environment when keeping records and writing reports. Different types of communication need different styles of writing and different ways of presenting information but all require **literacy skills**. Meaning has to be clear and writing needs to be well structured and legible, with grammar, spelling and punctuation used correctly. A more formal style of writing and language is needed when recording information about a patient.

Key terms

Literacy skills – abilities required to speak, read and write clearly, correctly and accurately.

Activity — Written communications

1 In the first column of a table, make a list of all the different forms of writing a health and social care professional might use in a day. In the next column write down by each form as many uses for that type of written communication as you can think of. When your partner has also done this activity share your ideas to see if you can find any more.

2 Reflect on your own verbal, non-verbal and written communication. For each area decide what you do well, what you do less well and what you are going to do to improve those you do less well. Be totally honest with yourself.

3 Write an action plan for the improvements, in the form of a table which has columns for (i) each improvement to be made, (ii) the date it will be made by, (iii) what you need to help you do this, and (iv) notes, so you can record your progress towards making each improvement.

continued

Activity *continued*   Example template for action plan

Improvement to be made	Date it will be made by	What you need to help you	Notes

Assessment activity 3.3   *English*   2C.P5 | 2C.M3 | 2C.D3

1 You are going to role-play a conversation between yourself and a partner, where you are the trainee nursery nurse and your partner is the nursery manager. The conversation should be a discussion based on the training materials you produced in Assessment activity 3.1 and the PowerPoint you designed in Assessment activity 3.2.

2 Practise this conversation until you are satisfied that you are using your communication skills as well as you can.

3 Your teacher should have a video camera available so the conversation can be recorded to allow you to peer-assess and self-assess the conversation afterwards.

4 Repeat this process but this time swap roles.

5 Then combine with another pair in your class. This time carry out a group discussion comparing the best points of the four sets of training materials. Be honest, but be careful to only say positive things so that no one gets offended.

6 Video the group discussion and again peer-assess and self-assess everyone's communication skills.

7 Now watch your own performance in both interactions again and in a written report (i) identify and write down what communication skills you used, (ii) describe their effects, (iii) explain how effective they were, and (iv) make recommendations for how you can further improve your own communication skills.

Just checking

1 What do we mean by the expression 'active listening'?

2 Identify three active listening techniques and explain how they can be used effectively with a person who is distressed.

3 How can speaking too slowly and with lots of hesitation affect communication?

4 Why are clarifying and repeating useful techniques in verbal communication? What are the similarities and differences between the two techniques?

Introduction

How do you know the difference between right and wrong? Have you ever wondered why people hold the beliefs and attitudes they do, or how an individual's relationships and social factors, such as lifestyle or education, affect their health and wellbeing? If everyone did exactly what they wanted in this world, life would be chaotic. Fortunately, this is not the case because social influences, such as our families and our community, provide us with expectations and behaviours to conform to within our society. This is called socialisation.

In this unit you will find out more about how we learn acceptable behaviour from our parents or carers and the rest of our families and how we learn social rules from those in the wider community, for example teachers and work colleagues. You will also learn how these different forms of socialisation affect our health and wellbeing.

You will develop an understanding of the effects of a range of relationships and social factors on our health and wellbeing. This understanding is important in determining the types of care and support required by individuals, and allows health and social care professionals to plan and deliver care to meet the needs of service users.

Assessment: You will be assessed by a series of assignments set by your teacher/tutor.

Learning aims

In this unit you will:

A explore the effects of socialisation on the health and wellbeing of individuals

B understand the influences that relationships have on the health and wellbeing of individuals

C investigate the effects of social factors on the health and wellbeing of individuals.

It's important not to judge people. When a young person comes into the clinic who is morbidly obese, it is easy to think they are stupid for getting in such a state, but often it is because their parents have encouraged them to eat junk food and haven't taught them about a healthy diet because they didn't know either.

Nathan, *19-year-old student dietician*

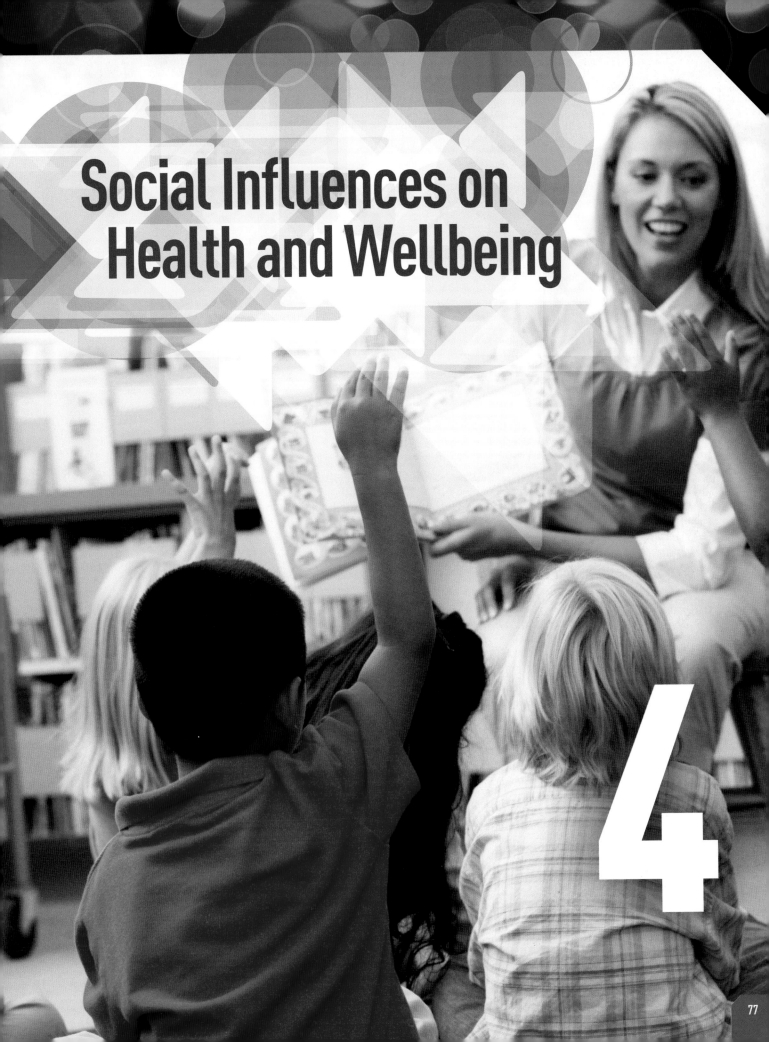

Social Influences on Health and Wellbeing

4

BTEC

This table shows what you must do in order to achieve a **Pass**, **Merit** or **Distinction** grade, and where you can find activities in this book to help you.

Assessment criteria			
Level 1	**Level 2 Pass**	**Level 2 Merit**	**Level 2 Distinction**
Learning aim A: Explore the effects of socialisation on the health and wellbeing of individuals			
1A.1 Identify agents involved in the primary and secondary socialisation processes.	**2A.P1** Explain the influence of agents of primary and secondary socialisation. **Assessment activity 4.1 See page 87.**	**2A.M1** Explain the effects of primary and secondary socialisation on the health and wellbeing of individuals, with reference to relevant examples. **Assessment activity 4.1 See page 87.**	**2A.D1** Evaluate the impact of primary and secondary socialisation on the health and wellbeing of individuals, with reference to relevant examples. **Assessment activity 4.1 See page 87.**
1A.2 Outline the main effects of socialisation on the health and wellbeing of individuals.	**2A.P2** Describe the effects of socialisation on the health and wellbeing of individuals. **Assessment activity 4.1 See page 87.**		
Learning aim B: Understand the influences that relationships have on the health and wellbeing of individuals			
1B.3 Outline the different types of relationships that have an impact on the health and wellbeing of individuals.	**2B.P3** Describe the influences that different types of relationships have on the health and wellbeing of individuals. **Assessment activity 4.2 See page 92.**	**2B.M2** Explain the influences that different types of relationships have on the health and wellbeing of individuals. **Assessment activity 4.2 See page 92.**	**2B.D2** Compare the potential positive and negative influences of different relationships on the health and wellbeing of individuals. **Assessment activity 4.2 See page 92.**
Learning aim C: Investigate the effects of social factors on the health and wellbeing of individuals			
1C.4 Identify the effects of social factors on the health choices of individuals.	**2C.P4** Describe how social factors can affect the health and wellbeing of individuals **Assessment activity 4.3 See page 99.**	**2C.M3** Explain how social factors can affect the health and wellbeing of individuals, with reference to relevant examples. **Assessment activity 4.3 See page 99.**	**2C.D3** Evaluate the link between social factors and the health and wellbeing of individuals, and the impact on health and wellbeing, with reference to relevant examples. **Assessment activity 4.3 See page 99.**

How you will be assessed

This unit will be assessed by either one, or a series of smaller, internally assessed tasks. You will be expected to show an understanding of socialisation in the context of health and social care sectors. The tasks will be based on a case study in which you are working in a local health or social care organisation where the staff want to reduce the number of preventable health problems. For example, your manager asks you to produce materials that can be used to help raise awareness of the positive and negative effects of social influences on people's health and wellbeing. You will produce a series of leaflets featuring fictional characters designed to show parents potential influences on their children as they grow up, and the impact these will have on health and wellbeing.

Your assessment could be in the form of leaflets accompanied by:

- a written report/article

or

- a verbal presentation with presentation notes and slides, and a signed observation record/witness testimony.

Whichever one you choose, you should look at one or a few case studies which highlight:

- the effects of primary and secondary socialisation on health and wellbeing
- the influences of relationships on health and wellbeing
- the effects of social factors on health and wellbeing.

Socialisation

Getting started

How do you know the difference between right and wrong? Who taught you this? How did you learn it? How do you know how to behave?

Think about these questions and then compare your thoughts with a partner.

Key terms

Agent – a person who causes a change.

Accent – a way of pronouncing a language.

Dialect – a way of speaking found only in a certain area or among a certain group or class of people.

Introduction

Socialisation is the process of learning to understand the expected roles, values and normal behaviours that allow an individual to become a part of a social group or culture and society in general. In this section, you will learn about primary and secondary socialisation, which groups of people are its agents, and the influence of these agents on speech, beliefs and values. It is important that you understand the difference between primary and secondary socialisation.

Primary socialisation

Primary socialisation usually happens within the family in the first five years of a child's life. Children learn about acceptable ways of behaving, mainly from family members and especially parents, before they reach school age. The **agents** of primary socialisation are:

- close family, e.g. parents, siblings, grandparents
- other carers, e.g. childminders and babysitters.

Speech

Children learn to speak from their families and other carers. An unborn baby tunes into the sound of the mother's voice while still in the womb, and after birth is able to recognise that voice among others. From the moment a baby is born, they are learning the rules of language and how others use it to communicate. A baby's first cry is followed by the absorption of sounds, tones and words from those around them, which will later shape the way they speak. Children usually learn to talk during the first two years of life; they learn what words sound like and how sentences are structured by listening to others speak. Research shows that children whose parents speak or read to them a lot when they are babies have much higher IQs and richer vocabularies than other children. Children also learn **accents** and **dialects** at an early age from their families and carers.

Beliefs

Beliefs are strongly held opinions and assumptions about the world that determine how an individual sees life. Have you ever thought carefully about what you believe in? Most people don't reflect much on what they believe, but their beliefs still influence their everyday thoughts, feelings and actions.

These beliefs stem from our upbringing, events that happen in our lives and the influences of others. They grow from what we see, hear, experience, read and think about and they affect not only ourselves but the way we see other people.

What behaviour may this baby learn to copy from its mother?

Children adopt their beliefs in the first years of their lives from their family and others who look after them. If a child is taken to church from an early age, they are likely to grow up believing in God. We tend not to question our beliefs because we are certain about them and many of them stem from our childhood; however, they can change as we grow older and are influenced by a greater range of agents.

Values

Our values are things that we consider to be important, worthwhile and morally right. These may include equality, honesty, dignity, respect, perseverance and loyalty. Our values are individual and they affect us at a deep subconscious level. Every decision we make is based on our values and we may either use them for avoidance or for aspiration. We start to learn these at a very early age when our parents or other carers teach us what is right and wrong and how to be polite to other people.

◤ Secondary socialisation

Secondary socialisation is usually as a result of what children experience outside the home. It takes place with other adults and children. The agents of secondary socialisation are shown in Figure 4.1.

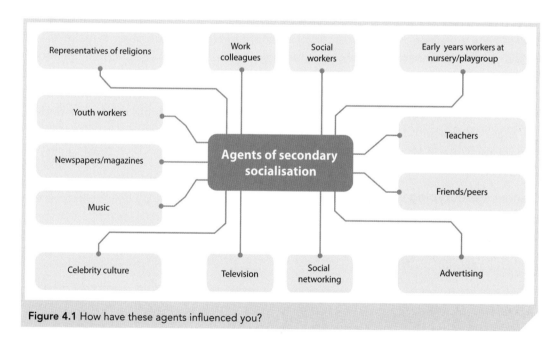

Figure 4.1 How have these agents influenced you?

Activity   Who has influenced you?

Think about the people or other factors that have influenced the way you behave and think. Think back as far as you can remember. Draw up a mind map showing each agent identified in Figure 4.1 and how they influenced you (you must be totally honest).Then decide who or what influenced you most: (1) during the first five years of your life, (2) during your time at primary school, and (3) during your time at secondary school.

Effects of socialisation (1)

Introduction

An effect of socialisation is the shaping of gender roles, for example the expectations of male and female behaviour. Another effect is the shaping of attitudes, such as the development of tolerance or prejudice.

Gender roles

A person's sex is determined genetically, but gender refers to the different expectations for male and female behaviour which start to be learned at an early age. Gender roles determine how males and females should think, speak, dress and behave in their interactions with others. Agents of primary socialisation, particularly parents, exert the greatest influence on the learning of gender roles, but secondary socialising agents teach and reinforce these roles throughout our lives.

Traditionally, mothers taught girls how to cook, clean, iron and sew, and fathers taught boys how to mend, build things and play ball games. In this way, the values of parents and society are passed from generation to generation. Even when parents make a determined effort not to reinforce this stereotypical behaviour, most children fall into these ways of behaving because of other influences around them. One example is toys. Many girls' toys are pink and involve nurturing or other stereotypical behaviours, such as dolls that need feeding and dressing, whereas boys' toys are rarely pink and are more often action figures or vehicles. This continues as we grow up, as there are assumptions made about financial responsibilities, housework, decision making and child rearing.

Gender **stereotyping** is often reinforced in the workplace, although this is less so than it used to be.

Key terms

Tolerance – the capacity to recognise and respect the beliefs or practices of others, even if we don't agree with them.

Prejudice – an unreasonable feeling against a person or group of people.

Stereotyping – thinking a group of people will all have the same attribute, for example, that all older people are deaf and forgetful.

Activity — Gender roles

1 On a large sheet of paper, write down expressions which adults use to children based on gender roles, e.g. 'Act like a man/woman'. On another sheet, write down words which are often used to describe males and females, e.g. 'handsome' or 'pretty', 'weak' or 'strong'.

2 Invite all members of the group to add their ideas and then discuss what this shows.

3 Traditionally males were expected not to show emotion in public; for example, they were supposed never to be seen to cry. Nowadays, males are more likely to show their emotions. Discuss whether you think this is a good or bad thing.

4 Think about your local medical centre and the roles of males and females within it. What sex do the receptionists tend to be? What sex are most of the nurses and doctors?

Shaping of attitudes

Attitude is the way a person views (or behaves towards) something or someone, often in an evaluative way. Our attitudes are central to who we are. Children watch their parents carefully and instinctively imitate their behaviour. Therefore, if parents are always bad-tempered, irritable and selfish, their children will grow up with a tendency to be the same. If parents always say 'please' and 'thank you', and praise their children for doing the same, the children are likely to have good manners.

Activity   Attitudes

Winston Churchill was a British politician, author and Prime Minister during the Second World War and lived between 1874 and 1965. One of his many famous quotes was that 'attitude is a little thing that makes a big difference'.

1 What do you think he meant by this?

2 Have you ever seen or been involved in a situation where someone displayed a negative attitude, for example being disrespectful to a teacher or the police? How did this attitude affect the way the people involved communicated with each other?

3 Think of another situation where someone's attitude affected a situation. Describe the situation to a partner and explain how the person could have made the outcome more positive.

4 Why do you think it is important for a person working in a health or social care context to have a positive and pleasant attitude?

Tolerance and prejudice

Someone may have a prejudice against a group of people for reasons such as age, gender, race, ethnicity, class, religion, sexual orientation, ability, health, disability or appearance. They might then treat them differently. Other people are more tolerant, accepting that a group of people has a right to be different from them if they are not causing anyone else any harm. This behaviour is learned early in life from families, and reinforced by others as we get older. Therefore, if children hear parents referring to someone who is not very clever in a derogatory way, they are likely to use the same language in the same situation and cause offence. If parents always speak about other groups of people in a positive and respectful manner, children are more likely to grow up to be tolerant adults.

Can you find any more of Winston Churchill's quotes about attitudes?

Effects of socialisation (2)

Getting started

Older people sometimes make comments about young people not having the high moral standards that they had when they were their age, lacking respect for adults and lacking the determination to work hard to succeed. Why do you think they believe this? Are they right?

Shaping of moral choices

Parents, or other carers, have the greatest influence on a child's life, as children learn by example. When children experience interactions inside and outside the home in which they feel safe and cared for and where anger and hostility are not present, they develop a strong sense of self which develops into a strong moral base. When they see or experience something such as violence that is different from their normal way of living, they instinctively know that it is wrong. Parents who talk about the basis of their moral principles and the expectations and rewards of following those principles usually succeed in teaching their children to hold to the same level of morals as they have.

Secondary agents also play a large part in shaping moral attitudes. Role models, such as other adults, have an important role to play because children tend to look up to them and believe what they say and do is correct. If any adult they know behaves inappropriately, children may think that is acceptable behaviour. Children need guidance to choose suitable role models. They also need the chance to interact with a range of adults and other children, of all ages. In learning how to get along with others, and learning the social conventions which help them fit in, their interactions reinforce or challenge a child's preconceived ideas about what is morally acceptable.

Religious and secular beliefs

Children are influenced by the culture that surrounds them, so if they are brought up in a culture that has strong religious or secular beliefs they will tend to accept those beliefs as their own.

Attitude to authority

Our attitude to authority is affected very much by the attitude of our parents or carers towards people in authority, which is often based on their experience of authority when they were young and which they subconsciously pass on to us. Parents are the first authority figures we have contact with and if they teach us to behave by using fear, then we will grow up to fear or resent other people in authority.

If parents tell their children that the police are there to help them and if they don't do anything wrong they won't punish them, they will grow up respecting the police. On the other hand, if parents say that the police are corrupt and call them derogatory names, children are likely to grow up with the same attitude.

Development of social norms and values

A social norm is behaviour that is expected by a family, social or ethnic grouping in any given situation and is based on the values of that grouping. Children develop views of what is right and wrong from primary agents and these are reinforced by secondary agents of socialisation. If parents do not provide clear boundaries, the child is unsure how to behave and as they grow older they will look to other people to provide a role model. This may be a good role model, but may equally be someone who shows them the wrong behaviour to model their own behaviour on.

Link

This topic links to Unit 7: Equality and Diversity in Health and Socal Care.

In teenage years the influence of friends or a peer group becomes very important. If it is the norm within a group to speak to authority figures rudely, swear, smoke, drink or take part in criminal activities, the group members will feel pressured to act in this way to be accepted.

Case study

From: Jay Patel (jay@rowshamyouth.org.uk)
Sent: 18 July 2012 15:19
To: Carol Charnley (manager@rowshamyouth.org.uk)
Subject: Kelly Perreira

Hi Carol

I thought I should let you know about a conversation I had with Kelly Perreira this evening.

Kelly is 15 and attends our centre regularly. She was very upset when she came in this evening as she was arrested last night for drunk and disorderly behaviour and narrowly avoided being charged with shoplifting.

Kelly missed school yesterday and said this is because she is being bullied about her weight by girls in her year. She now hangs around with a group of older boys and was with them last night. Kelly says her parents are very angry with her, but don't understand how unhappy she is.

I will be away next week, so I'd be grateful if you could keep an eye out for Kelly.

Jay

1 How are primary and secondary agents of socialisation influencing Kelly?
2 What effects are these having on Kelly's health and wellbeing?

Influence on lifestyle choices

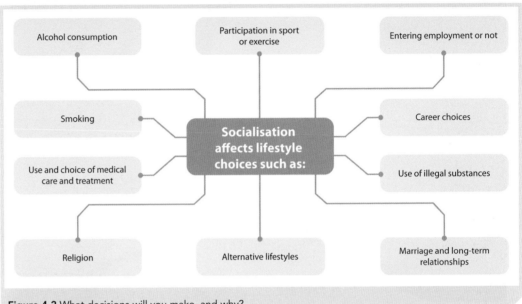

Introduction

Socialisation influences our lifestyle choices. Some of the lifestyle choices we make are shown in Figure 4.2. Although we will only look at one of these, you should understand how socialisation affects all these and other lifestyle choices.

Alcohol consumption

Participation in sport or exercise

Entering employment or not

Smoking

Socialisation affects lifestyle choices such as:

Career choices

Use and choice of medical care and treatment

Use of illegal substances

Religion

Alternative lifestyles

Marriage and long-term relationships

Figure 4.2 What decisions will you make, and why?

Smoking

the dangers of smoking around children.

As we are strongly influenced by our parents and other people we look up to, such as our peers and figures in the media, we have a tendency to copy their behaviour. Children whose parents smoke are approximately twice as likely to start smoking compared with those with non-smoking parents. Most smokers start in their teens, with girls more likely to smoke than boys. Peer pressure and the desire to create a certain image are strong influences. There is an almost immediate effect on the brain with the first cigarette smoked, so teenagers continue smoking to get this reward. Smoking can play an important role in friendships: offering a cigarette or light can be an ice-breaker and huddling together outside, maybe in some hidden place at school or college or outside at a workplace, creates a bond.

We are also influenced by the media. Actors smoking on television and in films can suggest a link with glamour, sex and risk-taking. Although adverts for smoking products are no longer allowed on television, the tobacco industry sponsors risky sports, such as motor racing. Deciding to give up can imply a criticism of others in the group, and so can cause a rift. Later in life smokers learn to associate having a cigarette with other activities, such as having a drink break at work.

Smoking is a biological addiction and a psychological habit, so smokers immediately have withdrawal symptoms when they give up. Smokers therefore keep smoking to avoid these symptoms. Awareness of the damage to a smoker's health takes years to build up, so it is easy to think that there is plenty of time to give up later.

Explore the effects of socialisation on the health and wellbeing of individuals

Below are some questions to test what you have learned. You can then complete a practice assessment assignment.

Just checking

1 What is meant by primary socialisation?

2 Name three groups of people who are agents of primary socialisation.

3 What is meant by secondary socialisation?

4 List three agents of secondary socialisation.

5 How do (i) primary agents, and (ii) secondary agents shape our gender roles?

6 Use an example to explain how we develop tolerance of, or prejudice towards, a group of people we see as different from ourselves.

7 How do we develop our attitude towards authority? How are we likely to react later in life towards authority figures if we have (i) a positive attitude towards authority, and (ii) a negative attitude towards authority? Use examples of certain groups of authority figures to explain your answer.

8 Give an example of what is meant by a social norm and how we develop it.

9 How do agents of socialisation affect our choice to (i) enter employment or not, (ii) use drugs, and (iii) use medical care and treatment?

Assessment activity 4.1
2A.P1 | 2A.P2 | 2A.M1 | 2A.D1

You are a youth worker at a youth centre in a big town. Staff at the local healthcare centre ask you to help raise awareness of the effects of primary and secondary socialisation on the health and wellbeing of young people.

They ask you to produce a series of leaflets featuring fictional characters and relevant examples to show parents and their children the potential influence of primary and secondary socialisation on the values, attitudes, behaviour and lifestyle choices of young people, and the ways in which these could affect their health and wellbeing.

Your leaflets should compare and evaluate the importance of the influence of different agents of socialisation in terms of shaping of gender roles, attitudes, the development of social norms and values, and the influence of lifestyle choices. Your teacher/tutor will provide you with a case study on which to base your leaflets.

Tips

To evaluate the impact of socialisation, you need to make a judgement on what is most important, backing up your arguments with at least three detailed examples. You should decide whether primary or secondary socialisation was more influential on the person studied, or which form of socialisation had a largely positive or negative effect.

Influences of relationships on individuals

Getting started

With a partner, discuss what the word 'relationship' means. Write down as many different types of relationships as you can.

Key terms

Family – a social group made up of people who are connected or related to each other, by blood, marriage or **cohabitation**.

Cohabitation – where two people live together as partners but without a legal basis for their relationship, such as marriage or a **civil partnership**.

Civil partnership – the legal equivalent of marriage between two people of the same gender.

Line manager – the person who is in charge of your department, group or project at work.

Colleague – a person you work with.

Did you know?

In the UK in 2011:

- there were 17.9 million families in the UK, of which 12 million consisted of a married couple with or without children
- 38 per cent of both married and cohabiting couples had dependent children
- there were 2 million single parents with dependent children.

For more information, look at the Office for National Statistics website.

Introduction

Different types of relationships, and changes in those relationships, influence the health and wellbeing of individuals.

Different types of relationships

Family

Almost everyone will live in a **family** unit at some stage in their life. There are various different types of family.

What are the advantages of a family unit?

- *Extended:* this type of family consists of at least three generations of one family, i.e. grandparents, parents and children, who live either together or close to each other and have very regular contact.
- *Nuclear:* this family consists of two parents living together with their children.
- *Reconstituted:* in this type of family a parent who already has children from a previous relationship sets up home with another person who may or may not also be a parent, so the children have a step-parent. The couple may go on to have children together.
- *Single parent:* this family is made up of one parent and that parent's child or children. This comes about because the parent has been widowed, divorced or separated, or the parent never married or lived with the parent of their children.

> ### Activity — Family units
>
> 1 Your class should divide into four groups. Each group takes one type of family and draws up a table to show its advantages and disadvantages. Be sensitive to the fact that there are likely to be members of the class from all four types of family.
>
> 2 Share your ideas with the other groups and add any other points that arise in the class discussion.
>
> 3 Each group should record how being a member of that type of family affects (i) the children's, and (ii) the parents' health and wellbeing by writing both positive and negative points under the PIES headings.
>
> 4 If you have time, research what percentage of families in the UK fall into each category of family.

Working

Working relationships also vary, but are either formal or informal. Formal relationships are with those who manage us, and any discussions are formal and professional. Examples are between a worker and their **line manger** or between a teacher and learner. Informal relationships develop with those we work alongside (**colleagues**), who may become close friends or even our partners.

Working relationships affect our health and wellbeing. They affect us physically (P) by the level of stress they do or do not cause us, intellectually (I) as we learn new skills and information from work colleagues, emotionally (E) by how happy we are at work, and socially (S) by the opportunities we get to become involved with colleagues socially.

Social

We form social relationships with friends and fellow members of groups, religious or **secular**. Friendships play an important role in our lives as they provide us with someone to give us practical support and advice, take part in activities such as exercise and leisure pursuits with (P), learn with (I), share our feelings with (E) and spend time with (S). We tend to become friends with those we consider to be like ourselves, with similar values, attitudes and interests.

Intimate and sexual relationships

When these are happy successful relationships, they provide us with someone with whom we can have a satisfying physical relationship. Together we can take part in a range of activities which keep us physically active, also travel, and take part in leisure activities and events, such as quizzes, which keep us intellectually stimulated. We can share our feelings and problems, so meeting our emotional needs, and take up social opportunities, as well as maybe have a family and so meet more of our needs.

> ### Remember
>
> Don't forget to use PIES to track how we develop throughout our lives, as in the example saying how working relationships affect our health and wellbeing.

> ### Key terms
>
> **Secular** – something that has no connection to any religion or place of worship.

Influences of relationships on the health and wellbeing of individuals (1)

Introduction

Relationships have an effect on us when they change, for example in marriage, divorce, bereavement and leaving education.

Relationship changes

When any relationship changes, it affects us in positive and negative ways. Any such change affects our **self-esteem**, levels of stress and anxiety, and can lead to **dysfunction**. Marriage is generally a very positive and happy event, leading to a happy settled life with a partner. Divorce is generally a negative event; even though a person may decide it is what they want and feel relief that they will no longer be living in an unhappy situation, it may still bring negative feelings and other consequences.

Table 4.1 Contrasting effects of marriage and divorce on health and wellbeing.

Aspects of health and wellbeing	Marriage	Divorce
Physical	**Positive**: Healthy sex life, someone to do activities with	**Positive**: May have more flexibility to choose food and exercise, rather than fitting in with another's choices
	Negative: May take on each others' bad habits of unhealthy eating or not exercising	**Negative**: May have less money, therefore affects diet, opportunities to exercise, general standard of living conditions
Intellectual	Positive:	Positive:
	Negative:	Negative:
Emotional	Positive:	Positive:
	Negative:	Negative:
Social	Positive:	Positive:
	Negative:	Negative:

Activity   Relationship changes

In groups, consider the positive and negative effects of marriage and divorce. Complete Table 4.1 on which the full aspect has been started for you. Share your ideas with the rest of the class.

Self-esteem

A positive and happy change in a relationship makes us feel good about ourselves, and it helps us to like ourselves and believe that others like us too. We are more confident and feel more capable and attractive.

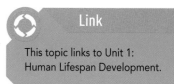

Levels of stress and anxiety

A change in a relationship which causes us to be upset or unsure of the future, such as bereavement, can raise our levels of stress and anxiety. This can lead to the effects shown in Figure 4.3 below.

A bereaved person suffers the physical effects of stress. These affect their intellectual needs as they will be distracted and lack concentration, their emotional needs as they will be unhappy, and their social needs as they will find it difficult to mix with others on their own.

Link

This topic links to Unit 1: Human Lifespan Development.

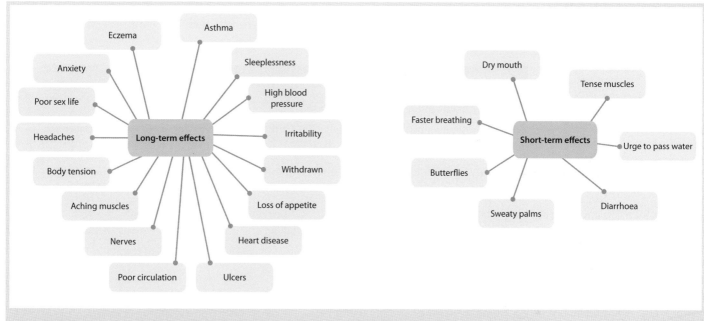

Figure 4.3 What situations have you been in when you have felt any of these effects of stress?

Dysfunction

A relationship change can lead to dysfunction, for example, when a couple marry and have a family but the relationship doesn't work out. In some cases this may be because one or both parents is addicted to substances such as alcohol or drugs, is suffering from an untreated mental illness, or is copying the behaviour of their own dysfunctional parents. This means that conflict, misbehaviour, and even abuse on the part of individual members starts to occur. Any major source of stress, such as moving house, unemployment and illness can cause existing conflicts affecting the children to become worse. Children who grow up with dysfunction may come to believe this behaviour is normal and can become dysfunctional parents themselves.

Dysfunction can lead to neglect of physical needs; the parents and children suffer from stress, poor diet, the effects of substances such as alcohol, and even abuse. This affects intellectual needs as it is very hard to concentrate on learning or using work skills in such a situation. It affects emotional needs as all concerned are unhappy, and social needs because there is no money to go out and if they do, a greater likelihood of a conflict arising.

Influences of relationships on the health and wellbeing of individuals (2)

Activity   Leaving education

Think about leaving education at the end of school, college or university. How will this affect a person's health and wellbeing? Draw up a table similar to Table 4.1, showing the effects on PIES. In pairs, compare your tables. Add any new ideas to your table.

Below are some questions to test what you have learned. You can then complete a practice assessment assignment.

Just checking

1 Name four different types of family.

2 How does being a single parent affect a person's health and wellbeing? Remember to include positive and negative points.

3 Give an example of (i) a formal working relationship, and (ii) an informal working relationship.

4 How does a negative relationship between an employee and their line manager affect (i) the line manager's health and wellbeing, and (ii) the employee's health and wellbeing?

5 Give an example of a social group, and explain what would make them likely to become a group.

6 How does having a successful intimate and sexual relationship help a person's health and wellbeing? Explain using PIES.

7 How does bereavement affect a person's self-esteem?

8 How does divorce contribute to a family's dysfunction? Explain your answer.

9 How does leaving education affect a person's levels of stress and anxiety?

10 How does marriage affect a person's health and wellbeing?

Assessment activity 4.2   2B.P3 | 2B.M2 | 2B.D2

As a youth worker at a youth centre in a big town, you have already produced a series of leaflets for the local healthcare centre to help raise awareness of the effects of primary and secondary socialisation on the health and wellbeing of young people.

The staff at the centre ask you to extend your leaflets to produce a report to show parents and their children the influence of different types of relationships, and the positive and negative ways these can influence their health and wellbeing.

Tips

When describing the influence of a range of relationships, which includes the influence of any changes in relationships, you should use evidence such as research from articles in the media or scientific and health-related reports, and give reasons to support the points you are making. Compare the likely negative and positive influences of the person's different relationships on their health and wellbeing.

WorkSpace

▶ AMAN BALLI

Youth Worker

I am a youth worker in a busy, big, town-based youth centre. I work in a team which includes other youth workers, one of whom is the manager, and a cleaner. We have regular contact with the police and social workers, and the Police Community Support Officers often drop in during the evening for a cup of tea (or a brew, as they call it!) and a chat with the young people who come here. We have one large open-plan room for the main activities. At one end is a pool table, and in one corner some video games, so people can sit on big bean bags on the floor and play games together. The other end of the room has easy chairs, books and magazines, so they can have some quiet time away from the games and pool table. One corner has a vending machine for snacks and a kitchenette so they can make themselves a hot drink.

My main task is to organise activities for those young people who want to take part, such as pool tournaments, card game evenings, gaming competitions, and occasional evening trips to the ice rink or somewhere similar when funds allow. The young people choose where they would like to go and help organise it, as this helps them to work together as a group and learn new interpersonal skills. I help keep accurate records on the attendance of the young people and any other necessary information, such as medical details and emergency contact details.

Think about it

1 Why are developing good relationships so important to Aman's job?

2 How is Aman likely to be able to help when young people have problems, such as changing relationships when a parent remarries?

3 What are your strengths when it comes to building effective relationships? And what are the areas that you would like to improve?

Social factors

Introduction

Social factors are connections with people that affect something else in our lives. There are various social factors that influence health and wellbeing. This topic looks at one of those factors, social class, in detail.

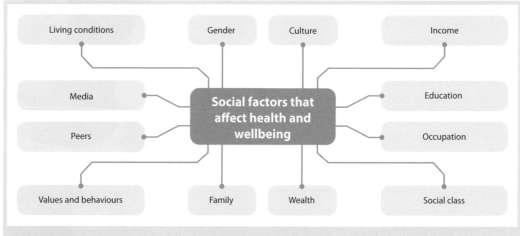

Figure 4.4 Which of these factors do you notice affecting your life?

Key terms

Hierarchy – a list or diagram of things or people arranged in order of importance, with each level considered superior to the level below.

Wealth – having riches, lots of goods and money.

Income – the amount of money people receive from their work, savings, pension or welfare benefits.

Manual work – work that requires the use of physical skills.

Non-manual work – work that depends primarily on mental skills.

Employment prospects – the ability to gain and keep a job which has a good income and the chance of promotion.

Poverty – having insufficient money to afford the essentials to live.

Material possessions – objects which can be bought, but are non-essential to live, e.g. designer clothing.

Social class

Social class is a person's position in a **hierarchy** of groups within a society and this is determined by their occupation and income. The British system was traditionally divided into three layers: working class, middle class and upper class. The higher up the class system a person belonged, the more power and influence they had. There were more working-class people than middle-class, and more middle-class than upper-class. Upper-class people tended to be those with inherited **wealth**. The middle class included industrialists, professionals and business people. The working class included agricultural and factory workers, people who work with their hands.

Due to the ever-increasing variety of jobs, the class system has become more complicated over the years and since 2001 has been divided into eight classes, according to occupation. Even this is not totally clear. Someone who is, for example, a factory worker, might win the lottery and become a millionaire but this alone does not make them upper-class.

Occupation

Most people spend a large part of their adult lives working. This provides the **income** to buy the goods and services they need for themselves and their family. Jobs can be **manual**, which means they may be very physically demanding, tiring and sometimes can lead to injuries, or **non-manual**, which usually means sitting at a desk. Sometimes the latter can be stressful and the work may involve little exercise, leading to the type of lifestyle that is linked to high blood pressure and heart disease.

Income

Most people's money comes from the income they earn for the work they do. Some people can't work for reasons such as disability, illness or caring for someone else, and so claim benefits from the state. The level of income a person earns is mainly linked to the skills, education, qualifications and talents they have, how hard they work and their area of work.

Influence on health and wellbeing

Social class affects health and wellbeing; a person in a lower social class is likely to have fewer opportunities and therefore poorer **employment prospects** and a lower income than a person in a higher social class. This makes life more difficult, as people can find it hard to meet even their most basic needs. There are still a large number of people in the UK who live in **poverty**.

People higher up the social class system tend to live longer than those from working-class backgrounds. People who can afford to buy healthy foods are more likely to be physically healthy, and can exercise more (P). They can go to a variety of places and take part in more activities, so have more opportunities to learn (I). They will be less stressed about financial problems and less likely to have failing relationships, so they will be happier (E) and have more opportunities to meet new people and enjoy time with friends (S). However, although wealth may allow people to buy private education, get private healthcare and have more **material possessions** than others, it does not guarantee health and wellbeing. Wealthy people can still become ill or have accidents. They may work so hard for their wealth that they don't have time to spend it, or time with their families. This can cause stress and failing relationships.

Activity | Social factors

In pairs, choose one of the social factors (other than social class) shown in Figure 4.4. Produce a mind map showing how that factor influences (i) a person's health choices, and (ii) their health and wellbeing (now and in the long term), including levels of stress and anxiety.

Is money the key to happiness?

Effects of social factors on health choices

Getting started

Reflect on your life so far. What health choices have been made for you by others? What health choices have you made yourself?

Introduction

Social factors affect health choices. These health choices include diet, smoking, living accommodation, use of recreational drugs, alcohol consumption, participation in sport or exercise, and seeking medical care. This topic looks at one of these choices, participation in sport or exercise, in detail.

Health-related choices

These are choices such as whether to pay for private healthcare, whether to take advantage of healthcare monitoring opportunities such as regular health checks with your doctor, optician and dentist, and how you choose to live your life, depending on a range of social and economic factors.

Some choices are in effect made for us, because although the UK is a welfare state with health and social care services provided for all, some people experience difficulty in accessing the services they need. This may be because they can't afford the costs of transport to a health provider, prescriptions, or dentist's or optician's fees. They may be in a rural location with no available transport to the services, or they may have a mobility problem or find travel uncomfortable, and therefore choose to stay away.

Participation in sport or exercise

All schools today teach children why it is important to take part in sport or exercise, so we are all aware of why we should do this. The social factors mentioned in the last section all affect our choice to exercise or not.

- *Physical benefits*: any kind of physical activity reduces the risk of developing many major illnesses and conditions which can lead to an early death, such as type 2 diabetes, heart disease, cancer, high blood pressure, osteoporosis and obesity. It also helps improve sleep, reduces stress, helps coordination and improves stamina, strength and suppleness.

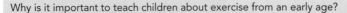

Why is it important to teach children about exercise from an early age?

- *Intellectual benefits:* it is believed that exercise is linked to our brain function and improves our ability to learn and solve problems, memory and recovery after injury. Playing for a team can lead to travel so we learn more about our country and other cultures. While exercising or taking part in sport we are also learning new skills and rules.
- *Emotional benefits:* exercise is believed to release endorphins form the pituitary gland in the brain and this not only gives us a sense of wellbeing and happiness after taking exercise but also helps to suppress pain. Even if it is not due to endorphins, actually doing some exercise can make us feel as though we have done something good for ourselves and achieved something, as can doing well when we compete and succeed. Exercise reduces stress and relaxes us, giving us space and time to think about things away from the pressures of everyday life.
- *Social effects:* many people take part in exercise or sport with a group of people or in teams, which can lead to making new friends or making friendships closer and stronger through a shared interest. This is not only based on the shared activity but also on the after-exercise opportunities, such as going for a drink together.

Choosing not to participate in sport or exercise

By choosing not to participate, all the opportunities to receive the benefits mentioned are missed. Although some people have very little free time or money or company, there are simple exercises which can be done at a desk at work or sitting in front of the television, which are quick and don't cost anything. If embarrassment is a problem there are ways round that; many public swimming pools, for example, have women-only sessions for women who feel uncomfortable wearing a swimming costume in front of men, or who have cultural reasons for not swimming at the same time as men. Activities such as gardening are also very good exercise and provide all the benefits mentioned without having to move out of your own garden. A person can burn up to 300 calories doing one hour of moderately active gardening.

Other factors stopping us exercising

Others factors prevent us from exercising. If we eat the wrong foods and become obese, it is harder to make the decision to exercise and harder work to start with. Smoking affects our lung capacity and leads to quickly becoming breathless when exercising, so making us more ready to give up. If we have very little money to buy clothes to wear for exercise, or poor living conditions where it is hard to wash and dry clothes, it also puts us off. The use of recreational drugs or drinking too much alcohol can also make us feel bad, as well as make us unfit, so again we are put off bothering to even think about exercise.

Activity	Health choices

The class should divide into small groups, each taking one of the health choices mentioned at the start of this topic. Discuss how the social factors identified in Figure 4.4 affects the health choice your group has chosen. Produce a PowerPoint presentation to show to the rest of the class.

Effects of social factors on the health and wellbeing of individuals

Introduction

In this topic you will learn how social factors affect our self-esteem and access to health and social care services.

Table 4.2 How social factors affect self-esteem and access to health and social care services.

Factor	Self-esteem	Access to health and social care services
Income	More positive if fewer money worries	More income, more able to pay for transport
Education	Better educated, feel better about self	More likely to realise the importance of accessing services
Occupation	Higher status job, feel good about self	All have access, some jobs make it easier to get time to access services
Social class	Higher social class, more positive and confident	More likely to access services if higher social class
Wealth	More wealth, often feel better, fewer money worries	Can afford private healthcare, including dental and eye care
Values and behaviours	Positive values and behaviours, feel better about self	Value self more so more likely to access services as soon as needed
Family	Loving supportive family, make you feel valued and worthy	Supportive and caring, will make sure you access services you need
Peers	Kind, supportive and caring, make you feel you belong and like yourself	Go with you or persuade you to go to services if need to
Media	Good stories about people like us, feel-good factor	Health promotion campaigns and reports raise our awareness of services
Living conditions	Comfortable, warm, pleasant home, feels good, not ashamed when peers visit	Good, less likely to need services, less reluctant to resent people providing services
Gender	Feel good if happy with gender role	Females likely to access services earlier than males
Culture	Depends on regard held in local community, if not resented or treated differently, feels good	Services able to address cultural issues as UK is multicultural; may need to raise awareness of this in certain cultures and areas

Below are some questions to test what you have learned. You can then complete a practice assessment assignment.

Activity   Effects of social factors on health and wellbeing

Choose three of the social factors in Table 4.2 and write a detailed report on how each factor affects (i) self-esteem, and (ii) access to health and social care services. Include up-to-date statistics and both positive and negative points. Finish with a conclusion which you will share with the rest of the class.

Just checking

1 Name three social factors and explain why each one is called a social factor.
2 How do (i) the media, and (ii) values and behaviour, affect health and wellbeing?
3 What is the difference between wealth and income?
4 Why doesn't winning the lottery and becoming a millionaire make a person upper class?
5 Identify six health choices and explain why they are referred to in this way.
6 How do social factors affect our health choices? Choose one factor to explain this.
7 How do social factors affect whether we seek medical care?
8 How do social factors affect our levels of stress and anxiety? Choose one factor to explain this.

Assessment activity 4.3   2C.P4 | 2C.M3 | 2C.D3

As a youth worker at a youth centre in a big town, you have already produced a series of leaflets for the local healthcare centre to help raise awareness of the effects of primary and secondary socialisation on the health and wellbeing of young people, and of the influence of different types of relationships and the potential positive and negative ways these can influence their health and wellbeing.

The staff at the centre ask you to extend your leaflets to produce a report to show parents and their children the effect of a variety of different social factors and their link to overall health and wellbeing, with relevant examples.

Tips

When describing how social factors can affect the health and wellbeing of individuals, you should include the effects of at least four social factors, such as income, education, family and the media, on the person's health and wellbeing. Explain the wider effects of these social factors on the overall health and wellbeing of individuals, supporting this with detailed examples of the effects of each social factor. Evaluate the link between social factors, and consider the impact on the health and wellbeing of individuals in terms of physical, intellectual, emotional and social wellbeing.

Introduction

How can we improve the health and wellbeing of the nation? Why do we need to try to do this and what are the benefits? Health and social care professionals can help people make healthy lifestyle choices and understand how to reduce risks to their health. This in turn can help prevent many diseases, illnesses and injuries.

Health promotion is the area of healthcare that raises awareness of these issues and educates us on how to follow healthier lifestyles. It helps us take more control over our own health and hopefully improve it. Health promotion is an important part of a number of roles in the health and social care sector, including health visitors, midwives, school nurses and GP practice nurses.

In this unit you will look at some of the reasons health promotion activities are carried out and the benefits of this work to both individuals and the general health and wellbeing of the nation. You will also explore the different forms of health promotion activities that are used by health and social care workers. Finally you will be given the opportunity to explore and research an area of health risk and then create materials for a health promotion activity for a specific target group. This will give you a valuable insight into this important aspect of health and social care work.

Assessment: You will be assessed by a series of assignments set by your teacher/tutor.

Learning aims

In this unit you will:

A explore the purpose, types and benefits of health promotion

B investigate how health risks can be addressed through health promotion.

> I found from listening to a GP practice nurse talk about her job that some people are not happy to be told how to live a more healthy lifestyle. However, by talking to them and explaining the benefits of making healthier choices, you can aid people's understanding. They are then more likely to take control of their situation and make their own decisions in choosing healthier lifestyle options.
>
> Hollie, *16-year-old would-be nurse*

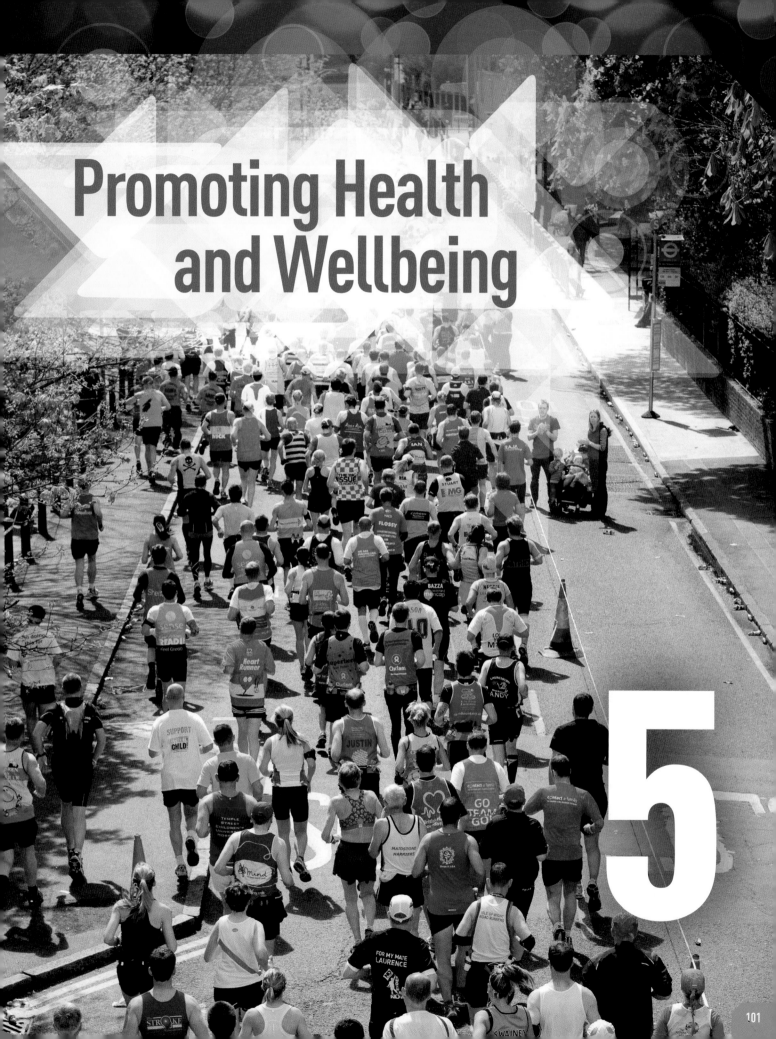

Promoting Health and Wellbeing

5

BTEC
Assessment Zone

This table shows you what you must do in order to achieve a **Pass**, **Merit** or **Distinction** grade, and where you can find activities in this book to help you.

Assessment criteria			
Level 1	**Level 2 Pass**	**Level 2 Merit**	**Level 2 Distinction**
Learning aim A: Explore the purpose, types and benefits of health promotion			
1A.1 State what is meant by health promotion, identifying the purpose and aim(s) of one health-promotion activity.	**2A.P1** Describe health promotion and the purpose and aims of three different health-promotion activities. **Assessment activity 5.1 See page 115.**		
1A.2 Outline how health promotion is used to benefit individuals.	**2A.P2** Describe how different types of health promotion are used to benefit the health and wellbeing of individuals and the nation. **Assessment activity 5.1 See page 115.**	**2A.M1 Maths** Discuss how different types of health promotion are used to benefit the health and wellbeing of individuals and the nation, using selected examples. **Assessment activity 5.1 See page 115.**	**2A.D1 Maths** Analyse the benefits of different types of health promotion to individuals and the nation, using selected examples. **Assessment activity 5.1 See page 115.**
Learning aim B: Investigate how health risks can be addressed through health promotion			
1B.3 Identify the main effects of the chosen health risk on individuals.	**2B.P3 English** Describe the chosen health risk and its main effects on individuals, using research findings from different sources. **Assessment activity 5.2 See page 125.**	**2B.M2 English** Explain how the chosen health risk affects individuals and how these effects can be addressed through health promotion, using research findings from different types of sources. **Assessment activity 5.2 See page 125.**	**2B.D2 English** Evaluate the strategies used to address the chosen health risk, using research findings. **Assessment activity 5.2 See page 125.**
1B.4 English Maths Produce materials for a health-promotion activity, with guidance.	**2B.P4 English Maths** Produce appropriate materials for a health-promotion activity, describing the health risk and health advice. **Assessment activity 5.2 See page 125.**	**2B.M3 English Maths** Produce materials for a health-promotion activity tailored to a target group, describing the health risk and health advice. **Assessment activity 5.2 See page 125.**	**2B.D3 English Maths** Make recommendations for how the health-promotion materials could be adapted for a different target group. **Assessment activity 5.2 See page 125.**

English English signposting   **Maths** Mathematics signposting

How you will be assessed

The unit will be assessed by a series of internally assessed tasks. You will be expected to show an understanding of health-promotion activities in the health and social care sectors. The tasks will be based on a scenario where you work in a local health or social care organisation. For example, the local youth service has become concerned about the health of young people in the area. They have approached your health and social care department to see whether there should be a local health promotion campaign.

Your assessment could be in the form of:

- an article or report on health risks faced by teenagers, which must include:
  - a description of health promotion and its purpose and aims, using three different examples
  - an explanation of a chosen health risk and how it affects teenagers
  - an explanation of how these effects could be addressed through health promotion
  - an evaluation of the benefits of health promotion to both teenagers and the nation

- an accompanying PowerPoint presentation, with slides and presentation notes
- a health-promotion campaign presented as an information pack containing posters, leaflets, booklets and a wall display, which could be given out locally and could be adapted for a different target group.

What is health promotion?

Introduction

Health promotion activities are an important part of a number of roles in the health and social care sector. In this topic you will learn what health promotion is and about its purpose and aims.

Key terms

Nation – a large community of people who share a common language, culture, ethnicity, descent, and/or history and usually a territory. In this unit 'nation' refers to the United Kingdom (UK).

Proactive – creating or controlling a situation by causing something to happen rather than responding after something has happened.

What is it?

Health promotion is the provision of information and education both to individuals and to the **nation,** which will enable them to make positive lifestyle choices. It enables people to take control over factors that affect their own health and so do something to improve their health and wellbeing. Health promotion cannot be imposed on people; it is done so that people are given sufficient good and accurate information for them to make up their own minds on actions to take that will make a positive change.

What is its purpose?

The purpose of health promotion is to inform people about current thinking on how to live healthily. It aims to motivate people to adopt healthy lifestyle choices. Health promotion should be **proactive** in tackling health-related challenges and issues. An example of an issue that can be targeted by health promotion is the rising incidence of obesity in this country and the problems that arise from this, such as cost to the NHS of treatment for conditions arising from obesity and the increase in obesity-related deaths.

What are the aims of health promotion?

Health promotion activities aim to:

- raise health awareness. An example might be a campaign to raise awareness of the dangers of high blood pressure and how to keep blood pressure down.
- encourage safety and reduce accidents. For example, a television campaign might show a child being hit by a car travelling at 30 mph, to demonstrate that even speeds considered quite slow still maim or kill. The aim of this would be to encourage people to drive more slowly and so reduce the incidence and severity of such accidents.
- reduce the number of people smoking. Health-promotion activities raise awareness of the dangers of smoking, explain how people can access help to stop smoking and provide strategies to help them give up.
- encourage healthy eating habits. Providing information about the hows and whys of healthy eating helps people make better food choices. This can have the effect of reducing the incidence of obesity or undernourishment in the population, and their effects, such as poor health, poorer quality of life and shorter life expectancy.

- reduce alcohol intake. Information on the risks of excess alcohol consumption and guidance on safe weekly levels may encourage people to cut down their alcohol intake, improving their own health and life expectancy, and reducing alcohol-induced antisocial behaviour.

Activity   Health promotion campaigns

1 Look at the material in the illustration. Do you recognise this health promotion campaign on strokes? If not, look at the website by visiting Pearson hotlinks. You can access this by going to www.pearsonhotlinks.co.uk and searching for this title. This campaign was launched by the Public Health Agency (PHA) in June 2011.

2 Make a list of the different types of health-promotion activities that form part of the campaign.

3 Download a FAST leaflet and read it.

4 Identify how the campaign meets each of the purposes and aims mentioned in this topic. To do this draw up a table with the purpose and the five aims in the left-hand column. Include two more columns for you to say how the campaign meets the purpose or aim, and what is good about the campaign. You may think that a campaign about strokes has nothing to do with healthy eating, smoking or alcohol, but it does. You will need to do some research into the possible causes of strokes to understand why.

5 What are the possible consequences of someone suffering a stroke not getting help fast enough?

6 In a group of two or three, role-play a person suffering a stroke with someone else being with them or finding them quickly and following the steps shown in the health-promotion campaign. If you have three in your group, the third person can be a paramedic or an emergency department doctor. Be prepared to show your role play to the rest of the class.

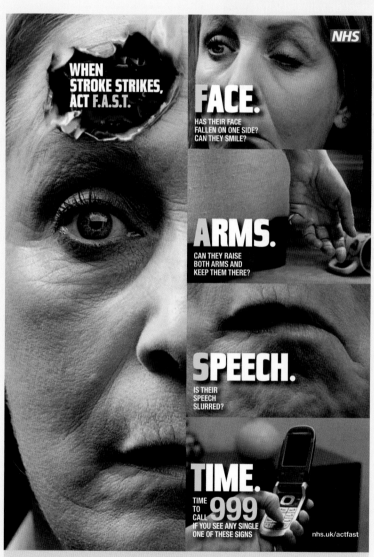

Do you recognise this health promotion campaign?

Types of health promotion

Getting started

Think about health advice you have been given during your time in primary and secondary school. What made the biggest impact on you and why? Be prepared to share this memory with the rest of the class.

Key terms

Screening – mass checking of sectors of the population for early signs of a particular disease or condition.

Immunisation – to make someone immune to a disease, usually by vaccination.

Vaccination – the introduction of a very small quantity of a weakened form of a disease into the body, usually by injection, to help the body develop antibodies to that particular disease.

Introduction

Health promotion activities can take the forms of health-risk advice, health-promotion campaigns and medical intervention.

Health-risk advice raises awareness of health-related issues and educates individuals to help them to make healthy lifestyle choices.

Health-promotion campaigns are local or national initiatives targeted at large audiences with the aim of raising awareness of health-related issues. There are various types of campaign, such as Department of Health national campaigns and national and local NHS campaigns. They use different media, such as television, cinema, the internet, magazines and newspapers, and leaflets.

Medical intervention is initiated by central government (e.g. the Department of Health) and includes programmes of **screening**, **immunisations** and **vaccinations** that are used to proactively reduce or eliminate disease.

Health-risk advice

There are many types of health-risk advice including:

- Peer education: rather than advice coming from health professionals, community members are supported to promote health-enhancing change among themselves, encouraging each other in healthy behaviour.

- Shock tactics: for instance, showing pictures of the inside of a dead smoker's lungs or close-up pictures of genitalia affected by a sexually transmitted infection.

- Advice from health professionals: in schools health professionals may be invited to speak to groups of learners on topics, such as drinking, smoking and safe sex. Health professionals also give advice in health and social care settings, such as doctors' surgeries or hospitals. They may be called upon, for example, to advise someone who has asthma and smokes or someone who needs an operation, but is too obese for this to be a safe option so needs to lose weight first.

- Advice from police and fire service: school-based police officers or police community support officers give advice in both primary and secondary schools as well as to other community groups on topics such as alcohol or keeping safe at Hallowe'en. The fire service talk about being safe on Bonfire Night, or any areas to do with fire safety.

Have you ever received health-risk advice at school?

- Testimonies from people personally affected by issues: this is when a person speaks about a health issue that has affected them. It can be in the context of a large-scale campaign, such as part of a television initiative against drink driving, or on a smaller scale such as an individual talking to a school or other community group, perhaps about the dangers of drug taking.

Examples of advice

Health advice can be given in a wide variety of forms and it can cover many topics.

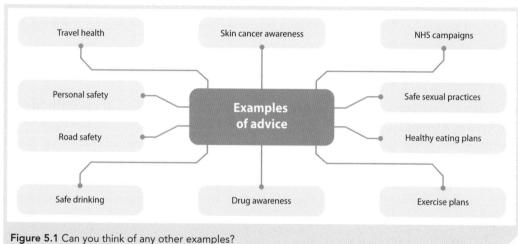

Figure 5.1 Can you think of any other examples?

One example of an area where health advice is needed in the UK is skin cancer awareness. The dangers of sun exposure in the development of skin cancer were not fully appreciated in Britain until relatively recently, with many people believing that in our temperate climate there was no need to protect ourselves from the sun. This is in stark contrast to Australia, where awareness is high because of the greater intensity of UV radiation from the sun there and the consequent very high incidence of skin cancer – four times higher than the UK, Canada and the USA.

There are many websites that help raise awareness of skin cancer. For example, the Cancer Research UK website explains that most skin cancers are caused by overexposure to ultraviolet radiation from the sun or sunbeds and recommends ways to enjoy the sun safely by staying in the shade, covering up and using at least SPF15 sunscreen for protection. There are video clips, information, photographs, an advice section and links to other useful websites, as well as details of their SunSmart campaign. The Skin Cancer Foundation website has similar information, including a Go With Your Own Glow campaign, which asks women to love and protect their skins, and videos aimed at teenagers showing the risks of sunbeds.

Activity   Skin cancer research

Do some research into the facts about skin cancer. Think about it. Do you, or any of your family or friends, ever go out in the sun without sunscreen? Do you ever use a sunbed? In a small group, discuss these questions and think about why people do these things.

Research the facts behind the causes of skin cancer to produce a poster that can be put up at school to persuade young people to:

- use sunscreen
- not use sunbeds.

Medical intervention and benefits

Introduction

In this topic you will learn about the different types and benefits of medical intervention.

◤ Types of medical intervention

Medical intervention falls into two main categories: vaccination, including childhood immunisations, and screening.

Vaccinations and childhood immunisations

A vaccine is a substance that contains a weakened or synthetic form of the **pathogen** that causes a particular disease. It cannot cause the disease in a person, but it stimulates the person's immune system to recognise the pathogen, so that if the vaccinated person comes into contact with the disease again, their body will recognise it and produce the correct antibodies to destroy it. Vaccines are usually given by injection and include HPV (human papilloma virus, to prevent cervical cancer), influenza and pneumonia.

The process of building up immunity by taking a vaccine is called immunisation. Through immunisations, diseases such as tetanus and diphtheria have practically disappeared in the UK. Europe was declared polio free in 2002 thanks to immunisation. These diseases could come back, though, which is why it is important that children continue to be immunised. Practice or school nurses usually do this and each immunisation happens at a certain age, for example babies up to 15 months are immunised against polio, diphtheria, whooping cough and meningitis, and measles, mumps and rubella (MMR). Girls aged 12–13 are now immunised against HPV.

Activity / Immunisation

Draw up a table, and in the first column write the names of three of the vaccines mentioned. Do some research and in the second column write down the categories of people they are given to, including age group.

Screening

Screening is a way of detecting cancer or other conditions at a very early stage, when they can best be treated. The NHS runs screening programmes for cervical, breast and bowel cancer and sight screening for people with diabetes.

The NHS Breast Screening Programme provides free breast screening every three years for all women aged 50 and over. Women are invited to have a mammogram. This is an X-ray of each breast taken while the breast is compressed. This can be uncomfortable, but it can detect small changes in breast tissue, which may indicate cancers that are too small to be felt either by the woman herself or by a doctor. In September 2000, research showed that the NHS Breast Screening Programme had lowered mortality rates from breast cancer in the 55–69 age group.

Women are invited for cervical screening from the age of 25.

WorkSpace

◤ Elaine White

Mammogram Operator

I am a health professional working as a mammogram operator, as part of a small team in a mobile breast screening unit. A mammogram is an X-ray of the breast, taken to look for any abnormalities and so find breast cancer at an early stage when there is a good chance of successful treatment and full recovery. We are all women, even the receptionist who books clients in on arrival and tells them what to do, and the unit is parked in different parts of the area for a couple of weeks at a time, usually in a hospital car park. Local women are automatically sent an invitation for screening if they are 47 or above, every three years.

My main task is to produce an acceptable mammogram for every person who comes for screening. The breasts are X-rayed one at a time. I have to position the breast between the X-ray machine and a clear plate at the correct angle and firmly compress the breast between the plates so that it becomes thin enough for the radiation to pass through the breast tissue to produce a clear image. Many women are nervous about having their breasts handled by a stranger the first time they come so it is important that I put them at ease, reassuring them while treating it as an everyday experience, and showing compassion if anyone is really worried or even frightened. The process can be mildly uncomfortable for a very short period of time but does not usually hurt. I also have to be careful to record which mammogram belongs to which client so there is no confusion when results are sent out by post after the mammogram has been looked at carefully. About one in twenty women is called back for further assessment but only about one in six of those are diagnosed with breast cancer.

It is a very satisfying job, because screening saves about 1,400 lives a year, and it is good to know that by doing my job well I have contributed to that number. I do mammograms on women who have undergone gender reassignment so started life as a man, and have X-rayed breasts of every shape and size, so no one need feel embarrassed. I also get to meet women from every walk of life and they all react slightly differently to the experience so no two days are the same.

Think about it

1 Why are communication skills so important to Elaine's job?

2 What qualities does Elaine need to do her job successfully?

3 Explain why breast screening is an example of health promotion. What are its benefits?

4 Look at the diabetes screening programme. How is it different to breast cancer screening?

The benefits of health promotion to the health and wellbeing of an individual

Getting started

Can you think of any piece of health promotion which has made you change your personal behaviour? If so, describe it to a partner.

Introduction

The World Health Organization has defined health promotion as 'the process of enabling people to increase control over, and to improve, their health'. In this topic you will look at the benefits of health promotion to the health and wellbeing of us all as individuals.

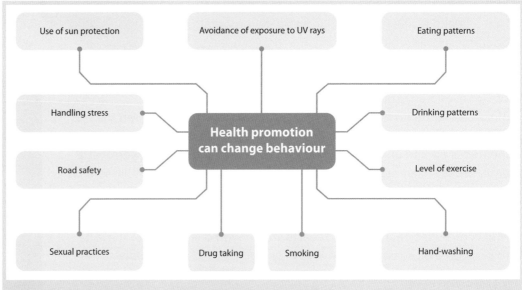

Figure 5.2 Can you think of any other changes to add to this spider diagram?

Key terms

Antibiotic – a prescribed drug that kills or prevents the growth of bacteria.

Superbug – a bacterial infection that is resistant to almost all antibiotics.

Life expectancy – the average number of years a person can expect to live from birth.

Benefits

Health promotion can do the following:

- Increase our understanding of health issues: for example, health promotion leaflets on the over-use of **antibiotics**, and the resulting consequences in the form of **superbugs**, have helped inform the public as to why the doctor won't prescribe antibiotics for a viral infection, such as a cold.

- Increase our responsibility for our own health: for example, understanding how to lift an object safely means a person is less likely to lift a heavy load wrongly (i.e. without bending the knees) and so help avoid back injury.

Activity   Safe working practices

1 There are many other examples of safe working practices that help us take responsibility for our own health, as well as examples of ways to take care of ourselves in other aspects of our lives. With a partner, write down as many ways as possible in which you can take responsibility for your own health.

2 Compare your list with those of other groups. Each group should then take one different point and prepare an information leaflet to promote it.

- Decrease risk of disease and/or injury: for example, health promotion about how the HIV virus can be transmitted has reduced the number of people developing AIDS.

- Improve quality of life: health promotion can raise awareness of ways to tackle a particular problem, e.g. giving obese people more strategies to help them lose weight and consequently improve their quality of life.

- Increase **life expectancy**: for instance, informing people of the levels of alcohol considered to be safe to consume in a week. By keeping to these limits people can increase their life expectancy.

- Change people's personal behaviour practices and lifestyle choices. For example, it is widely accepted that there is a correct technique to good hand washing, and separate studies from around the world show that good hand hygiene practices can reduce illness, sickness absence and the associated costs by up to 40 per cent. Hand washing is one of the most important ways of controlling the spread of infection, especially those that cause diarrhoea and vomiting, and respiratory disease.

  However, although most of us think we wash our hands thoroughly and effectively it is not until we watch a demonstration on the correct way to wash hands that we realise that we don't do it as well as we think.

  Another good example of the benefit to the individual of changing personal behaviour and lifestyle is smoking. It is better for people to improve their own health by giving up smoking rather than relying on health care professionals to try to help them once they have become ill with a smoking-related condition such as lung cancer or emphysema.

Activity   Washing your hands

1 Look on the internet at some of the information sheets on how to wash your hands properly. Decide as a class which you think are the best ones, print them off and have a go at doing it properly.

2 Think of a way of encouraging more learners in your school to wash their hands properly. Devise a health-promotion activity to do this, including facts as to how it will improve their personal health and wellbeing.

When should you wash your hands and use sanitizer?

The benefits of health promotion to the nation (1)

Introduction

This topic looks at how health promotion benefits the nation by reducing levels of illness and disease, taking pressure off the NHS and reducing costs; by reducing levels of crime and by increasing the uptake of vaccination and screening programmes.

Reducing levels of illness and disease

Reduction in the incidence of heart disease is an example of the positive effect of health promotion. A study by the British Heart Foundation Health Promotion Research Group at the University of Oxford in January 2012 reported that heart attack deaths dropped by more than half between 2002 and 2010, due in part to the prevention of heart attacks by better management of risk factors, such as smoking, high cholesterol levels and high blood pressure. Much of this improvement can be attributed to health promotion.

The study also showed that too many heart attack victims still died before medical help arrived, so the British Heart Foundation has made a video showing how to do hands-only **CPR**. This video has had high exposure on television and has a pop-up link on various websites. As well as the video there is a blog, T-shirts, a petition to get CPR taught in schools, an opportunity to download the music ('Stayin' Alive' by the Bee Gees) and a free mobile app. It is hoped that these measures will increase public awareness and knowledge so that more deaths can be prevented by early use of CPR.

Impact on crime levels

Health promotion has also been shown to reduce crime levels. The taking of recreational drugs has been tackled with programmes that help support people in living a drug-free life, such as the Home Office strategy promoted in 2010 aimed at reducing demand, restricting supply and building recovery for drug users. Other campaigns, including Talk to Frank, on both TV and the internet, have also had an impact. Getting addicts off drugs results in fewer drug-related crimes, such as people stealing to fund a drug habit. Similarly, there are national strategies and campaigns aimed at reducing alcohol consumption, and therefore alcohol-related violent crime, by raising awareness of the possible consequences of drunkenness, such as injury and death.

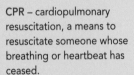

Key terms

CPR – cardiopulmonary resuscitation, a means to resuscitate someone whose breathing or heartbeat has ceased.

Cervix – the entrance to the uterus from the vagina.

Did you know?

There were 8,790 alcohol-related deaths in the UK in 2010, 126 more than in 2009.

1 Do some research to find three pieces of health promotion material that could have an impact on crime levels.

2 Produce a PowerPoint® presentation that includes these three pieces of health promotion. Pick the piece that is best in your opinion and find some recent statistics to back up how it could have contributed to reducing crime levels in the UK. For further information visit the Office for National Statistics website. You can access this by going to www.pearsonhotlinks.co.uk and searching for this title.

3 Show it to the rest of the class, explaining why you think this is the best piece and presenting your statistics.

Increased uptake in vaccination and screening programmes

By promoting the need for a certain vaccination nationally and, where possible, combining this with a screening programme, some diseases can be greatly reduced or even eradicated. One example is cervical cancer. Cancer Research UK reports that this is the second most common cancer in women under the age of 35, with 2,900 women a year in the UK diagnosed with the disease. The national Department of Health HPV (Human Papilloma Virus) vaccination programme was started in September 2008 for girls aged 12 and 13, to protect against the commonest cause of cervical cancer. It was also offered to older girls aged 14 to 17 over three years to make sure they didn't miss the protection. The 'cervical cancer jab' is delivered mainly through secondary schools. It is estimated that about 400 lives a year could be saved in the UK as a result of this programme.

The NHS Cervical Screening Programme was introduced in the 1980s. A cervical screening test, or smear test, is a way of detecting abnormal, pre-cancerous cells in the **cervix** of women aged between 25 and 64. By detecting and treating these cells about three-quarters of cancers can be prevented from developing. Since the programme's introduction the number of cervical cancer cases has decreased by about seven each year. Combined with the HPV vaccination, cervical screening continues to be an important step towards preventing cervical cancer.

What other screening programmes can you think of?

The benefits of health promotion to the nation (2)

Introduction

Other benefits to the nation of health promotion include addressing high-profile health and wellbeing concerns and reducing financial cost to the NHS.

Addressing high-profile health and wellbeing concerns

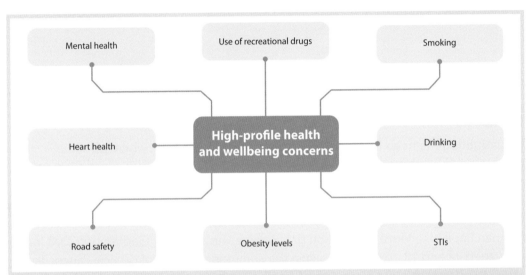

Figure 5.3 Are there any other issues you would expect to be on this diagram?

Obesity, especially in children, is a current high-profile concern. At the time of writing, the latest Health Survey for England (HSE) showed that nearly one in four adults (a quarter) and over one in ten children aged between two and ten (a tenth) are **obese.** Obesity can severely affect a person's health, increasing the risk of some cancers, heart and liver diseases, and type 2 diabetes.

Did you know?

The Foresight Report (2007) predicts that if no action is taken 60 per cent of men, 50 per cent of women and 25 per cent of children will be obese by 2050.

Key terms

Obese – having a **body mass index (BMI)** of 30 or more.

Body Mass Index (BMI) – a method of determining the proportion of body fat a person has, found by dividing a person's weight measured in kg by the square of their height in metres.

Activity — Health promotion work

Do some research on the internet into the health-promotion work being done by either Change4Life or Cancer Research UK. Produce a PowerPoint presentation to show what you have learned.

Reduced financial cost to the NHS and the government

Heath promotion also aims to help reduce financial costs. For example, the direct cost of treating obesity, plus the costs involved in treating conditions for which obesity is a likely contributory factor, are estimated to be £4.2 billion a year and are forecast to more than double by 2050 if we carry on as we are. As well as the conditions already mentioned, other health risks include stroke and osteoarthritis. There are additional costs for equipment, operations and other related services.

Other areas where health promotion aims to reduce costs are smoking and alcohol consumption. The British Heart Foundation research in 2005 showed that treating disease directly caused by smoking, such as lung cancer and emphysema, costs more than £5 billion a year in the UK. This figure is likely to be an underestimate, because it does not include indirect costs, such as lost productivity and informal care, the costs of treating disease caused by passive smoking, and other conditions associated with smoking. It also showed that smoking costs five times more than lack of physical activity, twice as much as obesity and about the same as an unhealthy diet.

Activity — Reducing health costs

1 These facts show how much obesity, smoking and alcohol are costing the NHS and the government. In pairs, research the most recent health-promotion campaigns on smoking and alcohol. One example is the hard-hitting television campaign showing children appealing to their parents not to smoke. Try to find videos of these campaigns and if there are any leaflets or posters produced as part of the same campaign. Put together a package to sum up each campaign you find, so you can report back to the rest of the class.

2 Another area where cost can be reduced by health promotion is the police and prison services. Do some more research to see how health promotion affects these two services. Find some current data showing trends to report back to the class.

Assessment activity 5.1 — *Maths*

2A.P1 | 2A.P2 | 2A.M1 | 2A.D1

You are a trainee nurse at a health centre in a big town. The local high school has become concerned about the health and lifestyles of some of the young people in the area and has approached your health centre to suggest that there should be a local health-promotion campaign. You have been asked to produce a report on health risks faced by teenagers. This must include the following:

- An introduction describing what is meant by health promotion with details of three different health risks that may affect teenagers and one health promotion activity that has already been carried out related to each health risk, describing the purpose and aim of each activity.

- An explanation of a chosen health risk relevant to teenagers in your area and at your school/college, such as obesity, drug taking or alcohol, and how it affects teenagers.

- How these effects could be addressed through health promotion.

- An evaluation of the strategies already being used in your area and nationally to address the chosen health risk.

- An analysis of the benefits of health promotion both to teenagers and to the nation, using selected examples.

You need to produce a PowerPoint presentation with notes on handouts to sum up your findings and conclusions to accompany your report.

Tips

You must use evidence to support your arguments, such as information from media articles and summaries of health reports, and should refer to the wider benefits of health promotion such as economic and social benefits.

When you analyse the benefits of health promotion, consider both the various benefits of health promotion and the links between benefits to individuals and the nation. You should refer either to a couple of examples in detail, such as one instance of health-risk advice and one instance of medical intervention, or to a wider range of illustrative examples if you decide to look at a range of health-promotion activities.

Targeting selected health risks

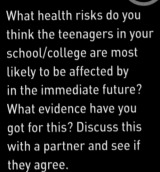

Getting started

What health risks do you think the teenagers in your school/college are most likely to be affected by in the immediate future? What evidence have you got for this? Discuss this with a partner and see if they agree.

Introduction

This topic suggests some possible health risks to young people. We will also look at some possible sources of information for your research.

◤ Topics for health promotion

Some of the health topics currently being promoted are:

- substance misuse, e.g. recreational drugs, solvents
- binge drinking
- safe sex
- healthy eating
- smoking
- road safety
- hand washing
- participation in sport and exercise.

For your assignment for this part of the unit you need to pick a health risk and research its associated effects on health. You will need to gather information such as is shown in Figure 5.4, for smoking.

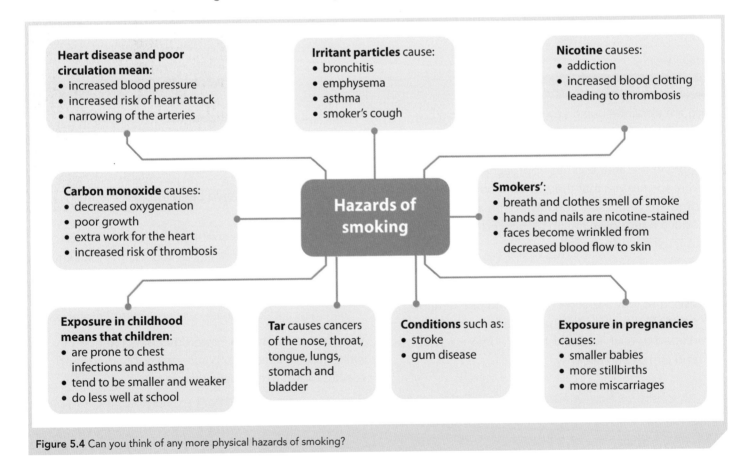

Heart disease and poor circulation mean:
- increased blood pressure
- increased risk of heart attack
- narrowing of the arteries

Irritant particles cause:
- bronchitis
- emphysema
- asthma
- smoker's cough

Nicotine causes:
- addiction
- increased blood clotting leading to thrombosis

Carbon monoxide causes:
- decreased oxygenation
- poor growth
- extra work for the heart
- increased risk of thrombosis

Hazards of smoking

Smokers':
- breath and clothes smell of smoke
- hands and nails are nicotine-stained
- faces become wrinkled from decreased blood flow to skin

Exposure in childhood means that children:
- are prone to chest infections and asthma
- tend to be smaller and weaker
- do less well at school

Tar causes cancers of the nose, throat, tongue, lungs, stomach and bladder

Conditions such as:
- stroke
- gum disease

Exposure in pregnancies causes:
- smaller babies
- more stillbirths
- more miscarriages

Figure 5.4 Can you think of any more physical hazards of smoking?

You will also need to work out the intellectual, emotional and social impacts of these possible physical effects to be able to fully understand the total effect of smoking on an individual's health.

Researching health risks

Choose the health risk you think you might want as the focus of your assignment. Do some research on its effects on an individual's health and divide the information up into effects on an individual's physical, intellectual, emotional and social (PIES) needs. You could do this as a mind map or in a table.

Forms of health-promotion materials

Health-promotion materials include posters, leaflets, games, presentations, web-based materials, CDs, DVDs, flyers, newspaper adverts or articles, TV and radio coverage and wall displays. They may accompany campaigns launched on the TV or internet. All should be easy to understand, attractive and accurate.

- Posters: should be eye-catching and not contain a lot of writing. They should give either telephone numbers or website addresses where help can be sought or more information can be found.

- Leaflets: contain more information than a poster, but should still be attractive, easy to understand, accurate and contain the information needed by the target group or groups, such as useful telephone numbers or websites.

- Games: examples include board games to persuade young children to clean their teeth and card games which teach facts about alcohol to teenagers in a fun way.

- Presentations: a popular form is PowerPoint and these can be very effective if each slide is kept simple, with a few bullet points and a diagram on each, so the person doing the presentation talks about each slide rather than reading them out. Special effects and diagrams can be incorporated and diagrams can be imported to make it attractive, hard-hitting and entertaining.

- Wall displays: the NHS website leaflet, *Effective Displays: A Guide*, suggests that the six rules for an effective display are (i) deliver the message, (ii) consider the display location, (iii) link to current campaigns, (iv) use a variety of materials to enhance your display, (v) make it readable, and (vi) arrange the display to give impact.

Did this poster catch your eye? Why?

Wall display

Download the guide from the NHS website if possible and produce your own wall display, based on the health risk you have been focusing on, following the six rules. You can do this in a small group with others who are working on the same risk. All groups should then judge the displays to see if they have stuck to the rules. Were any of them out of your control?

Promotional materials

Draw up a table showing each type of health promotion material mentioned, and any others you can think of, in the first column. Then add columns headed 'strengths' and 'weaknesses' for each type, and complete the table.

Research and data gathering (1)

Introduction

There are many different sources to use for research. Primary sources are first-hand sources of information where, for example, you speak to a school nurse about her work. You are gathering information that doesn't already exist. Secondary sources are those giving information which is second-hand, using sources such as books and the internet.

Research using different sources

Only use information that you understand yourself and put it in your own words.

Some examples of sources of information are:

- Websites: Remember that unlike books and journals, information on the net hasn't necessarily being checked. Search engines such as Google put the websites that are used most often at the top, so providing you search for the health risk in the UK by clicking on the 'Pages from the UK' option, check the date on the information and work from the top of the list of websites shown by a search engine, you should have current and useful information. Quote the website address in your bibliography.

- Books: always check the date a book has been published, as information in a book that is several years old may now be outdated. You can do this by looking on the copyright page. Use the contents or index to find the section you need. When quoting a book in a bibliography at the end of your work the correct way is to write the author (surname followed by initial/s), the year of publication, the title of the book and the publisher.

- Newspapers/magazines: these can be useful sources of information, but much of the content of these sorts of publication are the opinions of the author of the article, unless they are quoting from a specific piece of research. Be careful to distinguish between facts and opinions and quote not only the name of the newspaper/magazine and its date of publication, but also the title and author of the article or feature if known.

What are the advantages and disadvantages of using books instead of websites?

- Leaflets: these can be picked up from a wide range of places, such as libraries, health centres, hospitals and even supermarkets. Again, make sure they are up-to-date, quote the title and the body publishing the leaflet and any other information available, such as a date. Some leaflets show more of this sort of information than others.

- Journals: many professional bodies produce their own journals, such as the *Nursing Times* for nursery nurses. Quote sources of articles in the same way as those in newspapers/magazines.
- DVDs and TV programmes: these are useful as they often show real-life situations, can be watched by lots of people at once and are easy to use and engage with. When quoting information from them make sure you show you know what is fact and what is opinion or fiction, and that it is up-to-date.

Other research sources

- Department of Health: this government department is in charge of public health, adult social care and the NHS. It is headed by the Secretary of State for Health (who is a Cabinet minister), supported by health ministers (who are MPs), and professional officers (who are leaders in their professions and provide the department with expert knowledge about health and social care issues). The department produces a wide array of publications and has a very useful website. You can access this by going to www.pearsonhotlinks.co.uk and searching for this title.
- Health professionals: you can gather information from health professionals by interviewing them, giving them a **questionnaire** to complete or listening to them talk either in your school or in their place of work and making notes. You need to think carefully beforehand about what exactly you want to find out and have your questions ready, but also be prepared to ask supplementary questions depending on how the conversation goes. Don't ask questions that are too personal as these will make the person feel awkward or uncomfortable.
- Service users: again, you can conduct a **survey** with service users by giving the person a questionnaire. Be careful not to put too much reliance on one person's answers, because they may be biased.

> **Remember**
>
> Use the communication skills you learned in Unit 3.

> **Key terms**
>
> **Questionnaire** – a list of questions in writing, designed to gather information on a specific subject.
>
> **Survey** – a broad investigation of a subject, often informed by asking questions of a representative group.

Activity   Surveying school/college life

As a group, conduct a **survey** of an aspect of school or college life, such as the safety of the site or what learners prefer to eat at lunchtime. Discuss in your group what went well and what went less well. Write a report based on your findings and include an evaluation of how effective your techniques were for gathering the information you needed.

Research and data gathering (2)

Gathering data

Data is information, often in number form or statistics. It is important that you collect data on the health topic you select as the focus for your assignment. Before you start collecting data you have to be clear about what your aim is and what methods you are going to use so you don't end up collecting irrelevant data. When you have gathered the data you must decide how to present it, for instance in a report or in some form of diagram.

Examples of types of data include:

- National **statistics**: these are collected from a wide sample of the population of the UK by many national organisations, for example the UK Statistics Authority. One of the areas it covers is health and social care. The Office for National Statistics, the government statistics service, also has its own website. However, although you will come across these websites through search engines, the content is quite hard to understand, so you might prefer to use the Department of Health's website, as this has information that is more readily understandable.

- Local statistics: these are collected by many agencies, including local government. It is their responsibility to collect local data and submit it to the government when asked to. They provide information, advice and support for all local residents, so their websites provide a valuable source of data. You can also collect statistics from your community, such as your school or college, but be sure to ask a large enough sample of people to make your conclusions meaningful.

- Case studies: these are detailed descriptions of a person's life or work. Two useful sources are the CareUK and Macmillan Nurses websites. These provide a useful insight into how health issues affect individuals.

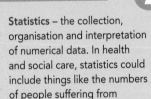

Key terms

Statistics – the collection, organisation and interpretation of numerical data. In health and social care, statistics could include things like the numbers of people suffering from particular conditions and the incidence of accidents.

Think about interesting and clear ways to present your data.

Activity | Local statistics

1 Go to your local council's website. Look to see what information they have on health issues in your area, in particular the one you are thinking of basing your assignment on.

2 Produce a PowerPoint presentation with no more than six slides to show to the class about a local health issue. It must include some data in diagram form.

WorkSpace

▶ April Forrester

School Nurse

I am a school nurse based in a small town. I work in a team that includes three early years workers, other health professionals and various support staff. We have a base, but I spend most of my time in the various secondary schools to which I am allocated.

My main task is to provide preventative health services to help the learners grow and develop in the best way possible. I identify problems and provide services, such as health education, and referral to other services and care, in order to prevent more serious problems developing later, which would be more difficult to deal with and more costly to address. I work with groups of, and individual, learners. I sometimes speak to a whole year group about an issue, and hold drop-in clinics at schools for any learners to come along and have a private chat with me. Issues they talk to me about are very varied, from unwanted pregnancies to personal hygiene or problems with parents and friends. I have a full range of printed health-promotion materials available, so I can give learners leaflets, which tell them where to find more help if needed. I can also refer them to more specialist agencies that can help them with their specific problems.

I help at school events, such as learning days, when a health input is required, and work with other nurses to carry out year group vaccinations, such as HPV. It is a very satisfying job, because although I speak to many learners when they are upset or worried, it is good to feel that I am helping them, and as no two problems are exactly the same it is a very varied job, so never boring. Sometimes it is very sad, such as when a relative, friend, learner or teacher has died, and learners need to talk through their feelings, but it is often fun, as I really enjoy working with young people.

Think about it

1 Why are communication skills so important to April's job?

2 How does April promote health among young people?

3 How can you make use of health-promotion materials to make sure you keep yourself fit and healthy?

Target groups in health promotion

Introduction

The target group of health-promotion materials can be almost anyone: children, adolescents, employees, men, women, the old, the young and so on. But what is important to note is that campaigns are much more effective if they are targeted at a specific group and tailored to meet that group's needs. General campaigns have been proven to be far less effective as people tend to feel the message is not aimed specifically at them.

Target-group appropriate health-promotion materials

There are many ways in which health-promotion materials can be made appropriate to a target group. They include:

- Language: plain language, without the use of jargon or technical terms, is very important in communicating health information to everyone. The level of readability of materials should be appropriate to the age and ability of the target group. It is important, for instance, that materials aimed at children have few words and are simple and straightforward. Materials should also be available in the range of languages that reflects the make-up of the target group.

- Images: images used for children should be appealing and make them feel safe, whereas those aimed at teenagers and older groups can be more hard-hitting and thought-provoking. Images can include photographs, movies, cartoons, symbols and artworks.

- Activity: some health-promotion materials ask that groups of people take part in a specific activity. The physical requirement of the activity should be appropriate to the target group. It would be inappropriate, for instance, to ask a group of people with limited mobility to do an exercise that involved doing star jumps.

- Position of display: think about your target group. If you have a display high on a wall, you will immediately rule out people below a certain height and wheelchair users. Similarly, if you have the display in a poorly lit corner, those with a visual impairment may not be able to read the display. Also think about the general environment where you place your display: there is little point, for instance, in putting something about childcare in an residential care home for older people.

- Timing: the timing of the use of health-promotion materials can be crucial; for instance, material about the safe use of fireworks and bonfires should be launched a few weeks before Bonfire Night and Diwali, and drink-drive campaigns are effective during the period of Christmas and New Year, when more people fall victim to this than at other times of the year because of all the extra parties.

Ethics

The consideration of **ethics** is very important when planning health promotion. The different aspects you need to think about are:

- Is the health promotion necessary?
- What can you do with regard to your health-promotion campaign that will place the smallest limit on people's **civil liberties**?
- Will it be effective?
- Is it proportionate? For example, the drink-driving laws are a serious curb on the freedom of individuals to drink what they want when they drive. However, the potential harm that drink-drivers could do to themselves and others makes the current laws fair and proportionate.
- Is there a public justification? A health promotion should affect the nation as a whole, not just the individual who changes their behaviour as a result of it.

Key terms

Ethics – a system of moral principles; the rules of conduct recognised in a group or culture.

Civil liberties – people's rights and freedoms in society, such as the right to privacy.

Activity   Ethical considerations in health promotion

In a group, take a recent example of a health promotion. Compare the health promotion to the list of ethical considerations above and come up with a list of reasons for and against each point. Present your arguments on both sides back to the class and allow them to vote on whether the health promotion was ethical or not.

Forms of media

The success of health promotion can often depend on the media used to do the promotion. For instance, women over 50 tend to read particular types of magazine and so using a young person's magazine to promote the Nation Breast Screening Programme would not work. Similarly, when targeting adolescents about an issue such as safe sex, it is better to use posters in places such as schools, colleges and youth centres, internet pop-ups, and adverts shown at the cinema before films aimed at teenagers.

Have you been influenced by adverts shown on social networking sites?

How materials could be adapted for different target groups

Introduction

The planning and producing of a national health-promotion campaign is very expensive. It is therefore more cost-effective if materials can be produced and then adapted for different target groups.

In adapting materials you would need to look at the following:

- Changing the language: making translated materials available to meet the unique cultural needs of a local population. Translation software or specialist agencies can translate documents and materials downloaded from websites, such as the Department of Health's.

- Changing the style of language: a campaign could use text message style spelling or street language to communicate with teenagers, whereas a more formal style of language would be used with older people.

- Using Braille: materials can be printed in Braille so that blind people can access leaflets and posters.

- Easier language: this is necessary so that people with learning difficulties can understand what they are reading or hearing. If you are adapting a message for children, it might also be necessary to simplify the language.

- Larger print: this enables people with sight impairments to access the information.

- Using a different media form: materials can be made into audio CDs for those who have sight impairment or made into videos for those with hearing impairments or learning difficulties or who don't read very well. The images can be changed to appeal to different groups.

One example is the NHS's free *NHS Stop Smoking Start Living* booklet, which is available as an audio CD, in Braille, in large print, and in an easy-to-read version for people with learning difficulties, as well as in 9 languages other than English. The website and the TV campaign, launched at the start of 2012, advertise a free Quit Kit – a box of practical tools and advice developed with experts, smokers and ex-smokers, which has helped thousands of smokers quit successfully – to use alongside the booklet.

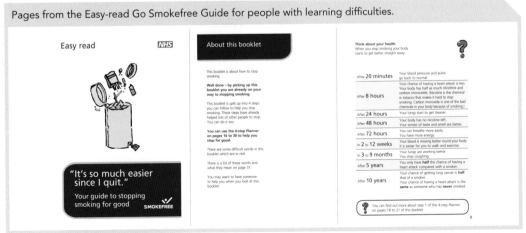

Pages from the Easy-read Go Smokefree Guide for people with learning difficulties.

Source: smokefree.nhs.uk © Department of Health.

Evaluation

It is important that all health-promotion materials are **evaluated** to make sure they are appropriate to the target group, and that the strategy used in producing and launching them is effective. Existing campaigns are evaluated and lessons learned from how successful, or not, they have been.

Assessment

Here are some questions to test what you have learned so far and a practice assessment assignment for you to try.

Key terms

Evaluate – gather and review evidence, and make a judgement as to success.

Just checking

1 Name three possible topics for health promotion.

2 Pick one of the topics you named in question 1, which is not the one you are basing your assignment on, and describe its effects on an individual's health and wellbeing.

3 Name three possible primary sources of evidence.

4 Name two possible secondary sources of evidence.

5 Name a source of national statistics.

6 Which body could provide you with local health statistics?

7 Explain why 'type of service user' is a target group? Give an example.

8 Name three factors in making health promotion materials appropriate to a target group.

9 How can health promotion materials be adapted for different target groups? Include at least three ways in your answer.

10 Why do groups producing health promotion materials evaluate the success of existing campaigns?

Assessment activity 5.2   *English   Maths*

2B.P3 | 2B.P4 | 2B.M2 | 2B.M3 | 2B.D2 | 2B.D3

You are a trainee nurse at a health centre in a big town. Following your successful report on health risks faced by teenagers it has been decided that it is necessary to run a health-promotion campaign.

You now need to pick a health risk and produce some materials that could be included in a pack that will be given out as part of this campaign in places such as youth and medical centres and libraries. The pack needs to contain posters, leaflets, booklets and material for a wall display that describe the health risk and give advice to teenagers.

You need to research and collect existing information on the health risk on which to base your materials. You will need to produce a short report on how the health risk can be addressed by health promotion and compare how successful different strategies have been in the past.

When you have produced your information pack, you will be expected to present the information to your peers, and recommend how the health promotion materials could be adapted for a different target group of your choice.

Tips

Don't forget to think about the effect of the health risk on physical, intellectual, emotional and social health.

Use research findings from at least two different sources.

Introduction

How often do you think about why you need to eat and what you are eating? Do you know how your body and health are affected by the food you eat? Although we know that some foods are not good for us, we might think that we have plenty of time to eat sensibly when we are older, but by then we might have developed a condition such as diabetes or coronary heart disease.

Health and social care workers must have a good understanding of the principles of nutrition so that they can maintain or improve their own health and that of service users or patients. You will learn what a balanced diet is and how an unbalanced diet can affect people's health. You will think about how dietary needs change over the lifespan, and conditions that require people to follow specific dietary plans or advice. You will explore the dietary needs of people of different religions, and other factors that influence what people choose to eat.

Assessment: You will be assessed by a series of assignments set by your teacher/tutor.

Learning aims

In this unit you will:

A explore the effects of balanced and unbalanced diets on the health and wellbeing of individuals

B understand the specific nutritional needs and preferences of individuals.

"I'm so glad I have learned something about nutrition. My dad had a heart attack last year, and the doctor told my mum it was because he was overweight and unfit. The whole family now thinks much more about what we eat and we are following a much healthier diet. We all take more exercise too. Doing it as a family has really helped Dad get better.

Jamie, *17-year-old Health and Social Care learner*

The Impact of Nutrition on Health and Wellbeing

6

BTEC
Assessment Zone

This table shows you what you must do in order to achieve a **Pass**, **Merit** or **Distinction** grade, and where you can find activities in this book to help you.

Assessment criteria			
Level 1	Level 2 Pass	Level 2 Merit	Level 2 Distinction
Learning aim A: Explore the effects of balanced and unbalanced diets on the health and wellbeing of individuals			
1A.1 Identify components of a balanced diet, giving examples of each.	**2A.P1** Describe the components of a balanced diet and their functions, sources and effects. **Assessment activity 6.1 See page 141.**	**2A.M1** Compare the effects of balanced and unbalanced diets on the health and wellbeing of two individuals. **Assessment activity 6.1 See page 141.**	**2A.D1** Assess the long-term effects of a balanced and unbalanced diet on the health and wellbeing of individuals. **Assessment activity 6.1 See page 141.**
1A.2 Identify three effects of an unbalanced diet on the health and wellbeing of individuals.	**2A.P2** Describe the effects of an unbalanced diet on the health and wellbeing of individuals, giving examples of their causes. **Assessment activity 6.1 See page 141.**		
Learning aim B: Understand the specific nutritional needs and preferences of individuals			
1B.3 Identify the specific dietary needs of an individual.	**2B.P3** Describe the specific dietary needs of two individuals at different life stages. **Assessment activity 6.2 See page 154.**	**2B.M2** Explain the factors influencing the dietary choices of two individuals with specific dietary needs at different life stages. **Assessment activity 6.2 See page 154.**	**2B.D2** Discuss how factors influence the dietary choices of two individuals with specific dietary needs at different life stages. **Assessment activity 6.2 See page 154.**
1B.4 English Create, with guidance, a nutritional plan for a selected individual.	**2B.P4** English Create a nutritional plan for two individuals, with different specific nutritional needs. **Assessment activity 6.2 See page 154.**	**2B.M3** Compare nutritional plans for two individuals with different nutritional needs. **Assessment activity 6.2 See page 154.**	

English English signposting

How you will be assessed

The unit will be assessed by a series of internally assessed tasks. You will be expected to show an understanding of nutrition across the lifespan. For example, the dietician at your health centre has planned a healthy eating week and has asked you to produce information for people that will provide a brief introduction to the components of a balanced diet, the effects on the body of an unbalanced diet, nutritional needs across the lifespan and specific dietary needs. You will also create a nutritional plan for two individuals.

Your assessment could be in the form of:

- a booklet
- a PowerPoint presentation to be shown on the TV screen in the waiting room
- case studies about individuals with specific dietary needs.

Components of a balanced diet (1)

Getting started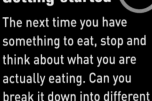

The next time you have something to eat, stop and think about what you are actually eating. Can you break it down into different nutrients? Make a list of everything you eat in your next meal and then try to identify the different nutrients you are eating.

Essential nutrients

A balanced diet is made up of carbohydrates, proteins, fats, vitamins, minerals, fibre and water. Carbohydrates, proteins and fats are known as macronutrients because they are required in the body in large amounts.

Carbohydrates

Carbohydrates provide the main source of energy in the diet. These are sugars, starches and fibre. They include grains, pulses, fruit and vegetables, and should make up about 50 to 60 per cent of the diet.

Glucose is a simple sugar which is found in fruit, plants and the blood of animals. Glucose syrups are used in the manufacture of cakes, sweets and jams. These are digested more quickly than starches, so they can be absorbed and used more easily, but they cause peaks and troughs in blood glucose levels, so energy levels are much less stable. Table sugar is sucrose, a combination of two simple sugars, glucose and fructose.

Starches are found in wholemeal cereals, such as oats, wheat, barley, rye and rice. This group also includes potatoes, root vegetables, some fruits, and pulses and beans, such as lentils, baked beans and chickpeas. Some starches are refined and are present in foods such as pizza, which are often high in fat so should be limited in the diet.

When carbohydrates are eaten and digested, they break down into glucose, which is what we need to provide energy for the body. The glucose is absorbed into the bloodstream and a hormone called insulin is released by the pancreas to control the absorption of glucose into the cells.

Polysaccharides or fibre cannot be digested by the body but play an important role in adding bulk to faeces and helping to prevent constipation. A daily intake of 25g of fibre is recommended.

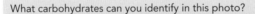
What carbohydrates can you identify in this photo?

Proteins

Protein is needed in the body for growth and repair. Proteins are made up of chains of amino acids and nine of them are essential. This means that you must obtain them from the food you eat because they can't be made in the body.

Proteins can be divided into animal and vegetable sources. Animal proteins include meat, fish, cheese and eggs, and contain all of the essential amino acids. Studies show that eating lots of red and processed meat can contribute to stomach and bowel cancer. Plant proteins include pulses such as nuts, beans, peas and soya or tofu. They are high in fibre, vitamins and minerals, and low in fat. They contribute to disease prevention and good health, but do not contain all of the essential amino acids.

Texturised vegetable proteins (TVP) and mycoprotein are developed from plant proteins and are used by vegetarians and vegans. They can be produced as slices, chunks, mince, burgers and sausages. Both will take up the flavour of other foods they are being cooked with.

Fats

The main sources of fat in the Western diet come from animal and dairy products. These are called saturated fats and are solid at room temperature, for example butter, margarine and fat on meat, and they can contribute to heart disease. Plant fats are usually liquid at room temperature, for example olive and sunflower oils. They are known as unsaturated fats. They are less likely to contribute to heart disease, because they do not have the same effect of blocking the blood vessels as animal fats. Olive oil helps to protect against heart disease.

Essential fatty acids are very important in the prevention of heart disease. They are the Omega 3 and Omega 6 fatty acids. Omega 3 is found in oily fish, such as mackerel, sardines, fresh tuna (not tinned), salmon, pumpkin seeds, linseed, soya, walnuts and leafy green vegetables. Omega 6 fatty acids are found in sunflower, grape seed and corn oil as well as cereals, eggs and poultry.

> **? Did you know?**
>
> If foods are mixed in the same meal, they will complement each other and become a complete protein, for example baked beans on toast. Bread is deficient in one essential amino acid and baked beans are deficient in another, so by eating them together, you can have a complete protein meal. Food combining is a way that vegetarians and vegans can obtain complete proteins in food without eating meat.

> **Did you know? ?**
>
> Fats have several important functions in the body:
> - They are a concentrated source of energy in the diet.
> - They help to provide insulation against the cold by preventing heat loss.
> - They protect body organs, such as the kidneys.
> - They help to transport and store vitamins A, D, E and K.
> - They provide taste to food and make it easier to eat.

> **Remember**
>
> A healthy balanced diet should be made up of:
>
> 50–60 per cent carbohydrate
>
> 15 per cent protein
>
> 20–35 per cent fat (but no more than 10 per cent of that should be saturated).

Components of a balanced diet (2)

Essential nutrients

Vitamins and minerals are known as micronutrients because they are needed in quite small amounts, but they are nevertheless essential to health. You will learn about the main vitamins and minerals in this topic.

| Activity | Dietary intake |

Make a list of everything you have had to eat and drink in the past two days. With a partner, decide which food groups your food came from. When you have done this, join up with another pair and discuss the following:

1 Do you think your two-day food intake was balanced?

2 What did you eat too much of?

3 What could you have eaten more of?

Keep your list and notes of your discussion as you will need them later on.

Vitamins and minerals

Vitamins cannot be made by the body and they are essential to life. There are two types of vitamins: water-soluble and fat-soluble.

Water-soluble vitamins are the B vitamins and vitamin C. They cannot be stored in the body, so we must have a daily intake of foods containing them.

Table 6.1 Sources and functions of water-soluble vitamins.

Vitamin	Sources in diet	Function
B_1	Bread, nuts, cereals, flour, meat, eggs, potatoes, poultry, milk	Converts carbohydrate to glucose; helps digestion; aids correct functioning of nerves; required for building of blood; essential for growth.
B_2	Milk, liver, kidney, cereals, yeast, meat extract, eggs, cheese	Converts glucose to energy.
B_3	Meat extract, yeast extract, wholemeal bread, eggs, liver, cereals	Converts glucose to energy; maintains healthy skin and nervous system; required for cell metabolism.
B_5	Animal products, cereals, legumes	Converts glucose and fat to energy; maintains healthy immune system.
B_6	Meat, green vegetables, bran, wholemeal flour, eggs, bananas	Required for protein metabolism; converts tryptophan to niacin; essential for formation of haemoglobin.
B_9	Yeast, leafy green vegetables, meat, avocado, bananas	Produces red blood cells and tissue cells; required for normal growth; maintains healthy digestive tract.
B_{12}	Widely distributed in animal foods	Involved in manufacture of red blood cells in bone marrow; maintains nervous system.
C	Blackcurrants, citrus fruits, green vegetables, peppers, tomatoes	Required in formation of bones and teeth; essential in building of blood; required for wound healing; maintains immune system, and healthy skin and gums.

Vitamin names

As well as letters and numbers, water-soluble vitamins also have names. Carry out some research to find out these names.

Fat-soluble vitamins are A, D, E and K. They dissolve in fat in the body, which is why we need to consume fat in our diet. They are stored in the body in the liver.

Table 6.2 Sources and functions of fat-soluble vitamins.

Vitamin	Sources in diet	Function
A	Fish oil, liver, butter, cheese, eggs, milk, fruit and vegetables	Aids night vision; keeps skin and epithelial linings healthy.
D	Fish liver, oily fish, eggs, milk, margarine, sunlight	Required for absorption of calcium in intestine; regulates calcium and magnesium in bone tissue.
E	Eggs, cereal oils, vegetables, nuts, seeds	Maintains healthy muscular system; anti-oxidant; protects cell membranes.
K	Green vegetables, fish liver oils, alfalfa tablets, molasses, yoghurt	Essential for blood clotting.

Minerals

Minerals are also known as micronutrients because, like vitamins, they are only needed in very small amounts in the body. They are found in the earth and in the sea. They are necessary for many processes in the body and these are shown in the table below.

Table 6.3 Sources and functions of minerals.

Mineral	Sources in diet	Function
Calcium	Milk, cheese, bread, flour, seafood, nuts and green vegetables. For some, the bones in canned fish are important	Builds strong bones and hard teeth; essential for blood clotting; helps muscles and nerves to work; activates certain enzymes; requires vitamin D for absorption.
Sodium	Naturally in eggs, meat, vegetables, milk. Added to many processed foods, such as meat and canned food	Maintains body fluid balance and blood pressure; excess is linked to high blood pressure; aids muscle contraction and nerve transmission.
Iron	Meat (offal), bread, flour, cereal products, potatoes and vegetables	Needed by all cells; needed to form haemoglobin in red blood cells and myoglobin in muscles; absorbed by body relative to need; vitamin C increases absorption of iron.

Water

The human body is made up of about two-thirds water, and we cannot survive for more than a few days without it as it is needed for many processes. The European Food Safety Authority (EFSA) recommends that men have 2.5 litres a day and women 2 litres a day.

 Take it further

Find out what the recommended daily allowance is for each of the vitamins and minerals in Tables 6.1 – 6.3. Make sure you use UK sources as there is variation in different countries.

Components of a balanced diet (3)

The five food groups and their functions

As well as thinking of food as belonging to different nutrient groups, you can also think of different types of food. The Food Standards Agency identified the five different food groups in *The Balance of Good Health* (2001), and this information is given below.

Can you think of any more foods that belong to this group?

Meat, fish and alternatives

This group is used in the body for growth and repair. It includes meat, poultry, fish, eggs, nuts, beans and pulses. Meat includes bacon and salami and meat products such as sausages, beefburgers and pâté. These are all quite high-fat choices. Beans and pulses are in this group and they are a good source of protein for vegetarians. Fish includes frozen and tinned fish, such as sardines and tuna, fish fingers and fishcakes. Aim to eat at least one portion of oily fish, such as sardines or salmon, each week. The main nutrients are iron, protein, B vitamins (especially B_{12}), zinc and magnesium.

The recommendation is to eat moderate amounts and choose lower-fat versions, such as meat with the fat cut off, poultry without the skin and fish without batter. Cook these foods without added fat. Beans and pulses are good alternatives to meat as they are naturally very low in fat.

Fruit and vegetables

The main nutrients in fruit and vegetables are vitamin C, carotenes, folates, and some carbohydrate. They also provide fibre in the diet. Fresh, frozen and tinned fruit and vegetables, dried fruit and fruit juice are all included in this group. Beans and pulses can also be eaten.

The advice is to eat lots – at least five portions a day. Beans, pulses and fruit juice count as one portion, however much you eat or drink in a day. You should eat a wide variety of fruit and vegetables of as many different colours and types as possible. Try to avoid adding fat or rich sauces to vegetables (e.g. butter on potatoes), and sugar or syrupy dressings to fruit (e.g. chocolate sauce on banana).

How many portions of fruit and vegetables do you eat each day?

Bread, other cereals and potatoes

This group is mainly made up of carbohydrate-rich food and provides much of the energy needed in the diet. Other nutrients in them are calcium and iron, B vitamins and fibre. Cereals are foods such as breakfast cereals, pasta, rice, oats, noodles, maize, millet and cornmeal. This group also includes yams and plantains. Beans and pulses can be eaten as part of this group.

You should eat a lot of foods in this group, and try to eat wholemeal, wholegrain, brown or high-fibre versions where possible. Avoid having them fried too often and adding too much fat (e.g. thickly spread butter, margarine or low-fat spread on bread), or adding rich sauces to pasta.

How many foods can you name in this group?

Milk and dairy foods

This food group includes milk, cheese, yoghurt and fromage frais, but not butter and cream. The main nutrients are calcium, protein, vitamins A, B_{12} and D. They are needed in the body to build strong bones and teeth and maintain healthy skin and eyes. The recommendation is to eat or drink moderate amounts, and choose lower-fat versions whenever you can.

Lower-fat versions mean semi-skimmed or skimmed milk, low fat (0.1 per cent fat) yoghurts or fromage frais, and lower-fat cheeses. Check the amount of fat by looking at the information on the labels. Compare similar products and choose the lowest; for example, 8 per cent fromage frais may be labelled 'low fat', but it is not actually the lowest available.

What are your favourite dairy products?

Foods containing fat/foods and drinks containing sugar

Foods containing fat include margarine, butter, other spreading fats and low-fat spreads, cooking oils, oil-based salad dressings, mayonnaise, cream, chocolate, crisps, biscuits, pastries, cakes, puddings, ice cream, rich sauces and gravies.

Foods containing sugar include soft drinks, sweets, jam and sugar, as well as foods such as cakes, puddings, biscuits, pastries and ice cream.

The main nutrients are fats, including some essential fatty acids, and fat is needed in the body to transport vitamins A, D, E and K, which are the fat-soluble vitamins. Some products also contain salt or sugar. Sugar is described by some people as 'empty calories', because it contains calories, but few, if any, nutrients.

You should eat foods containing fat sparingly and look out for low-fat alternatives. Foods and drinks containing sugar should not be consumed too often as they can contribute to tooth decay.

All foods and drinks containing sugar should be consumed mainly at mealtimes to reduce the risk of tooth decay.

Can you think of any healthy alternatives to your favourite snacks?

Components of a balanced diet (4)

Recommended Daily Intakes (RDIs)

A balanced diet will depend on the types of food you eat and your nutritional needs. The wider the variety of foods eaten, the more nutrients you will get from them. It is now known that some health problems are caused by dietary intake, such as too much fat causing heart disease and too much salt contributing to strokes.

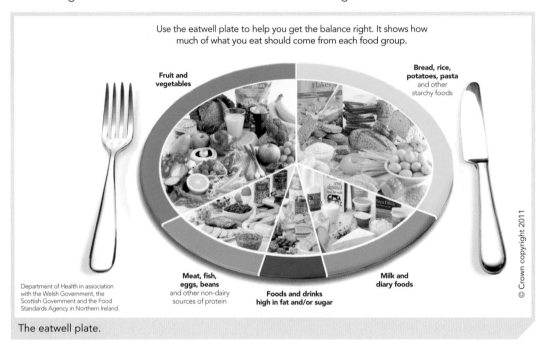

Use the eatwell plate to help you get the balance right. It shows how much of what you eat should come from each food group.

Fruit and vegetables

Bread, rice, potatoes, pasta and other starchy foods

Meat, fish, eggs, beans and other non-dairy sources of protein

Foods and drinks high in fat and/or sugar

Milk and diary foods

Department of Health in association with the Welsh Government, the Scottish Government and the Food Standards Agency in Northern Ireland.

© Crown copyright 2011

The eatwell plate.

Benefits of a balanced diet

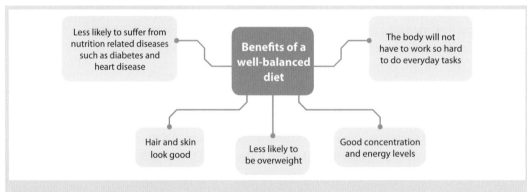

Less likely to suffer from nutrition related diseases such as diabetes and heart disease

Benefits of a well-balanced diet

The body will not have to work so hard to do everyday tasks

Hair and skin look good

Less likely to be overweight

Good concentration and energy levels

Figure 6.1 Can you think of any other benefits of a balanced diet?

Intake and needs

People have different dietary needs and intake depending on a range of factors:

- Height, weight and gender
- The level of exercise taken
- The type of job a person does
- Likes and dislikes
- A person's health
- Availability of food.

Are there any other factors that would determine what and how much a person needs to eat?

Dietary reference values

There are a variety of dietary reference values that can be used to identify different nutritional requirements for people of different ages and needs. They are shown in Table 6.4.

Table 6.4 Dietary reference values.

Dietary reference value	Definition
Estimated Average Requirement (EAR)	An estimate of the average need for food energy or a nutrient. Some people will need more than this average and some will need less.
Reference Nutrient Intake (RNI)	The amount of a nutrient that is enough for almost every individual, even those with high needs. The RNI is generally much higher than most people need. The RNI supplies enough of a nutrient for at least 97.5% of the population.
Lower Reference Nutrient Intake (LRNI)	The amount of a nutrient considered to be sufficient for the small number of individuals with low nutrient needs (only about 2.5% of the population).

In 2011, the Scientific Advisory Committee on Nutrition (SACN) published new guidelines on Estimated Average Requirements for the UK population. This is the average amount that individuals of average weight should consume. Table 6.5 shows the requirements in both megajoules and kilocalories.

Table 6.6 shows the recommended daily intakes for some common nutrients.

Table 6.6 Recommended daily intakes for common nutrients.

	Boys 11–14	Girls 11–14	Men 19–50	Women 19–50
Protein (g)	42.1	41.2	55.5	45
Calcium (mg)	1000	800	700	700
Iron (mg)	11.3	14.8	8.7	14.8
Zinc (mg)	9	9	9.5	7
Vitamin C (mg)	35	35	40	40

Source: DEFRA Manual of Nutrition, 12th Edition 2012.

Activity	Recommended daily intakes

Use the tables above to answer the following:

1 At what age are male and female energy needs greatest?

2 Explain why girls' and women's iron requirements are higher than boys' and men's.

3 Why is a male's protein requirement higher than a female's?

Table 6.5 Estimated Average Requirements.

Age (years)	Estimated Average Requirement	
	MJ/day (Kcal/day)	
	Males	Females
1	3.2 (765)	3.0 (717)
5	6.2 (1482)	5.7 (1362)
10	8.5 (2032)	8.1 (1936)
16	12.4 (2964)	10.1 (2414)
18	13.2 (3155)	10.3 (2462)
19–24	11.6 (2772)	9.1 (2175)
25–34	11.5 (2749)	9.1 (2175)
35–44	11.0 (2629)	8.8 (2013)
45–54	10.8 (2581)	8.8 (2013)
55–64	10.8 (2581)	8.7 (2079)
65–74	9.8 (2342)	8.0 (1912)
75+	9.6 (2294)	7.7 (1840)

Source: SACN Dietary Reference Values for Energy, 2011.

Long-term effects of a balanced diet

What is a balanced diet?

A balanced diet helps to maintain a healthy body. If you eat the right foods in the right amounts, you should be the right weight for your height and not have too much body fat. This means that your body will work efficiently, you will feel happy and you will be less prone to diseases, such as diabetes, heart disease and cancer. The eatwell plate shows the recommended amounts of each food group that should be eaten. It is also important to keep an eye on portion sizes.

Another recommendation is to keep to the 80/20 rule. If you eat healthily 80 per cent of the time, you can eat less healthy foods 20 per cent of the time with little ill effect.

Raised immunity to infections

The body's immune system helps to protect against disease. Fresh fruit and vegetables which contain vitamins A and E, and foods such as garlic and honey can help to maintain a healthy immune system. Foods high in zinc and omega-3 fatty acids also boost the immune system.

Greater energy levels

People who are overweight often have low energy levels. This is because they have to use up a lot of energy just to do a basic level of exercise, and have little or no energy to do more. Although we need to eat carbohydrates to give us the energy we need, it's important to make sure we don't eat too many, and get most of our energy from complex carbohydrates with a high fibre content. Getting into the habit of eating healthily will boost energy levels.

Having energy to exercise will boost your health and wellbeing.

Increased concentration

Research shows that children who eat breakfast have better concentration levels and do better at school than those who don't. Some believe that too many carbohydrates can lower concentration levels. Behaviour is also improved through a balanced diet. Studies carried out at the University of Southampton showed that children who had drinks with high amounts of additives were less able to concentrate and were more hyperactive than those who didn't.

Which drinks would you recommend to these children to help them concentrate?

Faster healing of skin, tissues and mucus membranes

A diet that is rich in vitamins A, C and E aids the healing of the skin, tissues and mucus membranes. Vitamin C in particular helps to form connective tissue in cuts. It also assists in making red blood cells and fighting infection, especially colds. Vitamin E helps to make less scar tissue and break down blood clots.

Did you know?

The Balance of Good Health is based on the Government's Eight Guidelines for a Healthy Diet. It forms the basis of the Food Standards Agency Nutrition Strategy. If people follow the recommended amounts and make sure that they choose different foods, this should ensure that they have a balanced diet.

The Government's Eight Guidelines are:

- Base your meals on starchy foods.
- Eat lots of fruit and vegetables.
- Eat more fish.
- Cut down on saturated fat and sugar.
- Eat less salt – no more than 6g a day.
- Get active and try to be a healthy weight.
- Drink plenty of water.
- Don't skip breakfast.

Long-term effects of an unbalanced diet (1)

◤ Malnutrition

Malnutrition can take different forms: too much nutritional intake can result in over-nutrition and obesity, and too little nutritional intake can result in under-nutrition or starvation.

Over-nutrition

Coronary heart disease – This can occur through eating too many animal proteins that are high in saturated fats. To maintain a healthy heart, people are advised to eat two to three meals containing oily fish such as salmon, mackerel, sardines or fresh tuna (not tinned) per week, and plenty of fresh fruit and vegetables. Regular exercise that raises the heart rate and maintaining a healthy weight will help to prevent this.

Weight gain and obesity – Any food that is eaten in excess will be converted to fat and stored in the body, which leads to weight gain and obesity. A healthy balanced diet together with exercise will help people to lose weight. Maintaining the correct weight for your height might require a lifestyle change, such as changing what you eat and taking regular exercise.

Type 2 diabetes – This is also known as late or adult onset diabetes, but it is seen today in children as young as nine years old. It is caused by eating too much fat and sugar. The pancreas is either unable to produce enough insulin for the cells to absorb glucose from the blood, or the body becomes resistant to the insulin that is produced. Symptoms of type 2 diabetes include thirst, excessive urination and extreme tiredness. It can be controlled by diet alone, or by diet and medication. Type 2 diabetics do not normally need insulin.

Stroke – A stroke occurs when brain cells die because the oxygen supply has been interrupted or stopped. Strokes are often caused by high blood pressure and one of the main causes of this is eating too much salt, but obesity and lack of exercise can also contribute to high blood pressure.

Under-nutrition

Specific nutrient **deficiencies** – This can result from a general lack of nutrients or a particular nutrient. It is not often seen in developed countries, but can be common in developing countries.

Diets low in thiamin (vitamin B_1) and magnesium may also cause low concentration span. A diet rich in fruit and vegetables, fatty acids, bread and meat will help poor concentration and behavioural problems.

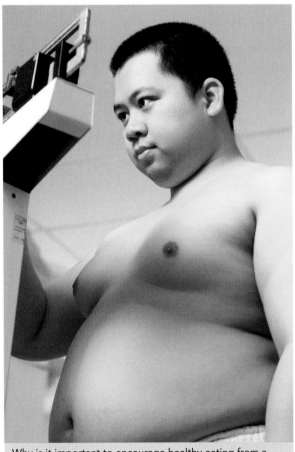

Why is it important to encourage healthy eating from a young age?

A vegetarian diet is usually high in fibre and low in fat and this makes it a healthy diet. As long as vegetarians are aware of the need to combine vegetable-based foods to make **high biological value proteins**, they can get all the nutrients they need.

Vegans can suffer from vitamin B_{12} deficiency as this is mainly found in animal products, although yeast extract is a good source, and provided vegans know about healthy eating choices, they can obtain everything they need from this diet. Nutritionists tend to advise that a vegan diet is not suitable for young children because it contains so much bulk that is filling that they may not eat enough to get the energy they need. However, a vegan diet containing a wide variety of foods will allow children to grow and develop normally, although they are likely to be lighter and leaner than meat-eating children.

Key terms

Malnutrition – lack of proper nutrition, caused by not having enough to eat, not eating enough of the right things, or being unable to use the food that one does eat.

Deficiency – a lack of a nutrient that is necessary.

High biological protein – a protein that provides the body with all eight essential amino acids.

Assessment activity 6.1

2A.P1 | 2A.P2 | 2A.M1 | 2A.D1

You have a part-time job at a local leisure centre and the manager is planning a 'get healthy week' for the people who use the facilities. There will be a variety of activities, including presentations and taster sessions. The manager wants you to help him prepare a booklet about balanced diets to be available for people to take home.

1 Using the information you have learned so far and carrying out further research, start your booklet by providing a table identifying and describing the components of a balanced diet and their functions, sources and effects on the body.

2 Create an eye-catching page that describes the effects of an unbalanced diet. Make sure that you link these effects to the causes: for example, a stroke is caused by high blood pressure due to a high salt intake.

3 Compare the effects of balanced and unbalanced diets on the health and wellbeing of individuals. Provide two case studies, one about someone who has a balanced diet and the other about someone who has an unbalanced diet, describing the effects of each and comparing them. Include an assessment of the long-term effects of a balanced and unbalanced diet on the health and wellbeing of individuals.

Tips

Remember that an unbalanced diet may include too much of some nutrients and not enough of others.

You need to make sure that the handout and leaflet that you provide is user-friendly, and that anyone who reads it can understand the information.

You must think carefully about the two people in your case studies. You may choose to use real people, but if you do, make sure you maintain confidentiality.

Long-term effects of an unbalanced diet (2)

Vitamin deficiency

Although it is possible to become deficient in vitamins, in the UK it is rare as many foods are fortified with vitamins to prevent deficiency diseases occurring. However, in developing countries some vitamin deficiency diseases can be fatal, especially in children.

Table 6.7 Effects of vitamin deficiency.

Vitamin	Effect of shortage
A	Night blindness (also known as xeropthalmia or dry eye). In its early stages, it can be cured by providing sufferers with vitamin A supplements such as palm oil or other foods high in vitamin A. However, in its later stages it is incurable and leads to complete blindness and in some cases death. Vitamin A deficiency can also cause itching, thickening of horny layer of the skin, ageing of the skin, dry skin and loss of taste.
B_1 (thiamin)	Beriberi, causing some or all of the following: neuritis (inflammation of the nerves), headache, fatigue, poor memory, diarrhoea, anxiety, insomnia, depression, irritability, eczema, dermatitis, acne, enlarged heart, muscle weakness, wrist and ankle drop, poor appetite, tenderness in calf muscles and pins and needles in legs.
B_2 (riboflavin)	Chapping of the lips, cracking at the corner of the mouth, soreness of the tongue, sensitivity to light, and skin rashes. It may also cause red, itchy eyes, night blindness, cataracts, migraines, peripheral neuropathy, anaemia and tiredness. There can also be some abnormalities associated with development, e.g. cleft lip and palate, growth problems and congenital heart defects.
B_3	Pellagra, causing redness of skin, exfoliation of hands and face, weakness, diarrhoea, memory loss, irritability and insomnia. Deficiency is rare and if supplements are needed, they should be given under medical supervision.
B_5	Weakness, depression, lowered resistance to infection, numbness, muscle cramps, restlessness, sleep disturbances, nausea, vomiting and abdominal cramps. Deficiency is very rare.
B_6	Anaemia, fatigue, nerve dysfunction, sore tongue, skin inflammation and depression.
B_9	Megaloblastic anaemia (abnormally large red blood cells), neural tube defects (e.g. spina bifida), nausea and headaches, memory loss, depression, loss of appetite and diarrhoea.
B_{12}	Pernicious anaemia, tiredness, loss of appetite, weight loss, breathlessness, diarrhoea, red and sore tongue, degeneration of nerve cells, a change in taste, ringing in the ears (tinnitus).
C	Scurvy, bleeding gums and loose teeth, incomplete cell repair, easy bruising, tiredness, and physical and mental stress.
D	Rickets, causing osteomalacia, spontaneous fractures, obesity, overactive parathyroid hormones, depression and fatigue.
E	Slow healing, poor muscle, circulatory and nerve performance. Vitamin E deficiency as a result of diet is rare.
K	Problems with blood clotting. It is very rare, but occasionally babies need a supplement at birth.

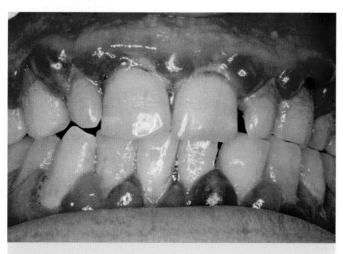

Bleeding gums are one of the symptoms of scurvy.

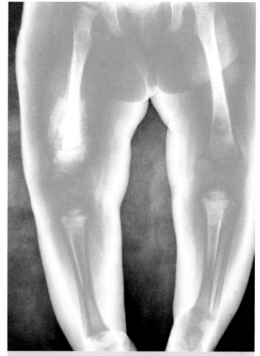

An X-ray of the bones of a person with rickets.

Mineral deficiency

Calcium

Osteoporosis is caused by loss of bone density. People with this condition are at greater risk of fracturing bones, especially wrists, hips and vertebrae. Any activity that promotes stronger bones will help to prevent osteoporosis, so walking and running are good. Calcium-rich foods, such as cheese, milk, bread and tinned fish should be included in the diet. It is important also to have enough vitamin D as calcium cannot be absorbed without it.

Iron

Iron deficiency is known as **anaemia**. Iron is required in the formation of healthy red blood cells, and helps the body to use oxygen efficiently. Symptoms of anaemia include fatigue, brittle fingernails, weakness and lack of energy. Asian people may become anaemic as they have a diet low in iron. Teenage girls are sometimes anaemic due to blood loss from starting menstruation. It can be easily treated by taking iron supplements and eating iron-rich foods, such as red meat and dark green leafy vegetables.

Nutrient excess

Tooth decay, which is also known as **dental caries,** is caused by an excess of sugar in the diet. Bacteria, food and saliva combine and form sticky deposits (**plaque**) which are deposited on the teeth. Plaque is acid and over time it will dissolve the enamel on teeth, causing cavities. If they remain untreated, they can kill the tooth's nerve and blood supply and eventually the whole tooth will die. Sugary foods and drinks should be kept to a minimum and good dental hygiene observed.

? Did you know?

You should follow these tips for looking after your teeth:

- Brush your teeth twice a day, in the morning and in the evening.
- Spend at least three minutes each time.
- Always use a fluoride toothpaste.
- Use a small toothbrush so that you can reach the back teeth, applying no more than a pea-sized amount of toothpaste for adults.
- Flossing is very important as the toothbrush does not always reach the gaps between the teeth.
- Do not brush too hard – this can damage gums.
- Limit your consumption of sugar and starchy foods.
- Visit your dentist regularly.

Source: NHS Choices

Factors influencing the diet of individuals and their associated dietary needs (1)

Getting started

In small groups, discuss what you all eat with your family. Are there differences in what you eat, and if there are, why? Is it to do with religion or culture, health, or just likes and dislikes? Show the results of your discussion as a picture or series of pictures.

Introduction

Although nutritionists and dieticians give advice to people about healthy eating and devise diets for people with particular conditions, they have to take other factors into consideration. There are many different factors that will influence what people eat, and you will explore them in this topic.

Religion and culture

Hinduism

Although some Hindus are vegetarian, many are not. Most avoid beef as the cow is seen as sacred in their religion, and some avoid eggs. Hindus who do not eat beef will also avoid cheese and yoghurt containing rennet as it is produced from cows. Strict Hindus avoid mushrooms, garlic, onions, tea and coffee (containing caffeine), and alcohol. Some Hindus will fast at times of special festivals.

An example of Kosher foods.

Judaism

Jewish people generally eat **kosher** foods. This means that they do not eat pork, and will only eat other meat where the animal has been killed according to kosher laws. They eat fish, but not shellfish, such as prawns, mussels and scallops. Orthodox Jews do not mix meat and milk products in the same meal, so would not have a cheeseburger or lasagne, for example. According to household custom, they would wait one, three or six hours to eat a dairy product after eating meat. Yom Kippur or the Day of Atonement is the holiest day in the Jewish calendar and traditionally requires Jews to fast for 25 hours. Children under the age of nine are not allowed to fast, nor are people who are pregnant or in poor health.

Islam

Muslims usually eat lawful or halal foods. This is similar to kosher in the Jewish faith, in that animals for meat must be slaughtered according to religious law. Unlawful or haram food includes pork and pork products, but cheese, fish and shellfish are halal foods. Alcohol is unlawful to Muslims, and some choose not to drink caffeinated drinks. Fasting takes place during Ramadan, the Muslim holy month, for 30 days. During this time, no food or drink may be eaten between sunrise and sunset.

Buddhism

There are no set dietary laws in Buddhism. Although most Buddhists are either vegetarian or vegan, some will eat meat and/or fish. Some avoid onion, garlic and leeks, but dietary choice depends on what branch of Buddhism is studied and in which country. Strict Buddhists do not drink alcohol.

 ## Moral reasons

Some people choose to follow a particular diet for moral reasons, rather than religious beliefs or particular customs.

Vegetarians

Some people don't eat meat and fish because they don't like the taste or texture, they disapprove of the way that animals are reared, or the way that animals and fish are killed.

There are different types of vegetarian:

Internationally recognised symbols for kosher and halal foods.

Table 6.8 Different types of vegetarian.

Vegetarian type	Diet
Semi- or demi-vegetarian	No red meat, but will eat fish and poultry
Lacto-vegetarian	Dairy such as yoghurt, milk and cheese, but not eggs, meat, fish or poultry
Ovo-vegetarian	Eggs, but not dairy, meat, fish or poultry
Lacto-ovo-vegetarian	Dairy products and eggs, but not meat, fish or poultry

Restaurant menus use a green 'V' to indicate vegetarian dishes, and labels on packaged foods are sometimes marked in the same way to show that the product is suitable for vegetarians.

Vegans

Veganism is a stricter form of vegetarianism, and vegans eat no animal foods at all. Many refuse to wear leather or wool goods as well. Vegetarians and vegans must combine different plant proteins in meals to ensure that they get enough protein in their diets.

Activity	Vegetarian and vegan food

Do some online research on vegetarian and vegan foods and recipes.

Produce a handout or booklet with recipes for one breakfast, lunch and dinner for a lacto-ovo-vegetarian and one for a vegan. Make sure that the meals are balanced and that you have combined the food to ensure that there is sufficient protein.

Factors influencing the diet of individuals and their associated dietary needs (2)

Environment

Access to food and food storage

In developed countries, people have access to a good variety of food which can come from all over the world, and the increase in air travel means that most foods are available all year round. For the population of developed countries, this can lead to over-nutrition. The longer fruit and vegetables are stored, the more nutrients they lose. In developing countries, people often have access to restricted diets that are high in carbohydrates and not so rich in protein and fats. This can lead to under-nutrition.

Location

Where you live will have an effect on your diet. Although there is enough food in the world, it is not evenly distributed. More wealthy countries can afford to buy food and so have a greater variety than countries that are poor. Food that is grown in poor soil will contain fewer minerals and so the quality of the diet will be poorer.

Climate

Many developing countries suffer from poor soil conditions, flooding and drought, which result in repeated years of lost harvests. In 1995 and 1996, severe flooding in North Korea destroyed crops and the harvest, including the reserve grain stores that were being stored underground. As a result, many people starved to death.

Socio-economic factors

Costs

The cost of food varies according to the region of the country where people live and the type of shop that sells it. Changes in the economy also have an effect, and the financial status of the country affects cost. Large chain supermarkets sell in large quantities, which means that they can sell at a lower price than independent shops that have much less space and stock.

Income

The ability to afford food is linked to social class. People who are in higher social classes have more money to spend on food and tend to buy better-quality food, and eat out more. People who have low incomes are more likely to buy food that is high in salt, fat, and sugar and provides concentrated sources of energy to help them feel fuller for longer.

A fast food snack.

Trends

Just as you might follow trends, such as wearing clothes that are in fashion, or downloading the same music or apps as your friends, some people follow trends in eating. In recent years there has been an increase in the number of bio yoghurts on sale that claim to strengthen the body's defences or aid digestion.

Family

There is not much evidence to suggest that there is a difference in food choice depending on an individual's position in the family, but it is known that mothers will often give more protein or fruit and vegetables, or larger quantities to their husband/partner or children. They will then fill up on lower-quality food and their nutritional status may suffer.

Class

There is some evidence that differences in social class influence dietary choices. In general, people from the upper social classes eat more healthy food, and poorer people eat less fruit and vegetables and more high-fat, high-sugar foods. Women in the lower social classes are more likely to be obese than women in the upper social classes. People in lower social classes usually earn less money than those in the higher social classes and are more likely to substitute cheap processed food for fresh food.

Peer pressure

Peer pressure can have an effect on the food choices that are made, especially by children and teenagers. Many young people develop a stereotypical view of people who eat healthy and unhealthy food and may choose less healthy options to copy their friends.

The media

Information in the media can influence food choice. Food scares can be caused by what is reported in the press. In 2006, products were recalled after there was a salmonella scare in a chocolate factory. More recently, there has been a lot of publicity about rising levels of obesity in the UK.

▶ Personal preferences

Although some people like almost everything that is put in front of them, there are others who only eat food they really enjoy. Often in a family household, the food is mainly chosen and cooked by one person, so their preferences may be dominant. However, as long as healthy eating guidelines are followed, the diet will be balanced. It is less easy to ensure a child has a balanced diet if they are fussy, and parents often need to come up with imaginative ways to make their children eat.

> **? Did you know?**
>
> In October 2011, the UK's Advertising Standards Authority banned an Actimel TV advert in the UK, after it ruled that claims it helped protect school-age youngsters against illness were not supported by evidence.

Factors influencing the diet of individuals and their associated dietary needs (3)

Illness

Effects on appetite and dietary requirements

How do you feel when you are ill? When we feel really unwell, we often lose our appetite until we start to feel better. Some conditions can increase appetite, such as an overactive thyroid gland.

Some illnesses may affect the body so that the food eaten can't be digested, and in some cases treatment for illness will affect dietary intake. People who have a poor appetite should be encouraged to eat small amounts of food which are high in nutrients, and it is well known that vitamins and minerals are necessary for health and healing.

> **Activity**   Effects on appetite
>
> Carry out some research into the causes of both loss of appetite and increased appetite. What other conditions may affect appetite?

An EpiPen: an instrument for giving medication for severe allergic reactions that people can use on themselves.

Underlying health conditions

Allergies

Do you have an allergy to peanuts, prawns or strawberries? Many people do. Allergic reactions to food vary in intensity. Similar symptoms and illnesses can be triggered by different allergens, yet the same allergens can also cause very different reactions in different people. Symptoms can include eczema, asthma, urticaria (hives) and other health problems. Anaphylaxis is an extreme reaction which must be treated by adrenaline injections. Failure to treat this promptly can result in death. Avoidance of food that causes allergies is the only way to prevent the onset of symptoms, although some people have desensitisation treatment which can be very effective.

Lactose intolerance

Lactose intolerance is an inability to digest lactose, the sugar found in milk and milk products. It is particularly common in people of African, Asian and Indian races and can lead to digestive disturbance, such as cramps, diarrhoea and wind. Milk should be avoided in the diet, but often sufferers can tolerate yoghurt and cheese because the lactose is converted to lactic acid during manufacture.

Coeliac disease

Coeliac disease is an autoimmune disease caused by the protein gluten, which is found in wheat, barley and rye. Symptoms include abdominal pain, cramping and bloating, nausea and vomiting, and diarrhoea. People with this condition should avoid foods containing gluten. This is quite difficult because many foods contain thickeners made of gluten, so people with the condition tend to become experts in reading food labels.

Diabetes

People who suffer from type 2 diabetes can help the levels of blood glucose by maintaining a diet low in fat and sugar. Complex carbohydrates should form a part of the diet, as low carbohydrate diets can be high in fat. There is a relatively high incidence of coronary heart disease in diabetics in the United Kingdom.

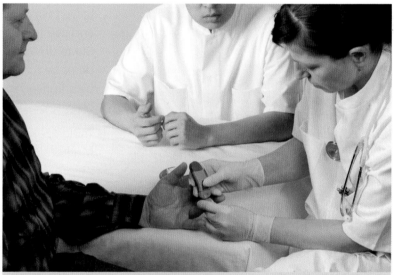

Why is it important to regularly test the blood sugar level of diabetic patients?

Crohn's disease

The cause of Crohn's disease is unknown, but it is a chronic inflammatory condition that affects the whole of the digestive tract. Symptoms include abdominal pain, diarrhoea, weight loss, fever and tiredness. Sufferers of the disease can go into remission and have no symptoms at times. Crohn's disease is treated by diet, usually an individual diet plan for each person.

Irritable bowel syndrome (IBS)

The cause of IBS is not known, but triggers may be stress or immune system problems. It usually affects people in their twenties and thirties. Symptoms include stomach cramps, bloating, diarrhoea and constipation. There is no cure, but changing diet and lifestyle can help.

Nutritional variation during life stage development (1)

Introduction

A person's diet changes during his or her lifespan, according to need and the ability of the body to digest the food. Although we all need the same macro- and micronutrients, we need them in different quantities and different formats at different stages in our lives.

Life stages

Infancy (0–2 years)

Weaning can help babies develop social skills.

From birth, breast milk contains all the baby's needs in the right amounts. Although it is low in iron and copper, the baby has enough of these stored until it starts eating solid foods at about six months. Breast milk is clean, provides immunity and does not have to be prepared. Some mothers can't or choose not to breastfeed and use formula milk, which is modified cow's milk. It must be made up according to the instructions provided to prevent damage to the baby's immature kidneys, and equipment must be sterilised to prevent infection. **Weaning** too early may cause obesity or allergies later.

Table 6.9 shows when different foods should be introduced. Mothers may find that they need to introduce foods several times before the baby gets used to the taste and texture. This can help to prevent children becoming fussy eaters.

Table 6.9 The weaning process.

Age	Weaning process
6 months	Start with spoonfuls of baby rice, mashed potato or puréed vegetables, such as carrot, peas or parsnips. When they are used to the spoon, introduce lots of tastes, such as puréed meat, pulses and fruit. As a baby gets used to eating, introduce food with soft lumps. Do not give nuts as infants may choke or be allergic to them.
9 months	Minced or finely chopped food can be given. Infants at this age should be given different textures to get them used to them.
12 months	Give a good mixed diet by this stage, including three meals and two to three healthy snacks each day.

Key terms

Weaning – introduction of solid food into the baby's diet from about six months of age.

Activity   Weaning

Use the internet to research weaning. Find out at what stage different foods should be introduced and produce a handout for new mums on weaning.

Childhood (3–8 years)

Children aged between three and eight years of age tend to be very active and are growing fast. Although their energy requirements are not as high as those of adults, they need almost the same amount of some vitamins and minerals.

Some children have big appetites because they have high nutritional needs. Children should be encouraged to eat healthy meals consisting of a mix of meat, fish or eggs and potatoes, pasta or rice with vegetables.

Table 6.10 Daily energy needs of babies and children.

Age range	Male		Female	
	MJ	Kcal	MJ	Kcal
1-2 months (Breast milk substitute-fed)	2.5	598	2.3	550
3 – 4 months	2.6	622	2.5	598
5 - 6 months	2.7	646	2.6	622
7 - 12 months	3.1	742	2.8	670
3 years	4.9	1171	4.5	1076
6 years	6.6	1577	6.2	1482
9 years	7.7	1840	7.2	1721
12 years	9.4	2247	8.8	2103

Source: DEFRA, *Manual of Nutrition*, 12th Edition, 2012

Adolescence (9–18 years)

The nutritional needs of adolescents are greater than for any other age group because they have large appetites and are still growing. Boys aged 11 to 14 need approximately 2,354 kilocalories a day, rising to 3,005 for 15 to 18 year olds. Girls need 2,175 and 2,432 kilocalories respectively. Adolescents should be encouraged to eat sensibly and healthily at regular intervals and to avoid phases of overeating or starving themselves in order to lose weight, and to take a regular amount of physical activity.

Both children and adolescents should avoid too many sweets, crisps, biscuits and fizzy drinks.

Activity	Healthy eating for children

Visit the Change4life website and find out what advice there is for encouraging children to eat healthy meals. You can access this by going to www.pearsonhotlinks.co.uk and searching for this title.

Make a poster for 7 to 10 year olds that gives them advice on making healthy food choices.

Nutritional variation during life stage development (2)

Introduction

Although our nutritional needs do not change a lot during adulthood, as we age our bodies can become less active and efficient. As a result, we need to make sure that we know how to maintain a healthy and balanced diet to suit our needs. Intake that is more than the amount of energy we expend will cause weight gain, and less activity can also result in weight gain, weakened bones and muscles, and loss of ability.

Discussion point

You may have noticed that different members of your family eat different things in different amounts. Do you eat more than your parents or grandparents? Who eats the most in your family? Why do you think this is?

Early to middle adulthood (19 to 65 years)

An adult's nutritional needs reduce with age. Men and women between 19 and 45 need approximately 2,550 and 1,940 kilocalories per day, but this will vary with the amount of activity or exercise taken. In general, adults need to eat a healthy diet consisting of complex carbohydrates, such as bread, potatoes, rice or pasta, protein, such as meat, eggs, cheese or fish and at least five daily portions of fruit and vegetables. Foods with high levels of fat, particularly saturated fat, and sugar should be kept to a minimum and adults are advised to carry out physical activity on a regular basis. Alcohol intake should be limited as it contributes extra calories to the diet.

Between the ages of 45 and 64 men need between 2,550 and 2,380 kilocalories per day and women 1,900. They should have at least five portions of fruit and vegetables a day to provide vitamins, minerals, fibre and water, which will help to prevent constipation. Osteoporosis can be a problem for older people, particularly women, so calcium-rich foods should be included in the diet, although they should be advised to stick to low-fat versions where possible. Walking and any exercise that is considered to be weight-bearing will help to strengthen bones too. A couple of meals a week containing oily fish, such as salmon, mackerel or sardines will help to protect against heart disease.

Pregnancy and breastfeeding

During pregnancy and breastfeeding a woman's nutritional needs are increased to provide nutrition for the growing baby and for making breast milk after the baby is born. Pregnant women are advised to avoid eating foods high in vitamin A, soft cheeses and patés which may contain listeria bacteria, as they can cause birth defects.

Although some people think that being pregnant means that a woman can 'eat for two', only about an extra 200 kilocalories a day are required in the last three months of the pregnancy, and about

Why is it important for pregnant women to have a balanced diet?

450 to 570 kilocalories a day extra during breastfeeding. This is to give the mother the energy she needs to carry the extra weight of the baby and to make breast milk. Women planning to become pregnant should be advised to eat a diet rich in folic acid to prevent damage to the foetus, particularly spina bifida.

Later adulthood (65+)

Although there is not much difference in the dietary needs of adults and older adults, as we age we become less mobile and we need less energy for our daily needs. Men and women between the ages of 65 and 73 need approximately 2,330 and 1,990 calories a day. Over the age of 75, they need 2,100 and 1,810 kilocalories a day respectively. Older people have smaller appetites, so the diet should provide concentrated sources of protein, vitamins and minerals in smaller portions. Gentle exercise should also be encouraged.

In old age, the body begins to slow down and does not work as efficiently as in younger days, so older people are more likely to become constipated. They should be encouraged to drink plenty, and to have at least five portions of fruit and vegetables a day. Taste sensation can alter in old age, which might make food seem tasteless and unappetising. Strong flavours, such as herbs and spices, can be used to improve taste and might encourage older people to eat more.

Old people who live alone often cannot be bothered to cook a hot meal for one person, so they should be encouraged to eat foods that do not require much preparation but are high in nutrients. It is a good idea for older people to make sure that they have some tinned or dried food in the cupboard and some longlife milk, in case of illness or bad weather.

There are some companies that provide ready-made meals that can be delivered frozen and a microwave oven to heat the food, but this might be too expensive an option for some elderly people. In some areas of the country, there are 'meals on wheels' services that deliver a hot meal once a day to older people.

? Think about it

Malnutrition in older people can be caused by poor-fitting dentures or bad teeth. Why do you think this is?

Hot food served at a day care setting may help vulnerable people meet their nutritional needs.

Considerations for nutritional planning

Introduction

There are times when healthcare professionals may see patients who need dietary advice, whether it is just to lose weight, or to help in the treatment of an illness or disease.

Remember

Some questions you might ask are:

- How old is the individual?
- Does he/she have a diet-related problem or illness?
- What foods does he/she like?
- Can he/she get to the shops?
- Does he/she have sufficient income to buy nutritional food?
- Are there any specific cultural or religious considerations?
- Does the individual live with other people?
- Who normally does the cooking?

A dietician or nutritionist normally provides a dietary plan for an individual on a long-term basis, but other healthcare workers can do so provided they have a sound knowledge and understanding of dietary intake, the long-term effects of balanced and unbalanced diets, and specific dietary needs of individuals at different life stages.

When planning suitable diets, it is important to get to know the individual and their eating habits, as many factors need to be considered.

A nutritional plan can then be put together taking into account as much of the information gathered as possible. An example of a one-week plan is shown in Table 6.11.

Jack is a 57-year-old sales executive who has had a heart attack. He has just been discharged from hospital following treatment and has been given a diet plan by Anoushka, the dietician. This is to be combined with taking regular exercise and drinking one to two litres of water a day.

You will see that there are three meals which include oily fish (tinned tuna is not included) and there are at least five portions of fruit and vegetables every day. There are a couple of treats as Jack is likely to be bored with this diet long term, and provided he sticks to the plan, he should remain healthy.

Assessment activity 6.2   *English*   2B.P3 | 2B.P4 | 2B.M2 | 2B.M3 | 2B.D2

As trainee dietician, you are working with a dietician in a GP practice. She runs a training session every two months for the doctors, nurses and healthcare assistants at the practice. She asks you to prepare a PowerPoint presentation for use at the next teaching session about individuals with specific dietary needs. She has given you two sets of patient notes and has asked you to make a sample nutritional plan for each patient:

- Sarah is a 22-year-old Jewish mother of two who is pregnant with her third child. Her husband has just been made redundant.
- Alan is a 45-year-old bank manager who is married to Helena, and they have grown-up children who no longer live at home. They are both vegan, and Alan runs about six marathons a year and trains every day.

1 Describe the specific nutritional needs for Sarah and Alan.

2 Explain the different factors that influence the diets of Sarah and Alan.

3 Discuss how the different factors will influence the diets of Sarah and Alan.

4 Show your nutritional plans for Sarah and Alan to the group, and compare them. You might want to create a handout showing the nutritional plans in detail.

Tips

You have been given the main points about the lifestyles of Sarah and Alan, but you can introduce more information that can be used to add further detail to your presentation. Make sure that it is realistic, so set aside enough time for research and preparation.

Table 6.11 An example diet plan.

	Breakfast	Snack	Lunch	Snack	Dinner
Sunday	Porridge made with skimmed milk and dried fruit Tea with skimmed milk	Banana Coffee with skimmed milk	Sandwich made with lean ham, salad and low-fat mayo Six cherry tomatoes Tea with skimmed milk	Low fat yoghurt Tea with skimmed milk	Roast chicken Dry roasted potatoes Carrots Cabbage Gravy Small portion of apple crumble, custard One glass of red wine
Monday	Two slices of wholemeal toast Low fat spread Marmite Tea with skimmed milk Orange juice	Two plums Coffee with skimmed milk	Jacket potato with tuna and sweetcorn (low-fat mayonnaise)	Two water biscuits with a small portion of reduced-fat cheese Celery	Vegetable curry Rice Low-fat chocolate mousse
Tuesday	Two poached eggs Two rashers of grilled bacon, fat removed Orange juice Tea with skimmed milk	Carrot and celery sticks Can of diet cola	Small can baked beans Two slices of wholemeal toast, no spread Water	Tea with skimmed milk Two Rich Tea biscuits	Grilled salmon New potatoes Peas Broccoli Fresh fruit salad Tea with skimmed milk
Wednesday	Porridge made with skimmed milk and seeds Tea with skimmed milk	One chocolate digestive biscuit Coffee with skimmed milk	Chicken breast Salad New potatoes Low-fat dressing One orange	Banana Tea with skimmed milk	Pork chop, fat removed Couscous Roasted Mediterranean vegetables Frozen yoghurt
Thursday	Bowl of cornflakes with skimmed milk One slice of wholemeal bread with low-fat spread and marmalade Tea with skimmed milk	Low fat yoghurt Coffee with skimmed milk	Tinned sardines on two slices of wholemeal toast Apple	Apple Orange juice	Vegetable lasagne Salad with low-fat salad dressing Low-fat chocolate mousse
Friday	Grilled tomatoes Two slices of wholemeal toast Orange juice Tea with skimmed milk	Cereal bar Coffee with skimmed milk	Bowl of homemade vegetable soup One wholemeal roll, no spread Apple	Two water biscuits with a small portion of reduced-fat cheese Celery	Cottage pie Courgettes Green beans
Saturday	Fresh fruit salad Two toasted crumpets with low-fat spread Coffee with skimmed milk	Pear Orange juice	Smoked mackerel Salad and tomatoes with low-fat dressing Frozen yoghurt Coffee with skimmed milk	One slice of malt loaf Tea with skimmed milk	Spaghetti Bolognese Fresh strawberries with a small amount of single cream Tea with skimmed milk

Introduction

How can you make sure you treat others of all ages, cultures and abilities fairly? Health and Social Care professionals meet people who look and sound different to them, and who have completely different backgrounds to them. This unit aims to help you understand and value the ways in which we are different so that you can better understand the diverse needs of service users in health and social care. You will learn what is meant by diversity and that it is important that all individuals have equal access to health and social care services to meet their diverse needs.

You will learn to recognise discriminatory and non-discriminatory practice in health and social care and their impact on both service users and those who work in the health and social care sector. You will then understand the importance of non-discriminatory practice in health and social care.

You will learn how health and social care practices can promote equality and diversity, looking at ways of adapting services to meet individuals' diverse needs and the benefits to service users of doing so.

The understanding you will gain can be used to help promote equality of opportunity for service users in health and social care environments. This unit covers the roles and responsibilities of service providers to promote diversity. You will also learn about legislation, codes of practice and charters that support this work.

Assessment: You will be assessed by a series of assignments set by your teacher/tutor.

Learning aims

In this unit you will:

A understand the importance of non-discriminatory practice in health and social care

B explore how health and social care practices can promote equality and diversity.

> When I went on placement to a dentist, I understood that when an older person called me 'love', he wasn't being sexist but was just speaking as all older people do in this part of the country, rather than asking my name and forgetting it.
>
> Sara, *18-year-old would-be dental nurse*

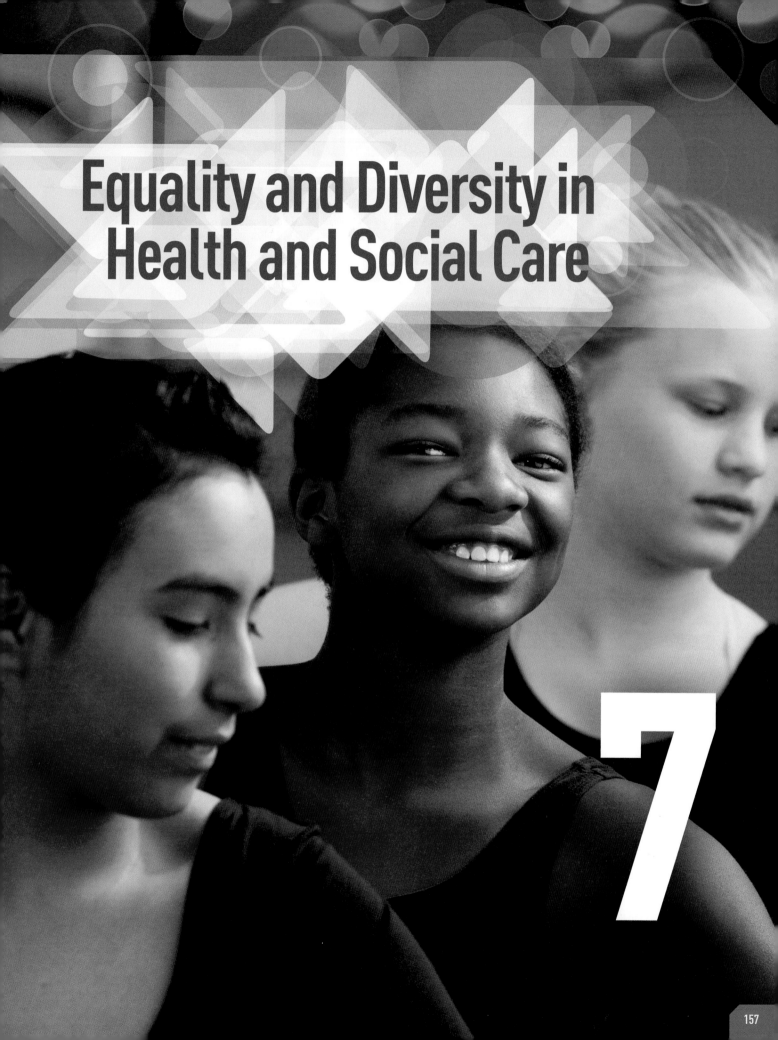

Equality and Diversity in Health and Social Care

7

Assessment Zone

This table shows you what you must do in order to achieve a **Pass**, **Merit** or **Distinction** grade, and where you can find activities in this book to help you.

Assessment criteria			
Level 1	**Level 2 Pass**	**Level 2 Merit**	**Level 2 Distinction**
Learning aim A: Understand the importance of non-discriminatory practice in health and social care			
1A.1 Define non-discriminatory practice in health and social care, using two examples.	**2A.P1** Describe non-discriminatory and discriminatory practice in health and social care, using examples. **Assessment activity 7.1 See page 168.**	**2A.M1** Explain the importance of legislation and codes of practice in promoting non-discriminatory practice in health and social care, using examples. **Assessment activity 7.1 See page 168.**	**2A.D1** Assess the impact of discriminatory practice for health and social care workers, with reference to selected examples. **Assessment activity 7.1 See page 168.**
1A.2 Identify how one code of practice or piece of legislation promotes non-discriminatory practice in health and social care.	**2A.P2** Describe how codes of practice and legislation promote non-discriminatory practice in health and social care. **Assessment activity 7.1 See page 168.**		
Learning aim B: Explore how health and social care practices can promote equality and diversity			
1B.3 Identify the different needs of individuals in relation to health and social care provision.	**2B.P3** Describe the different needs of service users in health and social care, with reference to examples. **Assessment activity 7.2 See page 181.**		
1B.4 Identify ways that health and social care provision can be adapted to meet the diverse needs of a selected individual.	**2B.P4** Describe how health and social care provision can be adapted to meet the diverse needs of different individuals, with reference to examples. **Assessment activity 7.2 See page 181.**	**2B.M2** Explain the benefits of adapting health and social care provision to meet the diverse needs of different individuals, with reference to two selected examples. **Assessment activity 7.2 See page 181.**	**2B.D2** Assess the effectiveness of health and social care provision for different individuals with diverse needs, with reference to two selected examples. **Assessment activity 7.2 See page 181.**

How you will be assessed

The unit will be assessed by a series of internally assessed tasks. You will be expected to show an understanding of diversity in the context of health and social care sectors. The tasks will be based on a scenario in which you are working in a local health or social care organisation. For example, you may be asked to produce materials for an induction programme for new care assistants at a residential care home for older people. The care home has a wide catchment area and many of the residents come from diverse backgrounds. The manager asks you to produce training materials that can be used during the work experience induction session.

Your assessment could be in the form of:

- an induction pack or handbook; training materials such as a presentation or display; a written report, based on a case study; and/or a DVD based in a health and social care setting, such as a care home, which will:

  - identify and describe non-discriminatory and discriminatory practice for the health and social care workers

  - describe how codes of practice and current and relevant legislation promote non-discriminatory practice

  - assess the potential impact of discriminatory practice for health and social care workers

  - identify and describe the diverse needs of two of the residents and how the home can adapt provision to meet these needs

  - identify and assess the benefits of the proposed changes in meeting their diverse needs.

A diverse society

Introduction

What do you believe in? Without sharing or discussing your ideas with your friends, write down five things you believe in. Then compare your list with others in a small group. Are you surprised at how many different things you have listed?

Link

This unit links to Units 2, 3, 4 and 8, as understanding diversity is an essential part of working with other service users and providers.

Key terms

Diversity – variety.

Culture – the beliefs, language, styles of dress, ways of cooking, religion, ways of behaving, etc. shared by a particular group of people.

Beliefs – strongly held opinions.

Discrimination – treating a person or group differently from others.

Prejudice – an unreasonable feeling against a person or group of people.

Diversity

Diversity means a variety or range of differences. To value diversity is to respect and value the **cultures** and **beliefs** of other people. If we are unwilling to accept that other people's cultures and beliefs may be different from ours, and so dismiss and ignore them, we will not be able to learn about them and understand them. Similarly, we must respect and value differences such as age, gender and disability. These factors are covered later in this unit.

A good service provider will get to know the people they work with and not make any assumptions about them. They will be open to other people's life experiences and differences, and value their diversity. They will form good relationships with their colleagues and the people who use services. A team of service providers who have different interests and skills is more likely to be able to handle the range of tasks when helping an individual, and the team will enjoy working together.

It is important to listen to and respect the beliefs of both colleagues and service users.

Non-discriminatory practice

An important aspect of health and social care work is promoting non-discriminatory practice. This means:

- not treating individuals or groups less fairly than others
- valuing diversity
- adapting care to meet diverse needs.

To really understand what non-discriminatory practice is, you need to understand **discrimination**.

Discrimination

Discrimination happens when someone has a **prejudice** against a person or a group of people. This might be for reasons such as age, gender, race, ethnicity, social class, religious beliefs, secular beliefs, family structure, sexuality, ability, health, disability, address, dress or appearance. They might then discriminate against that person or group and treat them differently.

There are four types of discrimination:

- Unfair discrimination is when a person is treated unfairly compared with someone else: for example, when someone is not considered for a job because they are older than another candidate, despite having the same qualifications and experience.

- Direct discrimination is when someone is rude, hostile or offensive to someone because they see them as being different: for example, when someone who is overweight is called names. This form of discrimination is easy to prove because it is heard or witnessed by other people.

- Indirect discrimination is harder to prove: for example, a manager may appear to be supportive and friendly towards a member of staff, but may show disrespect for their ideas by dismissing them in a jokey way.

- Positive discrimination is when a decision is made in a person's favour because there is something different about them: for example, when an advertising agency advertises for a person who has red hair and fair skin because they are to play the part of the sister of someone who has these characteristics; or when a service has few people from an ethnic minority at a certain level, so they appoint someone from an ethnic minority despite interviewing a cross-section of people.

Discriminatory and non-discriminatory practice in health and social care

Getting started

In a small group, discuss the care which is appropriate for a person who (i) is partially sighted and has an ear infection, (ii) has mobility problems but needs to visit his dentist who has an upstairs surgery in a large dental practice with no lift.

In a whole class discussion, identify the issues with these two service users.

Key terms

Judgemental – making decisions or forming opinions on the basis of something such as appearance, without proper evidence, and being too critical.

Adaptation – changing something, such as a service or device, so that it becomes suitable for a new situation or person.

Equality – equal treatment and respect.

▼ Discriminatory practice

Stereotyping and labelling

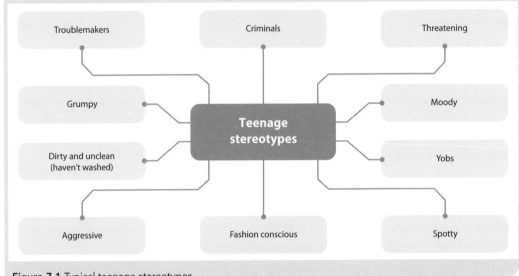

Figure 7.1 Typical teenage stereotypes.

A **stereotype** is a fixed idea about an individual or group of people: for example, someone may talk to an older person slowly, loudly and patronisingly because they assume they are deaf and intellectually less able. Other examples are shown in Figure 7.1.

When groups of people are labelled as though they are all the same, they lose their identity and assumptions are made about them; people can be very **judgemental**. Some may even decide to behave as expected, feeling that they are not valued.

Refusal of medical treatment

Refusing an individual medical treatment when another individual is given the same treatment is an example of discrimination. Examples include:

- denying a person surgery for reasons such as being morbidly obese, taking drugs or smoking
- denying a person lifesaving drugs which are very expensive but which a person living in a different area is allowed to have.

Offering inappropriate treatment or care

This may happen when a service is very busy and resources are stretched to the limit, when a health or social care professional is not being as careful as they should be, or when someone makes an assumption about a person who is behaving in a certain way. For example, when a person appears to be drunk, those around at the time may treat them with disgust and ignore them, so they are left to sleep it off, but in fact they may have suffered a stroke. By the time it is realised the person has had a stroke, it is too late for them to make a full recovery.

Giving less time than needed

If a service provider doesn't like a person they are caring for or is too busy they may not give that person as much time as is needed. For example, a person in a care home recovering from a hip replacement operation needs to keep the hip mobile by walking each day. If a carer does not make time to take the person for a walk, the hip will seize up and never give the degree of mobility it would have done if the person had been given the time to help them exercise.

Non-discriminatory practice

Providing appropriate health and social care to meet the needs of individuals

Individuals have varying needs and they must be given the appropriate health and social care to meet those needs.

Adaptations to meet diverse needs

Services can be **adapted** to meet individuals' specific needs, allowing them to maintain as much independence as possible. Some of the ways they are adapted are shown in Figure 7.2.

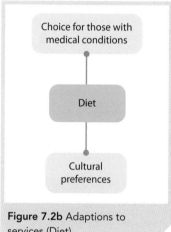

Figure 7.2b Adaptions to services (Diet)

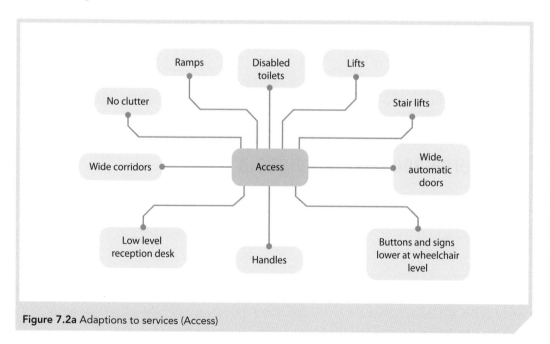

Figure 7.2a Adaptions to services (Access)

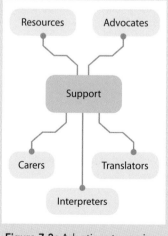

Figure 7.2c Adaptions to services (Support)

Providing equality of access to health and social care services

Providing **equality** of access means that all individuals have the right to access the same high quality of health and social care, and service providers have the responsibility to provide this. For example, a person who is in prison is just as entitled to access health and social care as those who aren't in prison. This means that prisons have to provide their own high-quality facilities or arrange transport to use facilities outside.

Impact of discriminatory and non-discriminatory practice

Introduction

There are many effects of discrimination on service users, which you will learn about in this topic. You will then go on to learn about how non-discriminatory practice meets the diverse needs of individuals and what the law says.

Effects of discrimination on service users

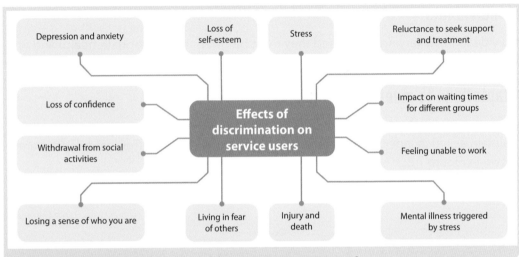

Figure 7.3 Can you think of other effects of discrimination on service users?

Did you know

Someone with a speech impediment, for example, may need an extra service such as an advocate (someone who speaks on their behalf) in order to access the healthcare they need.

Discussion point

What would happen in a school or college if there were no rules? Would you *really* like it? In pairs, write a list of rules you would have if you were headteacher or principal. Think about what would happen if you had your rules. Then discuss what would happen if we did not have rules, such as which side of the road we should drive on, or for sports such as football.

Non-discriminatory practice meeting the diverse needs of individuals

Everyone should receive a service of equal quality which meets their personal needs. This is not the same as everyone receiving the same service. For example, everyone should be able to register with a doctor but a more seriously ill person will require more of the doctor's time.

Treating people as individuals by taking into account their different beliefs and abilities is crucial when caring for others, and service users should acknowledge an individual's personal beliefs even if they do not share them. For example, a Muslim in hospital must be allowed to pray at certain times as this will make them feel that their identity is valued and will also help their recovery.

Meeting legal and workplace requirements

Workplaces need rules, and they come in various forms, which make sure that legal and workplace requirements are met.

- Legislation: Certain types of rules or customs may become law, and legislation (a set of laws) is introduced and passed by Parliament to make sure they are followed. One example is the law that says we drive on the left-hand side of the road in the UK. If laws are broken, the person or service breaking them can be charged with committing a crime.

- Non-discriminatory practice is a crucial part of meeting legal and workplace requirements, and includes adhering to current and relevant legislation, for example the Equality Act (2010). Equal opportunity is an approach which provides an environment in which people are not excluded from the activities of society, such as education, employment, or health and social care, on the basis of things they cannot change.

- Regulation means controlling human or society's behaviour by rules or restrictions. Regulation can be considered to be restrictions which lead to some sort of sanction or punishment, such as a fine, if they are broken.

- A charter is set out by the government and informs service users of their rights and what they can expect from **statutory** services. Many health centres and other organisations, e.g. the NHS, have charters to give service users information, such as how to access services.

Key terms

Statutory – set up and regulated by the government (according to statute or law).

Activity   Promoting non-discriminatory practice

1 Research the following legislation: Human Rights Act 1998; Equality Act 2010; Mental Health Act 2007, and Disability Discrimination Act 2005.

2 Draw up a table, showing the title of the piece of legislation in the left-hand column, and bullet points in the second column listing the importance of each Act for people who provide a health or social care service.

3 In a group, discuss why it is important in a health and social care environment for workers to understand these key pieces of legislation and how they affect their care of service users.

4 Discuss how providing halal food and a multi-faith prayer room for a Muslim hospital patient will help their recovery and promote non-discriminatory practice.

Case study

Sunshine Holidays arranges short breaks for young carers. Ben is 14 and the main carer for his mother who has MS, a condition that often reduces her ability to move around. Ben was offered a place on a two-day trip to London. Although Ben very much wanted to go on the trip, he and his mother were concerned that he would not be able to access kosher food, as the family is Jewish and follow the dietary laws strictly.

Katya, the trip organiser met with Ben and his mother and discussed how to accommodate Ben's needs on the trip. To keep the costs of the trip down, Katya was planning for the group to stay at a youth hostel with kitchen facilities, so they arranged for Ben to take some kosher ready meals. Katya also helped Ben and his mother use the internet to find a kosher take-away near to the youth hostel where he could buy a sandwich to eat for his lunch on the way home.

1 How do you think Ben felt about going on the trip before he met with Katya?

2 Identify what non-discriminatory behaviour Katya displayed.

3 Look at your notes on the Equality Act. How should this help people like Ben?

165

Following workplace and national codes of practice (1)

Introduction

Health and social care workers must protect service users and each other against discriminatory practice through their behaviour, attitudes and work. Non-discriminatory practice is the responsibility of both individual carers and the institution they work in. They are therefore provided with guidelines, which come in several forms. This topic looks at these and the bodies set up to enforce them.

Codes of practice

All **professional bodies** and services should have a code of practice (or code of conduct), which gives guidelines to people who work in that body or service. Any code of practice advises service providers on how to behave and standards of practice, not only to promote the individual rights of the service users, but also to protect themselves. There are many workplace and national codes of practice on different issues including non-discriminatory practice,

Regulatory bodies

These are bodies set up to make sure that the rights and responsibilities of all service users and providers are upheld, for example the Health and Care Professions Council (HCPC) regulates social workers in England. There are similar bodies that exist for the rest of the UK. They provide codes of conduct or standards of conduct, performance and ethics for social care workers and employers in a wide variety of formats.

The Health Care Professions Council's 'Standards of Conduct, Performance and Ethics' states that a social care worker must act in the best interests of service users.

You must not allow your views about a service user's sex, age, colour, race, disability, sexuality, social or economic status, lifestyle, culture, religion or beliefs to affect the way you deal with them or the professional advice you give. You must treat service users with respect and dignity.

In addition, social care workers must behave with honesty and integrity and make sure that their behaviour does not damage the public's confidence in them or their profession.

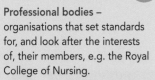

Key terms

Professional bodies – organisations that set standards for, and look after the interests of, their members, e.g. the Royal College of Nursing.

Litigation – the act or process of bringing or contesting a legal action in court.

Deregistration – to be removed from a register, e.g. no longer allowed to run a residential care home.

Safeguarding – a precautionary measure to prevent injury or abuse.

How legislation and codes of practice support non-discriminatory practice

Guidelines in their various forms, such as legislation and codes of practice, support non-discriminatory practice in health and social care by:

- protecting the carer and service user: both know the quality of care which is expected and how it will be provided. They can also be used as a basis for measuring quality of care, so provided the quality is good enough, both can be protected against unfair claims

- enforcing non-discriminatory practices and employer and employee responsibilities: both the employer and employee know their responsibilities as the guidelines make it clear what is expected of both of them

- helping avoid **litigation** and **deregistration**: carers want to avoid being sued or their institutions having their licence removed because for example, they are not providing the required quality of care. The guidelines can be used as a basis for measuring the quality of care provided.

- **safeguarding**: by having clear guidelines which support non-discriminatory practice, both carers and service users are safeguarded against possible injury or abuse. For example, safeguarding policies in schools and colleges protect children and young people under the age of 18 and provide guidance for all staff who may have any concerns of this nature.

Activity   The Nursing and Midwifery Council (NMC)

1 Look at the Code of Practice for Nursing and Social Work (May 2008) on the NMC website. In a group, discuss the ways in which it promotes non-discriminatory practice. How does it affect admission to hospital and access to advocates?

2 Imagine you are part of a group setting up a new hospital. Look at the table you drew up about key pieces of legislation and the NMC code of practice. How would these affect your plans for the new hospital? What would you need to do to make sure you follow these laws and this code of practice?

3 Think about the fact that these are just a few laws and one code of conduct; there are many more which would have to be considered if you were really setting up a new service. In your group, discuss what some of these might be.

Following workplace and national codes of practice (2)

Here are some questions to test what you have learned. You can then complete a practice assessment assignment.

Just checking

1 What is meant by diversity and why is it important to value it?

2 Name the four types of discrimination.

3 Is it ever right to use discrimination in the health and social care workplace? Explain your answer.

4 What is meant by being (i) judgemental, and (ii) stereotypical?

5 Give three examples of non-discriminatory practice in health and social care.

6 Give five possible effects of discrimination on a health and social care service user.

7 What is equality of opportunity?

8 What do we mean by legislation?

9 What is a charter? Give an example.

10 Why is it important to follow workplace and national codes of practice?

11 Explain three ways in which legislation and codes of practice support non-discriminatory practice in health and social care.

Assessment activity 7.1   English | 2A.P1 | 2A.P2 | 2A.M1 | 2A.D1 |

You are a trainee care assistant at a residential care home for older people on the outskirts of a small city. You have been asked to write a chapter of an induction handbook for new staff which describes non-discriminatory and discriminatory practice, how codes of practice and current and relevant legislation promote non-discriminatory practice, and assesses the potential impact of discriminatory practice for health and social care workers in the care home.

You should examine at least two codes of practice from two different local care homes and compare and describe the ways they support non-discriminatory practice and promote the diverse needs of service users.

Your chapter should include the use of at least two examples to explain the importance of non-discriminatory practice and to assess the impact of discriminatory practice for health and social care workers.

Tips

When describing discriminatory and non-discriminatory practices, you should mention at least three types of practice, as listed earlier in this unit.

WorkSpace

▶ SALEEM SINGH

Care Assistant

I am a care assistant in a busy residential care home for older people. I work in a team which includes many other care assistants, nursing staff, a manager, a matron, a chef, domestic workers who change beds and take food and drink to residents, and cleaners. We have ninety separate rooms, so residents can have their own room although a few rooms have married couples in them. There are also two TV lounges and two dining rooms, so residents who choose to can mix together for certain activities, as well as a staffroom where staff can keep their personal belongings and offices for the manger and matron.

My main task is to look after the residents in a number of rooms which are all in the same area of the home. I help them wash and dress each morning, get them settled either in their rooms or in the TV lounge, and do whatever else needs doing during the day. This includes taking their food orders, accompanying them to the dining room, keeping them company if they are feeling lonely or sad and want a chat, taking them to the toilet if they are unsteady on their feet, and arranging any visiting services for them, such as the hairdresser or chiropodist. I enjoy helping them to maintain as much independence as possible and making their lives easier and happier. It is lovely to meet their families too, although it can be very sad sometimes, such as when a resident is taken ill, has a fall, or dies, but I then try to make things as easy as possible for the family.

I love my job because I work with a wide range of people who are mostly very nice and who have a lot of experience of life and many stories to tell. I feel that I am making a real difference to them.

Think about it

1   Why is it so important for Saleem to understand the diverse needs of the residents of the care home?

2   Do you feel that you understand how diverse the needs of our multicultural society are? Does the area you live in reflect this diversity? If not, what do you think you can do to increase your understanding?

3   Do you think you carry out non-discriminatory practice in your everyday life? If not, how will you improve this?

Factors that may affect care needs (1)

Introduction

There are a range of factors which may affect the diverse needs of service users in health and social care. You will usually need to consider many factors at the same time. In this topic you will learn about three of these: gender, sexual orientation and gender reassignment.

Gender

Traditionally women were expected to stay at home and look after the house and family. As the years have passed, changes have occurred that have made men and women more equal, including legislation that makes it illegal to discriminate against someone because of their gender.

All individuals should have their personal preferences acknowledged and catered for where possible. Both genders should have the option of being treated in single-sex wards; patients often feel that being on a mixed-sex ward can reduce their privacy and dignity at a time when they are already feeling **vulnerable**. Some patients are opposed to mixed-sex accommodation for cultural or religious reasons. However, it is necessary to have mixed-sex accommodation when patients need urgent or highly specialised care.

Some people prefer to receive medical treatment and personal care from health and social care workers of their own gender, for example having a female doctor doing a smear test, while others have religious reasons for this.

Key terms

Vulnerable – open to being hurt emotionally or physically.

Remember

When working in health and social care, you need to ensure that you have a person's permission to share information about their sexuality. For example, a patient in hospital may not wish their parents to be given any information that would suggest that the patient is gay. This would include avoiding references to the patient being visited by their partner. Social care workers need to show respect for the sexual orientation of both carers and service users. Workers are also entitled to work without suffering discrimination for their own sexual orientation by either their employer or by people using their service.

Activity — Rights of women

1 Carry out some research to show how the rights of women have changed since the start of the nineteenth century. Draw a timeline to show key events.

2 Think about jobs in the health and social care sector. When you go to your local hospital, are the nurses and doctors mainly men or women? What about your dentist, GP and optician? Think about other jobs in this sector. Compare your thoughts with those of the rest of your group.

3 Discuss whether you think there are some jobs in health and social care that are better done by women than men, and vice versa. Explain why you think this.

Sexual orientation

A person's sexual orientation refers to the gender to which he or she is sexually attracted. Most people are heterosexual (attracted to the opposite sex), some are homosexual (attracted to the same sex) and some are bisexual (attracted to both sexes).

The Civil Partnership Act 2004 allowed homosexual people to have a legal partnership that gives them the same rights as married partners. Some people struggle with their homosexual feelings, sometimes hiding them for years and even marrying someone of the opposite sex, but this affects their health and wellbeing and care needs.

Case study

Aurel is homosexual, but has hidden his true feelings all his life. He is 45 years old, has a wife, two children and a high-profile job as a surgeon. Lately he has become more and more unsettled and has met a man in a gay bar he feels he could be happy with. He is afraid to tell his wife because he does not want to break the family up. He is worried that he will lose his children's love and his parents' respect, and that his colleagues and patients will be unhappy working with and being treated by a gay man.

1 In a group, discuss Aurel's predicament. (i) What do you think he should do? (ii) What do you think the effects will be on his health and wellbeing if he doesn't admit his true feelings? (iii) What do you think the effects will be on his health and wellbeing if he admits his true feelings?

2 Role-play the situation when he tells his wife and family, and then his work colleagues (i) where they are supportive, and (ii) where they are unsupportive.

Gender reassignment

Some people are born feeling very unhappy about their gender, and eventually go through gender reassignment therapy to become a member of the opposite gender. This consists of hormone replacement therapy to change secondary sexual characteristics, such as facial hair, and gender reassignment surgery to alter primary sexual characteristics, such as the sex organs and permanent hair removal for women.

Many people hide their desire for gender reassignment for many years, which is why some undergo therapy to cope with the mental health issues of anxiety, stress and various addictions. Service users and carers have the right to have their choice of gender respected and to be addressed in the correct way.

Activity   Gender reassignment

1 If you wanted to be the opposite gender, how do you think it would make (i) you, (ii) your family, and (iii) your friends feel?

2 Do some research into people in the public eye who either dress as though they are of the opposite gender, or who have undergone full gender reassignment. How has it affected their lives? What have been their health and social care needs, and how were they met?

Factors that may affect care needs (2)

Introduction

In this topic, you will learn about more factors that may affect the care needs of individuals: age, disability, marriage and civil partnership, pregnancy and maternity, and race.

Age

Two hundred years ago, if you lived beyond the age of 50, you were considered to be old and to have lived a long life.

More people are living longer nowadays because of advances in medical science and greater health awareness, so the population of the UK is increasing, with a greater number of older people in our society than ever before. Our society contains many active and healthy older people, as well as many who are less active and healthy and in residential care of some kind. This affects health and social care services.

The appropriate formal form of address and language should be used by carers of older people as they often do not like being called by their first name, feeling it is too informal and lacks respect. This can cause resentment and affect the service user's recovery or rehabilitation as they may not engage with the help being offered as readily.

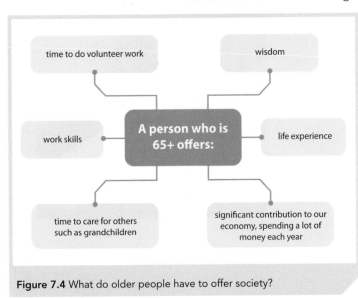

Figure 7.4 What do older people have to offer society?

Activity — Older people

1 In a small group, discuss the implications of people living longer on (i) society in general, (ii) their families, (iii) health services, and (iv) social care services.

2 Cut pictures out of magazines or print them off the internet of people over the age of 65. Divide them into positive images and negative images, and produce two separate collages.

3 As a class, discuss young people's attitudes towards older people. Look at Figure 7.4. If you don't know the meaning of 'wisdom' and 'life experience', your teacher/tutor will explain them to you.

Disability

Whatever condition a person has, their needs include all those of an able-bodied person, but they have important additional needs, especially in relation to accessing places and services. A disability may affect physical fitness, restrict access to learning activities, cause emotional distress and remove some social opportunities, thus affecting health and wellbeing. It may also affect the growth and physical development of the body and the development of new abilities and skills, as well as emotional development. It is therefore essential that a disabled person has equality of access to health and social care services.

Marriage and civil partnership

Many people choose to commit to their partner through marriage or a civil partnership, but others choose to just live together. Carers must show respect for the service user's choice regarding involvement of their partners or family in their care. Health and social care services may need to be adapted to provide accommodation for married couples to live together.

Pregnancy and maternity

A pregnant service user has a right to choose a birth plan, usually on the understanding that if things go wrong, the safest options for the mother and baby will be taken. The birth plan includes wishes such as having the baby at home or in hospital; pain relief or a natural birth; use of a birthing pool; choice of birthing partner, and the form of post-natal care (breastfeeding or not).

Race

The term 'race' is used to describe a person's genetic heritage, meaning **traits** that are socially significant, such as skin colour. **Ethnicity** refers to a person's cultural background.

Regardless of appearance, ethnic or national origin, everyone has an equal right to access health and social care services. Depending on their cultural background, people often have different expectations of how they wish to be addressed, or how they should interact with others. For people to be able to access health and social care services fully, their ethnic and national identity must be considered. Giving people appropriate choices about their lives and the treatment they receive maintains their dignity and improves the quality of the care they receive.

Key terms

Trait – a particular quality in someone's character.

Ethnicity – being part of a group sharing the same way of life and culture.

Case study

Mary is from the traveller community. Her two-year-old son, Damon, has been ill recently and had to spend some time in hospital. At the first follow-up appointment with the GP, Mary and Damon were accompanied by several members of their extended family, and the GP refused to allow them all into his room. However, after speaking to Mary, he learned that within the traveller community, family members expect to be included in discussions and decisions about health. He arranged for the extended family to wait outside while he examined Damon, and then to come back into his room for the discussion about his progress. When Damon is well again, the family plans to travel around the country for several months over the summer.

1 How did the GP adapt the health and social care service to Mary's needs?

2 What are the benefits to Mary and her family of the GP's actions?

3 When Mary's family starts to travel again, how might this affect their ability to access health and social care services?

4 Research how your local council helps travellers overcome these problems.

Factors that may affect care needs (3)

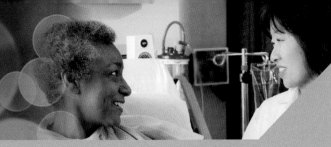

Introduction

The final factors affecting the care needs of individuals which you will learn about in this topic are religion and belief, social class, family structure and geographical location.

Religion and belief

A **religion** is a set of beliefs which is based on the idea of a sacred being, or god. **Secular** beliefs, however, have no connection to religion or a place of worship: for example, the beliefs of a political party. Individuals have different needs relating to their beliefs and practices. You will learn more about these needs later in this unit.

Social class

Social class is to do with the status that an individual has in society. This is based mainly on occupation, wealth and lifestyle. The higher up a class system a person belongs, the more power, influence and wealth they tend to have. All service users and carers should have a right to equality of access to health and social care services regardless of their social class.

Activity   Family tree

Draw a quick family tree for your family. How does it differ, if at all, from the others in your class?

Link

This topic links to Unit 4: Social Influences on Health and Wellbeing.

Family structure

A family is a social group made up of people who are related to each other by birth, marriage or adoption. Being part of a family shows others that those people are connected in some way. We can classify four different types of family:

- The extended family: this consists of three or even four generations of one family who live together (or near each other) and have very regular contact with each other. This type of family is becoming less common in our society, but remains important in countries such as Italy. The advantages of such a family are a strong support network for help when, for example, parents work or someone is sick. They also support each other financially and help the development of children. Health and social care services may need to be adapted to allow greater participation in care, and care planning, by family members.

- The nuclear family: this includes two parents (who may be married or **cohabiting**) and their children. This is a more common family structure than the extended family in the UK. Health and social care services may need to be adapted to take into account the working patterns of both parents.

- The single-parent family: this family has one parent, maybe because of divorce, separation, being widowed or never having had a relationship with the other parent. It is more usual for the children to live with the mother. These families are more likely to struggle financially. Health and social services may need to be adapted to take into account financial need, and that it may be difficult for a single parent to arrange childcare to attend appointments.

- The reconstituted family: in this type of family, an individual with children develops a relationship with another person who may or may not have children from a previous relationship. They may go on to have children together. The family therefore has at least one step-parent. Health and social care services may need to be adapted to take into account that children from reconstituted families often spend time in different locations, and may not always have easy access to their registered services.

Activity	Families

Draw up a table listing the advantages and disadvantages of living in (i) a nuclear family, (ii) a reconstituted family, and (iii) no family, and compare the three. Remember to include the impact on care needs.

Geographical location

Where people live affects their needs and their access to health and social care. Someone living in a rural area will have the benefit of less air, light and noise pollution, and the countryside to walk in, but may have to travel further to access a service. In a built-up area, there may be too many people trying to access a service, so longer waiting lists.

Access to health care can be difficult in rural locations.

Religion and belief (1)

Introduction

One of the main differences in our society and across the world is in the beliefs we hold. There is a wide range of religious or secular beliefs. For people working in health and social care, it is important to have an understanding about the beliefs of those you come into contact with. Some religious and secular beliefs directly affect care needs, but it can also be useful to know some background information about what people consider to be important. This topic looks at Christianity and Islam.

Activity   Places of worship

All hospitals, hospices and many other health and social care settings provide a multi-denominational room where people can worship or simply sit and reflect. In a small group, discuss why this is necessary and what the benefits are.

◤ Christianity

Key terms

Eternity – an endless amount of time.

- Beliefs: Christians believe in God. Christianity began in the Middle East over 2,000 years ago from the teachings of Jesus Christ. Christians believe that Jesus Christ lived a humble and selfless life, died to save humanity by taking our sins with him, and rose from the dead. God is the Trinity of the Father, Son (Jesus) and Holy Spirit. Christians believe that when they die, they will join God in the kingdom of heaven for **eternity**. They follow the Ten Commandments, which they believe were given to Moses by God.

- Festivals and holy days: The main Christian day is Sunday, which has traditionally been seen as a day of rest. Christians celebrate many festivals, including Christmas when they celebrate Jesus' birth, and Easter, the death and resurrection of Jesus.

- Food and diet: Some Christians fast or give up a food they enjoy for the 40 days of Lent, which come before Easter. Otherwise there is no special Christian diet.

- Forms of worship: People are baptised, usually as babies, by having a cross drawn with water on their forehead to welcome them into the Christian faith. Christians worship on a Sunday by going to church and taking part in a variety of services, at which they sing hymns of praise and pray to God. One of these services is Holy Communion, where those who have been confirmed eat a wafer of bread to represent Christ's body and drink communion wine to represent his blood.

- Dress: There is no Christian form of dress except for the church ministers, some of whom wear long robes to lead services.

- Symbols: The main symbol of the Christian faith is the cross on which Jesus was crucified. The holy book is the Bible, consisting of the Old Testament (shared with the Jewish faith) and the New Testament, which tells the story of Jesus' birth, life, death and resurrection, and contains his teachings.

- Health and medical beliefs: some Christian groups are opposed to abortion and stem cell research.

Islam

- Beliefs: Muslims have six main beliefs, called the Articles of Faith. They believe in:

  - Allah – the primary Muslim belief is that there is only one god, called Allah in Arabic, and that Muhammad is the messenger of Allah

  - angels

  - the holy book, which is the Qur'an

  - the prophets, or special messengers, such as Ibrahim (Abraham) and Muhammad

  - the day of judgement, when the life of every human being will be assessed to decide whether they go to heaven or hell

  - predestination, that Allah has already decided what will happen in the world, although this does not stop humans making free choices.

- Festivals and holy days: There are two main holy days in Islam, Eid ul Fitr, which occurs at the end of the holy fasting month of Ramadan, and Eid ul Adha, which commemorates Ibrahim's obedience to God in agreeing to sacrifice his son.

- Food and diet: the only meat Muslims will eat is halal meat that has been killed according to religious practice. Eating pork is forbidden. For the holy month of Ramadan, religious Muslims do not eat during daylight hours.

- Forms of worship: Muslims pray up to five times each day and some attend the mosque for these prayers. They use prayer mats and they must face Mecca, wherever they are in the world. Religious practices include the Five Pillars of Islam, which are five duties that unite Muslims into a community.

- Dress: Both men and women are required to dress modestly. Some Muslim women wear a headscarf to cover their hair and neck, and a few choose to cover their faces as well.

- Symbols: There are no official symbols in Islam, but the crescent and star are often associated with the religion.

- Health and medical beliefs: Muslim boys are usually circumcised, which may have some health benefits. Among many possible adaptations, health and social care services may need to be adapted to take into account a Muslim's wish to pray, to eat halal food and to fast during Ramadan. Muslims may wish to receive treatment in a single-sex ward and personal care from someone of their own sex.

Activity   Hinduism

1 Carry out research on Hinduism. Include details about (i) food, (ii) dress, (iii) symbols, (iv) health and medical beliefs, and (v) festivals and holy days. Use the information to produce an information leaflet with pictures.

2 In a small group, discuss how hospital staff would have to adapt their care to meet the needs of (i) a Muslim, and (ii) a Hindu patient.

3 Discuss how such adaptations would help the patient's recovery. Share your ideas in a group discussion. Visit Pearson hotlinks to view websites that will be very useful for this activity.

Can you identify these items?

Religion and belief (2)

Introduction

In this topic you will learn about Judaism and Buddhism, which some consider to be a religion and others a secular group. People who work in health and social care may find it useful to know details about the beliefs of service users in order to be able to adapt care where necessary.

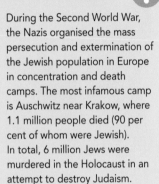

Did you know?

During the Second World War, the Nazis organised the mass persecution and extermination of the Jewish population in Europe in concentration and death camps. The most infamous camp is Auschwitz near Krakow, where 1.1 million people died (90 per cent of whom were Jewish). In total, 6 million Jews were murdered in the Holocaust in an attempt to destroy Judaism.

Key terms

Atonement – something done to make up for an injury or wrong.

Kosher – food that satisfies the requirements of Jewish law; for example, when an animal is slaughtered, all the blood must be drained from its body before it can be eaten.

Circumcision – male circumcision is the removal of some or all of the foreskin from the penis.

Judaism

- Beliefs: Judaism began in the Middle East over 3,500 years ago. Jews believe that God created the world and everything in it, and that God appointed the Jews to be his chosen people in order to set an example of holiness and ethical behaviour to the world. They follow the Ten Commandments. Judaism was founded by Moses. The Jewish holy book is known as the Tanakh.

- Festivals and holy days: Judaism has a number of festivals and holy days. The most important days in the Jewish calendar are Rosh Hashanah, which is the Jewish New Year, and Yom Kippur, the Day of **Atonement**. Other holy days include Pesach (Passover), which lasts for eight days and is celebrated in spring. It reminds Jews that their ancestors were once slaves in Egypt and that God helped them to flee from slavery. Shabbat (Sabbath) is the weekly holy day, which lasts from sunset on Friday evening to Saturday night.

- Food and diet: To celebrate Shabbat, Jews eat bread called challah, made in the shape of a plait, and drink wine. Jewish people buy their meat and other foods from specialist **kosher** shops and butchers. They do not eat pork, rabbit or shellfish and they have different sets of utensils, one to use with meat and one with milk, because meat and milk foods are never prepared or eaten together.

- Forms of worship: the Jewish holy book is made up of the Torah (five books of Moses), the books of the Prophets, and holy writings. Jewish people worship in the synagogue and their spiritual leaders are called Rabbis.

- Dress: Orthodox Jewish men wear tefillin (cubic black leather boxes with leather straps) on their head and their arm during weekday morning prayers. Orthodox Jewish men always cover their heads by wearing a skullcap known in Hebrew as a kippah or in Yiddish as a yarmulke.

- Symbols: The Star of David is the best-known symbol of Judaism. Another symbol is the Menorah, a seven-branched candlestick.

- Health and medical beliefs: The Brit Milah (**circumcision** ceremony) is an important initiation rite for Jewish baby boys.

Buddhism

- Beliefs: Buddhists believe that life is one long cycle (the samsar) which consists of birth, life, death and rebirth. After death, a person's soul is reborn in a new body and the only way to break the cycle is to reach enlightenment (nirvana), the end of everything that is not perfect such as greed, hatred, suffering and ignorance. The Buddha was simply a human being, called Siddhartha Gautama, who was born into royalty but left his privileged life to find enlightenment when he saw the suffering of others. Buddha means 'Awakened One'. There are various forms of Buddhism, each of which believes in different routes to reach enlightenment.

- Festivals: The most important Buddhist festival is Wesak (or Buddha Day), which is held on the first day of the full moon in May or June. On this day the Buddha is thought to have been born, gained enlightenment and passed away, all in different years.

- Food and diet: Most Buddhists are strict vegetarians because they are opposed to causing harm to any living creature.

- Forms of worship: Buddhists worship in a temple or monastery, and often meditate as well.

- Dress: Some Buddhist monks wear a red, yellow or saffron robe.

- Symbols: The wheel (Chakra) is one of the most important Buddhist symbols, as it represents the teachings of the Buddha.

What other Buddhist symbols are there?

- Health and medical beliefs: Since prayer is part of the healing and cleansing process, prayer and meditation are important to enable medications and other medical treatments to assist with healing. Some holy days include fasting from dawn to dusk, but considerations are allowed for the frail and elderly, for whom fasting could create problems. Terminal illness may be seen as a unique opportunity to reflect on life's ultimate meaning, and the meaning of one's relationship with the world. Therefore, it is important that medication does not interfere with consciousness.

? Did you know?

Richard Gere, Orlando Bloom, Harrison Ford, Keanu Reeves, Tiger Woods, Pamela Stephenson, Tina Turner and Joanna Lumley are just a few celebrities who have taken up Buddhism.

Adapting services

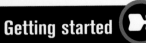

Getting started

In small groups, discuss *either* how you think the world began, *or* what you think happens to a person when they die. Discuss the ways in which your opinions differ and where your ideas came from.

Introduction

Atheists and humanists have their own beliefs which should be respected in the same way as religious beliefs, as it is important to value diversity in order to promote equality of opportunity for all service users. Health and social care provision is adapted to meet the diverse needs of service users. In this topic, you will learn about adapting services.

Secular groups

Atheists

Atheists do not believe in any god. They think that God and religion are man-made myths and legends, and so are not meaningful. Atheism is not a set of beliefs, but an absence of belief in God. Health and social care services may need to be adapted for atheists. For example, in a care home that holds a Christian service on Sundays, space needs to be available for atheists so that they don't feel their beliefs are being dismissed.

Humanists

Humanism is a positive set of beliefs about people and ethics. Humanists do not believe in any god. They celebrate events such as weddings, but the ceremony is centred on the people involved rather than a religion.

Activity   Humanists

Carry out some research on humanists. Prepare a PowerPoint presentation to show how humanists make the following non-religious: (i) naming ceremonies, (ii) weddings, and (iii) funerals.

Adapting services to meet needs

Service users in health and social care have diverse care needs and there are many factors that can affect these. Adaptations are made to services to meet service users' specific needs so that they can maintain as much independence as possible. You must be able to relate the adaptations to services to the factors that are covered in this unit.

In addition to the adaptations you have learned about in this unit, visiting arrangements in a hospital or care home are adapted to meet the needs of service users. Families and friends can visit at set times in the afternoon and evening. Outside of visiting times, service users are given as much rest as possible and their dignity preserved, and the staff can focus on providing the required care service.

Benefits of adapting provision

There are a range of benefits to service users of adapting health and social care provision to meet their diverse needs. If service users are happy with the provision they receive, this will aid their recovery and rehabilitation.

The benefits include:

- being respected
- being treated equally
- not being discriminated against
- maintaining dignity and privacy
- feeling safe
- receiving improved quality of care
- receiving personalised care
- improved accessibility of health and social care
- having their needs met.

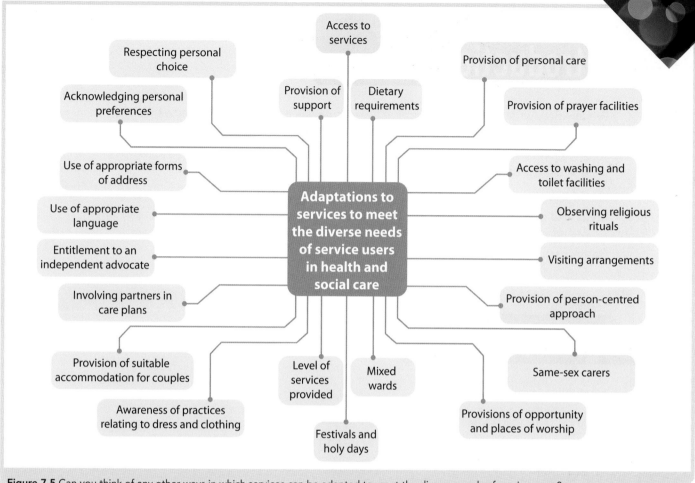

Figure 7.5 Can you think of any other ways in which services can be adapted to meet the diverse needs of service users?

| **Assessment activity 7.2** | English | 2B.P3 | 2B.P4 | 2B.M2 | 2B.D2 |

In your role as a trainee care assistant at a residential care home for older people on the outskirts of a small city, you are approached by two new care assistants who have read the chapter of the handbook which you wrote. They ask you how health and social care provision in the home could be adapted to meet the diverse needs of the two residents they are to care for. The manager asks you to produce a presentation for them, in which you will describe the residents' diverse needs and how provision could be adapted to meet these needs.

You must then explain how your ideas on how adapting services will benefit the service users, and assess how effective these proposed changes are likely to be in meeting their diverse needs.

Note that the residents of the care home have a wide range of health and social care needs as it is also a nursing home, and therefore accepts older people with conditions such as dementia.

Tips

You must give a clear description of the potential needs related to all the factors listed in this unit, using at least one example for each factor.

Activity Adapting services

Look at Figure 7.5. In a small group, discuss any adaptations which have not been mentioned in detail in this unit. How do you think they help meet diverse needs?

Introduction

We all know what is right and fair, don't we, so why is it so important that we have a whole unit devoted to this subject? But do we? Do you really know your 'rights'? And do we all have the same rights? Are people all treated the same, even if they do not look or act the same as others?

Health care professionals are quite likely to meet people who do not have the same ideas and behaviours as they do. This unit will help you understand why it is important to ensure all people who use health and social care services, and colleagues, are treated equally and fairly.

Assessment: You will be assessed by a series of assignments set by your teacher/tutor.

Learning aims

In this unit you will:

A investigate the rights of individuals using health and social care services

B examine the responsibilities of employers and employees in upholding service users' rights in health and social care.

> When I am at my Saturday job in the care home I always ask the residents if they want me to help them. I used to just do things for them without asking, but I now realise that I was often taking away their independence and not allowing them to make choices about what they wanted to do or wear.
>
> Martin, *16-year-old would-be social worker*

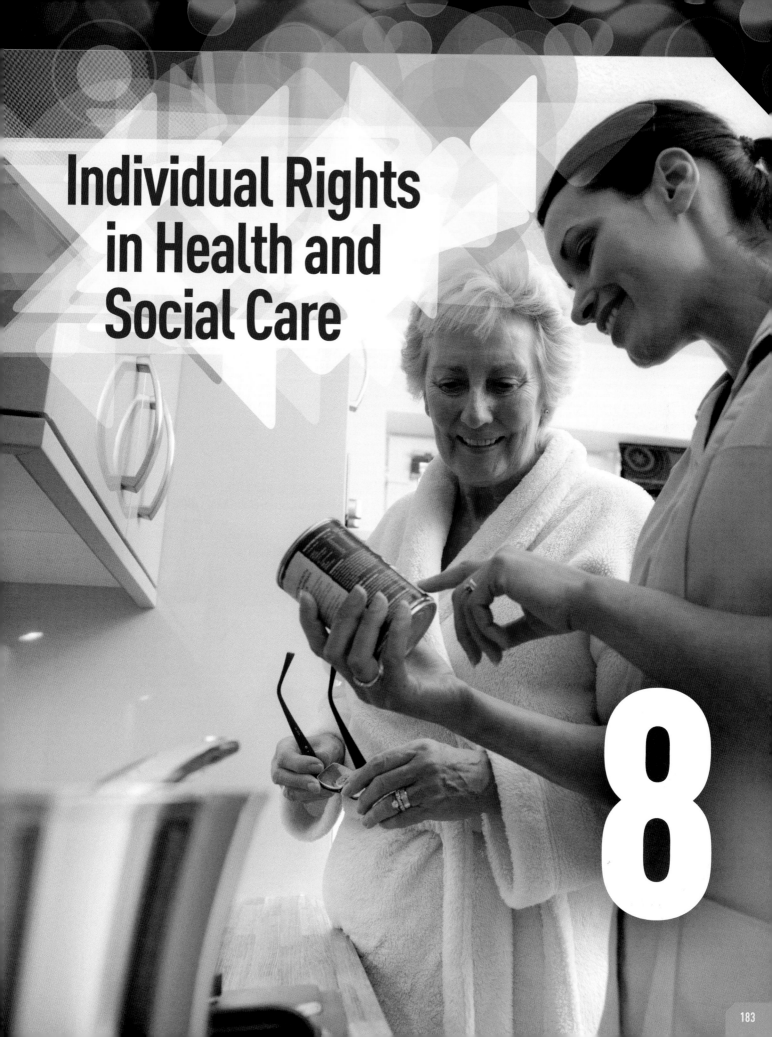

Individual Rights in Health and Social Care

8

BTEC
Assessment Zone

This table shows you what you must do in order to achieve a **Pass**, **Merit** or **Distinction** grade, and where you can find activities in this book to help you.

Assessment criteria			
Level 1	Level 2 Pass	Level 2 Merit	Level 2 Distinction
Learning aim A: Investigate the rights of individuals using health and social care services			
1A.1 Identify the individual rights of service users in health and social care.	**2A.P1** Summarise the individual rights of service users in health and social care. **Assessment activity 8.1 See page 194.**	**2A.M1** Explain ways in which service users' individual rights can be upheld in health and social care, using selected examples. **Assessment activity 8.1 See page 194.**	**2A.D1** Assess the benefits and potential difficulties of upholding service users' rights in health and social care, using selected examples. **Assessment activity 8.1 See page 194.**
1A.2 Identify how current and relevant legislation protects the rights of service users, with reference to one example.	**2A.P2** Describe how current and relevant legislation protects the rights of service users, using examples. **Assessment activity 8.1 See page 194.**		
Learning aim B: Examine the responsibilities of employers and employees in upholding service users' rights in health and social care			
1B.3 Identify how an employee can plan to maximise the safety of service users.	**2B.P3** Describe how an employee can plan to maximise the safety of service users. **Assessment activity 8.2 See page 201.**	**2B.M2** Explain why risk assessment is important in health and social care. **Assessment activity 8.2 See page 201.**	**2B.D2** Evaluate the importance of the use of risk assessments in health and social care, using selected examples. **Assessment activity 8.2 See page 201.**
1B.4 Identify how the right to confidentiality is protected in health and social care.	**2B.P4** Describe how the right to confidentiality is protected in health and social care. **Assessment activity 8.3 See page 205.**	**2B.M3** Explain why the right to confidentiality is protected in health and social care, using examples. **Assessment activity 8.3 See page 205.**	**2B.D3** Justify occasions where there is a need for an employee to breach confidentiality, using examples. **Assessment activity 8.3 See page 205.**

How you will be assessed

The unit will be assessed by a series of internally assessed tasks. You will be expected to show an understanding of communication skills in the context of health and social care sectors. The tasks will be based on a scenario where you work in a local health or social care organisation.

Your assessment could be in the form of:

- a written observation log based in health or social care settings

- training materials, such as leaflets, posters and PowerPoint presentations

- a training DVD demonstrating good practice through role play.

Rights of individuals using services

Getting started

Everyone in society has **rights** that are protected by law. When people are using health and social care services, they are often in a vulnerable position. It is very important that everyone working in health and social care understands what rights service users have and how to uphold them.

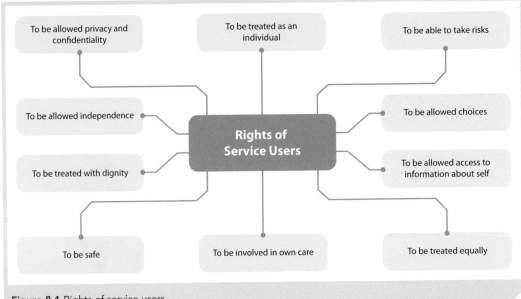

Figure 8.1 Rights of service users.

Key terms in the diagram:
- To be allowed privacy and confidentiality
- To be treated as an individual
- To be able to take risks
- To be allowed independence
- **Rights of Service Users**
- To be allowed choices
- To be treated with dignity
- To be allowed access to information about self
- To be safe
- To be involved in own care
- To be treated equally

Key terms

Rights – things that a person can claim they are free to do or that are due to them.

Dignity – a calm and serious manner/style suitable for the situation and to treat someone with respect.

Self-esteem – how much you like, accept and respect yourself as a person, how you value yourself.

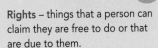

The spider diagram shows the **rights** of each individual using health and social care services, but what do these rights really mean?

- To be respected – we show respect to others by the way we address each other and the attitudes that we display. The way in which we listen to the views and opinions of other people and how we value privacy and confidentiality are all part of respecting each other.

- To be treated as an individual – we are each unique and expect to be treated as an individual person, not the same as everyone else. We should always treat others as individuals, trying not to generalise and not to lump people together in categories, for example, 'all teenage girls have long hair' or 'all old people have arthritis and walk with a stick'.

- Treating people with **dignity** ensures that they keep their self-respect and **self-esteem**. For example, many people – not just the elderly – can have a problem with incontinence, which means that they might not get to the toilet in time. This can make the individual feel embarrassed and ashamed. The behaviour and attitude of their care workers can help overcome these feelings and allow the individual to maintain their dignity.

- All individuals have the right to be treated equally and not discriminated against. This does not mean treating everyone the same, but behaving towards them fairly whatever their gender, social class, sexuality, age, race, ability, where they live, etc.

- Being allowed privacy means freedom from the attention or intrusion of others into an individual's private life and affairs, and that any information about them should remain confidential.

- To be allowed access to information about themselves. By ensuring that individuals have access to information held about them helps them make choices about their care and treatment. This in turn helps raise self-esteem and feelings of respect.

- By allowing individuals to have account taken of their choices (e.g. to communicate in preferred method/language) helps support their **independence** and raise their self-esteem.

- Allowing independence means that individuals are not dependent or controlled by another person or organisation.

- We all have the right to be safe and to be free from harm. All health and social care settings must have a health and safety policy that sets out rules, regulations and actions that must be followed.

- Being independent and able to make choices could mean that an individual might wish to take risks. Risks should be managed carefully to ensure that hazards are identified and eliminated or reduced.

- Being involved in their own care means that individuals feel their opinions and feelings are important and that they are respected as independent people.

Key terms

Independence – freedom from control by, or dependence on, others.

Protecting privacy: how does using a secure filing cabinet for records help to protect service users' rights?

Activity   Rights of service users

Look at Figure 8.1. Some of the rights seem to contradict some of the others.

1 With a partner, discuss an example of each of the rights.

2 Can you identify any problems in ensuring all of these rights are upheld?

3 Are some of the rights more important than others?

4 Make brief notes on your discussion so that you can present them to the rest of the group.

Upholding service users' rights (1)

Getting started

One of our rights is to have our choices taken into account.

We know how important it is that we can make our own decisions and that in order to make those decisions we need to have choices – but does everyone have that opportunity?

Consider these questions:

Did you decide what to wear today and what to eat? Did you decide whether to have a bath, a shower or just a quick wash?

How would you feel if your clothes and food were always decided for you – with no opportunity to choose something different?

Introduction

It should be the aim of all service providers to promote a way of life for service users that allows them to enjoy, as far as possible, their rights as individuals.

Through **empowerment**, individual users of a service can feel that their opinions are valued and respected. Too often individuals being cared for have their needs, wishes and expectations ignored. For example, the carer will select clothes to be worn because they are easy to put on, or food to be eaten because it is quick to prepare, not thinking that the individual might wish to choose their own clothes and food. Having choice in their lives helps people maintain their independence, dignity and positive self-image.

A person-centred approach

Taking a **person-centred approach** is one way of upholding service users' rights. By taking a person-centred approach carers ensure that the service user is the most important person. The service user should be included in planning and decision-making about their life. Their support should always be matched to their needs, not what is most efficient or practical for the care provider.

Taking part in writing their own care plan and in evaluating the care they are given can empower service users and help give feelings of **fulfilment**.

Key terms

Empowerment – enabling individuals to take responsibility for their own lives by making informed decisions.

Person-centred approach – working with individuals to identify their values, needs and expectations.

Fulfilment – the opportunity to accomplish personal goals and use abilities to the full.

Infringing – going too far, or overstepping the mark.

Case study

Thomas is 78 and lives in a care home. Recently a new care assistant has been assigned to Thomas. She visits Thomas's room at 9.30 each evening, and turns off the television and takes the remote control from the room. The care assistant then removes Thomas's hearing aid, saying that he will not need it as the television is now off.

1 How is this **infringing** Thomas's rights?

2 What choices is Thomas being given?

3 Should Thomas be given any options?

4 As a 78 year old, what time should Thomas go to bed?

5 Should Thomas be allowed to turn the television on during the night?

6 How much independence do you think Thomas feels he has?

Ensuring privacy during personal care

Just checking

1 What does 'empowerment' mean?
2 Give three examples of care that might empower a service user.

In the very recent past it was common practice for toilet doors in many care settings to not have a lock. While a lock on a toilet door is not a 'right' in itself, the lack of a lock meant that the right to privacy during personal care was not being respected. Imagine how you would feel if you could not use the toilet or bathroom in privacy.

Ensuring that a service user can use the toilet or bathroom with as much privacy as possible helps to maintain their dignity. Maintaining dignity can help to boost self-esteem and increase people's quality of life.

How do you feel if you have to use a toilet without a lock?

Activity Promoting rights

Shona is a young adult who has severe learning disabilities and lives in a care home. She also has similar needs and expectations to any other young person.

• Give at least five examples of how you might promote Shona's rights by supporting them in controlling their own life.
• Devise a set of guidelines that could be used to promote the rights of service users in a residential home for young adults with learning disabilities.

Upholding service users' rights (2)

Introduction

Making sure that you don't discriminate against service users and that you use empathy and honesty when communicating are important parts of upholding service users' rights.

Anti-discriminatory practices

Sometimes discrimination is deliberate (for example refusing to employ someone because of their gender or race), but it also happens because institutions or individuals have not thought about how their actions might affect others.

For people working in health and social care, it is very important to take an active role in ensuring that the service they provide does not discriminate against service users.

The right to be able to communicate in the method or language of choice is important for individuals being cared for, as this helps to ensure that users of services can take part in making decisions. If a service user is used to using British Sign Language (BSL) for instance, then the service provider should find someone who can communicate in BSL. The need for effective communication is of the highest importance.

Making sure that all service users have access to food that meets their dietary and religious requirements is another form of anti-discriminatory practice.

It is also important to ensure that all service users can physically access a service, for example making sure that buildings are accessible or that written information is available in large print, Braille or appropriate languages.

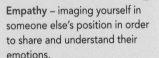

Key terms

Empathy – imaging yourself in someone else's position in order to share and understand their emotions.

Sympathy – feeling pity or sorrow for another person's feelings, emotions or distress.

Empathy and honesty

Care workers should try to ensure that service users are respected for being the people they are through **empathy** – not **sympathy**. In this way, a care worker can support an individual and enable the person to maintain their dignity.

Empathy is shown by the way that a care worker speaks to users of services, the words that they use and the non-verbal communication that they demonstrate.

When you sympathise with someone you feel sorry for them and have pity for their situation. Sympathy is often a negative approach and is not helpful in dealing with issues or problems.

Honesty and empathy are two major characteristics of the worker in health and social care.

When you empathise with someone, you show that you can identify with them, understand how they are feeling and put yourself in their position. However, this is not always easy if you have not experienced what the other person is feeling or the situation they are in, you might find it hard to put yourself in their position – but you can tell them this, and ask them to explain their situation and feelings to you.

Honesty means being trustworthy and truthful. It is an important principle and value and should always be practised by all health and social care workers. Being honest in a helping situation should encourage a relaxed feeling between the carer and the user of service, and this will help create the best environment for communication to take place.

An important factor of being honest includes the willingness to admit to your mistakes so that they can be corrected. However, it is not always easy to be completely honest.

Case study

Bill is 79 and lives in a residential care home. He is used to regular visits from his grandchildren, as they call in on their way home from school. Suddenly one of the grandchildren stops visiting. The care staff have been told that the grandchild is in hospital following a serious accident, they have been asked not to tell Bill as the news will cause him much worry and distress. The carers understand the wishes of the family but feel unhappy that they are not telling Bill the truth.

How would you handle this difficult problem without damaging the relationship between Bill and the carers?

Discussion point

You have learned that empathy is not the same as sympathy.

With a partner, give examples of using sympathy and examples of using empathy.

Legislation at work

Link

This topic links to Unit 7: Equality and Diversity in Health and Social Care.

Equality Act 2010

Imagine being told that you cannot use the same entrance into school or college as your friends because you are different; or that you are not suitable for your chosen career just because you would look different from your colleagues.

In the past such **discrimination** was accepted as normal. However, over time attitudes have changed and legislation has changed, making many discriminatory practices against the law. This Act should ensure that discrimination no longer occurs.

Activity   Similarities and differences

Work in groups of four or five.

- Investigate your differences and your similarities. Think about your eye colour, religion, food preferences and music taste. You might be surprised how similar you are – and how different!
- Produce posters showing the results of your investigations.

Why is this law so important?

The **Equality** Act brings together a number of existing pieces of legislation, and significantly adds to them and strengthens them. The existing laws in the Equality Act include those covering race and disability. One of the key changes is that it adds legal protection against discrimination in these areas:

- age
- disability
- gender reassignment
- marriage and civil partnership
- pregnancy and maternity
- race
- religion or belief
- **sex**
- **gender**
- sexual orientation.

The Equality Act can be used to help protect and support the rights of individuals in all walks of life, including in health and social care settings.

Did you know?

It is illegal to discriminate against people because of their gender, sexuality, religion, ethnicity, race or age.

Activity   Equality Act 2010

In pairs, devise a presentation that illustrates how the Equality Act 2010 can benefit service users.

Care settings – as all workplaces – must do all they can to promote equality and to value difference. Codes of practice or charters should have been put in place for staff to follow and adhere to. Codes and charters will be developed from the relevant legislation, and these can be used to provide information in the form of leaflets and posters to discourage **prejudice** and encourage non-discriminatory practice.

Human Rights Act 1998

Human rights are the rights and freedoms that everyone living in the UK has, regardless of their nationality or their citizenship status.

There are 16 basic human rights laid down in the law. These rights are based on the European Convention on Human Rights, written after the Second World War. The rights include freedom of religious beliefs and freedom of speech – that is, freedom for a person to speak as they see fit.

Mental Health Act 1983

Sometimes people using services need care and treatment for mental health problems that they are not willing to accept. This may include compulsory care to protect themselves or other people. This can conflict with an individual's right to choice and independence. The Mental Health Act 1983 sets out the criteria that must be met before compulsory measures can be taken, along with protections and safeguards for patients.

Key terms

Discrimination – treating a person or group differently from others.

Equality – equal treatment and respect.

Sex – the physical and biological differences between male and female.

Gender – the social and cultural differences between male and female.

Prejudice – an unreasonable feeling against a person or group of people.

Why do you think it might be difficult for patients to accept they are mentally ill?

Individuals' rights and diversity

Diversity and equality

Equality does not mean treating everybody the same, it means giving everyone the same opportunities. Diversity is the way in which people are different. In health and social care it is necessary to promote equality by respecting diversity. For example, everyone should be able to register with a GP (equality). However, someone with more health problems will need to take up more of the doctor's time (diversity).

Just checking

Bill and Thomas live in a care home and always go in to lunch together.

The chef always gives Bill and Thomas the same size of portions.

1   Are Bill and Thomas being treated equally?

2   What steps could the care home take to encourage their workers to treat residents equally while respecting their differences?

Assessment activity 8.1   2A.P1 | 2A.P2 | 2A.M1 | 2A.D1

You work as an assistant at the Good Days Community Centre. Several different community groups use the centre for their sessions. These include a lunch club for people with dementia, a music group for young adults with learning disabilities and an exercise class for people who are recovering from heart attacks. It is part of your role to help out at these sessions and to make sure that all the people using your community centre have their rights respected. Volunteers often come and help out at the sessions and your manager has asked you to put together some materials to tell them more about the rights of service users.

Put together a pack for the volunteers. This could include a poster outlining individuals' rights when using health and social care services and telling people how the law protects rights.

It could also include a leaflet for the volunteers about how they can help to support individuals' rights and what benefits there are to everyone when they do. It could include case studies about making difficult decisions about upholding conflicting rights.

Tips

You could use someone from each of the service user groups as an example when describing individuals' rights and how to uphold them.

When you are describing a difficult decision about rights, you could describe a conflict between the rights of two different service users, or a conflict between the rights of a service user and an employee or volunteer's responsibilities.

WorkSpace

► CLAIRE DAVIES

Healthcare Assistant

I have only been working as a care assistant for four months, but already I feel that I have changed because I have learned so much from so many different people. Not only have I learned from my supervisor and the team that I work with, but also from the service users themselves – I would never have thought this!

Although each working day follows a pattern, no two days are ever the same, so I am never bored. The service users all have different personalities and characters – they really keep me on the go! My job involves supporting the qualified staff in caring for and safeguarding service users. I also work with the activities coordinator and sometimes run the activities.

One of my main responsibilities is at meal times. I ensure that service users get to the dining room, or I will take a meal to someone who does not want to eat there. I often sit with service users at meal times and chat with them so it becomes a social occasion instead of just a means of getting nourishment.

I enjoy the personal care time that I spend with people. I can assist them when they ask, sometimes by just choosing an outfit for the day or helping put on some lipstick. Other times I might read articles from the magazines or newspapers that they really enjoy.

I love my job and would never have thought going to work could be so satisfying and worthwhile. I am hoping to continue studying and to start nurse training in the future.

Think about it

1 How might Claire be supporting service users' rights during her working day?

2 Do you think that Claire has to respect confidentiality in her work?

Responsibility for safety

Introduction

Service users have rights to be independent, to be safe and to take risks. In this topic we will investigate the employer's and employee's responsibilities in the area of ensuring safety and preventing harm, both to service users and to all who might be in the health and social care setting.

◤ Employer responsibilities

The employer in a health and social care setting has a variety of responsibilities towards their employees, service users and environment and just about everything that occurs on the premises.

Employers have a duty to ensure that they meet their responsibilities under health and safety legislation – the Health and Safety at Work Act 1974 – and must be aware of the action to take in order to safeguard both their workers and their service users.

Employers are responsible for seeing that any risks to health and safety are properly controlled. To do this, employers must provide risk assessment examples and checklists for staff training and for self-assessment.

Figure 8.2 What hazards can you see here?

Employee responsibilities

The employee also has many responsibilities, which often vary from day to day.

One of the most important responsibilities of an employee is to maximise the safety of everyone who is associated with the workplace.

As an employee your most important responsibilities are to:

- look after your own health and safety
- take care not to put other people at risk by what you do – or what you don't do – in the course of your work
- cooperate with your employer, making sure that you undertake proper training
- make sure that you understand and follow health and safety policies
- report any injuries or illnesses that you suffer as a result of doing your job
- tell your employer if something affects your ability to work, e.g. an injury or pregnancy, as your employer may need to change your duties.

Duty of care

Case study

An individual that you are caring for is pouring a cup of tea. The individual is very shaky and you are worried the tea will spill and burn him.

What do you do?

As a care worker who is aware of respecting the dignity of others, you might let the person carry on.

As a care worker who is aware of individuals maintaining their independence, you might let the person carry on.

As a care worker who is aware of the safety of individuals, you might offer to pour the tea yourself.

BUT – you want to respect dignity, help maintain independence AND keep the individual from harm, so you suggest that you work with the individual and so ensure that no harm occurs.

Care workers encourage people to live independently. That means enabling them to make decisions and take actions themselves. When someone in care decides to do something that is considered to be unsafe there is a dilemma (a difficult choice between two decisions). If we stop them doing it, are we denying them the right to take risks? If we let them do something dangerous, are we failing in our duty of care?

Care workers must know how to address dilemmas that arise between an individual's rights and the duty of care.

In the health and social care setting the service provider is a responsible person who has a **duty of care** to protect service users from harm.

Having a 'duty of care' means that the health and safety of the service user should be central to the carer's work. All treatment given must have a therapeutic benefit to the user or must be essential for saving life.

We saw earlier that employers are responsible for the health and safety of their employees while they are at work; this responsibility is covered by 'duty of care'. Employers are also responsible for any visitors to their premises such as customers, suppliers and the general public.

> **Key terms**
>
> **Duty of care** – responsibility to keep people in our care safe from harm.

Risk assessment

Getting started

Risks are related to hazards. For example the hazard is the cleaner's bucket at the bottom of the stairs, the risk is that someone could trip and fall over the bucket.

What risks and hazards can you see in the room you are sitting in?

Introduction

We take risks and assess hazards all the time, often without thinking. For example, when we cross the road (the hazard) the risk is that we could be knocked down by a car. To ensure that we don't get knocked down we do a quick assessment of the situation – is there any traffic coming? How fast is it going? Is there a crossing nearby? Can I get to the other side safely? This is a risk assessment.

When we take risks we weigh up the options and choices that we have – for instance, should I dodge between the traffic, or wait for a gap?

Individuals vary in their ability to assess hazards and risks. Some service users need more help in weighing up the options and choices before making a decision. For example, the very young might not understand when food is 'off' – when it is likely to cause illness – and might need more help when choosing food from the fridge.

Risk management

Part of risk management involves recognising and reporting adverse events, **accidents**, **incidents**, **errors** and **near misses**. Under the Health and Safety at Work Act 1974, employees are required to report problems like these to their employer. In some circumstances they may also need to report them to the **HSE** (Health and Safety Executive).

More accidents occur in the home than anywhere else. Care workers can often prevent injury and illness through careful monitoring of potential hazards and assessment of risks.

Falls and food poisoning are major causes of hospitalisation, but with care people can be kept well and free from harm. Fridges and freezers should be clean, set to the correct temperatures and the products should be used in date order – for example, if there are two bottles of milk dated the 10th and the 12th, use up the one dated the 10th first. Always ensure that food is not consumed after its use-by date.

Risk assessment and risk management are vital for all service users and should be reviewed and updated regularly, but especially when service users receive bad news, whether it is to do with their personal life outside the care environment or their progress through the health and care system.

Key terms

Hazard – a situation or object that could cause damage or hurt.

Risk assessment – investigating all hazards and offering precautions to prevent harm.

Accident – an incident, usually with negative results, that leads to harm, loss or damage to anyone in care, visitors or workers.

Incident – anything unusual that happens to individuals in care, visitors or workers.

Error – a mistake, a wrong decision or wrong action.

Near miss – an event that could have caused harm, loss or damage, but did not.

HSE – Health and Safety Executive, the body that regulates health and safety in the workplace.

Do you know the difference between 'best before' and 'use by'?

Activity   Risk assessment

The table below gives an example of a risk assessment sheet.

Concentrate on one area of your work placement setting, or a health/care setting that you have visited recently, identify hazards and fill in the rest of the table as shown in the example.

Table 8.1 Sample risk assessment

What are the hazards?	Who might be harmed and how?	What are you already doing?	Do you need to do anything else to manage this risk?	Action required by whom?	Action required by when?	Done – date
Falls	Staff and visitors could be injured if they trip over objects.	General housekeeping. All areas are well lit. There are no trailing cables.	Better housekeeping in residents' living room. Keep passages clear, put cleaning resources in cupboards when finished with.	All staff to monitor.		

Preventing harm to service users

Introduction

We all have the right to be safe and to be free from harm. All health and social care settings must have a 'health and safety' policy that sets out rules, regulations and actions that must be followed.

We have seen that there is legislation set down by government and there are policies and guidelines put in place by the work setting. All of these can help prevent harm to service users, visitors and service providers.

Figure 8.3 Do you always follow these steps to good hand washing?

Safeguarding

Safeguarding means protecting people's health, wellbeing and human rights, as well as enabling them to live free from harm, abuse and neglect.

In health and social care, employers and employees have a duty to safeguard the people in their care. Employers can do this by making sure that they employ the right people to work with service users, for example by doing a CRB check. They must also have good training in place for their employees, clear policies about what to do if abuse is discovered, and accessible ways for anyone to report suspected abuse. Employees need to comply with their workplace codes of conduct and report possible signs of abuse.

Other causes of harm

Harm can be caused by injury and by illness, but many injuries and illnesses can be prevented by using good risk-assessment procedures. However, this cannot cover everything that could possibly happen.

In most health and social care environments there are substances that could be harmful to the health of service users. These could include cleaning products that need to be stored correctly to avoid accidents involving trips and falls or unintended consumption. There may also be medicines stored on site. To avoid accidents such as dispensing the wrong medicine or overconsumption, medicines should be the responsibility of a trained member of staff.

If something has gone wrong in a health and social care setting, further harm, or future harm to anyone else can be prevented by having a clear complaints procedure. Employees working in health and social care need to know how their facility's complaints procedure works in order to be able to help those who need to complain and to assist in learning from previous complaints.

Enough clean toilets and washing facilities for service users and staff can help everyone to avoid infections and diseases.

The use of protective equipment – disposable gloves and aprons, for instance, should be worn when undertaking certain duties to prevent the transmission of bacteria and viruses.

However, the easiest way to prevent the spread of germs is by washing your hands.

The flu virus can also cause severe illness and death, especially in vulnerable individuals. The flu virus can live outside the body for 24–48 hours on hard surfaces; 8–12 hours on cloth, paper and tissues; and five minutes on the skin.

Service providers and service users should all be encouraged to take advantage of vaccinations – the spread of the seasonal flu virus can be greatly reduced if people take up the offer of vaccinations when offered.

Assessment activity 8.2   2B.P3 | 2B.M2 | 2B.D2

You are working in a local health and social care setting and it is part of your role to ensure that the health and safety of residents is protected. A new care assistant has just been appointed in a similar role and your manager has asked you to prepare some materials about how to maximise the safety of service users to share with the new employee.

Your materials could include:

1 An outline of the main ways you maximise health and safety for service users in your setting.

2 A completed risk assessment for a day out with a group of residents with an explanation of the importance of the risk assessment and why you have included some items on your assessment. You should also highlight where items on your risk assessment bring up conflicts between keeping service users safe and respecting their other rights.

Tips

You could relate this activity to a setting where you have done work experience, or somewhere you have done an observation visit.

You can draw your own risk assessment form based on the one shown earlier in the unit, or your teacher or tutor may supply a blank copy for you to use.

Take it further

Investigate the Management of Health and Safety at Work Regulations 1999. These cover the way previous legislation, for example the Health and Safety at Work Act 1974, should be implemented in the workplace.

How does the health and safety policy of a setting you have visited, or where you have completed a work placement, relate to the legislation?

Maintaining, storage and retrieval of information

Recording information

There is often a need to communicate information about service users between workers. Information must be checked and recorded accurately. Incorrect recording could be dangerous and lead to mistakes in care.

Storing and retrieving information

Not so long ago all information was stored on paper in filing cabinets. Although most health and care settings still record information on paper, much is now stored electronically online. Did you know that an EPR – electronic patient record – system is in place in many GP surgeries and hospitals? This records all the information about a patient's diagnosis and treatment.

Increasingly, people can make appointments, order repeat prescriptions and leave messages for their GP on the surgery's IT system via computer, smart phone or tablet.

A service user who has been issued with their own password can access some of the information that is stored electronically about them.

In order to make sure that these electronic records are not accessed by the wrong people, it is necessary to have secure passwords and networks over which to view the information.

Now that most people carry a smart phone, they are carrying the means to store and transmit data and photographs. It is important that people working in health and social care remember not to store information about service users on insecure devices. Since many people record their activities over social networking sites, it is also important to avoid sharing information about service users in such a public way.

Confidential information should not be shared over personal phones or tablets.

Confidentiality

Confidentiality is a main principle that protects the rights of individuals. It is part of the right to privacy and the right to dignity. Workers in health and social care have a duty of confidentiality – this means that when a service user gives personal information, it is expected that the information remains confidential.

The service user should always be asked if it is all right to let other people know information about them. The exception to this is that information can be passed to others who have a right and a need to know, for example other professionals involved in that service user's ongoing care.

Information should never be passed on to those who do not need it: for instance, friends or family members of the service user.

Health and care workers should never:

- discuss matters related to service users outside the care setting
- discuss a service user with colleagues in public where they may be overheard
- leave records unattended where they may be read by unauthorised people.

Maintaining confidentiality can also be a way of safeguarding service users. A service user may have a relative who has been abusive in the past. In a situation like this, even sharing basic information about someone's contact address can put them at risk of further abuse.

Key terms

Confidential – private; not available for general discussion or publication.

Remember

Information about service users is confidential, both legally and ethically.

What should you do if family members ask you for information about a service user?

Disclosing information

Key terms

Disclose – making something known that was previously unknown or confidential.

Ethical – morally right and decent; virtuous and honourable.

Data – this includes all information, whether it is facts, figures or images.

Introduction

Health and social care professionals will sometimes be asked to disclose information about people using your service. Sometimes they may want or need to share confidential information that a service user has shared with them.

There are legal and ethical reasons why information belonging to service users is confidential. It should not be used in a way that might identify a service user without their informed consent.

Disclosing information to service users

Service users are entitled to see information about themselves and their care. This is covered by the **Data** Protection Act 1998 and the Freedom of Information Act 2000.

Disclosing information to others

Information should never be shared about service users without their permission, unless it is directly part of their care or necessary to prevent harm to them or others. The type of information you can share and the circumstances under which you can do so are set out in the Data Protection Act 1998.

If it appears that information needs to be passed on it is important to first ask the individual for their agreement; it is wrong to pass on even birth dates or contact details without permission. It might be possible to agree a compromise where use or sharing of information is acceptable to the service user and the quality of care isn't compromised.

The Data Protection Act 1998

The Data Protection Act applies to all organisations that hold or process personal data. There are no exceptions.

The following provisions exist under the Data Protection Act 1998:

- Service users have a right to know what information is held about them and a right to access information about themselves.
- The Data Protection Act 1998 covers both paper and electronic records.
- Service users do have the right to refuse to provide information.
- Data held should be accurate and up to date; individuals have the right to correct wrong information about them.
- Data should not be kept longer than necessary.
- Information is confidential and should not be accessible to unauthorised people.
- Information must be kept secure.

Breaching a service user's confidence

Have you ever asked someone to keep a secret? Or promised that you would not tell?

Are there occasions when it is right to disclose something that has been told to you in confidence? Are there situations where it is not right to 'promise not to tell'?

Sometimes it is right and necessary to breach a confidence, despite confidentiality being an important right of individuals. An example of this is where it appears that a service user might harm themselves or others. Another example is if you know that someone is about to break, or has already broken, the law.

Activity   Breaching confidence

In groups of four or five consider the following points and decide the action that you should take. Discuss the possible advantages and disadvantages of your actions.

1 As a care worker at a training centre for young adults you are told by a service user with severe learning difficulties that she is going to have a baby. When you tell her that you must inform her key worker she bursts into tears, saying it should be kept secret.

2 Your best friend tells you that he would like to be a social care worker like you, but wants some more advice and insight. He knows that as a community care assistant you visit the Brown family on the street where he lives and he would like you to tell him all about them.

3 A nursery worker is asked by the father of one of the children for the child's address so that he can visit with a birthday present.

Assessment activity 8.3   2B.P4 | 2B.M3 | 2B.D3

You are a care worker in a residential home for older people. Following some examples in the media about breaches of confidentiality, your manager has decided that it is time to run a refresher course for all staff. As she knows you have studied this subject, she asks you to give a presentation.

The presentation should include a handout for the audience and cover the following:

1 Examples of recent breaches of confidentiality and the effect of these on the victims.

2 What the relevant laws mean for people working in health and social care, as well as the ethical reasons for maintaining confidentiality.

3 How to keep information private and confidential.

4 At least two examples of a time when you would need to breach a confidence.

Tips

This is a very tricky area and you should be aware of the implications for yourself, the service user and for your employer. Legislation does allow for breach of confidentiality in some circumstances, so you should research this to ensure you are acting in accordance with the law.

Introduction

Health and wellbeing are influenced by a range of biological and lifestyle factors. Some of the choices that you make can have a positive impact on your life. Eating healthily, for example, may have a short-term effect by making you feel good that you are helping yourself, but in the long term can help you better manage your weight and improve your general health. Other choices can have a negative effect, such as smoking and drinking. In this unit you will learn how a range of factors contribute to either good or poor health and wellbeing.

Helping people review and analyse their current health and wellbeing is an important part of many healthcare roles. The information gained can then be used to design and implement individual health-improvement plans. This unit will help you develop skills in analysing information and exploring strategies to improve health and wellbeing. It will also examine barriers and limitations that can influence the success of health improvement measures and how to help individuals overcome such barriers.

Assessment: You will be assessed by a paper-based examination lasting one hour.

Learning aims

In this unit you will:

A explore the factors that contribute to healthy and unhealthy lifestyles, and their effects on health and wellbeing

B explore ways of improving health and wellbeing.

I don't think people like being told to change their lifestyle, such as by exercising more. But a counsellor who came to talk to my group showed us that once people understand the effects their choices can have and that there are professionals who can help them, they are more likely to listen and make better choices. I'd like to help others like that.

Helen, *15-year-old would-be counsellor*

Healthy Living

9

Defining a healthy lifestyle

Introduction

If someone asks 'How are you?' you tend to say something vague, such as 'fine', because it is often too complicated to describe exactly. Health and wellbeing can change from day to day and from life stage to life stage. You will learn how to formally define health and wellbeing and understand its various aspects. Would you say you are healthy? How do you know?

Key terms

Physical – to do with the body.

Social – to do with interacting with other people.

Holistic – consideration of the whole – in this case, the whole person.

Intellectual – to do with the ability to understand things and think intelligently.

Emotional – to do with feelings.

Health and wellbeing

The World Health Organization (WHO) is an agency of the United Nations (UN) that coordinates international public health. It was established in 1948 and is based in Geneva, Switzerland. It defines health and wellbeing as 'a complete state of **physical**, mental and **social** wellbeing, and not merely the absence of disease or infirmity'. This **holistic** definition was agreed by all during the first World Health Assembly and has not changed since then. Therefore health and wellbeing may be regarded as a combination of physical, mental and social aspects of people's lives. Mental aspects are an integral part of health and wellbeing and refer to people's use of their **intellectual** and **emotional** abilities to function in society and meet the ordinary demands of everyday life.

Physical aspects

Physical aspects are the needs we have to keep our bodies working as well as they can. We all have different bodies, but the same basic needs, such as food, water, shelter, warmth, clothing, rest, exercise and good personal hygiene.

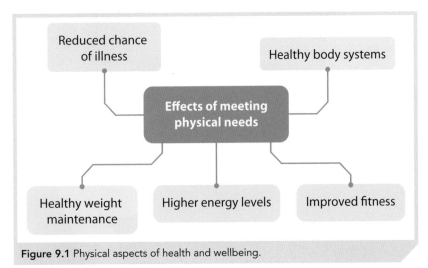

Figure 9.1 Physical aspects of health and wellbeing.

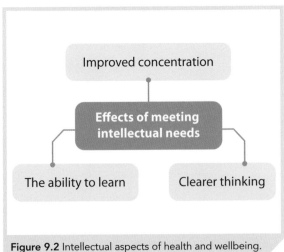

Figure 9.2 Intellectual aspects of health and wellbeing.

Intellectual aspects

Intellectual aspects are the needs we have to develop and think intelligently. They include mental stimulation to keep us motivated and interested, rather than bored, and the need to keep learning throughout our lives to keep our brains active.

Emotional aspects

Emotional aspects are those that make us feel happy and relaxed, such as being loved, respected and secure. We need to be able to feel, express and recognise different emotions in order to cope with different situations that arise throughout our lives.

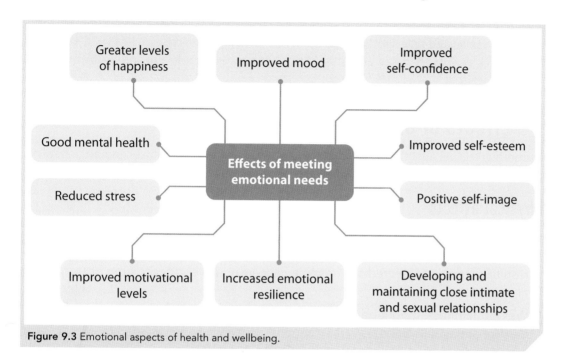

Greater levels of happiness

Improved mood

Improved self-confidence

Good mental health

Effects of meeting emotional needs

Improved self-esteem

Reduced stress

Positive self-image

Improved motivational levels

Increased emotional resilience

Developing and maintaining close intimate and sexual relationships

Figure 9.3 Emotional aspects of health and wellbeing.

Social aspects

Social aspects are those that enable us to develop and enjoy good relationships and friendships with others. Social needs include opportunities to mix with others in an appropriate environment and access to leisure facilities and activities.

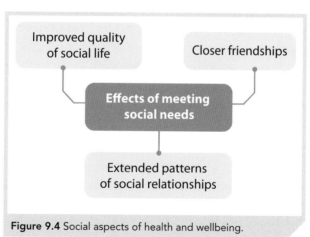

Improved quality of social life

Closer friendships

Effects of meeting social needs

Extended patterns of social relationships

Figure 9.4 Social aspects of health and wellbeing.

Why are outdoor activities with friends or with a club a good way of maintaining a healthy lifestyle?

Activity Physical, intellectual, emotional and social needs

Reflect on your own life. Think about your physical, intellectual, emotional and social needs (PIES).

1 Which are being met?
2 Which are not being met?
3 What effects are these having on your current health and wellbeing?
4 How do you think this may affect your health and wellbeing in the future?
5 Explain how one high profile athlete takes care so that his/her PIES are met.

Defining effects of an unhealthy lifestyle

Getting started

What do we mean by an unhealthy lifestyle?

With a partner discuss how someone with an unhealthy lifestyle might live.

Introduction

Your lifestyle is based on the choices you make about how you live, such as how you spend money, use leisure time, what you eat and whether/how you exercise. In this topic we move on to look at what effects an unhealthy lifestyle can have on our health and wellbeing.

Effects of an unhealthy lifestyle

Numerous factors affect how we feel at any point in our lives, but if we lead an unhealthy lifestyle it can have negative effects for us physically, intellectually, emotionally and socially.

Physical effects

- Disease and illness: we have no control over inherited conditions, but others can be caused by an unhealthy lifestyle, for example, sexually transmitted infections resulting from unprotected sex or some cancers and liver disease from obesity and alcohol abuse.

- Weight gain/loss: weight gain can make us more prone to illnesses such as heart disease and type 2 diabetes while eating less than we need can lead to weight loss and illnesses such as anaemia and stunted bone growth.

- Body fat composition: this is the percentage of body fat you carry. Someone who doesn't exercise will have more fat. Our bodies need some fat to regulate body temperature, cushion and insulate organs and tissues and store energy, however, too much can lead to health issues, such as those mentioned above.

- Short-term health problems: an unhealthy lifestyle can result in, for example, stress, which can produce faster breathing, heightened senses, tenser muscles, butterflies in the stomach and diarrhoea.

- Long-term health problems: for example stress for long periods of time can lead to conditions such as high blood pressure and nervous breakdowns; smoking can cause illnesses such as cancer, chronic bronchitis and emphysema.

Intellectual effects

- Reduced potential success in education: an unhealthy lifestyle can lead us to being ill more often and so having a poor attendance at school, or can lead to us eating a diet with insufficient vitamins and minerals for our brains to work well. For example, vitamin B6 is essential for our brains to develop properly and iron helps our brains function efficiently.

- Negative impact on long-term career prospects: illness, limited mobility or physical fitness and lack of educational success resulting from leading an unhealthy lifestyle can result in unemployment or only being able to get jobs with poor prospects.

- Inability to think clearly: having nowhere quiet and comfortable to study or feeling ill, whether from the after effects of, for example, alcohol and drug abuse, or from an illness such as a cold, prevents us concentrating effectively.

Emotional effects

- Lack of confidence: whether it is in your appearance, weight or behaviour.

- General feelings of unhappiness and worthlessness.

- Low self-esteem.

- Negative self-image.

- Feelings of stress and anxiety.

- Difficulties in developing and maintaining close, intimate and sexual relationships.

- Psychological dependence: this is an emotional need for a drug or substance or activity that has no underlying physical need. For example, people who stop smoking continually think they need the nicotine to stay calm, even though there is no physical need, so crave for a cigarette. Other examples include addiction to activities such as self-harming, gambling or shopping.

Social effects

- Loss of friends: people who lead unhealthy lifestyles may behave in ways that upset their friends, for example, people who behave aggressively or insultingly when drunk.

- Increased pressure on existing friendship groups: individuals may try to influence their friends to adopt their unhealthy choices, such as smoking.

- Negative impact on family relationships: family members may not approve of the lifestyle choices being made and feel that person adversely influences more vulnerable family members.

- Decreased levels of involvement in social activities: people who are ill may miss social opportunities; they may not be invited because of concern about their behaviour or hygiene or they may lack confidence to join in.

- Social isolation: someone living in, for example, poor housing conditions, may be too embarrassed to invite friends home so become more socially isolated.

- Increased potential for accidents, injury or criminal record: a person who becomes dependent on a substance, such as an illegal drug, may get hurt while under the influence and/or turn to crime to fund the habit and so end up with a criminal record.

Case study Lisa's lifestyle

Lisa is 16 years old and smokes a pack of cigarettes a day. She eats junk food at home and is continually snacking on chocolate and sweets at school.

1 Write 'Lisa' in the middle of a piece of A4 paper. In each of the four corners write one of the four types of effects discussed in this topic, i.e. physical, intellectual, emotional and social.

2 Think about each of the effects listed and note under the right heading how each might arise as a result of Lisa's smoking and diet problem.

Diet and exercise

Introduction

In the next few topics you will learn about the factors that contribute to healthy or unhealthy lifestyles and their effects. For each factor you will need to be able to make the link to physical, intellectual, emotional and social effects, including the general ones covered in the previous two topics and the more specific ones included under each featured lifestyle. In this topic we look at diet and exercise.

Diet and nutrition

A balanced diet is one that contains the correct **nutrients** in the right proportions to keep our bodies and minds healthy. The essential parts of a healthy diet, or food groups, are fats (saturated and unsaturated), carbohydrates (sugars and starches), proteins, vitamins, minerals, fibre and water.

The food we eat affects the way we feel and look, and is very important for our health, wellbeing and life opportunities. Although our dietary needs vary throughout life, what does not change is that if we eat more than we need it will get converted to fat by the liver and stored in our bodies. This can lead to obesity, and illnesses and conditions such as diabetes, coronary heart disease, high blood pressure, strokes and cancer. If we eat less than we need we can put ourselves at risk of heart failure, depression, anorexia, cancer and scurvy. Both over- and under-eating can result in premature death.

In addition, having the correct balance of vitamins and minerals is important. For example, our bodies cannot process calcium – essential for the maintenance of teeth and bones – if we do not have enough magnesium and we cannot absorb calcium without sufficient stores of vitamin D.

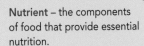

Key term

Nutrient – the components of food that provide essential nutrition.

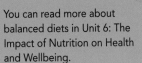

Link

You can read more about balanced diets in Unit 6: The Impact of Nutrition on Health and Wellbeing.

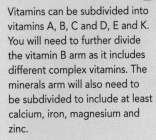

Take it further

Vitamins can be subdivided into vitamins A, B, C and D, E and K. You will need to further divide the vitamin B arm as it includes different complex vitamins. The minerals arm will also need to be subdivided to include at least calcium, iron, magnesium and zinc.

Activity   A balanced diet

Do some research to help you draw a mind map to show a balanced diet. This should have an arm for each food group, with sub-branches from each one showing:

- at least three foods from each food group
- why our bodies need the food group
- the recommended daily intake of that food group.

Following a balanced diet helps maintain a healthy weight and promotes higher energy levels. Reducing food intake and following a balanced diet will aid weight loss. It is not advisable to lose too much weight too quickly. Weight loss can be quite rapid at first as initially a lot of water is lost. A healthy weight loss to aim for after this initial stage is 0.5–1 kg (1–2 lbs) a week. This weight loss will be fat, and not water.

Exercise

Do you exercise on a regular basis?

Exercise improves our **strength**, **stamina** (or endurance) and **suppleness** (or flexibility) as well as our muscle and body tone. It also helps us maintain a healthy weight or lose weight, relieves stress, relaxes us, is enjoyable, makes us feel good, gives us a chance to meet others and gives us higher energy levels and personal satisfaction. Lack of exercise can lead to stiffening of the joints; poor stamina, strength and suppleness; obesity; coronary heart disease; respiratory conditions; osteoporosis and other conditions. Any of these mean our health and wellbeing suffer and we are less able to take life opportunities that come our way.

It is recommended that we are physically active every day. We should also take aerobic cardiovascular exercise between three and five times a week for a minimum of 20 minutes each time This type of exercise, which includes running, cycling and swimming, raises the heart rate for a prolonged period of time and improves fitness. There are appropriate levels of exercise for each life stage.

Key terms

Strength – the body's physical power.

Stamina – the heart's ability to work under strain.

Suppleness – the body's ability to bend without damage.

Activity Appropriate levels and types of exercise

Produce a PowerPoint® presentation showing an exercise plan you have devised that has the appropriate level and type of exercise for people of different life stages. Explain its likely physical, intellectual, emotional and social effects.

Exercise and diet can reduce Body Mass Index (BMI). This is a measure of the amount of fat in the body in relation to height. BMI is worked out using the formula:

$$BMI = \frac{\text{Weight in kg}}{(\text{Height in m})^2}$$

People with BMIs between 19 and 22 appear to live the longest. However, BMI has its limitations as it only takes into account weight and height and ignores the distribution of muscle and bone mass.

Table 9.1 BMI range.

BMI	Significance
Less than 18.5	Underweight
18.5–24.9	Normal
25–29.9	Overweight
30–39.9	Obese
40+	Morbidly obese

Home and work environments

Getting started

What is your dream home? Draw a quick floor plan showing what rooms you would like in your home. Note down what type of area you would like to live in and why.

Introduction

The next two factors which contribute to a healthy or unhealthy lifestyle are the home and work environments.

Home environment

Our home is where we spend most of our time. The following factors about our home affect our health and wellbeing:

- The type of home accommodation: in a semi-detached or terraced house occupants are more likely to be disturbed by noise from neighbours. This can cause arguments and affect concentration when studying or working.

  - The condition of the home environment: if a home is small, damp, dirty, cramped or cluttered, occupants are likely to be more prone to illness as lack of hygiene allows the growth and spread of pathogens and overcrowding causes infections and diseases to spread more quickly. Damp and mould can adversely affect respiratory conditions, such as asthma. There is also more chance of accidents and sleeplessness.

  - Location: town (urban) environments are more likely to be affected by pollution, including noise and light. Living in a high-rise flat with no garden and nowhere else for children to play outside can cause health and wellbeing to suffer. A detached house with a garden in the suburbs or countryside (rural) is likely to be quieter and provides an outdoor leisure environment. These factors can promote better sleep (physical), which is required for brain alertness (intellectual). A pleasant living environment tends to make people feel happier (emotional) and a healthy environment means people are less likely to fall ill and therefore able to enjoy an active social life (social). However, access to health and social care services can be more difficult in rural and isolated areas.

  - The amount of personal space: sharing a room with siblings means less privacy and less space for belongings, hobbies and school work. This can lead to disorganisation, demotivation and an inability to concentrate.

  - The influence of partners and family: the other people we live with affect us as they influence what we eat, how we dress, our moods and behaviour.

  - Level of conflict: living in poor housing conditions can cause conflict for many reasons, such as resentment, embarrassment, stress or living in close proximity to too many people.

What effect does your home environment have on your health?

Activity   Town or country?

Why might some people prefer to live in the town or city? Think about PIES.

Work environment

We also spend much of our adult lives in a work environment. The following factors at work affect our health and wellbeing:

- Manual/non-manual: manual work can be physically hard, but can aid physical fitness. It is generally less stressful and doesn't involve constant learning of new skills. Manual work can lead to accidents and injuries. Non-manual work can be sedentary and lead to loss of physical fitness. Responsibility and highly intellectual work can cause high levels of stress. People working in offices and with computers can develop eyesight and posture problems.

- Job satisfaction: routine jobs, both manual and non-manual can lead to boredom and dissatisfaction. Varied and stimulating work is much more enjoyable. High pay can also help towards job satisfaction.

- Career success: career progression with promotion and increased pay may lead to more confidence, self-esteem and happiness. The inability to earn sufficient money to make ends meet is extremely stressful.

- Mental stimulation: a stimulating job that provides opportunities to learn new skills keeps the mind active and alert and is generally more enjoyable than routine work.

- Support from colleagues and employers: we spend a lot of time with work colleagues so it is important to get on and be supportive of each other. Many people enjoy the social aspect of work and can form long-lasting friendships with colleagues. Employers that value employees and treat them with respect create a positive work environment.

- Work/life balance: demanding high-powered jobs are well paid but can also involve long working hours meaning less time to enjoy the benefits of the good salary. It is important to balance home and work. Remember we work to live, not live to work.

- Level of conflict: conflict, for example between employer and employee or a teacher and pupil, leads to stress and a lack of enjoyment in the job.

Would you like to work outdoors? What positive and negative effects can you think of?

Activity — Jobs and health

Divide into groups, each of which takes one of the following job roles: prison officer, plumber, teacher, refuse collector, a member of the armed forces, doctor, bricklayer, care assistant. On a large piece of paper, identify how the job may affect all aspects of the person's health and wellbeing.

Alcohol and smoking

Getting started

What do you think when you see groups of drunk people shouting loudly and swearing in the street? What do you think are the possible consequences of binge drinking?

Introduction

Another two factors that affect health and wellbeing are alcohol consumption and smoking.

Alcohol consumption

The drinking of alcohol is a socially accepted part of some cultures. In moderation it is both pleasurable and, in middle and later life, may be beneficial to health. However, it can also be addictive and excessive drinking causes many illnesses and problems.

Safe and unsafe drinking patterns

The Department of Health recommended weekly limits for alcohol consumption are:

- Men: no more than 21 units of alcohol per week, no more than four units in any one day, at least two alcohol-free days a week.
- Women: no more than 14 units of alcohol per week, no more than three units in any one day, at least two alcohol-free days a week.
- Pregnant women: pregnant women or women trying to conceive are advised not to drink alcohol at all. If they do drink, to minimise the risk of harm to the baby, they should not drink more than one or two units of alcohol once or twice a week and should not get drunk.

These guidelines can only be used as a rough guide, as different brands of the same drink can have different strengths, but even so, if they are exceeded regularly there is an increased risk to health. Smaller people, dehydrated people, women (because of their size and having more fat on their bodies), hungry people and less regular drinkers will find that alcohol affects them more. Parents are important role models, as their drinking habits tend to be followed by their children.

Underage drinking, due to peer pressure, the low prices and easy availability of alcohol, including from those parents who buy it for their underage children, contributes to alcohol-related problems.

Binge drinking among the young is a growing concern in the UK. The NHS definition of binge drinking is drinking heavily in a short space of time to get drunk or feel the effects of alcohol. The amount of alcohol this involves is less clearly defined, but both the NHS and National Office for Statistics suggest it is more than double the daily unit guidelines in one session. Binge drinking can result in vomiting, loss of sensory perception and blackouts.

Why do these friends find it harder to avoid binge drinking in a social environment?

Alcoholism is a disease. Binge drinking and alcohol abuse can develop into alcohol dependence when drinkers experience a craving for alcohol, a loss of control of their drinking, withdrawal symptoms when they are not drinking and an increased tolerance to alcohol so that they have to drink more to achieve the same effect. **Alcohol dependence** is a chronic and often progressive disease that includes a strong need to drink, despite repeated problems, and can result in death.

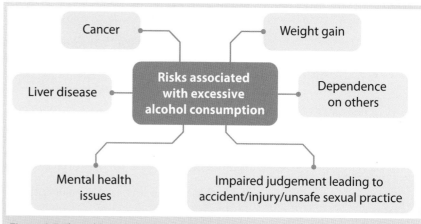

Figure 9.5 The risks associated with excessive alcohol consumption.

Smoking

Tobacco smoking, usually in cigarettes, is legal and more socially acceptable than the taking of other drugs. However, it is addictive and a major cause of ill health, preventable disease and death. All smoking material packaging and adverts now carry a government health warning.

Activity   How alcohol and tobacco affect the body

1 Draw the outline of a person showing the major organs in the middle of a large sheet of paper. Do some research into the short- and long-term risks to the body of:

   a) alcohol (there are many more than the ones listed in this topic)

   b) smoking.

   Label the drawing with the risks shown next to the part of the body likely to be affected. Label those for alcohol in one colour and smoking in another.

2 Describe how alcohol may affect health and wellbeing.

3 Do some research into the causes of smoking, and how the quantity smoked and the pattern of smoking affects health and wellbeing. Use the information to produce an information leaflet or poster.

Many smokers would like to give up, especially now that smoking is banned in public places. If you do stop smoking the body begins to repair the damage done quite quickly. The benefits include:

- risk of smoking-related diseases (e.g. cancer, emphysema, heart disease and bronchitis) is reduced
- blood pressure returns to normal
- breathing is improved
- the body is better able to cope with sudden exertion
- loss of smoker's cough with less phlegm being produced
- better personal hygiene
- improved sense of smell and taste
- sense of achievement
- saving money.

However, it is not easy to stop and requires a high level of motivation. There is a range of organisations dedicated to helping people give up, such as ASH, QUIT, GASP and the NHS Stop Smoking services.

 Key term

Alcohol dependence – anxiety and depression caused by alcohol can cause people to rely more on others as they may lose their jobs and develop financial and/or relationship problems/ mental health issues.

Recreational drug use, sexual practices, personal hygiene and sleep patterns

Introduction

Recreational drug use, sexual practices, personal hygiene and the quality of our sleep are another four factors which affect whether we have a healthy or unhealthy lifestyle.

Recreational drug use

Major concerns with recreational drug use are:

- increasing the levels of consumption as addiction takes hold
- the unknown composition of the drugs being sold illegally
- the trend of experimenting with drugs at a younger age because of the ill effects they have on developing brains causing potential mental health problems.

Physical effects of drugs include accidental death, illness and disease, and impaired judgement leading to accident/injury/unsafe sexual practice. The main emotional and social effects are dependence and mental health problems.

Activity   Drug use

Divide into groups, each of which picks one recreational drug to research.
Find out its short- and long-term effects and how it affects a user's health and wellbeing. Sum up the main points on an A4 poster that can be displayed in your classroom.

Safe and unsafe sexual practices

Two people can develop and maintain a sexual relationship, which can be both healthy and emotionally fulfilling. Safe sexual practices include the use of contraception and participation in sexual health screening.

However, sexual intercourse without the use of any contraception may result in an unwanted pregnancy and the contraction and spreading of a sexually transmitted infection (STI), both of which will affect the health and wellbeing of the persons involved. The contraction and spread of STIs, which include chlamydia, gonorrhoea, HIV/AIDS and herpes, can be greatly reduced with the use of barrier contraception. In the long term STIs can cause infertility, mental illness and even death. For this reason it is very important that if you find that you have an STI (or health status such as HIV) you must inform sexual partners, including previous sexual partners, to prevent it spreading further. The more sexual partners you have unprotected sex with, the greater the likelihood of contracting an STI.

Hygiene

Poor personal hygiene is not only unpleasant but it can affect your health and wellbeing. The main physical effects are contracting and spreading disease, especially to vulnerable groups, such as babies and older people. The emotional and social effects include loss of friends, social isolation, bullying and unemployment.

Why is it so important to ensure good personal hygiene after exercise?

Sleep patterns

Sleep is essential for health and wellbeing. The quality of your sleep affects the quality of your waking life, including your physical energy and your weight, intellectual sharpness, emotional balance and ability to mix socially. While you sleep your brain stays busy, overseeing a wide variety of biological maintenance tasks that prepare you for the day ahead.

Most healthy adults need between 7.5 and 9 hours of sleep per night to function at their best. Children and young people need more than this. Elderly people still need at least 7.5 to 8 hours of sleep. However it is not just the number of hours of sleep that is important, it is the quality of those hours.

Activity   Sleep

In groups research the following:

- the sleep cycle
- how shift work and stress affect sleep
- the short- and long-term effects of not getting enough sleep.

Make sure you present the information in an as interesting and different way as possible to the rest of the class.

Influences on adopting healthy and unhealthy lifestyles

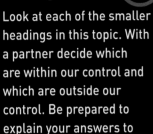

Getting started

Look at each of the smaller headings in this topic. With a partner decide which are within our control and which are outside our control. Be prepared to explain your answers to the rest of the class.

Introduction

There is a range of influences and factors outside our control that can affect lifestyle choices.

Factors

Partners and family

The ways our families and partners choose to live their lives can influence our own lifestyle choices. We may visit the dentist regularly, smoke, believe in a god, eat a certain type of diet, drink alcohol and so on, all because we are following the lifestyle choices of our parents, carers and partners.

Culture and religion

Our **culture** and religion influence the way we think, the food we eat, the people we mix with, how we spend our leisure time and our health and social care practices.

Link

You can read more about culture and religion in Unit 7: Equality and Diversity in Health and Social Care.

Peer group pressure

We are most influenced by our **peer group** when we are in our adolescence, when as teenagers we become less dependent on family for emotional support and turn to our friends for advice. Young people want to be accepted by their friends and this can sometimes lead to them behaving or dressing differently, taking up smoking or drinking, experimenting with sexual behaviour and changing attitudes towards education, because their friends do, even if they don't really want to. Peer pressure can cause problems because it can challenge many of the ideas learned from families.

Key terms

Culture – the shared beliefs, values and customs of a group of people.

Peer group – the social group a person belongs to which influences beliefs and behaviour.

Role models

We learn our roles through socialisation, which includes learning attitudes, behaviours and skills from role models. From about the age of 8 we start to choose who we will imitate instead of just copying those in our immediate surroundings. Therefore it is important that we have good role models.

Media influence

We are exposed to many more different forms of media than previous generations and this affects our ideas and how we think we should behave. For example, whether we have children vaccinated, what we eat, wear, drink, etc.

Link

You can read more about role models in Unit 4: Social Influences on Health and Wellbeing.

Self-esteem levels

Self-esteem is about how you value yourself and levels can vary throughout your life. If you have a high self-esteem you will be more confident and more likely to rise to challenges, seize opportunities and be successful.

Education and understanding

Educational successes increase our self-esteem levels by making us feel good about ourselves and giving us more choice of career and employment prospects. Education and understanding can make us challenge our existing values and give us the opportunity to explore new ideas and learn new skills.

Personal and family finances

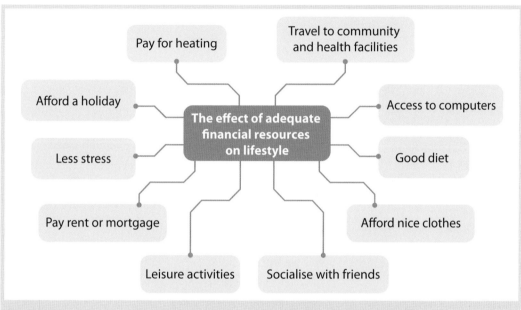

Figure 9.6 How does money make life easier? How might it sometimes make it harder?

Genetic inheritance (including predisposition)

Our genes carry the code for all aspects of our physical being and these are inherited from our parents. Sometimes genes are faulty code for disease or disability. This is why some diseases or conditions are inherited, i.e. passed from one generation to another.

Mental health and illness

Mental health covers a range of conditions including depression, anxiety, obsessive compulsive disorder, phobias, bipolar disorder and eating disorders. Mental illness can be genetic or brought on by stress, relationship breakdown, substance abuse, social isolation and economic deprivation. About one person in four in the UK will suffer from a mental health problem at some point in life yet there is still a lot of prejudice and fear associated with it. However, many conditions can be controlled by prescribed drugs or therapies, such as counselling. It is always important to seek help.

 Key term

Predisposition – a tendency to suffer from a particular condition, hold a particular attitude, or act in a particular way.

Activity   Influences

Working with a partner, pick a character from your favourite soap opera, or a famous person you know a lot about, and describe how that person's lifestyle may have been influenced by each of the ten factors listed in this topic. Present your findings in the form of an interview, where one of you plays the role of the character or person, and the other interviews you for a show such as 'This Morning'. Be ready to show this to the rest of the class if required.

Explore the factors that contribute to healthy and unhealthy lifestyles, and their effects on health and wellbeing

Introduction

On this page you will be given some questions to test what you have learned so far. Remember PIES! You will then try a practice exam question, and you need to look at how many marks each part is worth so that you know how many points you need to make in your answer.

Just checking

1 How does the World Health Organization define health and wellbeing?

2 Give three (i) physical (ii) intellectual (iii) emotional (iv) social effects of an unhealthy lifestyle.

3 How does diet affect us if we (i) eat more than we need (ii) eat less than we need?

4 Why is it important to take into account a person's age when designing an exercise plan for them?

5 How might the home a person lives in affect their existing health?

6 What effect does a good work/life balance have on a person's health and wellbeing?

7 How will binge drinking affect a person's health and wellbeing in the (i) short (ii) long term?

8 Identify three possible effects of (i) smoking (ii) taking recreational drugs (iii) having unprotected sex (iv) having poor personal hygiene (v) not having enough sleep.

9 How might (i) partners and family members (ii) culture and religion influence a person's lifestyle choices?

10 During which life stage does peer pressure have the most influence on us? Why is this?

11 How (i) do role models (ii) does the media influence the way we live?

12 Describe three ways having (i) a high self-esteem (ii) a good level of education and understanding (iii) sufficient personal and family finances influences a person's lifestyle.

13 Explain how poor mental health and illness might affect a person's (i) lifestyle choices (ii) health and wellbeing.

Assessment practice 9.1

Simon is 14 years old and lives with his mum and her boyfriend. He sees his father regularly, but doesn't get on with his dad's new partner. He has no siblings, but has a group of friends who all like the same hip hop and R & B music. They spend their leisure time eating junk food and listening to music. He does not smoke or drink alcohol. At school he is studying GCSEs in Maths, English, Double Science, Humanities and BTEC Health and Social Care. He wants to join the police so he can work with people.

1 Identify two each of Simon's social and emotional needs. (4 marks)

2 Explain how Simon's lifestyle choices are having a positive effect on his emotional and social wellbeing. (6 marks)

3 Explain how Simon's unhealthy diet might affect his health and wellbeing. (4 marks)

4 Describe three ways in which Simon's lifestyle choices may have been influenced by the media. (6 marks)

Tips:

- Remember to make sure that you answer the questions set.
- A list will be good enough to get the marks for a question that asks you to 'identify' or 'state' something.
- For 'explain' and 'describe' questions you will need to write in more depth, using full sentences and paragraphs.
- Make sure you do exactly what the question asks. If you are asked to give examples, for instance, you must give them to get the marks. Do not miss them out.
- Reread your answers at the end to make sure that you have completed all parts of the question and answered in a way that makes sense.

WorkSpace

Kirsty Steward

Operating theatre nurse

When I am in theatre I work as part of a team with consultants, anaesthetists and other theatre staff. Shortly before the operation patients come to the hospital for a pre-operative assessment, where a team of nurses do tasks such as calculate their BMI, do an ECG, take blood and urine samples and swabs from certain areas of the body. This ensures the patient is healthy and infection-free, so able to have the operation. I provide information about the operations and answer the patients' questions. If they have any issue which requires extra attention, such as asthma, or a larger BMI, they may also see the anaesthetist.

On the day of their operation a hospital porter delivers them to the room next to the operating theatre to be prepared for surgery. I reassure them while helping the anaesthetist to prepare and administer either a local or general anaesthetic. If they are awake during the surgery I speak to them frequently, to make sure they are comfortable and to keep them calm. I also work alongside the surgeon, providing instruments, needles, swabs and other materials as required. Another important part of my job is to keep track of surgical instruments, equipment and swabs throughout the surgical procedure to make sure that none are left inside the patient. After the operation I take patients to the recovery ward next door, where I monitor the patient's health and provide appropriate care and treatment until the patient has recovered from the effects of the anaesthesia and/or surgery and is stable enough to be taken back to a surgical ward. I love my job because I enjoy working as part of a team to help improve people's lives and I get great job satisfaction from knowing I have made them feel less frightened and looked after them as safely as possible.

Think about it

1. Why are interpersonal skills so important to Kirsty's job?

2. What needs does Kirsty set out to meet for her patients and how does she improve their health and wellbeing?

3. How does a person's lifestyle affect whether they can have the operation or not?

4. Would you have the interpersonal skills to be one of the nurses who does the tests on the patients, including weighing people who are overweight and embarrassed? What might you need to do to improve your skills?

Identify areas for improvement and assess difficulties

Introduction

In the following topics you will be exploring ways to improve health and wellbeing. The first stages, covered in this topic, are to identify areas for potential improvement and to draw up a health improvement plan to help a person change their lifestyle.

Identify potential improvements

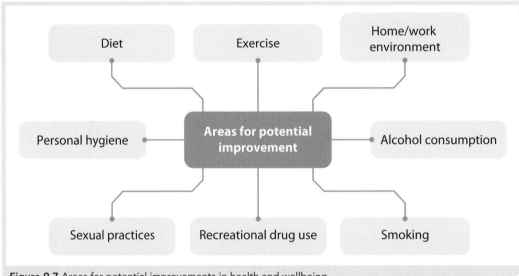

Figure 9.7 Areas for potential improvements in health and wellbeing.

Implementation

A health improvement plan should start by stating the problems to be tackled. It needs **targets** and should indicate what needs to be done to meet each target, people and resources required and an idea of costs. An idea of alternative options can also be included.

The plan then needs to be carried out and targets monitored. This could be by a practitioner, the person following the plan or a support group. For instance in a plan to improve diet, monitoring could involve recording everything eaten and drunk each day.

Assess and overcome difficulties

Before a person starts to follow a health improvement plan it is important to assess the difficulties that might be encountered in starting and keeping to the plan and looking for ways to overcome these difficulties. In order to get started and then successfully follow the plan it needs:

- realistic **goals** and targets (see next topic)
- support: for example, if a person is going on a diet they might ask their family to support them by following the same eating plan

Key terms

Targets – short- and longer-term challenges to help you meet your goal.

Goals – what you want to achieve in the long term; the final outcome.

- access to professional advice: the plan should include how to access professional support, such as joining a support group or seeing a doctor or counsellor (see next topic)

- a time commitment: this might mean setting regular time aside, for instance to exercise

- balance: for example, between exercise and home life and work commitments. This may mean rescheduling various aspects of someone's life, or getting up half an hour earlier in order to fit everything in

- identifying and managing potential difficulties: for example, reducing alcohol consumption on a special occasion, such as Christmas, is harder because there is more temptation. In this instance the person could offer to be the designated driver over Christmas so they are not tempted to drink when out at parties

- motivation to begin: as well as being aware of the likely benefits to their health and wellbeing it can be helpful to identify an optimum time to start. This might be at natural beginning times such as the new year or the start of the academic year, or, the lead-up to an event, such as a wedding or a holiday

- motivation to stick to the plan: reminders of the benefits, compliments and rewards are all effective motivators when the initial interest begins to fall

- pushing through difficult times: support and encouragement from others – family members, practitioners, interest groups and so on can help here. For instance, when a dieter stops losing weight a slimming club can provide vital support.

Case study   Changing Becky's routine

Becky is overweight and needs not only to be slimmer, but also to get more exercise. She is 36 and has two young children and a husband who seem to be able to eat whatever they want. She is a primary school teacher so has to do a lot of preparation work in the evenings and is often tired before she starts. She motivates herself every night by thinking about the glass or two of red wine and packet of chocolate buttons she will have as a treat when she has finished. She often goes to bed around midnight and gets up at 6.30 so feels tired all the time.

1 Assess the difficulties Becky will face if she tries to go on a diet and sleep and exercise more.

2 Identify what needs to be put in place to help her start and keep to a diet, sleep and exercise plan.

Setting realistic targets

Getting started ➡️

If your teacher told you that you have a year to do a piece of health and social care coursework and only gave you the title and no other guidance what is likely to happen? You might spend quite a long time working out how to do it, but not really start doing the coursework until the end of the year suddenly arrives. How would it help you to break the task down into smaller chunks, with deadlines for each part and guidelines on how to tackle each task?

Introduction

When drawing up a plan to improve health and wellbeing it is important to include targets not only to motivate the person following the plan but also so progress can be monitored. In this topic you will learn how to set realistic targets.

Targets

SMART targets

Targets must be:

- Specific – the target must be clearly stated, saying exactly what is meant, such as walk for 20 minutes a day for one week. This is clear and cannot be misunderstood or used as an excuse.
- Measurable – it is too vague to say do more exercise, an amount must be stated, so you can prove that you have met the target.
- Achievable – the person must feel it is possible to achieve the target set otherwise they will give up. Asking someone to exercise for 4 hours a day is not achievable but 20 minutes a day is reasonable.
- Realistic – the target set must be realistic; the person must be able to do it. It is unrealistic to expect someone who is older and not very fit to run for 30 minutes a day, but it is realistic to ask the same of a fit younger person.
- Time-related – there should be a deadline set by which to reach a target so that progress can be assessed.

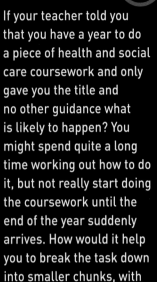

Figure 9.8 Are all your targets SMART?

Short-, medium- and long-term targets

It is important that a plan includes short-term targets, such as to lose 1 kilogram in the first week. This is easy to think of doing, as it is only a short time and not a major thing to achieve. The medium-term target might be to lose 5 kilograms in six months, and the long-term target to lose 10 kilograms in one year. By breaking down the path to the final goal into these smaller steps (short-term targets) the task seems less daunting and there is no excuse not to start that week.

Review

Setting SMART targets makes it possible to monitor progress regularly and amend the plan if necessary to meet the longer-term targets and goals. Designing a plan can be difficult because you are asking someone to change something about their lifestyle, something they may have often enjoyed doing.

People may not manage to change straight away so might fail to reach a particular target or their final goal. In this case it will be necessary to review the targets and possibly even start all over again. If a target is not being met you need to assess if it is realistic and it is sometimes necessary to see if a different target will improve the chance of success. This may happen several times until someone succeeds in making the lifestyle change permanent; for example, someone who is overweight might start many diets before they manage to get to, and stay at, their goal weight.

Activity	SMART targets

Set a SMART target for the first week for each of these three people:

- An 18-year-old male with a poor diet (eats junk food), who does not exercise and is obese.
- A 30-year-old female with a poor home environment (cramped and untidy) and poor work environment (noisy open plan office, lots of gossip, cannot concentrate and gets headaches) who smokes 30 cigarettes a day and has a problem with personal hygiene (body odour).
- A 24-year-old female who drinks 30 units of alcohol a week, uses cocaine once or twice a week and has unprotected sex with about two partners a month.

Intervention strategies and their effect on health improvement

These include:

- healthy lifestyle plans. Features of a good plan are:
  - a statement giving the problem to be tackled, based on the assessment of present health status through the use of physical measures of health and wellbeing and the factors that affect this
  - SMART targets
  - short- and long-term targets
  - statements of the benefits of meeting the targets
  - strategies to meet the targets, including health promotion materials
  - alternative strategies to overcome any difficulties that may arise
  - regular monitoring and reviewing of targets.
- strategies to maintain improvement in health and wellbeing
- support strategies (hypnotherapy, acupuncture)
- techniques to stop smoking, reduce alcohol consumption and recreational drug use such as face-to-face support and nicotine replacement therapy.

Activity	Planning lifestyle improvements

In groups, each pick a different health issue from Figure 9.7 in the previous topic. Research and produce an interesting handout, using clear headings, bullet points, up-to-date facts and diagrams, for the rest of the class on the current support strategies and techniques that will help a person make improvements in this area.

Support available and barriers to success

Introduction

We have already said that support is necessary to help people to have a healthy lifestyle. In this topic you will learn about the types and sources of support available.

Forms of support

Support can take the form of listening, **empathy**, encouragement or advice and guidance. People following a health improvement plan need support in maintaining a positive change, in keeping to the plan and maintaining a positive outlook. This support can be either formal or informal.

Formal support

This is provided by someone who is trained to give support.

Because these people have wide experience of dealing with particular situations they can offer sound advice and pass on useful information. They have a lot more knowledge and expertise than most family and friends. They also know of other sources of support, which they can readily refer people to if needed, and it is often easier to discuss difficult issues with a person who is not a family member or friend.

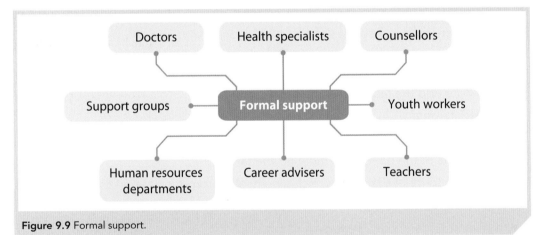

Figure 9.9 Formal support.

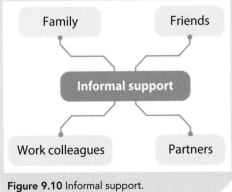

Figure 9.10 Informal support.

Informal support

This is provided by those who are not paid to give it such as family, friends, partners and work colleagues.

These people offer support because they care about the person and also usually feel a responsibility to do so.

Barriers

There are many limitations which prevent people being able to achieve a healthy lifestyle. These are outlined in Figure 9.11.

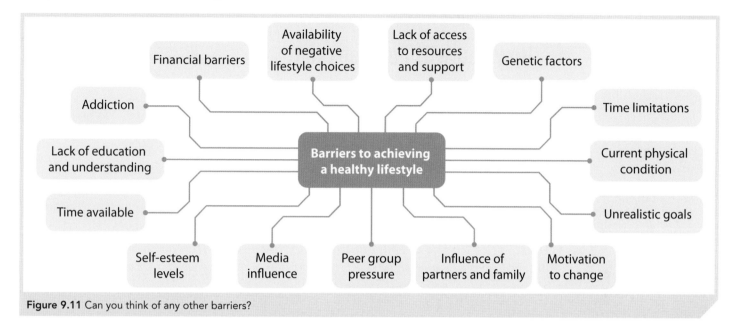

Figure 9.11 Can you think of any other barriers?

Just checking

1 Identify five areas for potential improvement in unhealthy lifestyles.

2 Identify three difficulties that may need to be resolved before starting a health improvement plan.

3 Identify the three stages in following a health plan where a person may particularly need motivation.

4 Explain what is meant by a SMART target.

5 List the main features of a good health improvement plan.

6 Identify three forms of support.

7 Explain why a youth worker gives formal support and a friend gives informal support.

8 Identify and explain three limitations on a person trying to follow a health improvement plan.

Assessment practice 9.2

Shama is 23 years old and single. She binge drinks at the weekend, but doesn't drink during the week. When she drinks she smokes and occasionally has unprotected sex, which she always regrets the next day. She works as a care assistant in a residential care home for young people with special needs and lives with her parents.

1 Identify three factors Shama needs to change to live a healthier lifestyle. (3 marks)

2 Identify and explain one source of support Shama could use to help her achieve a healthier lifestyle. (3 marks)

3 Explain the difference between formal and informal support. (2 marks)

4 Explain three barriers that Shama may face in trying to improve her lifestyle. (6 marks)

Tips

* Make sure that you answer all parts of the questions set, e.g. in question 2 you have to identify *and* explain.
* Write in more depth, using full sentences and paragraphs, for questions that use command words such as 'explain' or 'assess'.
* Check the marks available to make sure you have made enough separate points in your answers.

How you will be assessed

What you need to know about the examination

There are a number of key things you need to be aware of:

- The examination is 60 minutes long and there is a maximum mark of 50.
- Remember to read the questions, think about them, plan your answers, write your answers and check what you have written.
- There will be a range of questions on the paper – short multiple-choice-type questions, short answer questions and some longer questions. There may even be a calculation.
- There will be a range of different command words used in the questions, such as identify, describe, explain, assess and discuss. Make sure you know what they are asking you to do as some of them earn more marks than others.

How to approach answering the examination paper

You need to revise everything in this unit, including the areas where you have been set tasks to do some research, as not all the information you need would fit in this book. Your teacher/tutor is likely to give you some practice questions to complete and a mock/practice paper to complete. This is a good way to practise your examination technique and how to use your time well. This will mean that you are well prepared to sit the question paper.

When you open the paper it is a good idea to remember the following:

- Quickly look through the whole paper to see what it looks like. Be careful not to turn over two pages together and miss a whole question, and check the last page so you don't miss any questions. This will calm you down, as you will know what is coming. It will also help you plan how to use the 60 minutes you have to get the best results. Some people rush their answers and sit for 30 minutes doing very little, thinking they have finished, when they could have written better answers. Some people spend too long on the first part of the paper and never reach the end, losing out on many marks. Plan what time you want to start the second half of the paper and space your time evenly.
- There will be one long question at the end of the paper. Even if it looks hard, you will need to attempt it, especially if you are hoping to do well in the exam.

How to approach answering questions

You will be given some background information on which the questions are based. It is important that you read this very carefully and refer to it as you answer the questions.

Look at the sample and the practice questions that follow. At the end are some tips on how to answer each section well.

Background information

Shaun is 45 years old. He works hard in a job he enjoys to be able to give his wife and three children a nice home and standard of living. Shaun spends Saturday watching television and on Sundays he likes to take his family out for lunch and watch more television and drink a few cans of beer. He meets up with his friends in the pub once a week for the pub quiz and a few drinks. His wife is worried because Shaun is overweight so he has agreed to try to lose weight with her support. He is 2.0 m tall, weighs 125 kg and wants to lose 30 kg in the next year.

BMI	Significance
Less than 18.5	Underweight
18.5–24.9	Normal
25–29.9	Overweight
30–39.9	Obese
40+	Morbidly obese

(a) Calculate Shaun's Body Mass Index using the formula

BMI= (weight in kg)/(height in m)^2

Show your working out.

BMI =_____kg/m^2 **(2 marks)**

The examiners expect you to show your working out. You will get one mark for getting the numbers in the right place i.e. 125/(2.0 x 2.0) and another mark for the correct answer, 31.25.

(b) What does Shaun's BMI tell you about him? (1 mark)

Identifying Shaun as obese gets you the mark for part b.

(c) Explain two ways in which drinking too much alcohol could affect Shaun's health and wellbeing. (4 marks)

You need to identify two ways in which alcohol affects Shaun's health and wellbeing to get one mark for each and explain each to get the other two marks. For example, saying it will affect his concentration gets you one mark and explaining how that will lead to him doing less well at work gets you the other mark.

(d) Assess how successful you think Shaun will be at losing weight, including discussing some strategies he could use to try to do this. (8 marks)

This type of question will be worth the most marks on the paper. To gain really good marks you will need to be able to consider things from different points of view. You need to discuss the positives in Shaun's life, such as the support he will get from his wife and family, and strategies that will be available, like joining a slimming club, as well as identify barriers that will stop him succeeding, such as drinking with his friends at the pub quiz. You need to finish the answer with your overall conclusion as to whether you think he will be able to do this.

You will need to write in full sentences and use paragraphs to structure your written answer.

Disclaimer: These practice questions and sample answers are not actual exam questions and have been provided as a practice aide only. They should be used as practice material only and should not be assumed to reflect the format or coverage of the Edexcel external test.
Answers can be found on page 366.

Introduction

How often do you stop to think about how your body works? Probably not very often. In healthy people, the body's systems work together to maintain its function, so they don't normally give us cause to think about them very often.

This unit will give you the opportunity to study the human body, how it is made up and what it does. In the first part of the unit, you will learn about the structure and function of body organs and systems, and in the second part, you will learn about disorders that can affect the body, and about routine health checks and care that health and social care workers can give to their service users.

Assessment: You will be assessed by a series of assignments set by your teacher/tutor.

Learning aims

In this unit you will:

A understand the structure and function of main organs and major body systems, and their interrelationships

B explore routine care of disorders relating to body systems

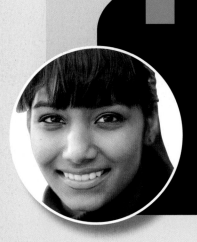

Learning about the human body has been really interesting. I know none of us really thinks much about how we do the things we do, but it has been great finding out much more about it and about how people are cared for when they have something wrong with them.

Sharmeen, *16-year-old, Health and Social Care learner*

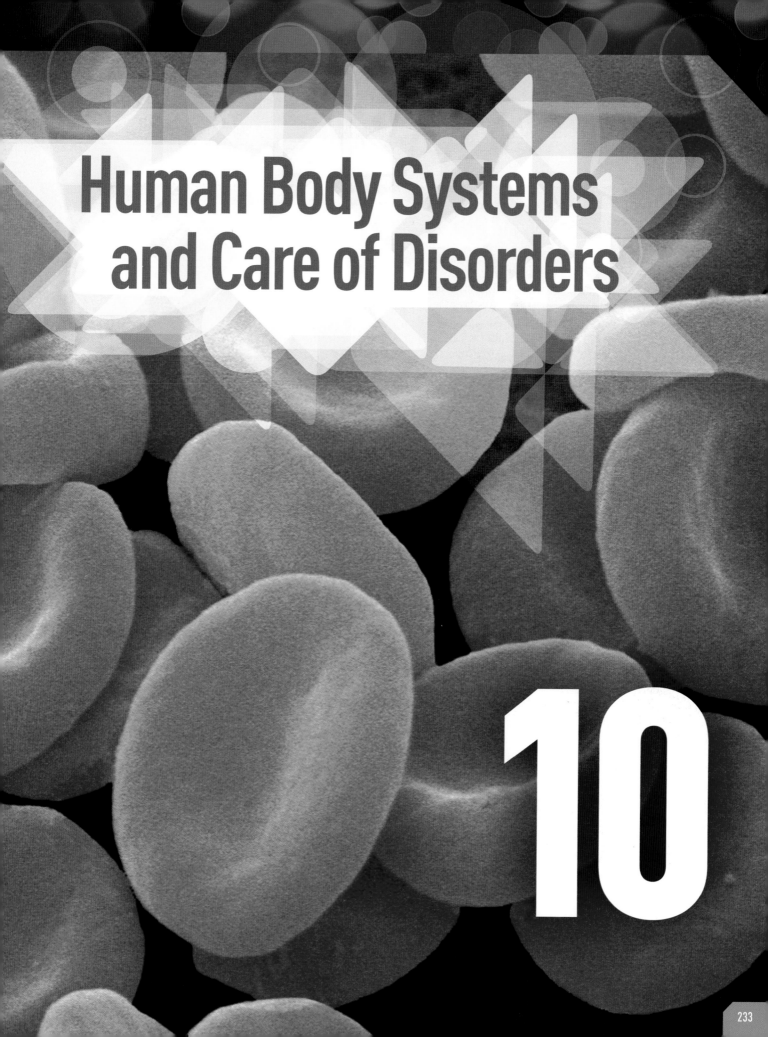

Human Body Systems and Care of Disorders

10

BTEC
Assessment Zone

This table shows what you must do in order to achieve a **Pass**, **Merit** or **Distinction** grade, and where you can find activities in this book to help you.

Assessment criteria			
Level 1	**Level 2 Pass**	**Level 2 Merit**	**Level 2 Distinction**
Learning aim A: Understand the structure and function of main organs and major body systems, and their interrelationships			
1A.1 Identify the structure and function of three main organs in the human body.	**2A.P1** Describe the structure and function of the main organs in the human body. **Assessment activity 10.1** See page 237		
1A.2 Identify the structure of one major body system.	**2A.P2** Describe the structure of major systems in the human body. **Assessment activity 10.2** See page 257		
1A.3 State the function of one major body system.	**2A.P3** Describe the functions of major systems in the human body. **Assessment activity 10.2** See page 257	**2A.M1** Explain the function of component parts of one major system in the human body. **Assessment activity 10.2** See page 257	
1A.4 Outline the relationship between three of the major body systems.	**2A.P4** Describe the relationship between major body systems. **Assessment activity 10.2** See page 257	**2A.M2** Explain how two major body systems interrelate. **Assessment activity 10.2** See page 257	**2A.D1** Analyse how body systems interrelate to maintain one example of homeostasis in the human body. **Assessment activity 10.2** See page 257
Learning aim B: Explore routine care of disorders relating to body systems			
1B.5 State one common disorder related to each of three selected major body systems.	**2B.P5** Describe one common disorder related to each major body system. **Assessment activity 10.3** See page 271	**2B.M3** Explain in detail the effects of three common disorders on the major body systems. **Assessment activity 10.3** See page 271	
1B.6 Identify the routine care given for one common disorder for each of three selected major body systems.	**2B.P6** Describe the routine care given for one common disorder related to each major body system. **Assessment activity 10.4** See page 279	**2B.M4** Discuss the impact of routine care given to individuals, with reference to a selected example. **Assessment activity 10.4** See page 279	**2B.D2** Recommend and justify appropriate routine care for a selected individual with a common disorder. **Assessment activity 10.4** See page 279

Assessment criteria			
Level 1	Level 2 Pass	Level 2 Merit	Level 2 Distinction
1B.7	**2B.P7**		
Carry out and record over a period of time one routine observation that can be used to support care.	Carry out and record over a period of time one routine observation that can be used to support care, interpreting your results in relation to norm values. **Assessment activity 10.4** **See page 279**		

How you will be assessed

The unit will be assessed by a series of internally assessed tasks. You will be expected to show an understanding of the structure and function of the human body and how routine care is given for common disorders. For example, your teacher/tutor could ask you to provide an electronic learning aid about human body systems, or common disorders, to be used in your school or college.

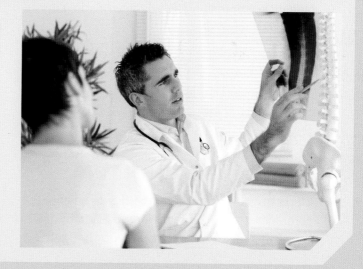

Structure and function of main organs and major body systems and their interrelationships

Getting started ⏩

With a partner, list as many different body organs as you can. Then draw an outline of a body and try to position the organs accurately on it.

Introduction

How much have you thought about how your body works? It is made up of organs and structures that work together to perform different functions. The table below lists the main organs of the body, showing their structure and function. You will learn more about these when you study the different body systems later in this unit.

Structure and functions of the main organs of the body

Table 10.1 Major organs of the body.

Organ	Structure	Function
Skin	The body's largest organ has two layers – the epidermis and dermis. Dermis contains hair, sweat glands, blood vessels and nerve endings.	Helps eliminate waste products in the sweat. Helps cooling by perspiration. Provides waterproof protection for the body.
Heart	About the size of an adult fist. Made of specialised cardiac muscle. It has four chambers, with valves to ensure blood pumps in the right direction.	Pumps blood round the body delivering oxygen to the cells and removing carbon dioxide.
Lungs	Network of branching air passages ending in alveoli (air sacs).	Maintenance of oxygen supply. Oxygen enters and carbon dioxide leaves the blood in the alveoli.
Stomach	Muscular J-shaped bag in the upper abdomen with sphincter muscles at entrance and exit. Mucus lining protects structure against stomach acid.	Produces acidic gastric enzymes to begin digestion and churns ingested food.
Bladder	Muscular bag in the pelvis. A ureter (tube) connects each kidney with the bladder.	The bladder stores urine until emptied by urination via the urethra.
Brain	Made up of the cerebrum, the diencephalon, the cerebellum and the brainstem. Divided into two hemispheres. Sits inside the skull for protection.	Receives and processes information. The cerebrum enables thought, speech, consciousness and movement. The cerebellum controls muscle contraction and balance, the thalamus interprets information from the brainstem and the brainstem links the brain to the spinal cord and controls vital functions such as breathing.
Eyes	Two eyes at the front of the skull. Globe shaped and lie in bony sockets (orbits) for protection.	Enable sight. The eye receives light rays which produce images that hit the back of the eye (retina). The optic nerve carries electrical impulses to the brain which translates them into sight.

continued

Table 10.1 (*continued*)

Organ	Structure	Function
Ears	One each side of the skull. Consists of outer middle and inner parts.	Enable hearing. Sound waves focused by outer ear cause eardrum to vibrate. Bones of middle ear transmit vibrations to inner ear where auditory nerve carries electrical impulses to the brain to be translated. Balance organs also make up part of the inner ear.
Pancreas	Leaf-shaped organ on left side of the abdomen about 12–15 cm long	Secretes enzymes to aid digestion and insulin – a hormone that regulates blood glucose).
Intestines	Small and large intestines are muscular tubes lined with mucus that lead from stomach and are coiled within the abdomen. The small intestine is about 6 m long and the large about 1.5 m long.	Digestion of food and absorption of nutrients take place in the small intestine and absorption of water in the large. Faeces are formed in the large intestine, stored in the rectum and expelled through the anus.
Liver	Largest internal organ weighing 1.5 kg and situated on the right side of the abdomen next to the stomach.	Among its 500+ functions, it controls blood composition, stores and releases glucose, stores vitamins, fats and minerals, removes toxins from the blood, makes bile.
Kidneys	One on either side of the spine at the back of the abdomen. Divided into cortex, medulla and pelvis.	Cortex and medulla filter the blood removing waste and excess water as urine.
Ovaries	In women: one ovary on each side of the uterus. White and about the size of a small plum, they are linked to the uterus by the fallopian tubes.	Female reproductive organs – store eggs (ova), releasing one a month.
Testes	In men: two testes in the scrotum behind the penis.	Male reproductive organs – produce sperm and hormones.
Uterus	In women: hollow muscular organ in the pelvic cavity behind the bladder and in front of the large intestine. Normally the size of a pear, but expands to contain the developing foetus.	Foetus develops in the uterus for 40 weeks. It is nourished during that time by the placenta – the blood-enriched lining of the uterus.

Assessment activity 10.1

2A.P1

Produce a poster showing the position of at least eight of the major organs described in the table. Label each organ and provide a short description of the structure and function of each organ.

The circulatory system

Cardiovascular – cardio – to do with the heart, **vascular** – to do with the blood.

Introduction

The circulatory or **cardiovascular** system is the network of veins and arteries, plus the heart, which keeps blood flowing round the body. The two main roles of the circulatory system are to:

- maintain the oxygen supply to all parts of the body
- transport substances such as nutrients and hormones to body tissues.

Main elements of the cardiovascular system

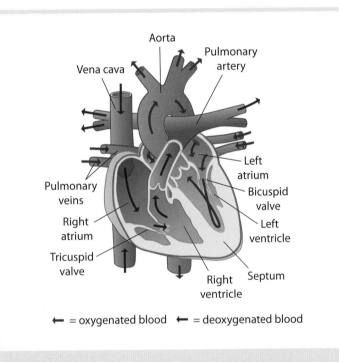

← = oxygenated blood   ← = deoxygenated blood

Figure 10.1 The heart is a double pump where each side works separately.

Heart

The heart is about the size of an adult fist and is made up of specialised cardiac muscle, which does not tire like skeletal muscle, so it keeps beating throughout a normal lifetime. Each side of the heart works separately – the right side pumps blood from the heart to the lungs; the left side pumps blood from the lungs via the heart to the rest of the body. It has four chambers. Each side has an upper atrium and lower ventricle and valves to ensure the blood always travels in the right direction. The heart has an electrical pacemaker to maintain a regular heartbeat.

Activity   Myogenicity

Cardiac muscle has the property of *myogenicity*. Find out what this means.

Blood

Blood is a body fluid in humans that transports necessary substances, such as oxygen and nutrients, to body tissues and takes away waste products to be removed by the kidneys or broken down in the liver or spleen. The liquid part of blood is called plasma and it carries different types of blood cells. Red blood cells (erythrocytes) contain haemoglobin, a protein that carries oxygen and makes the cells red. White blood cells (leucocytes) fight infection. Platelets (thromobocytes) are cell fragments that clump together at the sites of wounds and produce enzymes that help blood to clot.

Blood vessels

Blood has to reach all parts of the body. It does this via an efficient transport system of three different types of vessel – arteries, veins and capillaries.

Table 10.2 Blood vessels.

Arteries	Usually carry oxygen-rich blood away from the heart to the body tissues. The aorta is the main artery of the body. Arteries have relatively thick muscular walls.
Veins	Usually carry carbon dioxide-rich blood to the heart from the tissues. The vena cava is the main vein in the body. Veins have thinner walls than arteries, and valves to stop the back flow of blood.
Capillaries	So small that only one red blood cell at a time can pass through. The thin walls allow the exchange of water, oxygen, carbon dioxide, nutrients and waste between the blood and surrounding tissues.

? Did you know?

An adult's blood vessels stretched out end to end would measure about 100,000 miles – that is four times round the equator!

Blood circulation

Carbon dioxide-rich blood arrives in the right atrium from the vena cava and is pumped into the right ventricle. The blood moves into the pulmonary artery and on to the lungs where carbon dioxide passes into the alveoli to be breathed out and oxygen passes from the alveoli into the blood. The oxygen-rich blood travels back to the heart, through the pulmonary vein into the left atrium and left ventricle. The ventricle forces blood into the aorta, which takes the blood to all parts of the body delivering oxygen to and collecting carbon dioxide from the body tissues, which it delivers back to the right atrium.

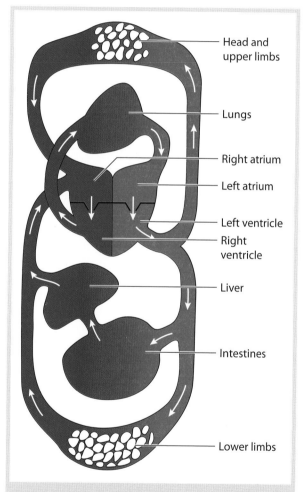

Head and upper limbs

Lungs

Right atrium

Left atrium

Left ventricle

Right ventricle

Liver

Intestines

Lower limbs

Figure 10.2 The circulatory system.

? Did you know?

When the electrical conduction of the heart doesn't work properly, the heart rate can change or become irregular. This can reduce quality of life or may even be life-threatening. A battery-operated artificial pacemaker, about the size of a matchbox, can be inserted under the skin and is set to maintain a regular heartbeat. In 2010 more than 40 000 people had a pacemaker fitted.
Source: NHS Choices

Just checking

1. What do the different types of blood vessels do?
2. Explain the journey one red blood cell takes from arriving at the entrance to the right atrium and completing a whole circuit around the body.
3. Find out more about the different parts of the heart such as the atria, ventricles, valves and the pacemaker.

The respiratory system

Getting started

Place your hands over your ribcage. Take several deep breaths and feel how your hands move. Can you describe what is happening?

Key terms

Respiration – the process whereby living organisms produce energy. This involves the intake of oxygen and the release of carbon dioxide.

Breathing – the action of taking air into the lungs and expelling it.

Introduction

The main function of the **respiratory** system is to maintain the supply of oxygen in the body and to remove the waste carbon dioxide. Oxygen and food are the body's fuel and carbon dioxide is the waste that needs to be removed.

◤ Main elements of the respiratory system

Air is **breathed** in through the mouth and nose where it is warmed and moistened. The nose is lined with hair like structures (cilia) that filter the air and prevent dust and debris entering the lungs. The air passes down the pharynx (throat) and through the larynx and trachea (windpipe). The trachea branches into two tubes (bronchi), which lead to each lung. They branch into smaller tubes (bronchioles), which end in sacs called alveoli.

The nose, larynx and pharynx make up the upper respiratory tract, while the trachea, bronchi and lungs make up the lower respiratory tract.

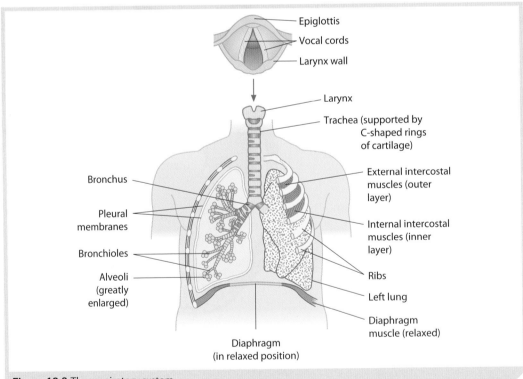

Figure 10.3 The respiratory system.

Larynx

The larynx lies between the pharynx and the trachea. At the top of the larynx there is a small leaf-shaped flap of cartilage called the epiglottis that closes over the entrance to the larynx to stop us choking when we swallow food.

There are also two membranes in the larynx called the vocal cords. These vibrate as air passes over them and produce sound that enables us to speak.

Lungs

The lungs enable us to take in the oxygen we need and excrete the waste carbon dioxide and water vapour made when we respire. The lungs are made up of a network of branching tubes, called bronchioles. At the end of the smallest bronchioles are the alveoli where **gas exchange** takes place. There are about 300 million alveoli in your lungs.

Gaseous exchange takes place by a process called **diffusion**. In the alveoli there is a high concentration of oxygen and a low concentration of carbon dioxide. There is a low concentration of oxygen and a high concentration of carbon dioxide in the blood. Diffusion allows the oxygen to move out of the alveoli and into the capillaries and the carbon dioxide to move out of the capillaries into the alveoli.

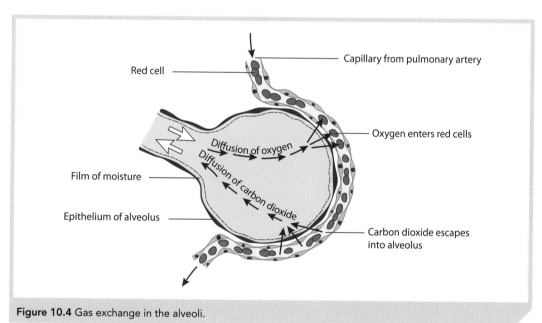

Figure 10.4 Gas exchange in the alveoli.

Labels: Red cell; Capillary from pulmonary artery; Diffusion of oxygen; Oxygen enters red cells; Film of moisture; Diffusion of carbon dioxide; Epithelium of alveolus; Carbon dioxide escapes into alveolus

Did you know?

Next time you add milk to a cup of tea or coffee, watch carefully. This is an example of diffusion as the milk, which has a high concentration when you add it, spreads out into the drink until it is evenly mixed.

Mechanism of breathing

During breathing in, or inhalation, the **intercostal** muscles between the ribs pull the ribcage upwards and outwards while the diaphragm, which is a sheet of muscle separating the chest and the abdomen, flattens. These two movements produce an increase in volume with a decrease in pressure, forcing air in and so the lungs inflate. During breathing out, or exhalation, the reverse happens; the diaphragm lifts back into a dome shape and the intercostal muscles pull the ribcage downwards and inwards. These two movements force air out of the lungs and they deflate.

Activity Respiration

- Find out how many litres of air the lungs can hold.
- Find out what the percentage of oxygen and carbon dioxide there is in inhaled and exhaled air.
- Revise what you have learned about respiration. Using diagrams explain the mechanism of respiration.

The nervous system

Introduction

The nervous system can be divided into the **central nervous system (CNS)**, made up of the brain and the spinal cord – the bundle of nerves that runs down the centre of the backbone, and the **peripheral nervous system** made up of all the nerve fibres in the rest of the body that connect to the CNS. Both systems receive and process information about what is happening to the body in the form of electrochemical signals.

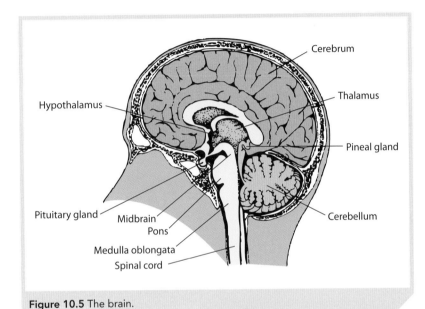

Figure 10.5 The brain.

Main elements of the nervous system

Brain

The brain acts like a control centre for the rest of the body, detecting changes and responding to them. It receives and interprets impulses from sense receptors in the body and sends impulses to make muscles and glands work. The brain co-ordinates the body's movements, allowing it to function efficiently. It controls feeding, sleeping, temperature regulation and salt and water balance (homeostasis). It stores information in the memory and deals with emotional and intellectual processes.

Table 10.3 The main parts of the brain.

The four main parts of the brain	
Brain stem (includes the mid-brain, pons, and medulla oblongata)	Controls involuntary reflex actions and vital functions, such as breathing.
Cerebellum	Maintains posture and coordinates movement. Receives messages from the cerebrum and muscles and joints.
Diencephalon (includes the thalamus and hypothalamus)	Controls homeostatic mechanisms and the autonomic nervous system.
Cerebrum	The largest part of the brain. It controls movement, thought, memory, emotions and personality traits and interprets sensory impulses.

The spinal cord is long bundle of nerves that lies in the spinal canal – a space inside the spinal column. Thirty-one pairs of nerves branch off the cord to all parts of the body.

Nerves

Nerves are made up of nerve cells or neurons. They vary according to where they are and what they do, but they all have a cell body containing the nucleus, usually located in the brain or spinal cord.

Motor neurons control the contraction and relaxation of muscles aiding movement.

Sensory neurons are concerned with the five senses: sight, hearing, touch, taste and smell. They pick up sensations such as light, sound, heat, taste and pain and transmit them to the brain or spinal cord where they are interpreted. This process is known as perception.

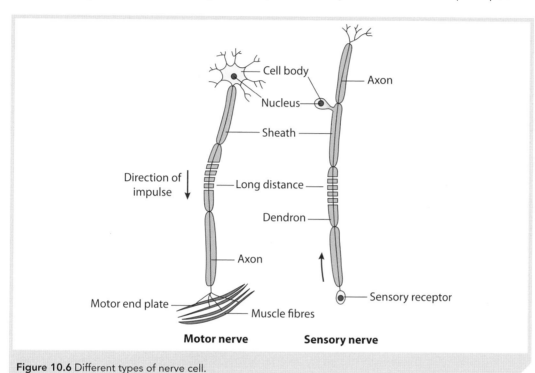

Figure 10.6 Different types of nerve cell.

? Did you know?

Neurons are the longest nerves in the body. One nerve may stretch from your brain to almost the end of your spinal cord. Another reaches from there down to your foot. There could be as many as 1,000,000,000,000 neurons in the body.

The autonomic nervous system

The autonomic nervous system works without us being aware of it. It is responsible for processes that happen all the time, such as maintaining homeostasis and blood pressure. It consists of the sympathetic and parasympathetic nervous systems.

The parasympathetic nervous system is in control most of the time, when we are relaxed. It slows heart rate and breathing and helps us to digest food.

However, in an emergency the sympathetic nervous system takes over. The hormone adrenaline is secreted and its effect is to raise heartbeat and breathing, and cause sweating and a dry mouth. It is known as the 'Fight, fright or flight' response, as it readies the body to do one of these three things in response to danger.

Just checking

1 Which part of your brain allows you to remember what happened yesterday?

2 What are the five senses?

3 What is perception?

The renal system

Introduction

Metabolism is the overall term for the chemical processes that take place in the body that allows us to convert food to energy and carry out the activities of daily living. During metabolism, carbon dioxide, water and urea – the breakdown products of protein – are produced as waste. They cannot be used in the body and may harm it. The urea combined with water is removed from the blood by the kidneys as urine. The system that does this is known as the excretory or renal system.

Main elements of the renal (or excretory) system

Kidneys

There are two of these bean-shaped structures, which lie either side of the vertebral column and are about the size of an adult fist. The right kidney is slightly lower than the left kidney to make room for the liver which is on the right side of the body. Each kidney is made up of an outer cortex and an inner medulla and hollow 'pelvis' in the centre where urine filtered from the blood in the cortex collects and drains out through the ureter.

In each kidney there are about one million microscopic structures called **nephrons**, which filter the blood, reabsorbing the useful materials such as glucose, amino acids, salts and water and getting rid of the products such as urea, which is produced following the breakdown of proteins.

Each kidney is supplied with blood by a renal artery, which branches off the aorta, the main artery of the body. Filtered blood is returned to the vena cava, the main vein of the body via a renal vein.

Key term

Nephrons – the functional units of the kidney, each consisting of a microscopic filtering capsule and long convoluted tubule. There are up to 1.5 million nephrons in a kidney.

Ureters

These are tubes about 3 mm in diameter and 25–30 cm long that carry urine from the kidneys to the bladder.

Bladder

This is a muscular bag situated in the pelvic cavity that collects urine. It can hold about 500 ml of urine.

Urethra

This is a tube leading from the bladder to the outside of the body through which urine is expelled. The male's urethra is 18–20 cm long, while the female's urethra is only 4–6 cm long.

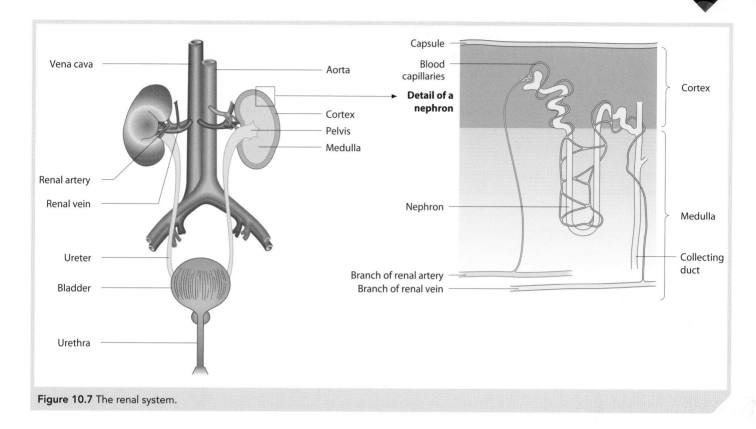

Figure 10.7 The renal system.

Water regulation

The body's water content is controlled by anti-**diuretic** hormone or ADH, which is produced by the hypothalamus and stored and secreted by the pituitary, a gland in the brain. ADH regulates how much water there is in the body by increasing the amount of water absorbed by the kidneys. If the blood is too concentrated ADH tells the kidneys to reabsorb some of the water. If there is too much water in the body, ADH will not be secreted and the excess water will be released by the kidneys for excretion.

The kidneys also regulate the chemical composition of body fluid (e.g. salt, potassium and calcium) and the pH or acid balance of the body.

About 150–180 litres of fluid are processed by the kidneys every day and about 1.5 litres of urine is manufactured.

In December 2010 approximately 7,000 people in the United Kingdom were waiting for a kidney transplant.

Source: NHS Activity Report 2009/10 Transplant Activity in The UK

| **Activity** | The renal system |

- What is urine made up of?
- Find out how the blood is filtered through the nephrons.

> **Key term**
>
> **Diuretic** – causing the increased flow of urine.

> **Did you know?**
>
> The kidney was the first internal organ to be transplanted. Although we have two kidneys, we can survive happily with only one. The first successful kidney transplant was carried out in America in 1954 when 23-year-old Ronald Herrick donated one of his kidneys to his identical twin brother Richard who was dying of kidney disease. Richard went on to live for another 8 years and Ronald died in December 2010 at the age of 79.

The endocrine system

Introduction

The endocrine system is made up of glands which secrete chemical messengers called hormones. When a change in the body causes an imbalance, the secreted hormones target specific cells and tissues. This stops the change and brings the body back into balance.

Table 10.4 Glands and hormones.

Organ/gland	Hormone	Process
Pituitary gland	Trophic hormones	Stimulate production of hormones from other glands
	Somatotrophic (growth hormone)	Growth of long bones in limbs
	Prolactin	Milk production
	Luteinising hormone (LH)	Triggers ovulation, controls menstrual cycle and sex hormones from testes
	Follicle-stimulating hormone (FSH)	Controls menstrual cycle, starts ripening of ova, assists in control of sperm production
Hypothalamus	Hormone releasing factors	Stimulates pituitary to produce hormones
	Anti-diuretic hormone (ADH)	Controls water balance
	Oxytocin	Helps uterine contraction in childbirth and stimulates the letting down (production) of milk for breastfeeding
Thyroid gland	Thyroxine	Controls rate of body processes and heat production and energy production from food, controls growth and development of the nervous system
Pancreas	Insulin	Controls blood glucose level
Adrenal glands	Adrenaline	Controls emergency action, response to stress
	Cortisol	Stress control. Conversion of fats, proteins and carbohydrates to glucose
	Aldosterone	Controls salt and water balance in the kidneys
	Androgens	Stimulate male sex hormones , beard growth, deepening of voice and muscle development
Testes	Testosterone	Controls sperm development, and growth and development of male features at puberty
Ovaries	Progesterone	Helps control normal progress of pregnancy. Interacts with FSH and LH and oestrogen to control the menstrual cycle
	Oestrogen	Controls the development of female features at puberty Interacts with FSH, LH and progesterone to control menstrual cycle
	Placental hormones (pregnancy only)	Control normal progress of pregnancy. Oestrogen and progesterone start milk production

The pituitary gland or 'master' gland controls the functions of the other glands that produce hormones, as well as producing its own hormones. When there is a change in the body, such as a high blood-glucose level after a meal, the hypothalamus in the brain receives a message about the change. It transmits the message to the pituitary gland, which instructs the pancreas to secrete insulin to bring the blood glucose level back to normal. Other glands receive messages to secrete hormones in response to other changes.

Adrenaline – the fight, fright or flight hormone

Adrenaline is secreted by the adrenal glands, positioned on top of the kidneys, in times of emergency or stress. It prepares the body for action by rapidly increasing the supply of oxygen and glucose to the brain and muscles. It is known as the fight, fright or flight hormone because it gives people the strength or speed to get out of difficult situations. It can also help to suppress pain for a short while.

Adrenaline produces specific reactions in the body.

- Stored glycogen in the liver is converted into glucose to provide energy.
- The rate and depth of breathing increases.
- Blood is diverted from other parts of the body to the brain and muscles.
- The heart rate increases.
- This can make people experience 'butterflies in their tummy', heightened senses, a dry mouth, pale face, and clammy hands.

Once the emergency is over adrenaline stops being secreted and the body returns to normal. However, people may shake for some time after the emergency.

? Did you know?

In the mid-nineteenth century, the average age that girls had their first period was 17, but today is at about 12. This is thought to be due to better nutrition leading to the achievement of a sufficient level of fat in the body to trigger the hormone that starts menstruation.

Adrenaline can also be useful in non-emergency situations. Can you think why?

Just checking

1 Where is the hypothalamus? What role does it play in the function of the endocrine system?

2 Draw an outline of the body and position all the endocrine glands on it.

The digestive system

Introduction

The digestive system or tract begins at the mouth and ends at the anus. Digestion includes four processes:

- ingestion – taking in food via the mouth
- digestion – mechanical and chemical breakdown of food by chewing and enzymes
- absorption – passing of nutrients through the intestinal wall into the blood system
- elimination – removal of undigested waste.

Activity   Digestion

The mouth is where digestion starts in the body. Research the mouth and teeth to find out what structures are used in the process of digestion. You should be able to identify and describe the teeth, salivary glands and taste buds.

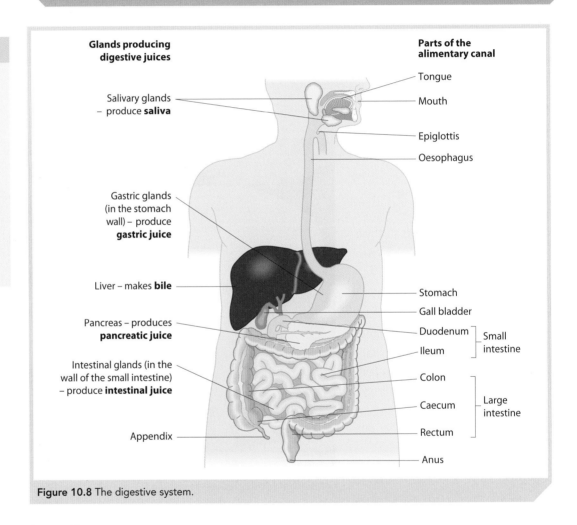

Figure 10.8 The digestive system.

Ingestion

When food enters the mouth the teeth cut and grind the food into small particles that can be swallowed. The food mixes with saliva, which moistens the food and starts digesting it. Amylase, an enzyme in the saliva, starts to break carbohydrates down to sugars.

On swallowing, the food moves down the pharynx (throat) into the oesophagus, a muscular tube about 30 cm long to the stomach. Muscles along the whole length of the **digestive tract** contract and relax automatically to push food onwards. This movement is known as peristalsis.

Key term

Digestive tract – the entire length of the gut, from the mouth to the anus.

Digestion

When the food reaches the stomach, it is churned and mixed with stomach acid and digestive enzymes. This breaks down the food even further into a mixture called chyme. After about five hours, the chyme moves into the first part of the small intestine (duodenum) where digestion continues. This takes about four hours, at the end of which carbohydrates will have been broken down into glucose and proteins into amino acids. Fats are **emulsified** by bile – an alkaline substance synthesised in the liver and stored in the gall bladder.

Key term

Emulsify – to disperse the particles of one liquid evenly in another.

Table 10.5 Digestive agents.

Location	Digestive agents	Action
Mouth	Salivary amylase	Starts to break down carbohydrates
Stomach	Hydrochloric acid	Kills bacteria
	Pepsin	Begins digestion of protein
	Rennin	Curdles milk
	Intrinsic factor	Helps body to absorb Vitamin B$_{12}$
Small intestine	**Pancreatic juice:**	
	Amylase	Converts starch to maltose
	Lipase	Converts fats to fatty acids
	Trypsin and chymotrypsin	Convert proteins to peptides
	Intestinal juice:	
	Maltase	Converts maltose to glucose
	Sucrase	Converts sucrose into glucose and fructose
	Lactase	Converts lactose into glucose and galactose
	Peptidase	Converts peptides into amino acids
From the liver	Bile	Emulsifies fats

Absorption and elimination

After digestion is complete nutrients are absorbed through the wall of the small intestine and into the blood. Fats are not absorbed directly into the bloodstream: they are absorbed from the small intestine into the lymphatic system first. After about seven to nine hours, food that has not been digested moves into the large intestine. Water is absorbed from it into the body leaving behind faeces, a semi-solid mass that is stored in the rectum and eventually eliminated via the anus.

Just checking

1 Identify the organs of the digestive system and explain the function of each.

2 Explain how a meal of fish, chips and peas is digested and absorbed in the digestive tract. You will need to identify the different types of food in the meal first. Make sure you state which enzymes act on which foods to break them down.

The reproductive system

Getting started

What are testosterone, oestrogen and progesterone? Why are they produced and what does each do?

Introduction

Reproduction is the fertilisation of an egg (ovum) by a sperm. The fertilised cell formed is called a zygote. After a few days, during which time it undergoes rapid cell division and implants in the lining of the womb, it develops into an embryo. After eight weeks of growth and development it becomes a foetus. After 40 weeks of pregnancy, hormones trigger the onset of labour and a fully formed baby is born.

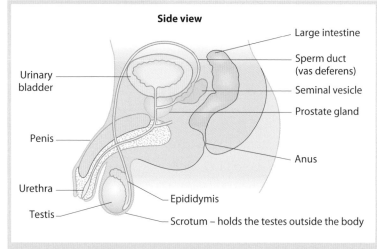

Figure 10.9 The male reproductive system.

The male reproductive system

The male reproductive system is made up of the penis and testes. Two testes are suspended in the scrotum outside the body and produce sperm and testosterone. When sexually aroused, the penis fills with blood and becomes erect.

The female reproductive system

The female reproductive system is made up of two ovaries, two fallopian tubes, the uterus and cervix (neck of the uterus) and the vagina. Although at birth a girl has 1–2 million potential eggs in her ovaries, only about 400 will develop and mature during her lifetime. Fertilisation usually takes place in the fallopian tubes and the fertilised egg is then transported to the uterus where it is implanted in the lining.

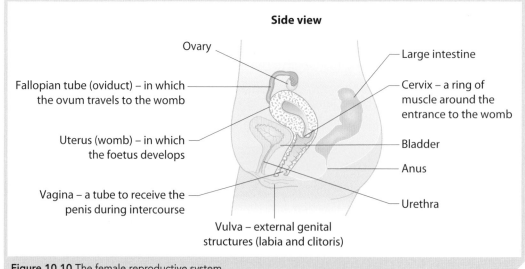

Figure 10.10 The female reproductive system.

Table 10.6 Male and female sex cells.

Sperm	Egg
Very small – $\frac{1}{500}$ mm	Very large – $\frac{1}{10}$ mm
Nucleus contains half of the male's chromosomes	Nucleus contains half of the female's chromosomes
Cytoplasm contains lots of mitochondria to provide energy	Cytoplasm contains lots of nutrients for embryo development
Can move on their own	Cannot move on its own
Several hundred million produced every day from puberty onwards	Present at birth and released one at a time about every four weeks from the onset of menstruation to menopause
Each ejaculate contains 200–400 million	One released every four weeks

The menstrual cycle

During approximately the first five days of the menstrual cycle the lining of the uterus is shed. This is commonly known as a period.

Follicle-stimulating hormone (FSH) stimulates an egg to mature in a follicle within the ovary. Oestrogen stimulates the uterus to start building its lining, and cause FSH to stop being produced and luteinising hormone (LH) to be secreted.

The LH causes an egg to be released from the follicle (ovulation). The follicle then folds in on itself to become corpus luteum (yellow body), which produces progesterone and thickens the lining of the uterus ready for an egg to implant. If a fertilised egg has not appeared in the uterus by day 24 of the cycle, the corpus luteum dies, the lining of the uterus breaks down and is shed as a period.

What happens if an egg is fertilised?

Fertilisation usually occurs in the fallopian tubes. The resultant zygote then travels to the uterus where it implants into the lining. The corpus luteum produces progesterone until the placenta starts to produce it about three months into pregnancy. Progesterone is essential for establishing and maintaining pregnancy.

The placenta provides nourishment to the embryo from the mother through blood vessels in the umbilical cord. It also produces hormones for the remainder of the pregnancy, which ensure that the lining of the uterus continues to develop and production of FSH stops so that no more eggs are produced. High hormone levels also stimulate the development of breast tissue in preparation for milk production. Just before birth the pituitary gland produces the hormones prolactin, which triggers the production of breast milk, and oxytocin, which initiates labour. During labour the muscles in the uterus contract to push the baby down the birth canal. At the same time the cervix or neck of the uterus dilates or opens. When it is fully open, the contractions push the baby down the vagina and it is born. The placenta is delivered shortly afterwards.

Just checking

Research what happens during pregnancy and produce a timeline of the main points of development of the foetus.

LINK A.2 A.3

The musculoskeletal system

Getting started

In small groups see how many of our 206 bones you can name. Do you know the formal and more commonly used names for some of them?

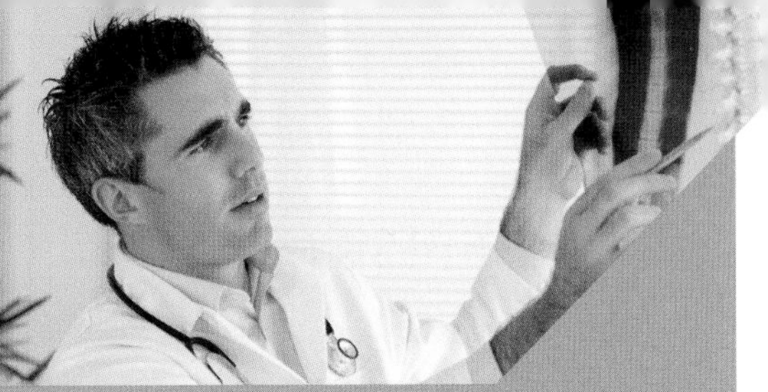

Introduction

As the name suggests the musculoskeletal system is all to do with our muscles and bones, and also includes ligaments and tendons. It is the body system that controls movement and coordination. The human body contains 206 bones and over 600 muscles.

Did you know

While the adult skeleton contains 206 bones, an infant's skeleton has about 300 bones. As a child grows, some bones, such as bones in the skull, fuse together.

The skeleton

The skeleton provides the rigid internal framework of the body and without it animals would not have a shape. It has several functions:

- to support the body and allow it to move in conjunction with muscles
- to protect vital organs of the body, such as the brain and heart
- to produce blood cells (in the bone marrow of some bones)
- to produce calcium, needed for blood clotting and muscle contraction.

There are two parts to the skeleton – axial and appendicular.

Skull
Clavicle
Scapula
Sternum
Humerus
Ribs
Vertebral column (backbone)
Radius
Ulna
Pelvis
Hand
Femur
Patella
Tibia
Fibula
7 tarsals (ankle)
Metatarsals
Phalanges

Figure 10.11 The skeleton.

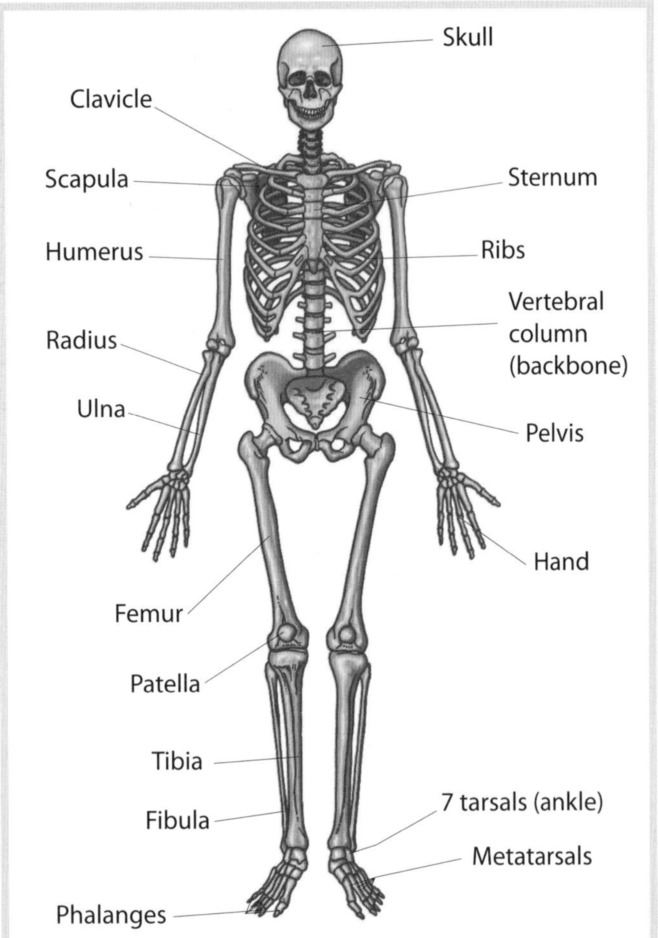

The axial skeleton

This consists of the skull, vertebrae and ribcage. The skull consists of 22 separate bones – eight are fused together to protect the brain, and the remaining 14 make up the face. It sits on the top of the spinal column (backbone). The 33 small bones (vertebrae) that make up the backbone protect the spinal cord. They are separated from each other by pads of cartilage, which act as shock absorbers. The ribcage consists of 12 pairs of ribs and protects the heart and lungs.

The appendicular skeleton

This consists of the arm and leg bones, the shoulder girdle, which attaches the arms to the vertebrae, and the hip girdle that connects the leg bones to the vertebrae. The pelvic girdle helps to protect the reproductive organs, and is strong enough to support the body's weight.

Joints and ligaments

Joints are where two bones meet. There are different types of joint that can be classed as:

- immoveable: fixed, such as the skull bones
- slightly moveable: such as the vertebrae of the spine
- freely moveable: such as the hip and knee joints.

Ligaments are strong elastic structures made of a strong protein called collagen. They hold bones together at a joint.

Bones cannot move by themselves. They need the action of muscles to allow movement.

Muscles

The muscle tissue involved in the movement of the body is known as striped or striated muscle because it looks striped under a microscope. There are more than 650 skeletal muscles in the human body.

Activity	Muscles of the body

Can you name any of the muscles in the body? If you can do you know where they are?

Muscles are attached to bones by fibrous tissue called tendons. When a muscle contracts, it pulls on the bone and moves the joint. Muscles can only work by contracting, which is why they need to work in pairs – for instance one muscle will contract to bend a joint, and another will contract to straighten it. Muscles are always slightly contracted so that they are ready for movement. This is known as muscle tone.

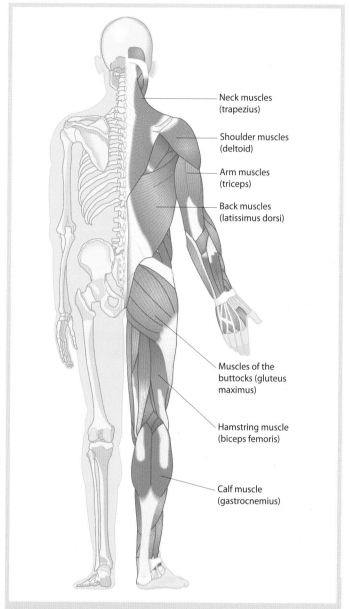

Neck muscles (trapezius)

Shoulder muscles (deltoid)

Arm muscles (triceps)

Back muscles (latissimus dorsi)

Muscles of the buttocks (gluteus maximus)

Hamstring muscle (biceps femoris)

Calf muscle (gastrocnemius)

Figure 10.12 Some of the main skeletal muscles.

Just checking

1 Find out what the following parts of the skeleton are then label them on a diagram of the skeleton: sutures, axis, femur, humerus, clavicle, patella, atlas, tibia, ulna.

2 Find out what different types of moveable joints there are and how they move.

Relationships between major body systems

Introduction

For the body to work efficiently, all its systems have to work together. In this section you will find out how some of them do this.

The circulatory and respiratory systems

The respiratory system supplies oxygen that the circulatory system delivers to all parts of the body, and the circulatory system transports carbon dioxide, a waste product of the body's metabolism, to be removed via the respiratory system.

Air is inspired (breathed in) via the bronchi and bronchioles to the alveoli where oxygen moves into red blood cells in the capillaries for delivery all round the body. Waste carbon dioxide passes from the cells and tissues into the blood plasma where it is carried to the alveoli for expiration (breathing out) from the mouth and nose via the bronchioles and bronchi. If oxygen is not delivered to the cells, then they will die and long-lasting damage or death of the organism might occur.

Activity   Cardiac arrest

Find out what happens to heart muscle cells if a person has a heart attack.

The musculoskeletal and nervous systems

The autonomic nervous system maintains many of the body's processes and works automatically without us having to think about it.

However, bones cannot move on their own. They require nerves to produce movement and have to rely on the muscles and ligaments to move for them. The brain has to tell the muscles what to do. The flow diagram below shows what happens when you press a key on your mobile phone.

> A motor neurone sends a stimulus (or message) from the brain to a receptor in the muscle.
>
> ↓
>
> The muscles in the thumb contract and relax to move the thumb bones. This is the response.

Figure 10.13 How the musculoskeletal system and nervous system work together when you press a key on a mobile phone.

The digestive and endocrine systems

The digestive and endocrine systems work together to keep blood glucose levels stable and ensure body tissues have sufficient glucose to be able to metabolise. After digestion, glucose from the digested food passes into the blood causing blood glucose levels to rise. The glucose needs to get from the blood into the body tissue where it is used to provide energy.

The pancreas responds to a stimulus in the brain that tells it that the blood glucose level is too high, and secretes the hormone insulin into the blood. Insulin changes the permeability of cell membranes, allowing glucose to be absorbed into the cells where it is needed and blood glucose returns to normal levels.

If you have not eaten for a long time, your blood glucose level becomes low. Then the pancreas secretes the hormone glucagon, which causes the liver to convert stored glycogen to glucose to raise the blood glucose level and maintain energy supplies to body tissue cells. The pancreas also secretes the hormone ghrelin, which makes us feel hungry, encouraging us to eat and thus provide the needed glucose.

The endocrine and reproductive systems

The reproductive system needs the endocrine system to direct puberty, trigger essential processes in the formation of gametes (sperm and ova) and in preparing for and maintaining pregnancy. The endocrine system controls the menstrual cycle in women. Various hormones stimulate ovulation (the releasing of an egg from the ovary), the build-up of the lining of the womb, and then the shedding of the lining if fertilisation does not take place.

In men, follicle-stimulating hormone, luteinising hormone and testosterone control the production of sperm. Two organs are involved in these various processes: the hypothalamus, a very small but vital part of the brain that stimulates the production of hormones, and the pituitary gland, which is known as the master gland, which both produces hormones itself and stimulates production of hormones from other glands.

Hormones play a vital role in puberty. For instance, the adrenal glands which lie on top of each kidney produce hormones that stimulate the development of secondary sexual characteristics, such as voice deepening and facial hair growth in boys. You can find out more about these in Unit 1: Human Lifespan Development.

Activity	Sperm production

Find out how sperm are produced and the role of testosterone in the process.

Activity	Body system synergy

Find out how some other body systems work together:

- the nervous and circulatory systems
- the respiratory and musculoskeletal systems
- the endocrine and renal systems.

Coordination of systems through homeostasis

Key term

Homeostasis – from the Latin meaning to stay the same, homeostasis is the process by which the body maintains a stable environment in which cells can function.

Introduction

The various body systems work together to maintain **homeostasis**, to ensure that the body functions efficiently. The nervous system is involved in all of these activities as it receives messages about changes in the body and passes them on to the relevant part of the body that controls where the change is happening. There is then a response, which brings the situation back to normal.

Temperature control

Many of the body's processes work best at a constant temperature of about 37°C so it needs to be able to make changes to maintain this temperature. Figure 10.14 explains how this happens.

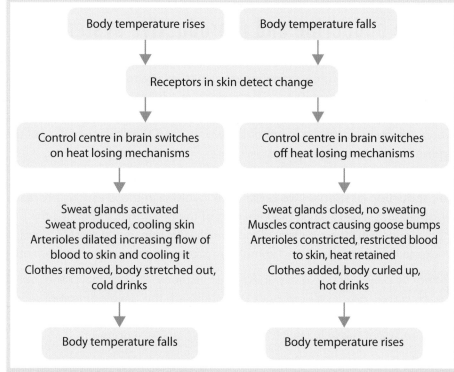

Figure 10.14 How the body maintains a constant temperature.

Negative feedback

Negative feedback is a mechanism used to detect and correct changes in the body.

Figure 10.15 The negative feedback mechanism.

Blood pressure control

Blood pressure is measured in millimetres of mercury and the normal blood pressure should be below 120/80 mmHg. The higher figure (120) shows the systolic pressure – the pressure in the vessels when the heart is beating. The lower figure (80) shows diastolic pressure – the pressure in the vessels when the heart is at rest.

Several factors can change the blood pressure, for instance stress can cause it to rise. Receptors in major arteries detect a rise in blood pressure and send a message to the medulla in the brain. Messages are sent out to slow the heart rate and widen the arteries, which lowers the blood pressure. In this instance, the systems working together are the nervous system and the cardiovascular system.

Oxygen control

The respiratory system maintains the oxygen supply in the body. In the brain there are two regions concerned with respiration. One changes the depth of breathing and the other the rate of breathing. The medulla contains clusters of neurons that control the respiratory centre. One cluster is responsible for inspiration (breathing in) and one for expiration (breathing out).

Receptors in the aorta and the carotid arteries in the neck are sensitive to chemical changes in the blood. If they detect a rise in carbon dioxide, they send a message to the brain telling it to increase the rate and depth of breathing. When carbon dioxide levels fall, the depth and rate of breathing returns to normal. This is an example of three systems working together: the nervous system, the cardiovascular system and the respiratory system.

Blood sugar control

Cells need glucose to function and a homeostatic mechanism works to keep the body's glucose supply constant.

Figure 10.16 shows how the nervous system works with the digestive system and the endocrine system to maintain steady blood glucose levels.

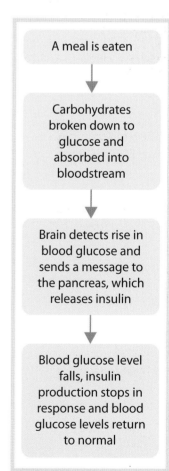

Figure 10.16 How glucose levels are maintained.

Assessment activity 10.2   2A.P2 | 2A.P3 | 2A.P4 | 2A.M1 | 2A.M2 | 2A.D1

You have been asked to create an electronic resource for your school or college about the different body systems and how they interrelate. You have been asked to do this under separate headings so that more junior students can study it in sections. You need to complete the following tasks:

1 Describe the structure of the major systems in the human body using labelled diagrams and clear explanations.
2 Describe how each system functions.
3 Explain how the different parts of **one** system work.
4 Describe how the major body systems relate.
5 Explain how two major body systems interrelate.
6 Analyse how body systems relate to maintain **one** example of homeostasis in the body.

When you have completed this, print it out and submit it to your teacher/tutor.

Circulatory system disorders

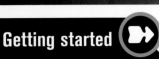

Getting started

If you have a friend or relative who has an illness or disorder such as asthma, diabetes, heart disease or osteoarthritis, ask if they are willing to talk to you about the disorder. If they are, ask about how they are affected and what treatment or care they receive.

Introduction

In this unit, you have learned about the structure and function of organs and systems in the human body, but have you ever thought about what can go wrong? Circulatory system disorders include those relating to the heart and the blood vessels.

Common circulatory system disorders

Hypertension

Hypertension, or high blood pressure, is when the pressure on the walls of the arteries caused by the blood pumping around the body is above normal. Blood pressure is measured as two figures in millimetres of mercury (or mmHg):

- **systolic pressure:** the pressure when the heart is beating
- **diastolic pressure:** the pressure when the heart rests in between beats.

Blood pressure is normally around 120/80 or 110 over 75 for a young person. A blood pressure measurement of 140/90 mmHg would be considered high and is known as hypertension. This can cause strain on your heart and arteries.

Hypertension can be reduced by cutting down the amount of salt in the diet. Currently the recommended daily allowance for salt intake is 6 g a day, which is about one teaspoonful. Risk factors include being overweight, family history of hypertension, lack of exercise, drinking a lot of caffeine and alcohol, not eating enough fruit and vegetables, being over 65 and being of African or Caribbean descent.

Deep vein thrombosis

A thrombosis is a clot. Deep vein thrombosis (DVT) is a clot in one of the deep veins, usually in the lower leg. It is usually caused by lack of movement, for example after surgery or a long flight. If part of the clot breaks off and travels through the blood vessels to the lungs, it can cause a pulmonary embolism, which can be very serious. Symptoms of DVT include:

- pain or tenderness and swelling in the calf
- a change in the colour and temperature of the calf. Blood that would normally go through the blocked vein is diverted to outer veins. The calf may then become warm and red.

A DVT is usually treated with anti-coagulant drugs that thin the blood and break down the clot and the wearing of compression stockings to support blood flow. The patient should keep active but elevate the legs when resting.

Coronary heart disease

The heart muscle needs a constant supply of oxygen from the coronary arteries. If fatty material builds up in the arteries, they can become partially or completely blocked. With partial blockage, people can experience chest pains known as angina due to the lack of oxygen reaching the heart muscle. If a coronary artery becomes completely blocked, the heart muscle stops receiving oxygen and the heart muscle cells die. This is known as a myocardial infarction or a heart attack. If too many cells die, the heart will stop beating and the person might die.

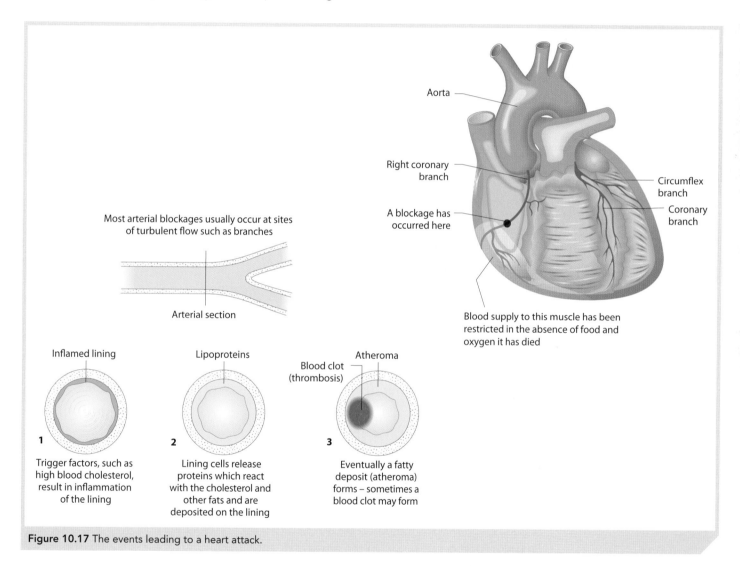

Figure 10.17 The events leading to a heart attack.

The symptoms of coronary heart disease are chest pain or discomfort (angina), pain in one or both arms, the left shoulder, neck, jaw or back and shortness of breath. The severity of symptoms will depend on how advanced the heart disease is.

Hereditary factors, lifestyle, age and gender affect a person's susceptibility to heart disease. Men are more likely to develop heart disease than women although women's risk increases after the menopause. Diabetics and some ethnic groups are more susceptible too.

Respiratory system disorders

Common respiratory disorders

Bronchitis

Bronchitis is inflammation of the bronchioles of the lungs, which causes them to narrow and fluid to be produced which makes it difficult to breathe. Bronchitis can be **acute** or **chronic**. People can recover from acute bronchitis relatively quickly, but may have a cough that lingers for a few weeks.

People with chronic bronchitis will not get better although some symptoms can be relieved. Continued coughing produces mucus or phlegm. Eventually the bronchioles become scarred, which makes them floppy and narrower, resulting in shortness of breath. Chronic bronchitis and **emphysema** can occur together, and is known as Chronic Obstructive Pulmonary Disease (or COPD). The most common complication of chronic bronchitis is pneumonia.

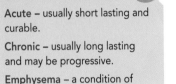

Key terms

Acute – usually short lasting and curable.

Chronic – usually long lasting and may be progressive.

Emphysema – a condition of the lungs where the alveoli are damaged and enlarged, leading to breathlessness.

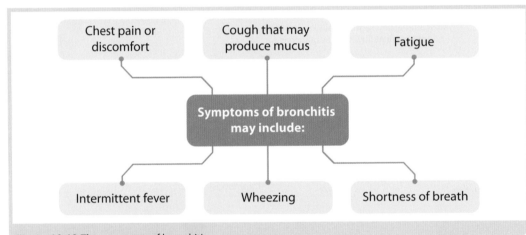

Figure 10.18 The symptoms of bronchitis.

Risk factors for developing chronic bronchitis are smoking, long-term exposure to smoke, pollution and certain jobs, such as coal mining and textile manufacture. Chronic bronchitis can also be caused by allergies.

Smokers with bronchitis should be advised to stop immediately and may also need to be prescribed drugs to widen the airways or antibiotics, if infection is the cause.

Overweight or obese people with bronchitis should be advised to lose weight as carrying extra weight causes the lungs to work harder and increases shortness of breath.

Gentle exercises to increase the muscle power of the diaphragm, chest muscles, arms and legs should be encouraged.

Emphysema

Emphysema is a chronic lung condition caused by gradual damage to the lung structure, which causes difficulty in breathing. The alveoli lose their elasticity and it becomes very difficult to inhale enough oxygen or exhale carbon dioxide. People with emphysema are constantly battling to breathe and get tired very quickly.

Risk factors are:

- smoking
- living in areas of high levels of air pollution.

Emphysema is more common in urban than rural areas and amongst people who work in dusty environments. More men than women suffer with this condition.

Affected people are advised to stop smoking and to use oxygen to help with their breathing. Infections need to be treated promptly with antibiotics to prevent further chest complications.

A woman using an inhaler to relieve her symptoms of asthma.

Asthma

Asthma is a condition that affects the airways of the lungs. It usually happens because of an allergy, which causes the airways to narrow as the muscles around their walls tighten, making it hard to breathe and causing sticky phlegm to be produced. Symptoms can include coughing, wheezing, shortness of breath and tightness in the chest. It can affect anyone of any age.

Infections and environmental factors are the main risk factors. Common triggers include cigarette smoke and other fumes, and allergies to pollen, dust and animals.

Treatment for asthma includes inhalers, which are either preventers or relievers. Preventers help to control swelling in the airways and help to reduce sensitivity to triggers. Relievers relax the muscles surrounding the airways and relieve symptoms.

Activity	Find out about asthma

Visit the Asthma UK website and find out how asthma is diagnosed, and what the indoor and outdoor triggers for an asthma attack might be.

Nervous system disorders

Common nervous system disorders

Stroke

Stroke can be thought of as a disorder of the circulatory system, but the effects are mainly on the nervous system. There are two types of stroke:

- Ischaemic stroke occurs when a blood vessel in the brain becomes blocked. The part of the brain beyond the affected vessel cannot receive the oxygen and dies.
- Haemorrhagic stroke occurs when a blood vessel that supplies the brain with blood is weak and bursts, causing brain damage.

Depending on where in the brain it occurs, a stroke can result in loss of movement in the limbs and speech difficulties. If it occurs in the left side of the brain, the right side of the body is affected. Speech may be affected as the speech centre is in the left side of the brain. If it occurs in the right side of the brain the left side of the body is affected.

Ischaemic strokes are often caused by high blood pressure which in turn can be caused by eating too much salt in the diet.

Parkinson's disease

Parkinson's is a progressive disease of the nervous system, which means that it gets worse over time. It affects about one person in 500 in the UK. It usually affects people over the age of 50, but younger people can get it too. Nerve cells in the brain die so less of a chemical called dopamine is produced. Dopamine helps to regulate movement so if there is not enough of it movement becomes slower. Some people with Parkinson's disease also develop a tremor or their muscles become rigid. Other symptoms might include tiredness, pain, depression and constipation. Parkinson's affects people differently and some people are able to have a good quality of life for a long time. Men are slightly more likely to develop Parkinson's disease than women.

It is difficult to diagnose the disease because no agreed tests are available.

> **Activity**   Parkinson's disease
>
> Find out what other symptoms people with Parkinson's disease may have.

Sensory impairment

Sensory impairment occurs when nerves are unable to pass on impulses or when the brain is unable to interpret the signals it receives. This can be the result of damage caused by injury or disease, or be due to other conditions. Sensory impairment can affect sight, hearing, smell, touch, taste and spatial awareness. A sensory impairment does not have to be total. It can have mild to severe effects; for example, many people who are registered blind can see or sense some light and movement.

The table below shows four of the most common causes of visual impairment:

Table 10.7 Visual impairment.

Disorder	Effects
Age-related Macular Degeneration (AMD)	A condition where the central part of the back of the eye (the macular, which plays an important role in central vision) stops working properly.
Cataracts	Where cloudy patches form on the lenses of the eyes.
Glaucoma	Where fluid builds up inside the eye, damaging the optic nerve (which relays information from the eye to the brain).
Diabetic retinopathy	Where blood vessels that supply the eye become damaged due to a build-up of glucose.

Some people are born with hearing impairment, but in other people it can develop, for instance noise-induced hearing loss from prolonged working in a noisy atmosphere, especially without ear protection.

Can you think of any other jobs in which people may be at risk from hearing loss?

Touch impairment can occur as a symptom of several different disorders. People who have had a stroke or have multiple sclerosis often experience numbness. People who cannot feel anything are at greater risk of injury or burns.

Activity   Sensory impairment

Either research the sensory impairment effects of multiple sclerosis or find out what ageusia and anosmia are.

Digestive system disorders

▼ Common digestive system disorders

Bowel cancer

Bowel cancer generally occurs in the colon (large intestine). It is sometimes called colon or rectal cancer, depending on where in the bowel it starts. It can start in the small intestine, but this is much less common than large-bowel cancer.

Symptoms include blood in the faeces, a change in bowel habits, such as diarrhoea or constipation, and weight loss that cannot be explained.

NHS statistics show that bowel cancer is the third most common type of cancer in England with around 40,000 new cases registered every year in the UK. Survival rates are high if diagnosed early. However, the chances of surviving more than five years drop from 90 per cent for early diagnosis, to just 6 per cent if diagnosed at its most advanced stages.

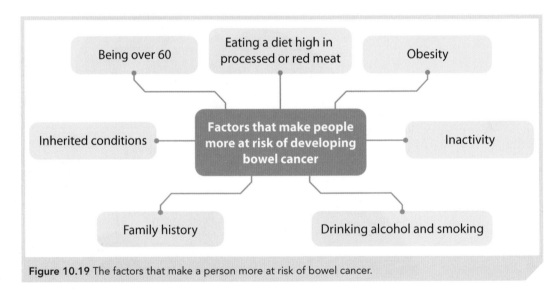

Figure 10.19 The factors that make a person more at risk of bowel cancer.

There has been an NHS bowel cancer screening programme since 2006, which recommends that people between the ages of 60 and 69 are screened every two years. The earlier the disease is caught, the better the chance of survival.

Cholecystitis

This is inflammation of the gall bladder. The gall bladder is a sac situated under the liver that stores bile, which is released into the digestive system when a meal is eaten and emulsifies the fat so that it can be absorbed.

Cholecystitis occurs when the bile crystallises into hard lumps called gall stones. Many people have gall stones without knowing about them because they cause no problems unless they get caught in the bile duct, the tube that transports the bile from the gall bladder to the small intestine. As the bile cannot get past the stone, the gall bladder enlarges and becomes inflamed, causing pain on the upper right side of the abdomen.

Initial treatment includes pain relief and following a low fat diet to reduce the inflammation. Keyhole surgery is then used to remove the gall bladder.

Irritable bowel syndrome

Irritable bowel syndrome (IBS) is a common disorder, but its cause is unknown. The affected bowel usually looks normal but does not function normally. IBS often develops during the teenage years or young adulthood and can affect anyone at any age, but women are more likely to have it than men.

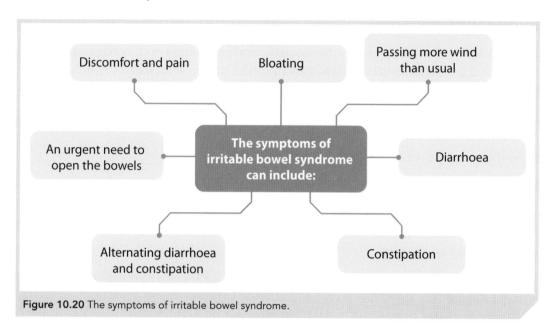

Discomfort and pain

Bloating

Passing more wind than usual

An urgent need to open the bowels

The symptoms of irritable bowel syndrome can include:

Diarrhoea

Alternating diarrhoea and constipation

Constipation

Figure 10.20 The symptoms of irritable bowel syndrome.

Other symptoms can include nausea, headache, belching, poor appetite, tiredness, backache, muscle pain, feeling quickly full after eating, heartburn and bladder symptoms.

There does not appear to be any pattern in how IBS occurs. Some people can have mild symptoms quite rarely and others can experience severe symptoms often.

Activity   IBS

Carry out some research into the dietary advice that is given to people with irritable bowel syndrome. What advice is given about fibre in the diet?

IBS can cause sufferers to have very bad stomach cramps.

Renal system disorders

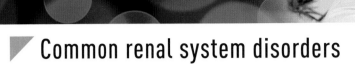

Common renal system disorders

Urinary tract infection

A urinary tract infection can be in the kidneys, bladder, urethra and, occasionally the ureters. It is usually caused by bacteria and women are more prone to them than men, mainly because the urethra in women is much shorter and is close to the anus. Symptoms include:

- burning on urination
- needing to pass water frequently
- urine can be cloudy, smell strongly and may be bloody.

More severe symptoms can be present if the infection is in the kidneys. They include:

- high temperature
- feeling tired and unwell
- shaking
- night sweats
- pain
- nausea and vomiting
- in elderly people confusion is often the only symptom.

Diagnosis is usually confirmed by testing a urine sample for the presence of bacteria and blood cells. If the infection is fairly mild then antibiotics are given and the infection will clear in a few days.

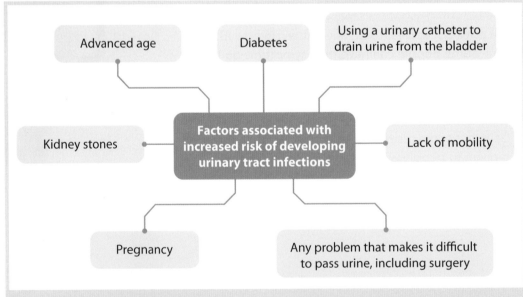

Figure 10.21 Factors associated with increased risk of developing urinary tract infections.

Activity   Treating recurring UTIs

What advice do healthcare workers give to people who are prone to repeated urinary tract infections?

Renal failure

In renal failure the kidneys function less efficiently or stop working altogether so waste products are not filtered and stay in the blood circulating around the body.

Renal failure can be acute or chronic.

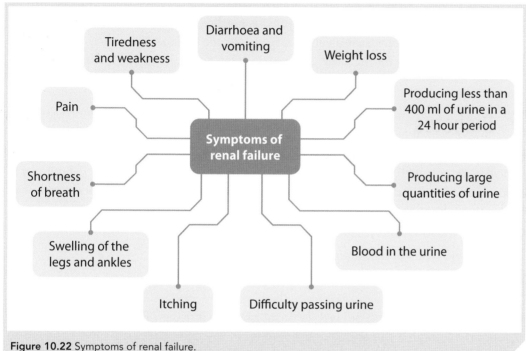

Figure 10.22 Symptoms of renal failure.

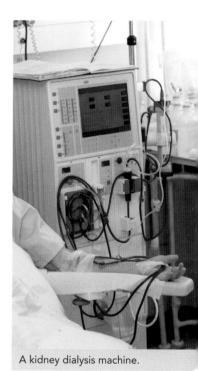

A kidney dialysis machine.

Table 10.8 Renal failure.

	Acute renal failure	**Chronic renal failure**
Causes	Can be due to injury, infection, dehydration, kidney stones or lack of salt	Complications related to diabetes or some inherited conditions, but may also be unknown. High blood pressure usually associated with chronic failure
Onset	Quick, over days or weeks	May occur over months or years

Renal failure can be treated by dialysis, which is a way of removing the waste products from the blood. There are two types of dialysis. Peritoneal dialysis uses the peritoneum, which is a membrane that covers the abdominal organs, as a filter. A tube is inserted into the abdomen and attached to large bags of fluid that flow into the body. The fluid is left inside the body for several hours so that the waste products from the blood filter through the peritoneum. The fluid is then drained out taking the waste with it.

Haemodialysis is done every two to three days using a dialysis machine. The blood leaves the patient's body via a vein usually in the lower arm, and is filtered by machine before being returned to the body. This takes several hours. Some people have a dialysis machine at home, but most have to be treated in hospital dialysis units.

Acute renal failure treatment is usually very successful and kidney function is restored, but chronic renal failure is normally not reversible. If it is severe, kidney transplantation will be necessary.

Endocrine system disorders

Introduction

You have already learned about the different glands that make up the endocrine system, the hormones that they produce and some of the functions that the hormones regulate. Endocrine disorders can cause an imbalance in hormone levels, with a serious impact on health. In this section you will learn about some of the more common endocrine disorders.

Diabetes

Blood glucose levels are controlled by the hormone insulin, which is secreted by the pancreas. People with diabetes either cannot produce insulin or the body cannot use it properly so blood glucose levels become uncontrolled. Untreated diabetics experience excess thirst, frequent urination, extreme tiredness and weight loss. Long term, more serious complications can affect the kidneys, blood circulation and eyesight.

There are two types of diabetes, Type 1 and Type 2.

Type 1 diabetes

This is known as childhood or juvenile onset because it usually first appears during childhood although it can appear in people up to the age of about 40. It is believed that it is either genetic or develops following an infection during which the insulin-producing cells are damaged and stop producing insulin. Because of this, injections of insulin are needed before each meal. About 15 per cent of people with diabetes have this type.

A young girl injecting herself with insulin.

Type 2 diabetes

This is also known as adult or mature onset diabetes, although children as young as nine have been diagnosed. Either a reduced amount of insulin is produced by the pancreas or the body cannot use the insulin that is produced. It is non-insulin dependent and usually treated by diet, exercise and tablets, although as it develops over years, some people might need to use insulin as well. It occurs more often in overweight or obese people and is more common in people of Asian or Afro-Caribbean origin. It can run in families.

Diabetics are advised to regulate the amount of fat and sugar in their diet and take regular exercise. Some Type 2 diabetics can control their condition by diet alone.

Exercise is used as part of the treatment for Type 2 diabetes. Can you think why this might be?

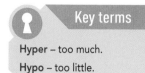

Thyroid gland dysfunction

Thyroxine, the main hormone produced by the thyroid gland, helps to maintain the body's metabolism in the regulation of heart rate and temperature. If the thyroid gland malfunctions it can produce either too much or too little thyroxine.

Overactive thyroid

This is also known as **hyper**thyroidism. The thyroid gland produces too much thyroxine, and this speeds up the metabolism.

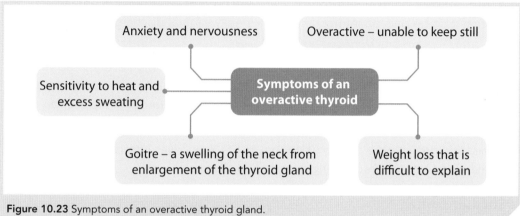

Anxiety and nervousness

Overactive – unable to keep still

Sensitivity to heat and excess sweating

Symptoms of an overactive thyroid

Goitre – a swelling of the neck from enlargement of the thyroid gland

Weight loss that is difficult to explain

Figure 10.23 Symptoms of an overactive thyroid gland.

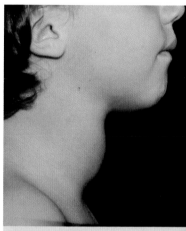

A patient suffering from hyperthyroidism.

It can be treated by taking radioactive iodine that shrinks the thyroid gland, making it less active, and in some cases by surgery to remove some or all of the gland. If the entire thyroid is removed then patients need to take thyroxine in tablet form to regulate its function.

Hyperthyroidism usually starts in young adulthood, although it can start at any age, and is much more common in women than men. It also affects white and Asian people more commonly than other people.

Underactive thyroid

This is also known as **hypo**thyroidism. The thyroid gland produces too little thyroxine and this slows down the metabolism.

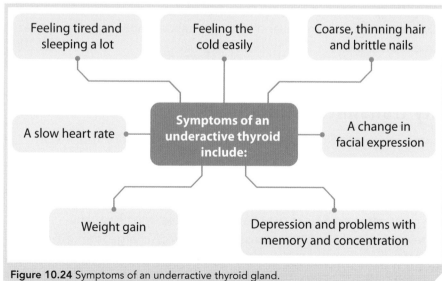

Feeling tired and sleeping a lot

Feeling the cold easily

Coarse, thinning hair and brittle nails

A slow heart rate

Symptoms of an underactive thyroid include:

A change in facial expression

Weight gain

Depression and problems with memory and concentration

Figure 10.24 Symptoms of an underractive thyroid gland.

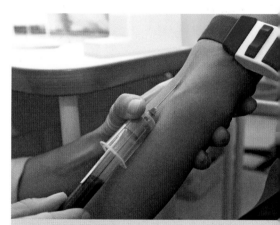

A patient having a blood test to check the levels of thyroxine in the blood.

Treatment is by taking thyroxine in tablet form. Blood levels need to be checked regularly to make sure that the dosage is correct and the gland is functioning normally.

Disorders relating to other body systems

The reproductive system

Cervical cancer

Cervical cancer has very few symptoms, especially in the early stages. Unusual vaginal bleeding can happen after intercourse, between periods or after the menopause. There may also be pain on intercourse and a smelly vaginal discharge.

Treatment is usually a hysterectomy – surgical removal of the uterus and cervix and/or radiotherapy. Women aged 24–50 are offered cervical smear tests every three years, and then every five years between the ages of 50 and 64. This involves scraping a few cells from the cervix and identifying any cancerous changes under a microscope.

Some types of the human papilloma virus can cause cervical cancer. A national immunisation programme of girls when they reach Year 8 was introduced in 2008, with the aim being to greatly reduce incidence of the disease.

Testicular cancer

This is the most common cancer among men aged between 15 and 35. Symptoms include:

- a painless lump in or enlargement of a testicle
- a dull ache or pain in the groin or abdomen
- pain and discomfort in the testicle or a feeling of 'heaviness' in the scrotum.

Treatment is removal of the affected testicle and insertion of an implant so that the scrotum does not look abnormal. Sometimes radiotherapy and/or chemotherapy may be needed, depending on the type of cancer. Doctors will always discuss side effects such as the impact on fertility.

Activity Cervical and testicular cancer

Carry out further research into cervical and testicular cancer, looking particularly at types of treatment available.

Sexually transmitted infections

Sexually transmitted infections (STIs) are passed on by having unprotected sex or genital contact.

Chlamydia

This is one of the most common STIs in the UK. Most people don't have any symptoms, but they can include pain when passing urine, a discharge from the penis, vagina or rectum. Women sometimes have vaginal bleeding between periods or after sex. It is easily treated with antibiotics, but if it is not treated it can lead to infertility from a condition called pelvic inflammatory disease.

Gonorrhoea

This is caused by bacteria present in discharge from the penis and in vaginal fluid. It is transmitted through unprotected sex but also by vibrators or other sex aids. Pregnant women can pass gonorrhoea to their unborn babies. Symptoms include discharge, pain on urination and vaginal bleeding but some people have no symptoms. It is easily diagnosed and treated with antibiotics. If it is not treated, it can lead to pelvic inflammatory disease and infertility.

Infertility

Despite having regular unprotected sex, some couples are unable to conceive. Infertility is diagnosed when a woman has not become pregnant after a year of trying. Normally about 85% of couples will conceive naturally within a year. Sometimes the reason why pregnancy does not occur is unknown, but there are also known causes and they can affect either the man or the woman. These include ovulation not occurring, blocked fallopian tubes, endometriosis or poor quality of the semen.

Living a healthy lifestyle can help couples to conceive but sometimes further treatment is offered such as medication to help ovulation, surgery or IVF treatment.

The musculoskeletal system

Osteoarthritis

Osteoarthritis is the most common type of arthritis in the UK. It most commonly affects the hips and knees but can affect any joint. The cartilage wears away, bony growths appear round the joints and the surrounding tissues become inflamed, resulting in severe pain and loss of movement, although the severity of the symptoms varies greatly. Osteoarthritis is more common in women and in older people. There is no cure, but it can be treated with pain killers, anti-inflammatory drugs and physiotherapy. Some people become so disabled that they need a joint replacement. The affected bone is replaced by metal or plastic joints.

Activity   Osteoporosis

Visit the National Osteoporosis Society website to find out more about osteoporosis.

Assessment activity 10.3   2B.P5 | 2B.M3

Your teacher has been so impressed by the work that you completed in the previous activity that she has asked you to add some more information about the disorders that you have been studying.

She has asked you to:

1 Produce a section describing one common disorder for each body system that you have studied. Make sure that you include information about how the disorder progresses and signs and symptoms.

2 Produce another section explaining in detail how three common disorders affect major body systems. You can use diagrams to illustrate your work and provide further explanation.

Regular monitoring and support of disorders by professionals

Introduction

You have already learned about some of the disorders of the main body systems and how they are treated, but you also need to research and understand other factors that professionals take into consideration when providing care.

Tests

Some conditions may be obvious to professionals, and they can quite quickly make a diagnosis just from the symptoms that their patients provide. But even though doctors usually know, they will often make sure that their suspicions are confirmed through laboratory tests. Blood and urine tests can usually be carried out at a GP surgery, but more complex tests such as X-rays or scans might require referral to a specialist at a hospital. Biopsies are sometimes carried out where a small amount of tissue from the affected area is removed and studied under a microscope.

Provision and use of aids

Some people with disorders may require equipment to help them with activities of daily living. This can range from something as simple as a walking stick, to a kidney dialysis machine. Sometimes an occupational therapist will assess an individual to identify the most suitable type of aid and items such as crutches, walking frames and specialist hospital beds may be provided.

Activity   Who supplies medical aids?

Find out about some of the companies that can supply equipment to individuals, and the types of aids that are available.

Prescribing of treatment and medication

We tend to think of prescribing as being just for medicines, but other types of treatment can also be prescribed. For instance, someone with a damaged ankle at an accident and emergency department may be referred to a physiotherapist, or certain types of dressing may be prescribed.

Why are patients referred to a specialist when X-rays or scans are required?

An elderly patient using a walking frame.

It used to be the case that only doctors and dentists could prescribe medication for patients, but the role of the independent prescriber has become extended over recent years and there are now other healthcare professionals who can be independent prescribers. These include:

- nurse prescribers
- pharmacist prescribers
- optometrist prescribers.

Nurses are allowed to prescribe some controlled drugs, but pharmacists and optometrists cannot prescribe any controlled drugs independently.

Self-administration of medication

Many people who need to take medication are reliable and remember to take the drugs they need. However, some people have mental health or physical conditions that make them forgetful or they are in the early stages of dementia. This means that they either forget to take medication or take more than they should because they have forgotten that they have already taken it. In the community district nurses visit people in their own homes one or more times a day specifically to do medication prompts, which means that they have to remind their patients that they need to take their medication, or check that they have already done so. People who have to take medication every day for the rest of their lives not only have to remember to take them, but also have to remember to monitor their stocks and order repeat prescriptions before their supply runs out. They may also need to be reminded of this.

In the community pharmacists are highly knowledgeable and can often give advice on appropriate over the counter medication which can reduce the need to see the GP.

Have you ever received a prescription from any of the professionals listed above?

Tablet boxes marked with the days of the week may help patients to remember to take their tablets every day.

Regular self-monitoring of disorders

Introduction

As medical science has developed over the years, it has become more common for people to manage illness in their own homes with support from healthcare professionals such as healthcare assistants, district and community nurses and GPs. This means that some patients can monitor their own medical status. There are a number of things that patients can do that help them to maintain a level of control over their care and treatment.

Tests

Some tests can be carried out by patients themselves. They can then record the results for monitoring by healthcare professionals. In some cases they can even upload information to different hospital departments so that their care can be managed remotely.

One of the main tests carried out regularly by individuals is blood glucose monitoring, for instance in the treatment of Type 1 diabetes. A small drop of blood is taken, usually from a finger, and wiped onto a testing strip that is placed in a monitor. This provides a read-out of the blood glucose level and allows a Type 1 diabetic to work out how much insulin they need to inject.

Lifestyle changes

There are instances where a change in lifestyle can make great improvements to an individual's health and wellbeing. These might involve weight loss, increasing activity levels by taking more exercise, giving up smoking, making a change in work/life balance, changing jobs or reducing stress levels.

A patient monitoring his blood glucose levels.

| Activity | Lifestyle therapy |

Find out what lifestyle changes might be recommended for the following conditions:

- coronary heart disease
- Type 2 diabetes
- high blood pressure
- osteoarthritis.

Support for self-administered medication

For many years patients in hospital have not played an active role in their medication and it has been given out to them on scheduled drug rounds by qualified nurses. Self-administration has been introduced because it was recognised that patients take their medication independently at home and there was no reason why they could not do so in hospital, provided their drugs could be stored safely. Assessment has to be carried out to establish that a patient is able to self-administer, and various factors are taken into account.

- Is the patient receiving medicines and willing to participate?
- Does the patient manage their own medication at home?
- Does the patient appear confused or forgetful?
- Is there any history of drug/alcohol abuse or self-harm?
- Can the patient read the labels and can they open the medicine containers?
- Can the patient open his or her medicines locker?
- Does the patient know what his or her medicines are for (and dosage, instructions and side-effects)?

If there is agreement after assessment that the patient can meet the requirements to self-medicate, then there is no reason why they should not do so.

Appropriate environment

Individuals being treated at home have a responsibility to ensure as much as possible that they live in an environment that will not cause their condition to deteriorate. However, some find it difficult to do this, especially if they are ill or not very mobile, and may require help and support. Someone needing dressings to be regularly changed, for instance may need help to ensure that there is a clean area for the dressing to be done so that the possibility of infection is minimised. A house that is too hot or too cold can have an impact on health; too cold and there is a risk of hypothermia and associated illnesses such as pneumonia, and too hot and there is a risk of infection from bacteria growing in warm environments.

How can carers ensure individuals being treated at home have an appropriate environment?

The impact of care on people with disorders

Introduction

Even though some people have conditions that are not curable, effective treatment and care can help them to live a full and enjoyable life.

The positive effects of care

There are a number of positive physical benefits that people can get from appropriate care and support.

Why is it important for individuals receiving care to remain independent?

Mobility

Greater mobility can enable an individual to be more independent and enjoy more of a social life as they might be able to go out more than they used to. This might be achieved as easily as providing a walking aid. There are also mobility schemes, such as mobility buses that can help people get out and about.

Pain relief

It can be very difficult for someone to be positive if they are in a lot of pain. People who experience a lot of pain find that when the pain is managed effectively they feel much better and this has the general effect of helping them to feel much more positive.

Breathing difficulties

Certain conditions cause difficulty in breathing and this can make a person conscious of taking every breath and they quickly become exhausted. It can sometimes cause panic if a person feels that they are not getting enough air into their lungs. Providing care such as oxygen or drugs to ease breathing gives a lot of relief to people.

Controlling diabetes

Eating a healthy diet, taking medication and taking regular exercise will all help to control the symptoms of diabetes. This means that diabetics will be less thirsty, will lose weight and become less irritable and tired.

Emotional and social benefits

Relief of symptoms by appropriate care and support creates a variety of emotional and social benefits for people with different disorders. When someone feels physically better, this has an impact on their emotional wellbeing, and their mood can lift a lot. This can have a knock-on effect of an improved social life, as people feel well enough to engage with others.

The negative effects of care

It is very easy to assume that all care provided can only have a positive effect on the individuals receiving the care, but this is not always the case.

Cost

The cost of certain treatment is very high and this means that some people will not receive it because their health authority will not fund it, and they cannot afford to pay for it themselves. This creates disparity of care and can cause discontentment and resentment.

Time

Some people have treatment that is very time consuming. Renal dialysis, for example, takes on average four hours three times a week. Prolonged treatment with radio- or chemotherapy can also take up a lot of time and some people find it difficult to adapt to a lifestyle that is limited because of the treatment they need to have.

Treatment side effects

The side effects of certain treatments can be very unpleasant and some people find that these are worse than having the condition or disease. Chemotherapy treatment can leave people feeling exhausted, weak and sick, and they are unable to do anything for several days after each treatment. Some patients lose their hair when undergoing chemotherapy. Radiotherapy can also make people tired.

Some drugs have side effects such as rashes, visual disturbance, gastric problems, pins and needles, nausea and vomiting and diarrhoea.

Activity   Drug side effects

Carry out some research into the side effects of the following drugs:

- Penicillin
- Metformin
- Vincristine
- Aldomet.

Carrying out and recording routine observations that support care

◢ Some common observations

Body temperature

Body temperature needs to be kept within quite narrow limits so that all the body's processes work properly. Temperature is taken with a thermometer.

- Ear thermometer: measures temperature by an infrared beam in the ear canal – not always accurate.
- LCD strip: placed on the forehead where the liquid crystal display strip will show the temperature – not very accurate but will show a rise in temperature.
- Electronic digital thermometer: has a digital readout to display the temperature – probably the most accurate but will vary according to the manufacturer.

Pulse rate

The pulse rate is recorded as the number of heartbeats per minute. The rate, strength and rhythm are all important. A fast pulse rate can indicate fever, fright or bleeding and a slow pulse rate can indicate heart problems, a brain injury or the fact that a person is very fit. The pulse rate is usually taken by pressing with the middle finger on an artery where it crosses a bone to feel the pulse. It is most commonly done at the wrist just below the thumb.

Breathing rate

The simplest method of measuring breathing rate is to count the number of times a person's chest rises and falls in a minute (or in half a minute, and double it). This can be done while the pulse is being taken as the person is usually unaware and does not change their breathing rate. Professionals should observe the type and rhythm of breathing as this can often indicate an underlying problem.

Blood pressure

This is normally measured by a battery or electrically operated instrument called a sphygmomanometer. An inflatable cuff is placed round the upper arm at the level of the heart and blown up. This blocks off blood supply to the arm. A valve is then slowly released and the cuff deflates, allowing blood to flow again. The machine records the data and displays the results on a screen. Often the pulse will be displayed as well.

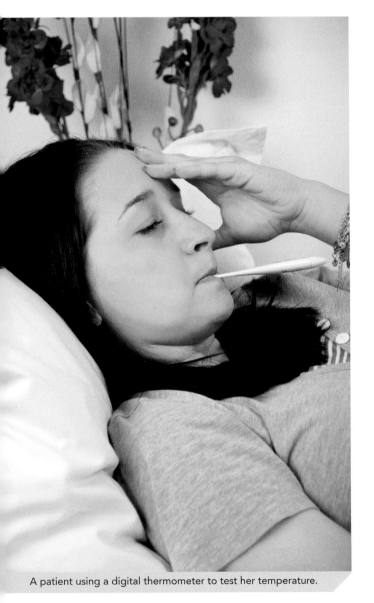

A patient using a digital thermometer to test her temperature.

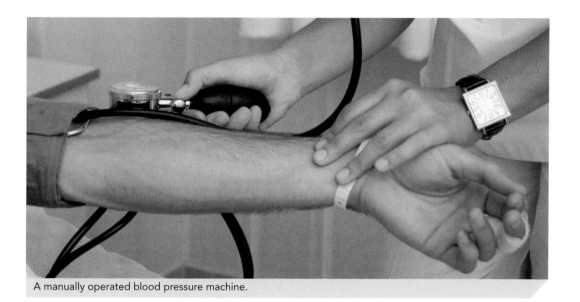

A manually operated blood pressure machine.

Interpreting results in relation to normal values

It is impossible to interpret observation results unless normal values are known for comparison. However, what is normal for one person may not be normal for another, but there are normal ranges that can be used. The table below shows the normal ranges of temperature, pulse, respiration rate and blood pressure.

Table 10.9 Normal values for body functions.

Measurement	Normal range
Body temperature	36.5–37.2°C
Pulse	60–80 beats per minute
Breathing rate	8–17 breaths per minute
Blood pressure	120/80 mmHg

Assessment activity 10.4

2B.P6 | 2B.P7 | 2B.M4 | 2B.D2

Your teacher/tutor is still working on the electronic resource for your intranet and wants you to produce information about one common disorder for each body system. She has asked you to provide the following:

- The routine care given for one disorder for each system.
- The impact of the routine care given to people with one of the disorders – you can do this as a case study.
- The recommended appropriate routine care that can be given to the individual with the condition, justifying your decisions.
- A record of one routine observation that can be carried out over time, which includes interpreting the results in relation to normal values.

Print out the work you have completed so that it can be checked before it is uploaded to the electronic resource.

Introduction

By studying for this qualification, you have already shown your interest in health and social care, but you may not be aware of how the different services work together.

For example, who decides whether a young adult with physical and learning disabilities is supported at home or in a residential setting? Why are some people with a medical condition cared for solely by their GP, while others regularly visit a hospital?

This unit will give you an insight into how health and social care services and staff communicate, and work together. You will look at the implications of good team working and at what happens if professionals do not work together effectively.

For some people, gaining access to health and social care services can be difficult. You will look at some of the reasons for this, and will learn how professionals work with individuals, to minimise barriers and provide high-quality services to all who need them.

Assessment: You will be assessed by a series of assignments set by your teacher/tutor.

Learning aims

In this unit you will:

A understand the provision of health and social care services

B explore factors that affect access to health and social care services

C examine partnership working in health and social care.

> When I went on placement to a nursing home, I thought I would only see care staff. But I was surprised to see that there were a lot of different professionals, some from outside agencies, all working together to support the service users. I saw a physiotherapist, chiropodist, GPs, a psychiatrist and an occupational therapist.
>
> Sam Tyler, *16-year-old would-be healthcare professional*

Services in Health and Social Care

11

Assessment Zone

This table shows what you must do in order to achieve a **Pass**, **Merit** or **Distinction** grade, and where you can find activities in this book to help you.

Assessment criteria

Level 1	Level 2 Pass	Level 2 Merit	Level 2 Distinction
Learning aim A: Understand the provision of health and social care services			
1A.1 Outline the provision of health and social care services.	**2A.P1** Describe the provision of health and social care services. **Assessment activity 11.1** See page 295	**2A.M1** Discuss the differences in the different types of health and social care provision, with reference to examples. **Assessment activity 11.1** See page 295	**2A.D1** Compare national provision of health and social care services to local provision. **Assessment activity 11.1** See page 295
1A.2 English Outline one effect of current and relevant legislation on the provision of health and social care services.	**2A.P2** English Outline how current and relevant legislation affects the provision of health and social care services. **Assessment activity 11.1** See page 295		
Learning aim B: Explore factors that affect access to health and social care services			
1B.3 Identify factors that positively affect access to health and social care services.	**2B.P3** Describe factors which positively affect access to health and social care services. **Assessment activity 11.2** See page 301	**2B.M2** Assess how factors affect access to health and social care services. **Assessment activity 11.2** See page 301	**2B.D2** Make recommendations on how to improve access to health and social care services for a selected individual. **Assessment activity 11.2** See page 301
1B.4 Identify factors that negatively affect access to health and social care services.	**2B.P4** Describe factors which negatively affect access to health and social care services. **Assessment activity 11.2** See page 301		
Learning aim C: Examine partnership working in health and social care			
1C.5 Identify professionals who might work in partnership in health and social care.	**2C.P5** Describe how professionals could work together in partnership in health and social care, using selected examples. **Assessment activity 11.3** See page 307	**2C.M3** Explain the potential benefits of partnership working in health and social care to service users. **Assessment activity 11.3** See page 307	**2C.D3** Assess potential difficulties of partnership working in health and social care. **Assessment activity 11.3** See page 307

English / English signposting

How you will be assessed

The unit will be assessed by a series of internally assessed tasks. You will be expected to show an understanding of the differences between the various types of health and social care services, and how each meets the needs of individuals.

You will also need to show an understanding of the laws which govern health and social care, and how they affect the ways health and social care services are provided.

You will consider the factors which have a positive effect on access for individuals to the health and social care they need, and also those factors which have a negative effect.

Finally, you will need to show an understanding of the different ways in which health and social care professionals work in partnership to support the people who use the services.

The tasks will be based on work in a health or social care organisation. To complete the tasks you will need to apply the information you have gained from your teacher/tutor and your personal research to the scenario.

Your assessment could be in the form of:

- a series of newspaper or magazine articles about health and social care services
- an information pack for people who are uncertain which health and social care career pathway to take
- materials such as leaflets, booklets and PowerPoint® presentations.

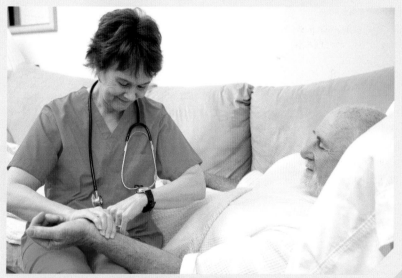

Structure of health and social care services (1)

Getting started

How many different health and social care services can you think of? What type of care do they all provide?

Introduction

It is important for you to understand that although this unit is divided into different topics, each one has an impact on the others. For example, the ways in which services are structured will have an effect on how well people are able to access them. The legislation and regulations form a framework in which all health and social care services in the UK must be contained. None of the services, statutory, private and voluntary can function outside laws, regulations and codes of practice. If you see the topics within this unit as being interrelated, you will find the information much more logical and easy to understand.

In this topic you will learn about the structure of health and social care services.

Key terms

Health and social care services – the services that provide health and social care.

Access – the ways in which service users receive the services they need.

Legislation – laws set by Parliament, which state how things should happen.

Look at Figure 11.1. Which types of health and social care services can you identify? The different types of services will be discussed in the next section of this unit.

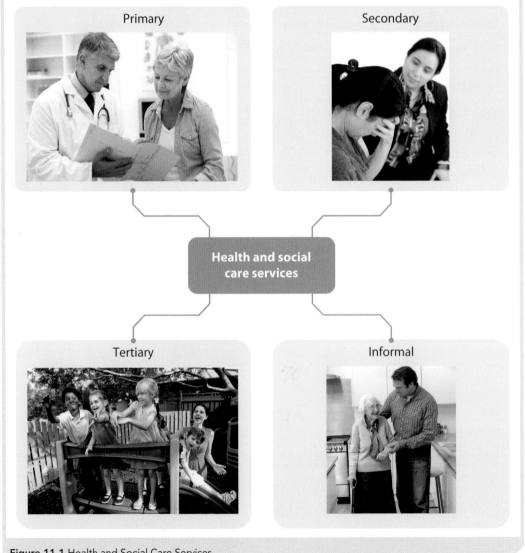

Figure 11.1 Health and Social Care Services.

WorkSpace

▶ Frank Romero

Occupational Therapist

I am an occupational therapist employed by my local primary care trust. I am attached to a team of health professionals who work in a medical practice in a large city. In addition to working in the medical centre I often visit the homes of service users, who find travel difficult. I am really glad that I learned to drive because I could not do this part of my job without a clean driving licence.

Some occupational therapists work in NHS Trusts and Mental Health Trusts, with a variety of people. Others work in research or are attached to schools for children and young people who have additional needs, such as learning disabilities. Other areas where occupational therapists have a role are sheltered housing projects, supporting older people to retain as much mobility as possible, prisons – where we support the teaching of life skills, residential and nursing homes and also charities, such as Age UK and the National Autistic Society.

My main role is working with individuals to prevent or reduce the effects of disability and to encourage them to function independently in all aspects of their daily life. Some of the disability experienced is due to medical conditions, such as arthritis or stroke, or injury from accidents. Other people have dementia or other mental ill health; my aim is to work with the team to improve the quality of life for individuals.

I completed my BTEC First Award Health and Social Care at school and then went on to college to the Diploma, followed by the BTEC Level 3 National in Health and Social Care where I achieved a full Distinction profile. I worked for a while as a receptionist at my local medical centre and then decided to apply to university to complete a Bachelor of Science degree in occupational therapy. My job is really satisfying – working with the whole team to provide best-quality care and support for our service users.

Think about it

Sometimes the patients in Frank's care display aggressive behaviour, as a symptom of their illness.

- Why is it important that Frank remains calm and polite when working patients who become aggressive?
- Why is it important that Frank records any incidents of aggressive behaviour in his patients?

Structure of health and social care services (2)

Introduction

There is a range of health and social care services designed to cope with particular needs so that individuals can have access to the appropriate care at any given time. For example, if you have a sore throat you would go to a pharmacist or to your general practitioner (GP) rather than the Accident and Emergency department of your local NHS Trust. On the other hand, a family with a disabled child would access Social Services for support.

Primary care

Primary means first, and these are the services you would approach first for help and support. Examples of **primary care** are:

- GPs who deal with everyday illnesses, medical conditions and minor injuries and who monitor more long-term conditions and pregnancy, often in partnership with secondary care services, such as NHS Trusts.

- Dentists who treat most normal dental problems and help with the care and maintenance of teeth. They may refer you to secondary care services, such as orthodontists or the oral surgical department of an NHS Trust.

- Opticians who monitor people's sight and eye health and fit glasses and contact lenses. They may refer you to secondary care services, such as the ophthalmic department of an NHS Trust, if there are concerns about your eyes.

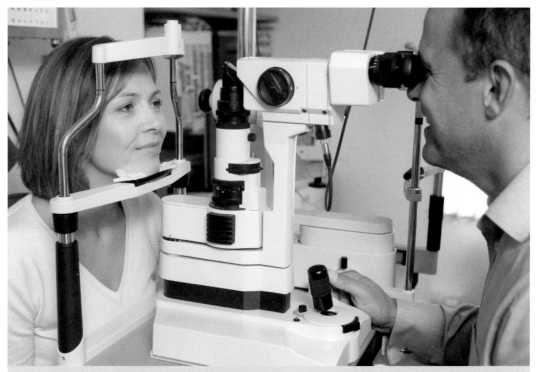

Why might a doctor refer you to your optician if you had a problem with your eyes?

- Health visitors who are usually attached to a local medical practice. Health visitors work closely with other professionals in the medical practice; for example, GPs, practice nurses and midwives. They give support and advice to families with young children, and also to older, more vulnerable, people who attend the medical practice. Health visitors are registered nurses, who also hold an additional diploma in Health Visiting.

- Midwives who care for pregnant women in the community. Some also work in NHS Trusts.

Secondary care

Have you had any experience of secondary health and social care services?

People are referred to **secondary care** by primary care professionals. For example, your GP may refer you to a specialist at the NHS Trust, if they think your symptoms require further investigation. Another instance might be a health visitor referring a family to Social Services if their home was not suitable for a new baby and they needed rehousing.

Examples of secondary health and social care services are:

- Hospital care – usually in NHS Trusts for physical illness, mental ill health and surgery (both planned, such as a knee replacement, or emergency, such as the removal of a burst appendix).

- Therapists – for example, physiotherapists who support mobility, occupational therapists who support skills for independent living, and speech and language therapists.

- Counsellors – for people who have problems they need to discuss with someone outside the family. For example, those who work with families, providing therapy to enable families to discuss the issues they have with different family members, in a safe environment.

- Social workers – for example, providing support for individuals with mental health issues and safeguarding children who are at risk.

 Key term

Secondary care – based in centres such as NHS Trusts, Ambulance Trusts, Mental Health Trusts and Children's Trusts.

Structure of health and social care services (3)

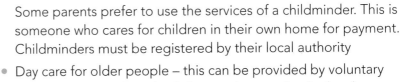

Tertiary care

Usually people receive **tertiary care** following a referral from a member of the primary or secondary services. Examples of tertiary care are:

- Day care for young children who have additional needs, or who have a parent in hospital and another in full-time work.

Some parents prefer to use the services of a childminder. This is someone who cares for children in their own home for payment. Childminders must be registered by their local authority

- Day care for older people – this can be provided by voluntary organisations, such as the Salvation Army, or by the local authority. Individuals may be recommended by Social Services in response to a request from the individual or a relative.

Individuals usually stay for the full day and participate in a variety of activities. A midday meal and snacks are also provided.

- Nursing homes – for people discharged from hospital but not ready to go home. Individuals receive nursing care from registered nurses and healthcare assistants. Individuals are referred either by hospital doctors or GPs. Nursing home places are often privately funded, either by the individual or by relatives, but some beds within the home are designated for the care of older people with mental illness, such as dementia, and are funded by the NHS.

What are the benefits of a child being placed in day care?

- Residential care homes – for individuals who need support with personal care. Individuals may refer themselves when they can no longer care for themselves at home. Individuals may also be referred by Social Services. Some relatives may contact Social Services to discuss a referral, if they cannot manage the care at home.

Many residential care homes are privately funded, but some residents are funded by the local authority, if they do not have the means to pay. Many local authorities have closed their care homes, and choose to pay the fees needed to support individuals in private care.

Why might a nursing home be better than a patient receiving care in their own home?

- Fostering arrangements – for children who cannot be cared for by their own families. Foster carers are trained and approved by Social Services and care for children within the foster carer's home. Children are placed in foster care by Social Services.

- Hospices – for individuals with terminal illnesses. Hospices receive some funding from the state, but also rely on donations from individuals, organisations and money-raising events to provide the remainder of the funds required. Individuals may be referred by their GP or, if they are currently an inpatient, by the NHS Trust.

- Specialist care units – for example renal units for individuals with kidney disease and oncology units for individuals with cancer. Individuals may be referred by their GP or, if they are currently an inpatient or attending an outpatient clinic, the NHS Trust.

All of these services work together to provide a good standard of care for individuals. Some individuals may receive support from all three types of care. For example, a person with diabetes may be monitored regularly by their GP, attend an NHS diabetic clinic and, if the diabetes has affected their kidneys, an NHS Trust renal unit for dialysis.

Informal care

Much social care is provided by informal carers; these are relatives, neighbours and friends. Some people may give up their paid employment to support people who cannot take care of themselves. Individuals may be supported informally by home carers; for example relatives who live within the family home and meet the person's daily needs. Although they may be eligible to claim a 'carer's allowance', informal carers work mainly out of concern for their relatives and are a valuable community resource.

Some informal carers have formed self-help groups to provide a forum for discussion and mutual support. These groups are a valuable source of support for families who can otherwise feel very alone as they manage the challenges presented by the people they care for on a daily basis.

Carers of individuals with long-term conditions may receive support from organisations such as the National Autistic Society. Charitable organisations such as Macmillan can provide support for those suffering from cancer and their families.

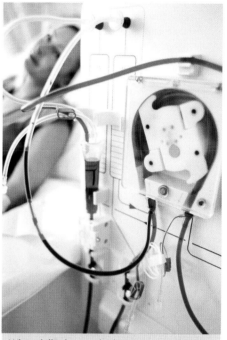

What skills do you think someone working in a specialist care unit may need?

Case study   Caring for the family

The Alonso family

The Alonso family consists of Javier, aged 36, his wife Monica (32) and their two children, Carmen (6) and David (12).

- Monica is six months pregnant and attends the antenatal clinic at her local GP practice.
- Javier damaged a tendon in his foot while running. He attends an outpatient clinic at the local general hospital every week.
- Carmen has eczema and attends the dermatology clinic at the local children's hospital.
- Monica's mother normally also lives with them, but is currently in a nursing home, following a stroke.
- David has recently visited the orthodontist and has been fitted with braces.
- Javier visits his grandfather three times a week and does his ironing and a weekly shop.

Questions

1 What types of care are the family receiving?
2 Are any of the family members providing care?
3 What is the name for care provided by the family?

Types of health and social care provision (1)

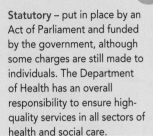

Introduction

There are different ways of providing health and social care in the UK but these fall broadly into three categories: statutory, private and independent, and voluntary. Statutory care is care that must be provided by law, and is generally government funded. Private and independent are two ways of describing care that is paid for by the service user, and voluntary care is provided by charities and unpaid workers, such as hospital visitors.

Statutory care

The government provides most statutory care, which is care that must be provided by law. Everyone who has a particular need as identified by the government must be able to access the service. Money to support these services and to pay the wages of people who work in these services is provided by the government. However, some people may choose to pay for their care. They still have a statutory right to have the care, but would rather pay for services.

Statutory services may change from time to time but currently include:

- Social Services – provides a variety of social care services, including safeguarding children, young people and vulnerable adults and supporting families of children with disabilities.
- The National Health Service – a national service that oversees hospitals, GP practices, dental practices, school nursing services and community nursing services .
- National Health Service Trusts – usually based in hospitals and clinics.

Ambulance Trusts are an example of statutory care. They manage all ambulances and professionals including paramedics and technicians within their region.

- Primary Care Trusts – cover services which are based in the community, including GP practices, dental practices, opticians and community nursing services.
- Mental Health Trusts – deal specifically with mental health and include mental health hostels, inpatient facilities, secure psychiatric units and community-based services.
- Children's Trusts – incorporate a variety of services for children. They include supporting families in bringing up their children and therapy and support for children with disabilities.

All of these organisations are funded primarily by the government, but there are other sources of funding. Some comes from charges made to users of health services, for example prescription charges, dental and optician's fees for adults over 19 and under 65 who are not entitled to some form of benefits. All of these services are statutory; however, the charges are intended to enable people who cannot afford to pay, to have a good standard of care.

Some support provided by social services is **means tested**. For example, fees for residential care, community home support and the mobile meals service. In addition, some statutory care facilities, such as hospitals and hospices are supported by groups of volunteers and fundraising to pay for particular projects, such as special equipment or care units.

Private and independent care

Some health and social care services are privately funded. This means that people either pay directly for the services or have private healthcare insurance. Some people prefer to use private care because of the shorter waiting times for appointments compared to services provided by the state. They may also prefer the greater choice, for example, of which hospital to choose, and the dates and times of treatment.

Examples of private care services include:

- private medical and nursing care including hospitals
- private dental treatment
- private therapies, including physiotherapy, osteopaths and chiropractics
- cosmetic clinics
- domiciliary care
- private residential care – this includes social care for older people who cannot cope at home due to age or reduced mobility, and younger people who have significant disabilities. Sometimes individuals are funded in private care by local authorities if this meets the needs of the individual more appropriately. Some residential schools for young people with complex needs are also privately funded, but may receive funding from local authorities for individuals whose needs cannot be met in other schools
- sheltered housing complexes for older and/or disabled individuals. A warden is attached to the complex, to ensure that the residents are safe, and that all of their needs are met.

Key term

Means testing – someone's income is assessed and taken into account to see if they are eligible for free or subsidised services. If income is over a certain level, they may have to pay for some or all of the cost of the service.

Sheltered homes usually have these cords in every room; do you know what they are for?

Types of health and social care provision (2)

Voluntary care

Other support is provided by voluntary groups, which support people who have a particular need. These organisations may have paid, professionally qualified staff working for them, but they mainly rely on donations from individuals and many of the staff are volunteers.

Organisations that provide voluntary care include charities and local voluntary initiatives.

Volunteering is a good way to increase self-confidence and learn new skills.

Charities are defined as organisations that are not run for profit and are involved in education, religion or services to individuals of all ages; these include:

- The Salvation Army – a Christian faith-based organisation funded by donation. The Salvation Army has branches all over the world and is involved in a variety of work including day care for children and older people, visiting vulnerable individuals and families in their own homes and giving out food to homeless individuals.

- The Samaritans – a national organisation funded by donation. Trained volunteers answer telephone calls from individuals who are in need of support. Sometimes individuals who call the Samaritans are in desperate straits and might even be contemplating suicide.

- Mencap – supports individuals with learning disabilities of all ages. It also provides support for families of individuals with learning disabilities. Mencap is funded by private donation.

Charities can apply for some funding from the local authority if they are providing a service within the community. However, this funding is now being reduced.

Local voluntary initiatives are usually formed by groups of individuals who want to help others. Sometimes people involved in local groups have experienced health and social care services themselves either directly or through the experiences of a friend or relative.

Local voluntary initiatives include the following:

- groups attached to local NHS Trusts and known as 'Friends of . . . ', for example, a hospice, hospital or local authority care home. These groups provide services such as running a mobile library for service users who are in hospital, manning hospital shops, or providing Christmas or birthday presents for older people who do not have visitors

- groups of volunteers who visit older and disabled people in their homes, and spend time chatting to relieve loneliness

- carers support groups – groups of informal carers who meet together to support each other and discuss issues related to caring for their relatives. Carers support groups also act as pressure groups to lobby for improvement in service provision.

The impact of different forms of service provision on individuals who use the services

Being able to choose the way in which health and social care is delivered can impact the health and wellbeing of individuals. For example, being placed on a long waiting list for surgery or treatment can result in the worsening of a condition. However, the state also runs services, overseen by the Department of Health, which offer good-quality care to many individuals.

Private and independent health and social care may offer more choice to individuals, and may also be better resourced. Individuals may enjoy a greater choice with regard to facilities, and waiting times for appointments, treatments and surgery are usually shorter. Nevertheless, care delivered by both types of service can be just as effective, and both types are monitored by the Care Quality Commission, which is an organisation overseen by the Department of Health, to ensure high quality of care delivery.

Activity — Caring for Mrs Jones

Write a list of all the different services you think will be available to Mrs Jones, who lives in a residential care home. Share your ideas with three others in a group. Then go online to look at the services available at a local care home. Are there any you missed? Are there any you are surprised to find offered? Why are you surprised?

Figure 11.2 Caring for Mrs Jones.

Just checking

1 Name three types of statutory care.
2 Name one way of paying for private healthcare.
3 Name three types of private care.
4 Name two types of tertiary care.
5 Name four voluntary organisations.
6 Who do hospices care for?
7 Name one group of people who could be helped by local volunteers.

Current and relevant legislation

Getting started

Do you think that laws and regulations are important in health and social care? What would happen if we did not have these? Are these laws and regulations strong enough?

Key terms

Legislation – laws laid down by Parliament.

Regulations – rules in this context that state how services should be delivered.

Discrimination – treating one group or individual less fairly than another.

Introduction

All health and social care services are governed by **legislation** and **regulations**. This is to make sure that the services do people good and not harm, and also that everyone who needs them has access to the services. The main pieces of legislation that apply to health and social care are outlined below.

Main pieces of legislation

The following pieces of legislation along with other regulations are intended to ensure that a high quality of provision is available for all who need it. They also state the rights of individuals who use the services, such as being treated with dignity and having care that meets their individual needs.

Health and Social Care Act 2008

This regulates the standards of care and support provided for individuals and introduced the Care Quality Commission, an organisation that monitors the quality of health and social care, aiming to ensure that everyone receives the same high standard of care and there is no **discrimination**. It also oversees the registration of health and social care workers.

This act ensures that complaints about health and social care professionals are investigated thoroughly. People who have caused harm to service users, either by accident or intentionally, can be removed from professional registers and no longer allowed to work in health and social care.

The act also regulates the way medication is dispensed by pharmacists.

Care Quality Commission (Registration) Regulations 2009

Inspectors from the Commission make regular visits to health and social care settings to ensure that care is of a high quality. Organisations that do not meet the right standards will be given action plans and a date by which these must be completed. The Commission has the right to close down organisations and remove their licence to practise.

Mental Health Act 1983

This legislation aims to ensure that individuals with mental health problems receive the appropriate care and treatment. This can sometimes mean that people are kept in hospital for treatment against their will, if they are at risk of causing harm to themselves or to other people.

Other legislation

Other pieces of legislation support health and social care workers, for example in agreeing pay scales, hours worked, and protecting them from workplace bullying. This is important so that workers can provide the high quality of care required.

Equality Act 2010

This legislation applies to many aspects of life in the UK, including health and social care services. It states that health and social care workers must not discriminate against:

- people with mental health problems
- older and disabled people who are being cared for in their own homes
- people of all ages who attend day centres
- residents in social care homes and nursing homes.

Legislation and regulations have been put in place to ensure fair and equal health and social care provision for all. Under the legislation, health and social care services are required to provide appropriate services, meet set targets for providing care which meets the needs of individuals and attends to all people on waiting lists, within set time limits.

The legislation also states that individual service users have rights; for example to complain about treatment or care, to be treated with respect and to be communicated with, using their preferred method of communication. Individuals who are detained in hospital due to mental ill health also have the right to a review, and to appeal against decisions made about their care.

The Department of Health has agreements, known as Service Level Agreements, on the agreed level of services to be provided for the people who use the services. These are monitored and organisations who do not meet the required level will be given action plans for improvement.

Why is it important that health care professionals are up to date with the latest legislation?

Assessment activity 11.1   2A.P1 | 2A.P2 | 2A.M1 | 2A.D1

Michael and Maria are lifelong friends from their school days. Both have mental health issues and attend the local drop-in centre run by the Community Psychiatric Nursing Service. They live in sheltered housing owned and managed by a charitable trust. They often go for their midday meal at the Salvation Army Day Centre. As Michael and Maria are unable to work, due to their mental health issues, they find the free lunch helpful. Michael also attends the renal unit at the local NHS Trust, as his kidneys were damaged as a result of medication.

Michael and Maria both have qualified social workers as key workers who support them with their daily living. Michael's mother visits them once a week to clean the house and do the washing and ironing.

Maria's cousin takes her out for lunch once a month. She noticed that Maria was having difficulty eating.

Maria explained that her dentures did not fit properly. Maria's cousin arranged for Maria to visit a private dental clinic for new dentures, and asked the clinic to send the bill to her.

1 Describe the different types of service provided for Michael and Maria.

2 Discuss the differences between the different services used by Michael and Maria in terms of the funding and the needs being met.

3 Compare the national and local services that are supporting Michael and Maria (you may need to research some of the organisations for information on this).

4 Outline the different pieces of legislation that ensure that Michael and Maria receive a high quality of care.

Factors that affect access to health and social care services (1)

Introduction

The aim of government and health and social care organisations is that everyone should have the access to services that they require, regardless of geography, finances, age, sex, gender, culture or ethnicity. In reality, however, there are many barriers to access that often have to be overcome.

Geographical location

People in rural or isolated areas may have less choice and further to travel for services. For example, a GP practice might provide services for more than one village and the nearest Social Services centre could be in a town several miles away.

There may be a problem with transport for people with no car in areas with poor public transport services. This can prevent people seeking assistance soon enough or often enough because it is too difficult to access the service. Some people might find that a long journey aggravates their condition or increases their discomfort so much that they prefer to stay at home. Others are concerned that their admission to hospital will mean further expense and travel for relatives.

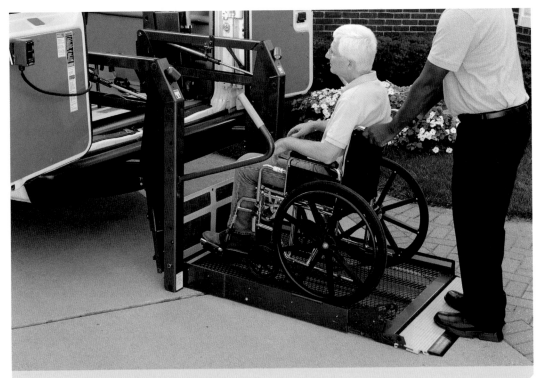

How can a patient transport service help those service users who live in rural locations?

Socio-economic

Education, social background, economic status and lifestyle can inform choices that will affect health. For example, healthy or unhealthy food choices, the decision to smoke, drink excessively or take drugs, and whether or not people choose to take exercise.

Lack of education can result in people making unhealthy choices and also being unaware of the benefits of things such as free screening. This can result in the early signs of diseases such as cancer and STIs being missed.

All of these reasons can result in individuals requiring health care due to the late diagnosis of disease and the effects on body systems from unhealthy choices.

Equality and diversity

Some people do not access health and social care services because their particular needs are not addressed, for example:

- unsuitable physical access, such as no ramps for wheelchair users, or no provision of induction loops for individuals with a hearing impairment
- appointments not offered outside prayer times to prevent disruption to religious practice
- guaranteed same-sex carers to meet personal and cultural preferences, for example due to religious requirements or sexual orientation
- shared accommodation for same-sex couples
- provision of activities in residential care, which meets the requirements of different age groups
- the use of appropriate and preferred methods of communication; e.g. British Sign language, Makaton, community languages
- financial support to meet the cost of travel to services, and replace loss of income created by visits
- direct and indirect discrimination from professionals e.g., not providing information in suitable formats, large print, or the individual's preferred language
- disrespectful treatment from professionals; e.g. use of impolite tone, shouting at service users, not using preferred names and titles.

Communication

People with English as their second language may prefer to be communicated with in their first language. This is particularly important when people are ill or under stress in order to ensure that they are properly understood and their needs are fully met. Other people may use alternative methods of communication, such as British Sign Language (BSL), automated speech or Makaton and will need interpreters or practitioners who can communicate with them.

It is vital that professionals use appropriate language for service users' age and level of competence. An adult with learning difficulties, for instance, will need something explained in ways that they can understand, but the tone of the professional should still be polite and not patronising. It is important not to use **jargon** or **acronyms**, but speak in clear language, which does not leave people confused.

Key terms

Equality – providing the best services for individuals in ways which meet all of their needs.

Diversity – difference between people, in terms of gender, race, culture, age, sexuality, ability etc. Diversity should be acknowledged when delivering services.

Jargon – terms used by the profession, but not widely understood outside.

Acronyms – letters which stand for terms, such as SIDS, for sudden infant death syndrome.

Remember

For all service users, it is important to use preferred names and titles. For example Doctor, Mr, Mrs, Miss or Ms, in order to show respect for the individual. Only use first names if specifically requested or permitted by the service user.

Factors that affect access to health and social care services (2)

Financial

For people on low incomes the cost of travelling to a service can be a barrier to access. Other charges may also be a burden, for example prescription, dental and optical charges may mean that some people have to choose between healthcare and other necessities. Such choices reduce access for many people.

Some people, for instance the self-employed, are not paid if they are not able to work or are absent from work for appointments to receive treatment. This may lead to people deciding to miss appointments or not have treatment rather than lose pay.

Local funding arrangements can also affect access, with different regions offering different services. For example, bus services in some isolated areas may be reduced or absent. If demand for a service is low in an area, then the local NHS Trust, Social Services or local authority may consider that it is not worth funding, meaning that people have to travel further for care.

Some services, such as home care and mobile meal services are means tested. The ability of individuals to pay for services will affect the level of service received. Individuals may choose not to pay for services, even when judged able to do so, and this can affect their health and wellbeing.

What other situations can you think of where home health visits may be necessary?

Accessing services

There are a variety of ways to ensure that services are accessible for everyone who needs them. For example, providing information in different languages, large print, Braille or sound-recorded; having interpreters available, and using technology to support communication. Not everyone needs to travel for services; care can be made more accessible by bringing it to the service user. For example, community nurse, social worker and social care worker home visits can be arranged. Also volunteers, such as Friends of the Elderly, will visit older people at home and organisations such as the British Red Cross can provide additional nursing support at home.

Quality of care provision

If the care delivered is not good quality, for example if the professional is incompetent, or individuals are not treated with respect or dignity, they may decide not to attend appointments because their previous experience was unpleasant.

Dignity is important for all of us, and when this is removed, for instance if individuals are not given privacy when being medically examined, or are discussed as though they were not in the room, people will not want to repeat the experience.

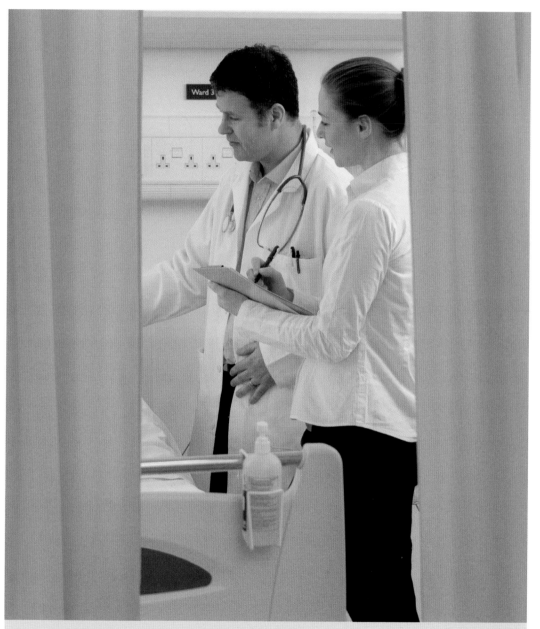

What other examples of ensuring dignity can you think of?

Factors that affect access to health and social care services (3)

Figure 11.3 How would you expect to be treated in each of these situations?

Case study   Respect

Ruth and Michael Jones live with their 3-year-old son Peter in a pleasant suburb at the edge of a large city. Peter has autism and attends a special nursery four times a week. Because Peter's speech is not progressing at the rate expected for his age, the family's GP referred him to Rhia, a speech and language therapist.

Rhia has worked with Ruth and Michael for several months, showing them how to encourage Peter. She asks them for information about Peter, calling them 'experts'. Ruth and Michael have asked her a lot of wide-ranging questions too. Rhia always listens carefully and allows them to finish before she replies. She does not laugh or show surprise at any of the questions because she recognises how concerned they were about their son. Rhia always explains issues clearly without using jargon, and uses a polite tone when speaking to them.

Ruth and Michael feel that Rhia shares the support and planning for Peter with them and this encourages them to work with her as partners.

1 How does Rhia demonstrate respect for Ruth and Michael?

2 Why is it important not to laugh or show surprise at the questions asked by service users?

3 How would Ruth and Michael have felt if Rhia had laughed at their questions?

4 Why does Rhia call Ruth and Michael experts?

5 Why does Rhia not use jargon when explaining issues to Ruth and Michael?

Assessment activity 11.2

2B.P3 | 2B.P4 | 2B.M2 | 2B.D2

Rebecca Goldsmith is 18 years old and was born with a visual impairment. Rebecca visits the ophthalmic (eye) clinic at her local hospital three times a year for a check-up. The clinic has recently received a large donation of money and the staff decided to use this to redecorate the waiting room and buy new furniture and a new carpet.

Before the redecoration, Rebecca found the clinic easy to access and move around; there was a brightly painted rail at the steps up to the clinic. Each step was brightly outlined in yellow and the door had a large handle which was easy for her to locate.

Inside the clinic, there was a bright yellow line to follow which led to the reception, the carpet edges were easy to see and the furniture was in bright colours. All of this made the clinic easily accessible and Rebecca felt confident and safe.

Unfortunately, the redecoration has reduced access to the clinic for Rebecca. The donation came from a building society whose brand colours were pale green and yellow and the building society manager insisted that the clinic be redecorated in these colours, which are difficult for individuals like Rebecca who have a visual impairment to see. There was no money left over to repaint the edges of the steps and the rail beside them; they are now faded and more difficult to see. In addition, the bright yellow line leading to reception has faded and needs repainting, and the carpet, which has a busy pattern, is confusing for Rebecca.

1 Describe the factors which made visiting the ophthalmic clinic a positive experience for Rebecca before the redecoration.

2 Describe the factors which made visiting the ophthalmic clinic a negative experience for Rebecca after the redecoration.

3 Assess how both the positive and negative factors affected Rebecca's access to the ophthalmic clinic

4 Read through the case study and make recommendations for ways in which the clinic manager could improve access for Rebecca.

Remember

- Every citizen has a legal right to access health and social care services.
- Different people need the same services provided in different ways.
- Without appropriate access, some individuals will not receive the care and support they need.

Take it further

Think about a health or social care setting you have visited, for example, your local GP, dental surgery or optician.

How accessible was it for people who:

- are visually impaired
- use a wheelchair
- are hearing impaired
- use a mobility aid such as a stick or walking frame.

Partnership working in health and social care (1)

Introduction

Much of health and social care is delivered by teams; even if someone is being supported by a community nurse or a social worker, these professionals are part of a team, which includes other health and social care professionals, administrative support and often technical support. Teamwork is essential if the individual is going to receive all of the support they need. Some people work best as team leaders, while others are more efficient and comfortable working as team members.

There are several different ways of working in teams that are used in health and social care services. These are two examples.

Multi-agency working

This means that professionals from different health and social care services or agencies work together to support an individual or family. An example would be Social Services working with a Mental Health Trust to support an individual who has mental ill health, enabling them to live in the community. Another example would be a local authority Children's Services unit working with the justice system to support an adolescent who has become involved in street crime. Working together, the two services would support the young person to complete their education.

Multi-disciplinary working

This means that professionals from the same service who have different roles work together to support an individual or family. An example of this would be a health visitor, a GP, a psychiatric nurse and an occupational therapist working together to support an individual with dementia and their family.

A team of healthcare professionals discussing treatment with a patient and his partner.

Case study   Supporting Tariq

Read the case study and decide whether Tariq is being supported by a multi-agency or a multi-disciplinary partnership.

Tariq is 28 years old and has mental ill health. He is supported by a group of professionals who enable him to live independently.

- The community psychiatric nurse visits him each day to ensure that he is taking his medication.
- Tariq has a key worker, who is a social worker, trained to support individuals with mental ill health.
- The housing officer worked with Tariq's key worker and the community psychiatric nurse to arrange sheltered accommodation for Tariq.

Benefits of working in partnership

Service users benefit from effective partnerships in health and social care. Professionals use their skills more effectively if they are not trying to meet all of an individual's needs, but can concentrate on what they do best. In this way, individuals who use the services really do receive expert care and support. Of course it is still important that all professionals take a holistic approach, which means that they still meet the need for respect and deliver care in a way which takes account of preferences, likes and dislikes, including cultural and religious requirements. Partnership working also means that individuals receive a 'seamless approach' to their care and support; in other words, there are no gaps because all of the professionals are working together, communicating with each other and functioning as a team, even when they are from different services. This approach also means that costs are reduced, as the care is planned and resources are not wasted.

Why is it so important to work as a team in health and social care?

Partnership working in health and social care (2)

▶ Difficulties of working in partnership

Not all partnership working is efficient and positive. There are various reasons why this is sometimes the case.

Professional animosity

Sometimes professionals from different agencies resent having to work together and may not communicate well with each other. This may be due to an individual's previous negative experience of working with other agencies, for instance because of clashing personalities. It could also be due to 'historical factors'. For example, in the past professionals from different agencies or disciplines may have worked in separate teams, often supporting the same service users but not cooperating with each other. Because they did not communicate, each team may have regarded themselves as being more efficient and more able to provide high-quality care. Lack of knowledge about the work of other teams may mean that everyone assumed that the 'other team' were inefficient and less qualified. All of this misinformation creates resentment which is not supportive for the service users.

Poor communication

This could be due to many different factors, for instance lack of time and overwork, with the large case loads each professional has to manage, reducing the time for communication with members of the team who work in different organisations. Breakdown in communication systems, for example information technology networks, can also cause problems, for instance with emails or voicemails not being sent or received; busy professionals may not find the time to access full inboxes, resulting in email messages 'bouncing back'. Sometimes fellow professionals answer the telephone for a team member, and do not pass on the message. Poor communication is not always intentional, but will still reduce the quality of care received by users of the service.

What measures can be put in place to improve communication within a team?

Activity   Poor communications

Research a high-profile case in the media where a service user did not receive appropriate care because of poor communications.

How could the service have been improved?

Manipulation by service users

Sometimes service users may attempt to manipulate professionals, trying to persuade one agency to provide more than they have agreed. This can sometimes happen when service users do not receive the required support as quickly as they would like. For example, by telling the social worker that the health visitor agreed to arrange a new flat and has not bothered to do this, when what the health visitor actually said was that they would contact the housing officer but could not promise a quick response as the housing department was very busy.

This can result in a build-up of resentment between professionals and demonstrates the need for clear and regular communication between professionals and the service user(s).

Logistics

When professionals work in separate organisations, it can be difficult to arrange team meetings at a time and place that matches everyone's schedule. Booking a room which is vacant for long enough and is large enough to accommodate the whole team may be difficult. Some organisations have team meetings in other venues, because all of the rooms in the building are constantly occupied.

Another reason might be that professionals have to visit service users at home, over a wide geographical area. Therefore attending a meeting on some days would be difficult due to having to travel.

Financial constraints

All sectors of the health and social care services have limited budgets. It is not always financially possible for each organisation to provide all of the support agreed as their part of the care and support plan. This may be due to other priorities, for example having to meet government targets to reduce waiting times, or having budgets cut by local authorities which have to make spending cuts.

Breakdown in services

Sometimes there is a breakdown in services because one or more of the organisations may face particular problems. For example, the pressures of managing with a reduced workforce due to illness, adverse media coverage of serious cases or inefficient reorganisation of departments which made key staff redundant.

Whatever the reasons for the difficulties are, it is important to remember that the service user must always come first. It is the professional duty of all health and social care employees to work together in order to provide the high quality of care which all service users deserve and which is required by law.

CONTINUED ▶▶

Partnership working in health and social care (3)

Case study   Rehabilitating Chad

Chad Riskin has just been released from prison where he has served a four-year sentence for possession of illegal substances with intent to supply. Chad has been referred to the Probation Service and has to meet with his probation officer three times per week.

Chad's house was repossessed whilst he was in prison, so the prison service has also referred him to the city housing officer to help him find accommodation.

1 Why is it important for the professionals to work in partnership when supporting Chad?

2 What could happen to Chad if the professionals do not communicate with each other due to a breakdown in systems?

3 Should the professionals consider Chad as partner in his own care and support?

Discussion point

In small groups, discuss:

- why groups work in partnership
- is it important to include the individuals receiving care in the partnerships?
- is it important to include family members in the partnership? Can you think of a situation where it would not be good for a family member to be involved in the partnership?

Figure 11.4 Working in partnership.

Link

This topic links to Unit 7, Equality and Diversity in Health and Social Care and Unit 8, Individual Rights in Health and Social Care.

Activity   Health and social care partnerships

1 In groups of three or four, make a list of all the health and social care partnerships you can think of.

2 Conduct an internet search and see if you can find any more.

3 Conduct an internet search of cases where partnership working was not effective.

4 Can you identify what went wrong with the partnerships?

5 How could the problems have been solved?

Assessment activity 11.3

2C.P5 | 2C.M3 | 2C.D3

Marissa Llewellyn is a social worker who works with people who have mental ill health. Boris Williams is one of her clients. He is 32 years old and is also asthmatic. Boris has just been discharged from hospital following treatment for a serious episode of his mental illness. Marissa knows that Boris is still not feeling completely recovered, but the hospital believes he can now be cared for in the community.

Boris is married with a 3-year-old son Patrick who attends the local village nursery. Patrick has cerebral palsy, which affects his mobility but not his speech or intellect. Boris's wife, Anya, is on probation for shoplifting, as she ran out of money while Boris was in hospital.

1 Name the professionals who would work in partnership with Marissa to support Boris and his family and describe the ways in which they would work together.

2 Give two reasons why Boris and Anya should be included as partners in the care delivered to them.

3 What could happen if Boris and Anya were not informed of any decisions that affected them?

4 Explain the potential benefits for Boris and his family of Marissa working in partnership with other professionals to plan and deliver their care.

5 Assess any potential difficulties that may arise from working in partnership to support Boris and his family.

Presenting your evidence

Remember that it is not sufficient just to name the professionals; you will also need to describe the ways in which they will work, for example through multidisciplinary and/or multi-agency partnerships. You should also include the ways in which Boris and his wife are part of the partnerships.

Be realistic when you explain the potential benefits of partnership and check your work against the unit content for Topic C1. You must also remember to explain how each factor you mention really does benefit the family. Your work must be more than a description of the benefits.

Remember, you must assess each potential difficulty in turn, considering exactly why this would provide difficulties for both the professionals and the family.

Finally, always check the assessment criteria on the specification and/or the end of your assignment brief given by your teacher. It is important to read the **verb**; for example **explain**, **describe** etc., so that your work has the right focus. It is not enough just to write about the content; you have to provide evidence of your understanding of the topic.

Just checking

1 Name three types of primary health care.

2 Name three types of primary social care.

3 Name one type of tertiary care.

4 What does the word statutory mean when referring to health and social care?

5 Name two examples of statutory health care that might involve charges.

6 Name one voluntary group that supports health or social care.

7 How is private health and social care funded?

8 Name two pieces of health and social care legislation.

9 Name three groups of people who are protected by the Equality Act 2010.

10 Name two ways of working in partnership in health and social care.

11 Name three benefits of partnership working to people who use health and social care services.

12 What could cause a breakdown in communication between health and social care partners?

13 What does an occupational therapist do?

14 What qualification does an occupational therapist require?

15 Should an individual receiving care be regarded as a partner?

Introduction

Do you take part in any creative or therapeutic activities, or know someone who does? Have you ever thought about how creative and therapeutic activities can be used in health and social care?

Health and social care settings can provide many such activities to benefit the health and wellbeing of service users. This unit will help you to understand the creative and therapeutic activities available, the settings that use them and how they can benefit service users.

Usually service users will need the support and expertise of specialist professionals to access and take part in activities. You will learn how these specialists support and encourage individuals to become involved.

You will also learn how to plan and implement activities in a health and social care setting and you will have the opportunity to plan and carry out a creative or therapeutic activity for an individual service user or a group. You will then assess the selection, planning and implementation of the activity and recommend any improvements.

Assessment: You will be assessed by a series of assignments set by your teacher/tutor.

Learning aims

In this unit you will:

A explore different creative and therapeutic activities used in health and social care and their benefits

B understand how professionals support and encourage individuals who take part in creative and therapeutic activities

C be able to plan and implement appropriate creative and therapeutic activities in a health and social care setting.

> When I did work experience in a care home I realised that the service users need something to do or they get bored, just like I do when there's nothing to occupy me. I have seen how much some of them enjoy taking part in different activities, and when they do the whole place seems much happier.
>
> Sharim, *17-year-old Health and Social Care learner*

Creative and Therapeutic Activities in Health and Social Care

12

BTEC
Assessment Zone

This table shows what you must do in order to achieve a **Pass**, **Merit** or **Distinction** grade, and where you can find activities in this book to help you.

Assessment criteria			
Level 1	**Level 2 Pass**	**Level 2 Merit**	**Level 2 Distinction**
Learning aim A: Explore different creative and therapeutic activities used in health and social care and their benefits			
1A.1 Identify three creative and therapeutic activities suitable for individuals or groups in one health and social care setting.	**2A.P1** Describe three creative and therapeutic activities suitable for individuals or groups in two different health and social care settings. **Assessment activity 12.1** See page 335		
1A.2 Outline the benefits of three creative and therapeutic activities for individuals or groups in one health and social care setting.	**2A.P2** Describe the benefits of three creative and therapeutic activities for individuals or groups in two different health and social settings. **Assessment activity 12.1** See page 335	**2A.M1** Assess the suitability of creative and therapeutic activities for an individual or group, with reference to a case study. **Assessment activity 12.1** See page 335	**2A.D1** Make recommendations to improve creative and therapeutic activities for an individual or group, with reference to a case study. **Assessment activity 12.1** See page 335
Learning aim B: Understand how professionals support and encourage individuals who take part in creative and therapeutic activities			
1B.3 Outline the role of professionals who plan and implement activities in one health and social care setting.	**2B.P3** Describe the role of professionals when planning and implementing activities in one health and social care setting. **Assessment activity 12.2** See page 343	**2B.M2** Compare and contrast the role of two professionals when planning and implementing activities in two different health and social care settings. **Assessment activity 12.2** See page 343	**2B.D2** Evaluate the impact of professional support on a selected individual participating in creative and therapeutic activities. **Assessment activity 12.2** See page 343
Learning aim C: Be able to plan and implement appropriate creative and therapeutic activities in a health and social care setting			
1C.4 Describe three factors that affect the selection, planning and implementation of creative and therapeutic activities.	**2C.P4** Describe three factors that affect the selection, planning and implementation of creative and therapeutic activities in one health and social care setting. **Assessment activity 12.3** See page 355		
1C.5 Plan one creative and therapeutic activity for service users of one health and social care setting.	**2C.P5** English Select, plan and implement one individual or one group creative and therapeutic activity for service users of one health and social care setting. **Assessment activity 12.3** See page 355	**2C.M3** Assess the selection, planning and implementation of the creative and therapeutic activity. **Assessment activity 12.3** See page 355	**2C.D3** Recommend improvements to the planning and implementation of the creative and therapeutic activity. **Assessment activity 12.3** See page 355

English English signposting

How you will be assessed

The unit will be assessed by a series of internally assessed tasks. You will be expected to explore different creative and therapeutic activities and their benefits to individuals and groups. You will also need to show your understanding of how professionals support and encourage individuals and groups to participate in activities. You will also plan, implement and evaluate an activity for an individual or a group.

An example could be that during your work experience placement in a day centre you are asked to shadow one of the professionals who comes in to lead activities and observe what they do. The manager then wants you to plan and implement an activity for a small group of adults with learning disabilities and evaluate the activity afterwards. They ask you to write up the activity including the different activities you considered, how they benefited the participants, how your role as a professional allowed you to support and encourage them, how you planned and carried out the activity and then your evaluation of what went well and what you could improve if you planned another activity. They want you to produce this as an article for the group's newsletter, which goes out to the relatives, friends and supporters of the day centre. The manager would also like some photos of the activity, provided you have gained permission from the participants to take and use them.

Creative and therapeutic activities (1)

Getting started

With a partner, think about the types of activities that could be carried out in different health and social care settings. When you have done this, have a whole group feedback session and list all the activities you all came up with. Then identify which are creative activities and which therapeutic.

Discussion point

How do you think people can use the medium of drawing and painting to tell their stories or express their feelings? As the person running the session, what things would you be looking for as clues to how an individual is feeling or saying?

Introduction

You may not have thought very much about what happens in a health and social care setting, other than providing basic care, but as Sharim in the Learner Voice realised, service users need the opportunity to take part in activities, both for enjoyment and for therapeutic reasons.

Art, crafts and performing arts

Creating a piece of artwork or making something that is decorative or useful can give people an opportunity to express themselves in a way that does not need words and can provide a great sense of satisfaction. This can be particularly important in helping people to come to terms with emotional or physical difficulties that they might be experiencing.

Drawing and painting

Some people are highly artistic and are able to draw extremely well, while others will have only a very basic ability. But it is not the level of competence that matters, what is more important is that art is a way to express oneself and it can give someone a great sense of having achieved something. There is a range of materials that can be used for painting, including water, oil or poster paints and drawing can involve using black or whiteboards as well as paper, and a variety of drawing implements, such as pens, pencils, charcoal, chalks and pastels. Collage, stencilling, and simple printing are other techniques that can be done by people of all abilities. Subjects can be naturalistic or abstract. Some people will be happy to display the results for everyone to see, but others will want to keep the work private. Self-expression through painting and drawing can have a therapeutic effect in helping service users to tell their own particular stories.

Photography

Photography includes capturing both still and motion pictures, with cameras, mobile phones or tablets. People who still use film may also choose to develop their pictures themselves in a darkroom, or they may have them developed and framed. Digital images can also be printed. Depending on how interested an individual might be in ICT, various image manipulation techniques can be used to create artwork.

Movies can be recorded on digital camcorders, cameras or phones and transferred to hard disk drives or onto DVD. People who have an interest in filming can create their own storyboards with the appropriate software.

Why do you think photography can be therapeutic?

Photography can be used in many ways in a care setting. It can help people to explore their identity and memories; it can help overcome barriers to verbal communication and increase self-esteem. Therapeutic photography is sometimes used by counsellors as a technique in psychoanalysis. People who use this technique see it as a way to effect active change in their lives.

Therapeutic photography does not need to be practised by a counsellor as it can be a way of using photography to work on personal issues or to make sense of life events.

? **Did you know?**

If you are working with service users whose hobby is photography, you need to bear in mind that they will need to obtain consent from anyone who is to be photographed.

Creative and therapeutic activities (2)

Knitting, sewing, embroidery

Knitting projects can be as simple as scarves or squares sewn together to make blankets or it can be complicated and skilled such as when making an Aran sweater. Although knitting is seen as a female pursuit, men can enjoy it too.

Hand-sewing techniques, such as embroidery and tapestry, are popular hobbies, although older people whose eyesight is deteriorating may need additional magnification to see what they are doing. As people age, they may become less able to maintain their fine motor skills, so using bigger needles to knit and sew, coarser canvas for tapestry or changing to a freestyle footless sewing machine, can help people to continue to follow their hobby, despite their physical limitations.

Knitting gifts for other people may help someone to feel they are still useful and independent. What other benefits do you think it may have?

Tapestry

Tapestry involves using a needle and wool to sew stitches onto canvas, creating a picture or pattern. It is quite easy to do, but like embroidery requires good light and mobile fingers. Some people enjoy this type of work as they find it restful and enjoy watching the pattern emerge as they work on a piece.

Drama

Belonging to a **drama** group or society is a very popular pastime. It is a very creative activity and people who do not necessarily have a condition or illness can use drama as a way of expressing themselves and purely for enjoyment. Drama can also be used to strengthen and build relationships.

Drama and **role play** are active approaches that can help service users to tell their stories, to solve problems and to understand the meaning of situations. It can help to set up a supportive and safe environment for service users to express themselves and explore areas that they may have otherwise avoided. This is particularly useful when working with children whose language may not be advanced enough to express themselves accurately.

Key terms

Drama – involves acting out situations and characters, either improvised or following a script.

Role play – similar to drama but more to do with taking the specific role of someone else and exploring reactions and motivations.

Do you feel you are able to express yourself through drama or music?

Singing and music

We all respond to music and it can often provide a sense of relaxation or therapy either for individuals or groups. A group of people could sing and/or listen to music or songs together or an individual may wish to do this as an activity while alone.

Using music as a therapy may be expensive considering the cost of instruments, but they can be made quite inexpensively out of many household items, e.g. yoghurt pots with lids filled with rice as a shaker.

Music therapy is often used with children and young people with challenging behaviour or with people who have mental health problems. There is some evidence to suggest that singing and music can be helpful in caring for people with Alzheimer's disease.

Sport and exercise (1)

Introduction

Many people enjoy taking exercise and some do this by playing a sport. Sometimes it is just for enjoyment, although many people will play competitively on a regular basis. It is well known that taking exercise releases hormones in the brain called endorphins, which give us a feeling of wellbeing.

Activity   Exercise and you

Do you take any exercise or play a sport? In a small group, draw up a table listing the types of activity done by each member and why each person has chosen their activity. How do you feel after you have taken part in an exercise session?

Exercise

Take it further

The Department of Health's website contains information on the UK's physical activity guidelines for daily exercise for different age ranges. You can access the website via Pearson Hotlinks (www.pearsonhotlinks.co.uk).

There are lots of different ways in which people can take exercise, from simply going for a brisk walk to playing soccer at a top-class level. Equally, people can do exercise that costs nothing or they can join an exercise class or gym for which they might pay a subscription or for each session. People of all ages and abilities can do some form of exercise that will contribute to health and fitness, even those with very limited mobility. Exercises done in a chair can help to lower blood pressure and is good for people with osteoporosis and arthritis who may not want to place extra strain on their legs, hips and arms. People with Down's syndrome often have poor muscle development and a tendency to obesity so can benefit greatly from exercise. For everyone, taking exercise can help maintain a healthy heart and control weight.

Activity   British paralympians

Stoke Mandeville Stadium in Aylesbury, Buckinghamshire was the birthplace of the Paralympics. Find out how many British competitors won medals and in which events in the 2012 Paralympics.

Having a disability does not prevent people from taking part in sport if the right adjustments can be made to an activity.

Swimming

Swimming is good all-round **aerobic** exercise. It is a holistic activity that benefits the whole body and can be done by all ages. When an individual is in water the buoyancy of the water reduces the weight and strain on the body's joints and so it is a great activity for those who have arthritis or other joint problems as it keeps them moving with reduced pain.

Key terms

Aerobic – exercise that improves the efficiency of the heart and lungs in and the transportation of oxygen around the body.

Fibromyalgia – a condition that causes widespread pain and severe fatigue.

Ellie Simmonds racing in the Paralympics. Have you been inspired by any Olympic athletes?

Service users with **fibromyalgia** can get benefit from a variety of different water therapies and not just swimming. Not every swimming centre has a warm-water pool but warm-water exercise can reduce pain, improve the pain threshold, relax muscles and lessen anxiety and depression. Many hospitals have hydrotherapy pools, which are used to treat patients with certain physical and mental conditions. Some special schools have pools so that pupils with disabilities can swim as part of their school routine.

Did you know?

Aquarobics is a great way of exercising as the water allows the body to move under much less strain. It is often recommended for people with mobility problems as the water helps to keep them buoyant.

Sport and exercise (2)

Yoga and Pilates

Yoga is a mental and physical discipline that uses a series of postures, breathing and meditation. It can be done as a group activity or on an individual basis and many people practise yoga every day to help them to feel calm and balanced. Some types of yoga focus on spirituality and others can be very physical.

Chair yoga is a more gentle form adapted from traditional yoga that can be done in seated and standing positions to aid physical and mental fitness.

Pilates is a body conditioning routine designed by Joseph Pilates in Germany in the early 20th century to develop strength in muscles of the arms, legs, abdomen and back. It uses apparatus specifically designed to exercise different muscles. Toning and strengthening the abdomen and back helps to develop a strong core or centre, which helps with coordination and balance. The exercises can build up in intensity as the body adapts and becomes used to the exercises. Pilates was a great believer in the interrelationship between physical and mental health and believed that his exercise regime promoted this.

Horse riding

Equine Assisted Psychotherapy helps people to explore their feelings and behaviour and is mainly used with people who have mental health problems. Most of the work is ground-based and does not tend to involve horse riding.

As well as helping people ride and interact with horses, the Riding for the Disabled Association also provides opportunities for people to try carriage driving.

Why is yoga good for improving health and wellbeing?

Activity   Riding for the Disabled

Research Equine Assisted Psychotherapy and list five benefits of this type of therapy. The Riding for the Disabled Association's website provides useful information, which you can access via Pearson Hotlinks.

Dancing

Dance is used as a therapy in a variety of settings, including children's settings, day care centres, community clubs, residential homes and hospitals. It has benefits for people with emotional, social, physical or cognitive conditions and concerns.

Dancing is therapeutic because it uses movement to improve the physical and mental wellbeing of a service user. It is a holistic activity as it focuses on the connection between the mind and body to promote coordination, a sense of wellbeing and, where appropriate, healing.

Dancing comes in many styles and is lots of fun. It is an inclusive activity as people of all ages, backgrounds, states of health and levels of physical and mental ability can get involved. Some health or social care settings may organise dance activities but individuals can also access dance at classes and clubs within their own communities.

Dance can be used as a complementary method of reducing stress for people with an illness and also for caregivers.

Walking and running

Walking is one of the best forms of exercise and has significant health benefits. Walking between 30 and 60 minutes a day five days a week helps to reduce the risk of developing heart disease, cancer, Type 2 diabetes, **depression** and anxiety. It also increases **endurance** and bone density and can lower cholesterol levels. It is thought to be helpful in preventing dementia and Alzheimer's disease.

The benefits of running are similar to those of walking. Additionally, running can help with weight loss and control and improve cardiovascular and respiratory function. However, there is an increased risk of injury with running, for example ankle, knee and hamstring injuries. People who run are advised to warm up properly, allow enough time to recover and to use ice for sore muscles.

Key terms

Depression – a mental disorder. It can be a chronic condition or a short-term one related to a life circumstance.

Endurance – the ability to withstand prolonged use or strain.

Take it further

Find out more about the benefits of walking and about the services that Walking for Health provides.

Walking is a good way of exercising while enjoying time with friends or family.

Just checking

Is swimming best for a particular age group or is it good for anyone? What benefits can it give?

Games and quizzes

Introduction

Games can include board games, bingo and various card games. Something as cheap and simple as a pack of playing cards can be used to play a variety of games either alone or with a group of people. Many games are suitable for a wide age range, which means that they can be played by families. If you are planning to play a game, it is important that you consider the ages and abilities of the client group you are working with.

Activity   Traditional games

Carry out some research to find out what traditional games such as Aunt Sally are still played in the UK, how they are played and where they originated.

Crosswords, Sudoku and other puzzles

Many people enjoy the challenge of completing crosswords, whether they complete the quick crossword or have a go at the cryptic crossword in various daily newspapers. Crosswords help with vocabulary, word recall and can increase or maintain people's problem-solving abilities and improve focus and attention.

Sudoku is a number game set out in a nine by nine grid where the numbers one to nine must be inserted such that every number appears once in each horizontal line, vertical line and square. It was developed in Japan in 1986, but became internationally popular in 2005.

Sudoku puzzles range in difficulty from very easy to almost impossible and can take minutes or hours to complete. It is believed they help with critical thinking, patience, focus and creativity.

Quiz and puzzle magazines are also good for both entertainment and maintaining people's mental ability.

Key term

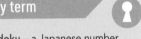

Sudoku – a Japanese number puzzle. Sudoku means single number.

Board games and jigsaw puzzles

Most board games require at least two people to play and many can involve up to six players, or even teams playing against each other. This means that some games are suitable for playing in day and residential centres where a large number of people can participate. Some board games can be very expensive, but you can make your own for a fraction of the price and can develop your own theme.

Jigsaw puzzles are available for every age and ability range from a small number of large pieces that need to be fitted into a board, to complicated puzzles where there are 1000 pieces or more. Simple puzzles with large pieces or that fit into shapes onto a board are good for children as well as people with learning difficulties or problems

What benefits are these children getting from completing the puzzle together?

with fine motor skills. Jigsaws are also an excellent pastime for people who prefer solitary pursuits, but can equally be done by small groups of people together. One problem with jigsaw puzzles is that they can take up quite a lot of room and take several days to complete. However, special jigsaw cases and wraps are available, which can be closed or rolled up and stored without causing the puzzle to fall apart.

General knowledge quizzes

TV quiz shows are popular and can be enjoyed by a number of people watching together within a setting. Some quiz shows, such as 'Mastermind', require contestants to have a high or specialist level of knowledge, whereas others are more accessible or just fun, such as 'Who Wants to be a Millionaire', or 'Never Mind the Buzzcocks'. Many people enjoy being part of a team playing in pub quizzes or for a local community and this could be encouraged or facilitated for some service users. Settings could also organise internal quiz events, or written quiz sheets and picture quizzes for service users.

Other activities

Introduction

Any activity that helps service users can be employed by carers as long as it is safe and carers have the skills and equipment to provide it. Below are some commonly used activities that are often used therapeutically in health and social care.

Gardening

Gardening is something that many service users miss most when they enter residential care. It can provide a variety of benefits for people with learning and physical disabilities, mental health problems, dementia and sensory impairment. Horticultural therapists work with people both individually and in groups.

Why might gardening be good for wellbeing?

Activity · Gardening therapy

Visit the Thrive website, which you can access by going to www.pearsonhotlinks.co.uk and find out how gardening can help people with dementia and disabilities.

Create two posters listing the benefits for both groups.

Cooking

Cooking can be done with any age group and with people of different competences. Carers might have to supervise cooking sessions for health and safety reasons.

Preparation and planning can also help people to develop organisational skills with opportunities to shop for ingredients, deal with money and follow instructions to make simple items.

Activity · Cooking

In small groups discuss any issues that you would need to consider if you were planning to cook with the following:

- seven teenagers with mild to moderate learning disabilities
- three older people with varying degrees of dementia.

ICT

Information and Communication Technology (ICT) is popular with people of all ages for recreation – such as gaming, as a source of information, as a study tool, to keep in touch with friends and family and as a necessary workplace skill. Some programs can help service users with communication difficulties. However, although stimulating, extensive computer use can be very solitary leading to isolation. People should also be reminded that other sources of information, such as books, are equally useful learning tools, and that some websites may not contain reliable information.

Concern about how the internet is used, especially on social networking sites, has led to the government providing guidance on how to protect the vulnerable from possible danger.

Why might cooking be good for wellbeing?

Reading

Reading is an important life skill and leisure activity that can help memory, concentration and focus and develop self-esteem and self-concept.

People who cannot read are often at a disadvantage, for instance with form filling, such as job and benefit application forms. In some cases being unable to read will prevent an individual from getting a job.

Massage

Massage involves stroking, kneading, rubbing and pressing on different parts of the body to aid relaxation and help with the circulation of blood. It can reduce pain and stiffness. Massage is not seen as a cure for any ailment, but more as a way of relieving pain and discomfort.

It is very important for service users to ensure that their therapist is a qualified practitioner to ensure that no damage is done during the treatment. Some people do not like to be touched so massage may not be appropriate for them, even if it might help them.

Activity	Massage therapy

Find out how many different types of massage there are and what they might be used for.

Record this information in a table format.

Multi-sensory stimulation

Multi-sensory stimulation or Snoezelen® is a method of providing soothing stimulation in rooms specially equipped to stimulate all the senses. This includes the use of light, sound, colour, music and scent and of different fabrics for texture. Snoezelen® can be beneficial for many different service users, both children and adults, with conditions ranging from profound and multiple learning disabilities and autism to dementia and brain injury. The rooms are not used in any formal way, and the equipment can be adjusted according to the mood of the service user at any given time.

What senses do you think may be stimulated by this Snoezelean® room?

Interaction with animals

A wide range of animals, including dogs, cats, horses, dolphins, rabbits and birds, can be used in various ways to help people with disabilities or illnesses. Each has specific characteristics and can become a fundamental part of the therapy.

The organisation Pets as Therapy (PAT) sends volunteers with temperament-tested dogs and cats to care settings for service users to stroke and cuddle.

Appropriate settings (1)

Getting started

How many different types of care settings can you think of? List as many as you can. Compare your answers with the rest of your group. Did they have some that you didn't think of?

Introduction

There are many different health and social care settings that provide a variety of services for many service users. These can be related to age, physical or learning disabilities or mental health, and be community based, day centres or residential care. You may have to take any or all of these factors into account when you are planning creative or therapeutic activities for service users. As you read about each setting below, think about the factors that would affect any activities you might plan. For example, can service users be away from the setting, or do activities have to take place on site? How much space is available? What else might be going on around you?

Pre-school care

Pre-school care includes any care provided for children aged five and under before they go to school. In England every 3 and 4 year old is entitled to 15 hours free early learning per week, taken over at least three days for 38 weeks per year. Over and above this provision, parents have to pay. Childcare settings providing this care include nurseries, preschools and playgroups, primary schools that admit 4 year olds, accredited childminders and Sure Start Children's Centres. All of these settings receive government funding so that the provision is free at the point of delivery. They have to be inspected by OFSTED, be in the local authority Directory of Providers and be helping children work towards the Early Learning Goals in the Early Years Foundation Stage.

Take it further

Search online for the Early Years Foundation Stage Framework. Investigate the Early Learning Goals.

What benefits do you think a child receives by attending preschool?

Day care

Day care can include childcare, and care for older people or people with disabilities who live in their own homes independently, but need some support. Hospital day care provides services for people who require medical care or other treatment, such as physiotherapy. Social Services provide day care for people who may be socially isolated and lonely. Some day centres provide services and activities ranging from hairdressing and podiatry to lunch, games and outings.

Activity Day centres in your area

Find out if there are day centres for elderly people and adults with learning disabilities in your area. If possible, arrange to visit them to see what activities they provide. Can you think of any other activities that would be suitable in either setting, taking into account the needs of the service users and the resources that are available?

Hospitals

Hospitals provide different types of care to all types of service users. Some will be local with limited services and others will be much bigger and cater for all or nearly all of the medical specialities. Some will be regional specialist units for specific problems. Pinderfields General Hospital in Wakefield, for instance, has a regional burns unit, while the Churchill Hospital in Oxford has a regional endocrine and diabetes centre.

Hospitals are open 24 hours a day to provide care, but not all departments will be open all the time – some have staff on call out of hours who come in if needed. Many patients are treated as day cases, and advances in technology such as keyhole surgery mean that people do not need to stay as long in hospital as they used to.

Private hospitals are also used for treatment and operations. Everything that is provided has to be paid for, and this can be done by an individual or by a health insurance scheme. An individual will pay a monthly sum of money into a health insurance scheme, which can then be used to pay for their care if it should be needed.

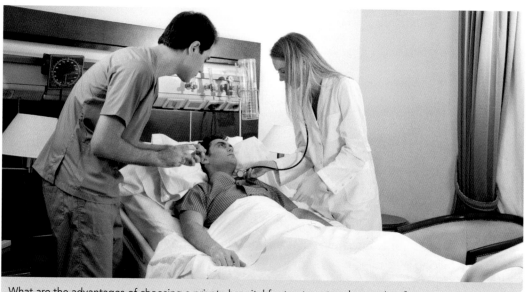

What are the advantages of choosing a private hospital for treatment and operations?

Appropriate settings (2)

Residential care

Residential care varies from large homes that cater for lots of residents to a house where three or four service users can live together with support. Residents have meals provided and are supported with personal care and management of any medication. There is staffing 24 hours a day, although where residents are quite independent there will be an alarm system to call a member of staff in an emergency. Most homes allow individuals to bring their own furniture and some might allow pets.

Discussion point

How can respite care benefit families and carers?

Although we tend to think of residential care as being for people nearing the end of their lives, there are homes for looked-after children whose families cannot look after them. Short-term residential care can be used for convalescence after an illness or operation, and respite care can give families and carers who look after people with long-term conditions a break.

Residential homes are for people who do not require nursing care and are staffed mainly by care workers. Nursing homes are for people who require nursing and/or medical care and there must be qualified nursing staff on duty at all times.

Residential care enables users to be able to socialise with other people in a similar position.

Domiciliary care

This is provided at home and helps clients to remain as independent as possible. The care provided might include helping clients to get up and washed and dressed to doing shopping or going on outings. It is provided on a temporary or permanent basis, and can be provided by live-in carers.

Community groups

Community groups cater for various ages, genders, abilities and interests. They usually meet on a regular basis to share interests and include Brownies, Beavers and Cubs, Guides and Scouts for children and teenagers; support groups, such as Gingerbread for lone parents; the Women's Institute; religious groups; sports teams and activities, and drama, music and singing groups. These can all provide support and social contact for a range of people. A day centre can be classed as a community group.

Supported living

Introduced in the UK in the 1990s by the National Development Team for Inclusion (NTDi), supported living helps people with learning disabilities to live in their own homes and have control over how much support they require, how they live and who they live with. This means that care and support is personalised and tailored to the needs of the individual.

The NDTi principles of supported living

- I choose who I live with.
- I choose where I live.
- I have my own home.
- I choose how I am supported.
- I choose who supports me.
- I get good support.
- I choose my friends and relationships.
- I choose how to be healthy and safe.
- I choose how to take part in my community.
- I have the same rights and responsibilities as other citizens.
- I get help to make changes in my life.

Special needs schools

Some children who have **special educational needs** can be taught in mainstream schools with extra support, but others may attend special schools where their needs can be met more appropriately. Schools have policies on special educational needs available to parents, and parents and schools can request assessment for a child, after which the child may be given a statement of special educational needs. The local authority must agree to send a child to the school the parents want, provided certain criteria are met, such as the suitability of the school, that the child's presence will not negatively affect others in the school and academic reasons for sending the child to the school that show local authority resources are being used efficiently.

Key term

Special educational needs (SEN) – refers to children with learning difficulties or disabilities that make it harder for them to learn or access education than most children of the same age.

Training centres

Courses run by training centres range from learning new skills or updating existing ones to the provision of staff training by employers. Skills taught include how to create a curriculum vitae and IT. Training centres also help people to develop self-confidence and will usually issue certificates for the training courses undertaken.

Benefits of creative and therapeutic activities (1)

Introduction

When someone has a specific problem, it is tempting to focus only on that and forget about other aspects of their lives. Taking a holistic approach to care, where you look at the person as a whole, is a much more balanced and effective approach. Keeping someone fit and active, encouraging their intellectual ability and supporting their self-esteem, sense of self and emotional health are vital aspects in their overall care.

Key terms

Serotonin – a neurotransmitter that affects mood and also has an effect on learning and cognition.

Wellbeing – a sense of contentment.

Cardiovascular – cardio – to do with the heart, vascular – to do with the blood.

Physical benefits

Physical activity is thought to reduce the risk of developing many major illnesses and premature death. Exercise causes the level of **serotonin**, a chemical in the brain, to increase, improving feelings of **wellbeing**. **Cardiovascular** activity during exercise, when the heart works faster, results in physical benefits that include reducing the risk of developing Type 2 diabetes, coronary heart disease and some cancers, lowering blood pressure, protecting against osteoporosis by building bone density, developing muscle strength, helping to maintain a healthy weight, countering depression and helping to improve sleep and reduce stress. Many types of sport and exercise help to improve hand–eye coordination, for example darts, snooker, pool and billiards.

Craft activities

There are physical benefits to certain art and craft activities. Wood and metalwork, such as making furniture, can involve physical exertion. Outdoor and wildlife photography will almost certainly involve walking. Activities such as knitting, sewing or using a computer keyboard can help to keep fingers nimble.

Gardening

Gardening can be surprisingly physical. A person can burn up about 300 calories doing one hour of moderately active gardening. If gardening includes producing fruit and vegetables then these can provide the basis for a healthy diet and a great sense of achievement to the grower, improving self-esteem.

Dance

Dance improves mobility and muscle coordination and reduces muscle tension. People can lose weight and tone up at the same time and often enjoy it so much that it does not feel like taking exercise. There have been claims that exercise strengthens the immune system and can prevent disease. Dance can also help people with physical disabilities. There has been a growth in the popularity of dance, and there are venues all over the country offering classes including ballroom, tap, salsa, hip hop and even belly dancing! Dance may help some service users who have suffered loss of mobility following a stroke or accident regain some movement.

Why do you think gardening may be particularly beneficial for people who spend all day in an office?

Swimming

Swimming provides an all-over body workout, as nearly all of the body's muscles are used. It increases flexibility, tones muscles and builds strength. It also builds endurance and cardiovascular health. Swimming provides a low-impact therapy for some injuries and conditions.

Activity	Swimming and obesity

Find out why swimming is a particularly good physical activity for people who are very overweight to undertake.

Drama and music

People of any age benefit from the movement and flexibility that drama can provide as it can help to develop both gross and fine motor skills.

Anyone playing any kind of musical instrument has to have good hand–eye coordination and dexterity. Energy expenditure will depend on the instrument being played, and musicians playing brass or woodwind instruments will have to learn how to use their diaphragms and respiratory systems to breathe properly while playing.

What other benefits do you think a person may gain from drama?

Gaming activities

A Wii™ uses interactive technology and many games and activities including golf and tennis will provide physical benefits such as improving hand–eye coordination for anyone who uses them.

Cooking

Cooking can be a learning opportunity for service users to explore the value of healthy eating. Information about the components of a balanced diet and how to cook healthily can help service users to maintain a healthy weight and help to prevent ill health. Producing delicious meals, cakes and so on, also boosts self-esteem.

Benefits of creative and therapeutic activities (2)

Cognitive benefits

The brain is a bit like a muscle – it needs to be stimulated to prevent boredom and keep it exercised. Any activity that means that you have to think about what you are doing helps to keep the brain active. Just as with any other organ and muscle in the human body, if the brain is not used and stimulated it starts to deteriorate. This can be manifested in things such as loss of memory. Problem-solving activities that require concentration help to retain and maintain memory and improve communication and organisational skills.

Activity   Brain training

Find out about brain training games and how they can help to keep the brain active.

Drama

Drama and role play can stimulate the brain to remember how to play as well as providing practice for language and memory skills. People recovering from a stroke or brain injury can find drama helpful in regaining their speech and improving their interaction and communication skills. Drama can stimulate the brain by providing opportunities to think, reason and remember lines. A person's imagination can be developed through drama as it allows the expression of feelings.

Games, puzzles and quizzes

Playing games and quizzes can help keep the brain active. Taking part in quizzes stimulates memory and working on puzzles such as Sudoku can help to develop analytical skills and logic. Doing crosswords helps to maintain or develop vocabulary and spelling.

Other games can help young children learn colour, number and word recognition, spatial awareness and manual dexterity among other things. Board games help with understanding the concept of fair play and taking turns as well as the general development of social skills such as communication.

Gardening

A study in Australia that lasted for 16 years and followed nearly 3000 people over the age of 60 found that the risk of their developing dementia reduced by 36 per cent when they gardened every day. The opportunity to learn new practical skills or information about plants and flowers can help to keep the brain active and provide a sense of achievement for those taking part.

Source: Medical Journal of Australia 2006; 184(2): 68–70.

Why do you think quizzes and puzzles are particularly beneficial for elderly people?

Cooking

Cooking is often used as a learning opportunity, especially in primary schools. Children can contribute to their intellectual development by learning about weighing and measuring and the nutritional value of food. People with learning disabilities in supported living can be helped to prepare and cook their own meals. This can help with reading, weighing and measuring, and understanding and following instructions.

Why is it beneficial for children to learn about cooking from an early age?

Music

Listening to or playing music can be very stimulating for the brain. Remembering how to read music, play an instrument or sing a song word-perfect ensures the brain keeps working and benefits the service users' overall health and wellbeing. Research indicates that the benefits of music for people with Alzheimer's disease can include improved sleeping patterns and behaviour as well as helping to trigger memory and reality awareness.

Exercise

Researchers are beginning to establish a link between exercise and brain function in humans. It is believed that exercise improves learning and intelligence scores. It improves memory, and can promote recovery after a brain injury. Exercise in childhood is also thought to make the brain more resilient. Some sports can help participants to develop problem-solving skills.

? Did you know?

The brain is made up of different areas. The medial temporal lobes control the part of the brain which processes memories. The cortices and subcortices areas control the part of the brain which processes music. Music can be used to 'code' information which some dementia suffers find easier to remember.

Benefits of creative and therapeutic activities (3)

Emotional benefits

Improved **self-concept** and **self-esteem** are emotional benefits that help service users to remain positive. Being able to create or produce something gives people a sense of achievement and satisfaction, and can provide the motivation to develop new interests.

Art and photography

Visual expression through painting, drawing or photography can allow the world to be seen through the eyes of the service user. This inside knowledge can then be used by healthcare workers to develop an understanding of how someone feels, especially if they have communication difficulties. These activities also provide a sense of satisfaction and achievement, which can boost self-esteem and help a service user to feel valued.

Dance and drama

Dance and drama can improve a person's self-awareness, self-confidence and interaction with others. Mime, body language and facial expressions can all be used in drama and dance to convey a message.

Some people find dancing a good way to improve their mood. Why do you think this may be?

Music

Music often aids relaxation and can be used to help people to change their moods and feelings when they listen to music or create different types of music. Taking part in music making positively develops an individual's self-esteem and self-concept.

Exercise

Many people report that they have a real sense of wellbeing after taking exercise. It is thought that physical effort stimulates the release of **endorphins** in the brain. These can produce a sense of wellbeing and suppress pain. Taking part in a sport where there is a competitive element can make people feel good when they win, whether it is a solo effort or as part of a team. Being part of a team fosters cooperation and communication skills and a sense of belonging.

Gardening

Gardening can help to relieve stress and tension; it has a very calming influence and produces a sense of achievement.

Cooking

Cooking is a very good way to encourage service users to create something and then allows them to enjoy eating and sharing what they have made. This can produce a real sense of achievement raising self-esteem. Research suggests that children who eat with their families regularly tend to do better at school and are less depressed, less likely to smoke, drink alcohol and smoke cannabis than children who eat with their families less than twice a week.

Games, puzzles and quizzes

Playing games where there is a chance to win can be very good for an individual's self-esteem and confidence, but it is important to be aware that children and some adults sometimes struggle with the concept of losing. It is unlikely that children under the age of six will be able to understand the concept of fair play so it is important that a balance is found between winning and losing. Making sure that the game is pitched to the right age or ability is important, otherwise participants will soon lose interest and feel that there is no point in continuing. Junior versions of popular games, such as Scrabble® and Monopoly® can be more enjoyable both for children and adults with learning disabilities.

> **Key term**
>
> **Endorphins** – hormones secreted in the brain that have a number of effects, including relieving pain and affecting mood.

Why do you think children may experience benefits from eating with their family?

Doing quizzes in whatever form can provide a sense of satisfaction when they are completed. Many people enjoy the challenge of working things out, and usually the harder something is, the more enjoyment can be had when it has been successfully completed. Puzzles, such as Sudoku, can be attempted at different levels of difficulty so they can be suitable for people of differing abilities.

Benefits of creative and therapeutic activities (4)

◤ Social benefits

Many activities provide the opportunity for people to interact with others, developing and maintaining new and existing relationships. Sometimes people take up a hobby for their own amusement, but there are many who join a class or club for the social contact. Sometimes a hobby can be so successful that it helps people develop enough confidence to start a new career. Using computers can allow isolated people to keep in contact with friends and family.

Dancing and drama

Dance and drama can help service users to form and develop friendships. Music brings people together and is an excellent way of including people and making them feel welcome in a new environment, and it may help them to make new friends. Going to concerts or festivals to listen to music and see bands performing is a very social activity. Music therapy groups are very useful to some people.

Do you belong to any clubs or groups?

Team activities

Team games and activities provide opportunities to develop social friendships. This is not only based on the team effort required to win a football match for example, but the after-match activities that take place where genuine friendships can develop from a shared interest.

Swimming

Many swimming pools and leisure centres offer free swimming for the elderly, which can be a real benefit for people on low incomes and they get to meet other people rather than being on their own. Many public pools also offer women-only sessions for women who prefer not to swim in front of men, or because there are cultural or religious reasons why they cannot swim at the same time as men. Muslim women who swim use these sessions.

Gardening

Gardening can be a very social activity when people work together to achieve a shared goal, such as designing a garden from scratch. Friendships based on a common interest can make a huge difference in the life of someone who might previously have lived a very isolated existence. The charity Thrive supports about 900 gardening projects throughout the UK benefitting many service users.

Cookery

Working together on the common goal of producing a dish or a meal can strengthen a friendship and give a shared sense of achievement. Eating together has always been seen as a very social activity and families who eat together and discuss the day's events around the dinner table tend to be closer.

Assessment activity 12.1   2A.P1 | 2A.P2 | 2A.M1 | 2A.D1

1 Choose two different health and social care settings which provide care and support for two different client groups. Spend some time considering the needs and abilities that each of the client groups might have. Describe three appropriate creative and therapeutic activities that you could organise for individuals or groups in each setting.

2 What physical, cognitive, emotional and social benefits could each of the activities have for the individuals or groups?

3 Davina is 27 and is tetraplegic following a horse riding accident two years ago. She has recently been discharged from a spinal unit and her home has been adapted for independent living with 24-hour care. She has no movement in her legs or hands but has some limited mobility in her arms. She has always been very active. She is worried that she will be bored sitting in her wheelchair all day. She has always felt frustrated when she has found it difficult to learn new things. Her carers have come up with the following suggestions for activities that they think she would be interested in doing despite her limited movement. They are:

- learning to drive an adapted car
- learning to paint and draw
- horse riding
- developing computer skills to enable her to work
- watching TV and playing video games
- regular swimming sessions.

Research these activities and assess how suitable each one might be for Davina, taking into account her level of physical ability and social and emotional wellbeing.

After you have assessed the suitability of the activities, make recommendations that could improve them so that they might be of more interest to Davina.

The role of professionals in supporting and encouraging individuals

Introduction

When you decide to take part in an activity, you probably do it because you have developed an interest in it, such as football or art. Although you might need some instruction or training, you probably feel that you can join in and have a go without thinking too much about it. But for some individuals, taking part can be a huge challenge and they need support and encouragement from professionals. In this section you will find out about different professionals who are involved in providing support and encouragement and how they do it.

The role of professionals in supporting and encouraging individuals

There is a range of professionals who are involved in supporting and encouraging individuals to take part in different activities. In this section you will find out about some of those professionals and develop an understanding of what is involved in their roles.

Activity coordinators

Activity coordinators are often employed by residential homes to plan and provide activities for residents. They could be educational or social and are usually based on the existing interests of individuals but they may also organise new activities for residents to experience. An important part of the activity coordinator's job is to get to know the people they are working with so they can plan activities that interest them. If some of the activities are therapeutic, then the activity organiser will be involved in assessment of needs and reviews.

Physiotherapists and occupational therapists

Physiotherapists work with people who have movement and function difficulties that may have occurred through illness, disability, injury or ageing. They work in health centres, hospitals, private practice and sports clubs. They assess individuals and then provide treatment to help to promote healing and/or relieve symptoms. This may include massage, exercise and ultrasound treatment. They will also provide advice about how to prevent further injury. Some treatments will need to be carried out over a long period of time.

Occupational therapists work with anyone who has difficulties or disabilities that present a challenge to everyday life. They assess individuals to find out what they can do, then develop a programme to help with rehabilitation or to make daily activities easier. They will advise on specialist equipment that might be required and adaptations to the home or office, such as making changes for wheelchair use. They also help with the development of social and practical skills to enable an individual to live independently and with confidence. They review treatment programmes so they can adapt the provision to meet the changing needs of the individual.

A physiotherapist working with a woman with physical disabilities.

Speech and language therapists

These professionals work with people who have speech, language and communication problems and with people who have swallowing difficulties. Like other therapists they assess the needs of their clients before they start working with them. The problems may have arisen from congenital disorders, such as a cleft lip and palate or from a stroke or other injury, or from cognitive problems. They will devise a treatment programme that might involve other healthcare professionals, family members or friends and will monitor and review the treatment according to the individual's progress.

Health care assistants and social care assistants

Health and social care assistants work in a variety of healthcare settings, such as hospitals, residential and nursing homes and in domiciliary settings. They are supervised by qualified professionals and carry out duties that include washing and dressing service users, feeding, being involved in physiotherapy or occupational therapy programmes, toileting and taking some basic observations such as temperature, pulse and respiration. Many organisations require that health and social care assistants are trained to NVQ Level 2. Senior health and social care assistants are usually trained to NVQ Level 3 and can take up training opportunities to extend their role.

 Take it further

To find out more about these roles, follow the link to the Prospects website at www.pearsonhotlinks.co.uk

Ways that professionals support activities

Planning and running creative and therapeutic activities

Therapeutic activities must be planned carefully to ensure that they are appropriate for the individuals involved.

Getting to know the individuals helps you to establish their interests and abilities and to select and plan appropriate activities. Some activities, such as certain physiotherapy exercises, may not always be enjoyable, especially if they cause pain or discomfort, but if service users are given pain relief beforehand and they are well designed and their purpose is explained, individuals will usually respond to them.

Giving resources and offering practical help and advice

Two of the most important and useful resources are money and time. Service users might indicate that time is the resource that they most want, for instance, something as simple as someone having a cup of tea and a chat with them.

Offering practical help can take many forms, from making sure that a service user has money or transport to attend an activity to helping to provide equipment or clothing. Respite care for families with a severely disabled family member is one example of practical help that health and social care workers can give.

Offering expertise and motivating individuals and groups

Health and social care professionals develop expertise to assess and plan activities that can improve physical, social, emotional or cognitive ability. However, some professionals may also have expertise in other areas, such as cooking or gardening that they can use in their work. There may also be opportunities to invite experts in to work with an individual or group on a one-off or regular basis.

Motivation is very important for people to respond effectively to professional health and social care input. People who require treatment may not be motivated if they are depressed or in pain. Health and social care professionals can make the difference to service users by helping to motivate them to improve their state of mind or physical ability. It is useful to spend time talking to clients to find out their interests or if they would like to try something new. It will often be easier to get someone motivated if you are offering something familiar. People can lose motivation if they cannot see progress being made and prefer to give up rather than keep going. If this happens with a therapy as important as physiotherapy, it could lead to reduction or loss of movement in a limb or other part of the body which could well be permanent.

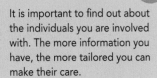

Remember

It is important to find out about the individuals you are involved with. The more information you have, the more tailored you can make their care.

Adapting activities to meet individual needs

Many activities and sports can be adapted to meet the needs of people with different physical disabilities. For instance, tennis for people with visual impairment uses larger balls with bells inside so that players can detect their position. There are organisations that provide adventure holidays for people with disabilities, and many local clubs provide activities such as sailing.

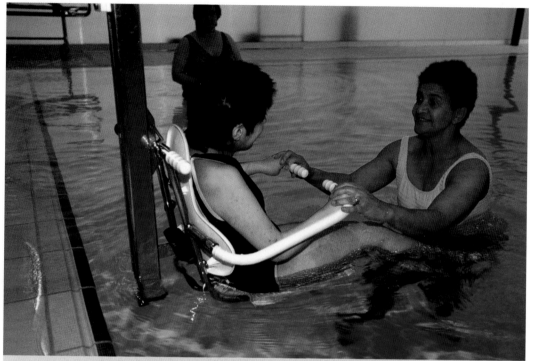

A lack of physical ability should not prevent service users from enjoying physical activities.

? Did you know?

PHAB is a charity that brings together able-bodied people with people with disabilities to take part in activities together. You can find out more about PHAB by visiting Pearson hotlinks.

Case study Bern Goosen

In October 2007, 28-year-old Bern Goosen from South Africa broke his own record for the fastest ascent of Mount Kilimanjaro in a wheelchair. He has cerebral palsy and is classified as quadriplegic. He took 6 days, 3 hours and 20 minutes to reach the summit and is the only man in a wheelchair ever to have achieved this. One of the other successful members of the team was Neil Stephenson, another South African, who had lost his leg in a shark attack a few years previously.

Health and social care workers need to assess an individual's level of intellectual ability and pitch activities at the right level so that interest is maintained with sufficient achievement to promote self-confidence and self-esteem.

People who have problems with verbal communication can find it difficult to take part in an activity, with the result that their needs are not being met. Alternative communication methods, such as picture books can help.

Carers need to ensure that service users are being given choices and are getting enjoyment and satisfaction in their lives.

Principles and values

Introduction

As a carer, you must ensure that you do not discriminate against service users and respect the diversity of the people in your care. It is very important that you do not prevent service users from receiving the best possible care because of their race, gender, ability, religion, sexuality or age.

Anti-discriminatory practice

When you are planning activities for a group of people everything should be done to ensure that they can all take part and enjoy it. This may mean you have to provide extra resources so some people can participate. This provides equality of opportunity. An example might be going to a swimming pool where there is a hoist to lower people with physical disabilities into the water so that they can swim.

Respect for cultural diversity and beliefs and equality of opportunity

Britain is a **multicultural** society made up of people of **diverse** cultures, religions and beliefs.

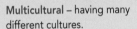

Key terms

Multicultural – having many different cultures.

Diverse – different.

What can carers do to ensure they respect diversity?

Learning about other cultures and customs helps us to find out how other people live, and using this as an educational tool in activities can help to develop understanding and respect. Carers should ask clients or check on the care plan for any religious beliefs when they are planning activities. Jewish or Muslim service users would not want to take part in any cooking activities that involved pork, for instance, and Muslim women would only swim during a women-only session at a public swimming pool. Failure to be observant about diversity, culture and beliefs can be offensive and negatively affect self-esteem.

Equality of opportunity means treating people without prejudice or preference. It does not mean that everyone should be treated the same. The Equality Act 2010 bans unfair treatment and helps achieve equal opportunities in the workplace and in wider society.

Empowerment and promoting independence

Empowerment means giving people control over their lives, or the ability to do something. This can be achieved in many ways, for instance through active listening and providing opportunities for individuals to develop skills enabling them to become more involved in choices relating to their care and to control how they wish to live their lives.

Promoting independence helps people to develop a positive self-image and good self-esteem. Supporting clients to do things for themselves rather than doing things for them prevents them from developing 'learned helplessness' where someone becomes dependent on carers even though they are capable of doing things for themselves. Taking part in activities can be a way of encouraging service users to remain as independent as possible for as long as possible.

Ensure dignity

Ensuring dignity means that people are respected and treated as being of worth. When planning activities it is important to ensure that dignity is maintained at all times. This involves considering factors such as the physical environment, the culture of the individuals you are working with, and making sure your attitudes and behaviours show respect for them. Treating people with dignity and respect will help them to feel valued, confident and in control of their lives.

Activity	Dignity in healthcare

Dignity applies equally to those who have mental capacity and those who lack it. Everyone has equal worth as a human being and must be treated as if they are able to feel, think and behave in relation to their own worth or value. Visit Pearson hotlinks at www.pearsonhotlinks.co.uk to view the Royal College of Nursing Guidance on dignity in healthcare for people with learning disabilities

Confidentiality

Confidentiality is one of the most important components of caring for others. Inappropriate disclosure of information to other people about a service user can destroy trust and the relationship between client and carer. Safety may be put at risk if sensitive information is disclosed to people who should not have access to it. You need to understand when disclosure is necessary, for instance discussing information with another professional involved in someone's care. You need to ensure that you do not discuss sensitive issues that might embarrass or hurt any of the service users.

Ways professionals support inclusion

Introduction

Inclusion means ensuring that everyone within society is engaged in what is going on around them and has goals that relate to the society in which they live. Organisations now recognise the importance of increasing opportunity and provision for all, with everybody in an organisation celebrating and valuing the abilities of everybody else.

Development of relationships

Can you remember how you felt on your first day at school or college? The place was different and unfamiliar and you probably remember feeling lost and uncertain. While some people make friends and settle in quite quickly, others do not always find this easy. It is the same for people in health and social care settings. Some service users will find it difficult to settle and may have difficulty in communicating, making it challenging for them to form friendships. Carers can contribute greatly in helping service users feel comfortable in new surroundings and organising activities can help people to develop friendships and a feeling of belonging.

Organised games in residential homes can help to prevent users from feeling lonely.

Use of preferred methods of communication

In Unit 1 you learned about the value of different methods of communication for people who have difficulty communicating verbally. There are other ways of communicating that can be as effective as speaking, and with patience carers can make a big difference to a service user's communication skills. Using signs and symbols such as Makaton or British Sign Language can help to open a new world to some service users and learning signing can help carers to improve their own communication skills as well as those of their clients.

Encouragement of participation and new experiences

Sometimes service users can be fearful of taking part in activities or trying new experiences and will resist any attempt to get involved. Carers who have developed a trusting relationship with service users might over time be able to use that trust to encourage them to participate. It is important to be aware that there might be a particular reason why someone might not want to participate in an activity, such as not going to the cinema because the sound is too loud or it is too dark. It is also important to know when it is not right for the client to enforce participation.

It might be necessary to build up slowly, so if a carer wants to encourage a service user to swim, for example, it might be necessary to start with a visit to a swimming pool. It may be some time before an individual will even get into the water because the steps need to be taken very gradually.

If you are working as a carer and an activity is a new experience for you, doing this with one of your service users can help them to gain the confidence to have a go themselves.

Assessment activity 12.2   2B.P3 | 2B.M2 | 2B.D2

You have already met Davina in Assessment activity 12.1 where you assessed the suitability of certain activities for her. The information has been repeated below so you can complete the next assessment activity.

Davina is 27 and is tetraplegic following a horse riding accident two years ago. She has recently been discharged from a spinal unit and her home has been adapted for independent living with 24-hour care. She has no movement in her legs or hands but has some limited mobility in her arms. She has always been a very active person. She is worried that she will be bored sitting in her wheelchair all day. She has always felt frustrated when she found it difficult to learn new things. Her carers had have come up with the following suggestions for activities that they think she would be interested in doing, despite her limited movement. They are:

- learning to drive an adapted car
- learning to paint and draw
- horse riding
- developing computer skills to enable her to work
- watching TV and playing video games
- regular swimming sessions.

1 Describe the role of professionals in planning and implementing the activities that were organised for Davina.

2 Organise a visit to one or two settings and observe some activities taking place. Compare the role of the different professionals when planning and implementing activities in the settings.

3 Assess the impact that the professionals you observed had on the individuals who took part in the activities.

Plan and implement appropriate activities

Introduction

You might be wondering why you are learning about legislation in a unit about creative and therapeutic activities. This is because everything that you do that involves service users is governed by the laws that are made by Parliament. You need to have an understanding of the most relevant ones that must be taken into account when planning and implementing creative and therapeutic activities.

Legislation, regulations and guidelines

Legislation

The **Health and Safety at Work Act 1974** is the main piece of legislation covering health and safety in workplaces, and both employers and employees have to make sure that all work is carried out as safely as possible. Employers have to protect employees and other people, and employees have every right to expect that their employer is doing all they can to protect them at work. But employees are also responsible for protecting themselves and others.

Activity	HASAWA

Look up the Health and Safety at Work Act 1974 and find out what the responsibilities of the employer and employee are. Create a poster that clearly outlines these responsibilities.

The **Equality Act 2010** was introduced to simplify many pieces of legislation relating to equality and discrimination. The main areas covered are:

- race
- sex
- sexual orientation (whether being lesbian, gay, bisexual or heterosexual)
- disability (or because of something connected with someone's disability)
- religion or belief
- being a transsexual person (transsexuality is where someone has changed, is changing or has proposed a sex change; this is called 'gender reassignment' in law)
- being pregnant or having just had a baby
- being married or in a civil partnership (this applies only at work or if someone is being trained for work)
- age (this applies only at work or if someone is being trained for work).

Employers will be held responsible if they know that an employee has been harassed repeatedly at work and have done nothing reasonable to stop it happening.

Activity   Equality Act 2010

Go online and search Equality Act 2010: What do I need to know? A summary guide to your rights.

Regulations and guidelines

Control of Substances Hazardous to Health (COSHH) Regulations (2002) state that employers have to control hazardous substances that employees and others may be exposed to at work. Hazardous substances are any products that could pose a risk to health if they are not controlled. They can include glues, paints, cleaning agents, fumes, dust and bacteria. Warning labels on packaging will show whether the product is subject to COSHH regulations. In a health or social care setting they will apply to certain substances that might be used for cleaning.

The **Reporting of Injuries, Diseases and Dangerous Occurrences Regulations 1995 (RIDDOR)** allow the Health and Safety Executive and local authorities to identify where and how risks arise. The HSE can then give employers advice on how to reduce injury, illness and accidents at work. Some work-related accidents, diseases and dangerous occurrences must be reported by an employer or self-employed person, and a record of them must be kept for at least three years.

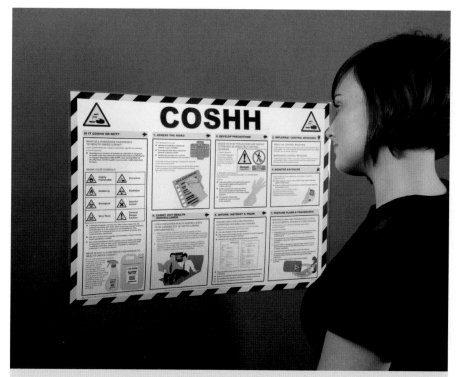

It is important that employers display a poster next to hazardous substances to warn employees of the danger.

Policies of the organisation

All organisations should have policies on issues such as health and safety, equality and diversity and these should be openly available. The commonest form of this is in a manual for employees. This is a crucial tool as it sets out guidelines on the working practices of the business and how they should be implemented. It should also inform employees about what is expected of them.

Codes of practice

Codes of practice set out the standards of conduct expected of employees in the workplace. They are drawn up to protect clients and to ensure the integrity of the profession. Disciplinary action can be taken against people who fail to practise according to the code. In some professions the code of conduct is statutory, which means that breaching it could result in court action.

The needs of the individual or group

Introduction

As human beings, we all have needs – from basic physical needs to keep us alive, to emotional and social needs. You should be aware of all these needs, for both individuals and for groups, when working with people in health and social care settings.

Physical

Basic physical needs are the minimum requirements that we have to keep us alive and our bodies working efficiently – food, water, shelter and safety. Health and care settings often work with people who have very specific physical needs over and beyond this; people for whom an accident, an illness or genetic disability affects their physical health or ability to live normally. People who are sight and hearing impaired, for instance, can find it very difficult to live in an environment where they cannot see and hear everything that is going on around them. They will require extra help to cater for their physical needs and to help them adapt. It is also important to remember that some physical needs will change across a person's life.

Guide Dogs and Hearing Dogs for Deaf People train dogs for sight and hearing impaired people.

Activity   A helping paw

Find out more about guide dogs, PAT dogs and hearing dogs from the organisations' websites. You will find links at www.pearsonhotlinks.co.uk

Cognitive

Although physical growth usually ends as we reach adulthood, we continue to develop throughout our lives, and our needs will change accordingly. Intellectual, language, emotional and social development in children is rapid and activities for children should aim to support and assist that development. Adolescents, adults and older people also need to be supported to develop, but some may be more able to do this independently and will gain a great boost to their self-esteem if they can. It is important to plan activities so that they will meet cognitive developmental needs and are designed at the right level for people's understanding and enjoyment.

Social

We all have a need to make friends and build relationships. If people have to move into residential accommodation because they are no longer able to cope in their own homes, it can be very upsetting as they will not know anyone. They could be moving some distance from their home and leaving friends. People can become very lonely and they will need plenty of support and activities that will help them to settle in and get to know other people.

What are the social benefits of being involved in a team sport?

Emotional

Emotional needs vary throughout a lifetime. At adolescence hormonal changes cause mood swings and insecurities. Teenagers may start comparing themselves to others and begin to explore their sexuality. At this age peer pressure may also have an effect on the individual.

In middle adulthood these hormones change again and many people experience a change in feelings and emotions that lead them to review their life so far. If the person does not feel that they have achieved much and has a lot of regrets it may cause depression.

There are many other causes for depression, such as loneliness, the loss of a partner, child or job, and clinical depression. People experiencing negative feelings often develop low self-esteem and lose interest in the world around them. It can become a vicious circle as depression leads to withdrawal and social isolation, which can make depressed people feel even worse.

Encouraging people to take part in creative and therapeutic activities and develop new interests can help them to meet new people. The activity may stop the cycle of negative feelings and they may feel able to enjoy themselves and overcome feelings of grief or depression.

Factors affecting choice of activity

Introduction

Health and social care workers need to understand how activities benefit client groups in different ways and activities should be based on the needs and abilities of service users.

Settings

Assessing the physical environment before starting to plan activities is important. Trying to organise a dancing session might be difficult if there is not much room; the lack of a sink and running water might make a painting activity challenging.

Potential benefit

When thinking about planning an activity for an individual or client group, it is essential to balance the benefits they would gain from taking part against any downside, such as a resistance from the service users to participate. Swimming, for example would provide physical benefits to almost anyone who takes part, but it would be pointless to arrange this for someone who is afraid of water.

Age, intellectual and physical ability

Children need to develop cognitive, social and gross motor skills so planning activities that include opportunities to develop these will provide lots of developmental benefits.

Peer pressure can affect how older children, teenagers and young adults respond to attempts to involve them in activities. For instance, they often won't want to be seen doing something that might be considered 'uncool'. A group activity that involves everyone so no one individual stands out can help. Activities combining physical and intellectual elements could be used to develop new skills or improve existing ones.

Some older people might be limited in what they can do because they are less physically able or they suffer from memory loss. Activities that are less physically demanding or help to support memory could be suitable. It is important that any activity allows them to retain their dignity and as much independence as possible, even if this means them not participating.

Activity

Think about how you would plan an activity for a group of mixed-ability individuals in a care home. What are the things you need to consider? Create an action plan.

Activities for people with disabilities may need to be adapted for their individual needs. For example, Paralympic athletics demonstrates how many activities and sports can be adapted to provide for the needs of many people with disabilities. Care workers must assess the level of ability and pitch activities appropriately. They also should not assume that lack of ability will result in lack of enjoyment. Some specialist organisations and local clubs provide activities such as rowing, sailing and adventure holidays for people with disabilities.

Communication skills

A lack of communication can mean that a client is unable to take part in an activity and their needs are not being met. Although it can be difficult, carers need to persevere to ensure that service users are being given choices and are getting enjoyment and satisfaction in their lives.

Culture

When planning activities it is necessary to consider all aspects of a person's culture such as beliefs, religion and way of life. If someone is a strict vegetarian it would be unprofessional and insensitive to ask them to join in a cookery activity using meat.

Gender

No activities should be gender stereotyped. Craft activities that might traditionally be thought of as female, such as knitting and sewing, for instance, are enjoyable and therapeutic for anyone. Contact sports, such as rugby, although male dominated, can also be played by both sexes.

Health and fitness of individuals

Planning activities must take into account the health and fitness of the individuals taking part. It is no good planning something beyond people's abilities. Some activities may need to be adapted according to the health status of the individual. For instance, someone with asthma will struggle with strenuous exercise.

Availability of resources and facilities and time and cost restrictions

Cost may often be a factor in planning activities. It is possible to source things such as art materials more cheaply, for instance from charity or discount shops or scrap stores. It is also possible to be creative and use natural resources, such as fallen leaves, and scrap materials. The value of free activities, such as going for a walk in a local park, should not be discounted.

Activity	Scrap stores

Look up Scrap stores on the internet and find out what they are. Find out where your nearest Scrap store is.

Sometimes activities depend on staff being prepared to work longer to fit them in. It is possible to organise activities, such as holding a coffee morning with cakes made by service users, at little cost, which can be used to fund raise for a more expensive activity.

Planning

Introduction

It is your responsibility to ensure that any activities undertaken with service users are properly planned. This can involve a number of factors, including assessing suitability for all participants, undertaking a risk assessment, ensuring you have enough space and time, organising resources and having enough helpers.

Risk assessment

Risk assessments identify any risks associated with a particular event or activity and how severe they might be. Carrying out a risk assessment is compulsory in many settings before an activity can take place, and carers should ensure that this is done and action is taken to minimise any risks identified.

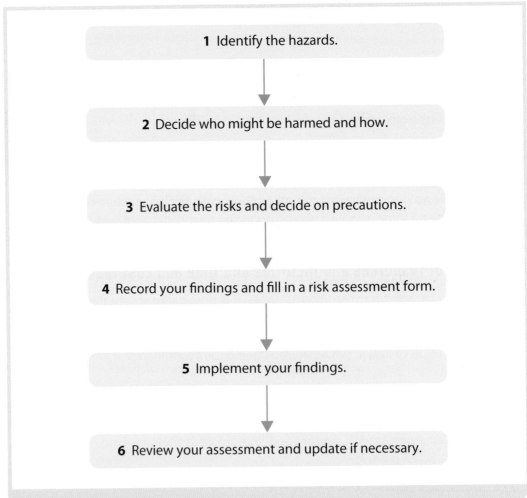

1 Identify the hazards.

2 Decide who might be harmed and how.

3 Evaluate the risks and decide on precautions.

4 Record your findings and fill in a risk assessment form.

5 Implement your findings.

6 Review your assessment and update if necessary.

Figure 12.1 The six steps of risk assessment.

Time for setting up, completing and clearing away

Planning activities means taking into account the amount of time needed to set up each activity and clear it away afterwards. Some may need very little, but more complicated ones might require a lot of time if there is a lot prepare. In addition, will service users need time and assistance to get to where the activity has been set up and prepare themselves? This needs to be taken into consideration and time allowed.

There also needs to be enough time for people to complete the tasks and to clear away within the time frame that has been allocated. For instance if cooking, time for washing up must be included, and gardening or painting needs time for cleaning and putting away implements. Planning and implementing an activity does not mean that the less pleasant bits of it are left for someone else to do!

Resources needed

There is nothing worse than having everyone ready to start a painting activity and then finding that there is no paper. There must be sufficient resources and the budget to acquire them. Resources required could range from cameras and computers, to CD players and cookery equipment. There also must be any required personal protective equipment (PPE) or clothing, such as goggles or dust masks.

Availability of location

Some activities may need a specific location, such as for a play or musical evening where a large performance space might be needed. Forward planning is essential to ensure that it is available for rehearsals and the performance dates. In addition, any hire costs must be budgeted for.

Selection of appropriate space

When deciding on activities there needs to be an appropriate space to do the activity, and if there are health and safety issues relating to space the number of service users who can do the activity may need to be limited. Sporting activities often need large spaces, either inside or outdoors.

Availability of helpers if needed

If a group activity is being organised, helpers may be needed to assist clients in participating in the activity or for safety reasons. Issues such as using public conveniences need to be planned for, as this affects things such as the right mix of male and female helpers being available.

Resources: appropriate equipment

Introduction

We have touched on the need to ensure that you have the right equipment when planning activities with service users. Here is some more specific guidance for common activities you might undertake.

Art and craft materials

Care workers need to ensure that service users can make use of the equipment available. Large brushes and non-spill containers can be useful, as can left-handed scissors and easy-grip equipment.

Musical instruments and CD players

Some musical instruments, such as drums and tambourines, can be played by people with little or no musical skill. Others, such as guitars and keyboards, do require a particular skill, so need to be chosen carefully for the individual service users. However, it is not necessary to use instruments to make music; a saucepan and wooden spoon can be used effectively as a drum, so be creative.

CD players are still used in many care settings to provide music, a fairly basic CD player is cheap to buy and some will have large controls which are easier for service users to use. Many people use MP3 players to listen to music, but might need help to download music. Costs and any appropriate licenses should always be taken into account when buying resources such as music players, CDs and downloads.

How will service users benefit from learning how to use a computer?

Cameras

Cameras can be cheap and simple to use, such as a disposable camera, or expensive and complex like digital single-lens reflex cameras costing hundreds of pounds. Digital cameras create instant pictures and can be downloaded onto a computer for storage or can be printed out. Many have a camcorder to record movies. The choice of camera to use will depend on cost and the ability of the people using it.

Computers

Most healthcare settings have computers and many individuals own their own desktop, laptop, netbook or tablet. Some service users use computers to communicate. There is also a lot of assistive software available to help with reading and writing activities. Other programs that might be of interest to clients include art and photographic manipulation software, music software and games.

Puzzle books and games

Puzzle books and games are useful and inexpensive resources. They are produced in a variety of type sizes and formats so that they can be enjoyed by people with different levels of ability.

Cookery ingredients and equipment

Choice of ingredients will depend on likes and dislikes, cultural preferences and allergies as well as cost. There is lots of equipment available for people who might need some assistance, ranging from food mixers to non-slip mats and easy-grip utensils.

Gardening equipment

Residential or nursing homes that have gardens may have gardening equipment that can be used by service users. Even homes with limited space and money can encourage the creation and maintenance of window boxes, hanging baskets or small herb gardens. Wheelchair users can still enjoy gardening if raised beds that they can reach are created. Remember, gardening is seasonal, so activities must be planned around the growing season and the weather.

Activity	Special equipment and art ideas

Go to www.pearsonhotlinks.co.uk for websites to research the different aids that could be used for cookery, gardening and art and craft. Try to find three of each and explain how they are used. Also visit Activity Village and Family Corner websites for free art activity ideas.

Appropriate clothing and protective equipment

For health and safety reasons it may be necessary to use special clothing or equipment for some of the planned activities. Aprons and gloves will be needed if service users are making food for other people to eat or for messy artwork to protect clothing. The manager of the setting can be asked about any health and safety issues if necessary.

Specialist helpers

It can be beneficial to have a specialist helper who either has expertise in an activity, or experience in working with adults or children with particular learning or physical disabilities. They can be a very valuable resource, providing specialist support and advising on how to plan and implement an activity.

Specialist resources

Introduction

In order to facilitate activities for some service users you may need to use specialist equipment. You need to know what is available, what is appropriate, and how to use the resources so you can help users with them. Some common resources are described here.

Large print items

People with impaired vision or whose eyesight has deteriorated over time may be very upset if they cannot read easily. Providing large print books can allow them to enjoy independent reading. Large print resources are available to buy or to borrow from libraries.

Talking books

Talking books are for people with a sight impairment or who find reading difficult for any other reason. The RNIB has a talking-book service. Subscribers can choose from almost 20,000 books, which then will be delivered to their door. The books are produced using DAISY audio which is an easy-to-use system.

Left-handed scissors

Left-handed scissors have the blades reversed so they cut properly if used with the left hand and the user can see what they are cutting.

Easy-grip tools

Easy-grip tools are designed to be used by people who struggle to grip or have limited movement in their hands and fingers. They are often moulded to fit the hand better and have textured surfaces.

Non-slip mats

Non-slip mats can have a variety of uses, from preventing slipping on a floor to stopping things from slipping when working at a table. They can also improve the stability of objects.

Computer touch pads or screens

Touch pads can be used by people who have difficulty moving their hands, wrists and arms as they require less movement and dexterity of the hands and fingers than a mouse. Touch screens, for example on a tablet or on some mobile phones, are also useful for people who have difficulty with hand movements.

Take it further

To find out more about talking books and DAISY follow the link to the RNIB website at www.pearsonhotlinks.co.uk.

Touch screens can give service users access to many resources.

Assessment activity 12.3

2C.P4 | 2C.P5 | 2C.M3 | 2C.D3

1 What factors do you think affect the selection, planning and implementation of creative and therapeutic activities in one health and social care setting? Create an illustrated poster showing them.

2a With a partner, select, plan and implement one suitable activity for an individual or a group in one health and social care setting. Although you are working together, the work you submit must be yours. You must ask permission to implement the activity and you should be supervised while you are doing it. Your supervisor should provide you with a written witness testimony of what you did. You need to provide a plan indicating:

- what the activity is
- who the activity is for (individual or group of how many?)
- how long it will take
- any extra help you might need

- all the resources required
- any health and safety issues you need to consider.

2b After you have implemented your activity, assess its selection, planning and implementation. Evaluate how successful it was, what went well, what did not go so well, how much it was enjoyed and what improvements you could make to the activity if you were to repeat it.

The evidence you need to submit is:

- your plan
- your witness statement from your supervisor
- your assessment and evaluation.

You may also submit photographs of what you did and/or the completed products if there were any, but you must make sure that you have permission to photograph any individuals who took part. You do not need permission if you are only submitting photographs of the work you completed.

Glossary

A

Abstract thinking – the ability to think about something that might not be there or even exist.

Accent – a way of pronouncing a language.

Access – the ways in which service users receive the services they need.

Accident – an incident, usually with negative results, that leads to harm, loss or damage to anyone in care, visitors or workers.

Acronyms – letters which stand for terms, such as SIDS, for sudden infant death syndrome.

Acute – usually short lasting and curable.

Adaptation – changing something, such as a service or device, so that it becomes suitable for a new situation or person.

Advocate – a person responsible for acting and speaking on behalf of someone who is unable to do so.

Aerobic – exercise that improves the efficiency of the heart and lungs in and the transportation of oxygen around the body.

Agent – a person who causes a change.

Alcohol dependence – anxiety and depression caused by alcohol can cause people to rely more on others as they may lose their jobs and develop financial and/or relationship problems/ mental health issues.

Anaemia – a medical condition in which there are too few red cells in your blood.

Antibiotic – a prescribed drug that kills or prevents the growth of bacteria.

Appropriate terms – ways of addressing individuals that do not offend them.

Atonement – something done to make up for an injury or wrong.

Autonomy – freedom to make your own decisions.

B

Beliefs – strongly held opinions.

Beneficence – doing good and not harm to an individual.

Body Mass Index (BMI) – a method of determining the proportion of body fat a person has, found by dividing a person's weight measured in kg by the square of their height in metres.

Bond – to form an attachment with a parent/carer.

Breathing – the action of taking air into the lungs and expelling it again.

C

Cardiovascular – cardio – to do with the heart, **vascular** – to do with the blood.

Cardiovascular – related to the heart and lungs.

Cervix – the entrance to the uterus from the vagina.

Chronic – usually long lasting and may be progressive.

Circumcision – male circumcision is the removal of some or all of the foreskin from the penis.

Civil liberties – people's rights and freedoms in society, such as the right to privacy.

Civil partnership – the legal equivalent of marriage between two people of the same gender.

Clarification – making something clear and understandable.

Code of practice – list of rules which state how health and social care must be delivered.

Cohabitation – where two people live together as partners but without a legal basis for their relationship, such as marriage or a civil partnership.

Cohabiting – people living together in an emotionally and/or sexually intimate relationship.

Colleague – a person you work with.

Communication – the exchange of information between people.

Confidential – information that is secret. It has been entrusted to only the person to whom it has been communicated. It is private and not open for general discussion or publication.

Context – the circumstances and setting in which an event occurs.

CPR – cardiopulmonary resuscitation, a means to resuscitate someone whose breathing or heartbeat has ceased.

Culture – the shared beliefs, values and customs of a group of people.

D

Data – this includes all information, whether it is facts, figures or images.

Deficiency (nutrition) – a lack of a nutrient that is necessary for wellbeing.

Dementia – an illness that affects the brain and memory, and makes you gradually lose the ability to think and behave normally.

Dental caries – the formation of dental cavities as a result of bacteria.

Depression – a mental disorder. It can be a chronic condition or a short-term one related to a life circumstance.

Deregistration – to be removed from a register, e.g. no longer allowed to run a residential care home.

Dialect – a way of speaking found only in a certain area or among a certain group or class of people.

Diffusion – the movement of molecules from an area of high concentration to an area of low concentration.

Digestive tract – the entire length of the gut, from the mouth to the anus.

Dignity – a calm and serious manner/style suitable for the situation and to treat someone with respect.

Disclose – making something known that was previously unknown or confidential.

Discriminate – to treat a person or group differently from others.

Discrimination – treating one group or individual less fairly than another.

Diuretic – causing the increased flow of urine.

Diverse – different.

Diversity – difference between people, in terms of gender, race, culture, age, sexuality, ability etc. Diversity should be acknowledged when delivering services.

Drama – involves acting out situations and characters, either improvised or following a script.

Duty of care – responsibility to keep people in our care safe from harm.

Dysfunction – when the physical or emotional aspects of a relationship are not working as expected.

E

Egocentric – seeing things from only your own perspective or viewpoint.

Emotional – to do with feelings.

Empathy – the ability to understand and share the feelings of another.

Emphysema – a condition of the lungs where the alveoli are damaged and enlarged, leading to breathlessness.

Employment prospects – the ability to gain and keep a job which has a good income and the chance of promotion.

Empower – to give service users control of their own lives.

Empowerment – enabling individuals to take responsibility for their own lives by making informed decisions.

Emulsify – to disperse the particles of one liquid evenly in another.

Enablement – ways and means to act independently.

Endorphins – hormones secreted in the brain that have a number of effects, including relieving pain and affecting mood.

Endurance – the ability to withstand prolonged use or strain.

Equality – equal treatment and respect.

Error – a mistake, a wrong decision or wrong action.

Eternity – an endless amount of time.

Ethical – morally right and decent; virtuous and honourable.

Ethics – a system of moral principles; the rules of conduct recognised in a group or culture.

Ethnicity – being part of a group sharing the same way of life and culture.

Evaluate – gather and review evidence, and make a judgement as to success.

F

Family – a social group made up of people who are connected or related to each other, by blood, marriage or **cohabitation**.

Fibromyalgia – a condition that causes widespread pain and severe fatigue.

Fine motor skill – the ability to control and coordinate the movements of the hands and fingers, e.g. writing, painting, tying shoelaces and holding a spoon.

Formal – polite, respectful or conventional.

Fulfilment – the opportunity to accomplish personal goals and use abilities to the full.

G

Gas exchange – when the body takes in oxygen and gets rid of carbon dioxide.

Gender – the social and cultural differences between male and female.

Gender role – a role that is determined by a person's gender.

Goals – what you want to achieve in the long term; the final outcome.

Gross motor skill – the ability to control and coordinate the movement of the large limbs of the body, e.g. crawling, walking and running.

H

Hazard – a situation or object that could cause damage or hurt.

Health and social care services – the services that provide health and social care.

Hierarchy – a list or diagram of things or people arranged in order of importance, with each level considered superior to the level below.

High biological value protein – a protein that provides the body with all eight essential amino acids.

Holistic – consideration of the whole – in this case, the whole person.

Homeostasis – from the Latin meaning to stay the same, homeostasis is the process by which the body maintains a stable environment in which cells can function.

HSE – Health and Safety Executive, the body that regulates health and safety in the workplace.

Hyper – too much.

Hypo – too little.

I

Immunisation – to make someone immune to a disease, usually by vaccination.

Incident – anything unusual that happens to individuals in care, visitors or workers.

Income – the amount of money people receive from their work, savings, pension or welfare benefits.

Independence – freedom from control by, or dependence on, others.

Informal – casual.

Infringing – going too far, or overstepping the mark.

Intellectual – ability to understand things and think intelligently.

Intercostal – between the ribs.

J

Jargon – technical words used by a professional person as a short way of saying things. These can be hard for non-professionals to understand.

Judgemental – making decisions or forming opinions on the basis of something such as appearance, without proper evidence, and being too critical.

K

Kosher – food that satisfies the requirements of Jewish law; for example, when an animal is slaughtered, all the blood must be drained from its body before it can be eaten.

L

Language development – the process which children go through as they learn to communicate with others using words and speech.

Legal requirement – something that has to be done by law.

Legislation – laws set by Parliament, which state how things should happen.

Life expectancy – the average number of years a person can expect to live from birth.

Life stages – a number of distinct phases people pass through during their lives.

Line manager – the person who is in charge of your department, group or project at work.

Literacy skills – abilities required to speak, read and write clearly, correctly and accurately.

Litigation – the act or process of bringing or contesting a legal action in court.

M

Malnutrition – lack of proper nutrition, caused by not having enough to eat, not eating enough of the right things, or being unable to use the food that one does eat.

Manual work – work that requires the use of physical skills.

Material possessions – objects which can be bought, but are non-essential to live, e.g. designer clothing.

Means testing – someone's income is assessed and taken into account to see if they are eligible for free or subsidised services. If income is over a certain level, they may have to pay for some or all of the cost of the service.

Menopause – the natural and permanent stopping of menstruation (periods), occurring usually between the ages of 45 and 55.

Mid-life crisis – a dramatic period of self-doubt caused by the passing of youth and the move into later adulthood.

Multicultural – having many different cultures.

N

Nation – a large community of people who share a common language, culture, ethnicity, descent, and/or history and usually a territory. In this unit 'nation' refers to the United Kingdom (UK).

Near miss – an event that could have caused harm, loss or damage, but did not.

Nephrons – the functional units of the kidney, each consisting of a microscopic filtering capsule and long convoluted tubule. There are up to 1.5 million nephrons in a kidney.

Non-manual work – work that depends primarily on mental skills.

Nutrient – the components of food that provide essential nutrition.

O

Obese – having a body mass index (BMI) of 30 or more.

Oestrogen – a hormone produced in a women's ovaries that controls the development of sexual characteristics and stimulates changes in the reproductive organs.

Offence – words that cause offence can include racist terms or terms that insult an individual's gender, disability or sexuality.

Osteoporosis – a medical condition in which your bones become weak and break easily.

P

Parallel play – children play alongside each other, but not together.

Pathogen – a microorganism that causes disease, such as bacteria and viruses.

Peer group – the social group a person belongs to which influences beliefs and behaviour.

Person-centred approach – working with individuals to identify their values, needs and expectations.

Personal space – the area immediately surrounding a person that they consider to be their own personal territory. People generally feel uncomfortable if others 'invade' this personal space. Everyone's idea of personal space is different.

Physical – to do with the body.

PIES – four groups of human growth and development: Physical, Intellectual, Emotional and Social.

Plaque – a harmful substance which forms on your teeth, which bacteria can live and breed in.

Poverty – having insufficient money to afford the essentials to live.

Predisposition – a tendency to suffer from a particular condition, hold a particular attitude, or act in a particular way.

Prejudice – an unreasonable feeling against a person or group or people.

Primary care – usually based in the community; provided for example by GPs, GP practice nurses, dentists, opticians.

Private – paid for by individuals either directly or by health insurance. Private health and social care organisations are monitored by the Care Quality Commission to ensure a high quality of care.

Proactive – creating or controlling a situation by causing something to happen rather than responding after something has happened.

Professional bodies – organisations that set standards for, and look after the interests of, their members, e.g. the Royal College of Nursing.

Proximity – the distance between someone or something.

Q

Questionnaire – a list of questions in writing, designed to gather information on a specific subject.

R

Regulations – rules in this context that state how services should be delivered.

Religion – a set of beliefs based on the idea of a sacred being.

Respect – showing recognition of the value of an individual.

Respiration – the process whereby living organisms produce energy. This involves the intake of oxygen and the release of carbon dioxide.

Rights – things that a person can claim they are free to do or that are due to them.

Risk assessment – investigating all hazards and offering precautions to prevent harm.

Role model – someone whose behaviour and/or attitudes people try to copy because they admire them.

Role play – similar to drama but more to do with taking the specific role of someone else and exploring reactions and motivations.

S

Safeguarding – a precautionary measure to prevent injury or abuse.

Screening – mass checking of sectors of the population for early signs of a particular disease or condition.

Secondary care – based in centres such as NHS Trusts, Ambulance Trusts, Mental Health Trusts and Children's Trusts.

Secular – something that has no connection to any religion or place of worship.

Self image – the mental picture we have of ourselves.

Self-concept – how you see or perceive yourself.

Self-esteem – how much you like, accept and respect yourself as a person, how you value yourself.

Serotonin – a neurotransmitter that affects mood and also has an effect on learning and cognition.

Sex – the physical and biological differences between male and female.

Slang – the use of informal words and expressions that are not considered standard in the speaker's dialect or language.

Social – to do with interacting with other people.

Social class – a group of people who share a common place in society.

Social development – the ability to interact with others in society and build relationships.

Social isolation – when people live without regular contact with other people, especially family and friends.

Social play – children play together, sharing their toys.

Solitary play – children play alone using their imagination and do not interact with other children.

Special educational needs (SEN) – refers to children with learning difficulties or disabilities that make it harder for them to learn or access education than most children of the same age.

Stamina – the heart's ability to work under strain.

Statistics – the collection, organisation and interpretation of numerical data. In health and social care, statistics could include things like the numbers of people suffering from particular conditions and the incidence of accidents.

Statutory – put in place by an Act of Parliament and funded by the government, although some charges are still made to individuals. The Department of Health has an overall responsibility to ensure high-quality services in all sectors of health and social care.

Stereotype – a fixed idea about an individual or group of people.

Stereotyping – thinking a group of people will all have the same attribute, for example, that all older people are deaf and forgetful.

Strength – the body's physical power.

Sudoku – a Japanese number puzzle. Sudoku means single number.

Superbug – a bacterial infection that is resistant to almost all antibiotics.

Suppleness – the body's ability to bend without damage.

Survey – a broad investigation of a subject, often informed by asking questions of a representative group.

Sympathy – feeling pity or sorrow for another person's feelings, emotions or distress.

T

Targets – short- and longer-term challenges to help you meet your goal.

Tertiary care – specialist care provided by, for example nursing homes, day care centres, oncology units.

Testosterone – a hormone produced by the testes that controls the development of male sexual characteristics.

Tolerance – the capacity to recognise and respect the beliefs or practices of others, even if we don't agree with them.

U

Underpin – to provide a supporting framework.

V

Vaccination – the introduction of a very small quantity of a weakened form of a disease into the body, usually by injection, to help the body develop antibodies to that particular disease.

Values – the ideas that lie behind and inform good health and social care practice.

Voluntary – usually funded by donations and money-raising activities. Volunteers do not receive payment. Volunteer organisations are monitored by local authorities and government inspectors to ensure that people are safe and cared for correctly.

Vulnerable – open to being hurt emotionally or physically.

W

Wealth – riches, lots of goods and money.

Weaning – introduction of solid food into the baby's diet from about six months of age.

Wellbeing – a sense of contentment.

A

BTEC Assessment Zone answers for Unit 1 and Unit 9

Unit 1 answers

Q: Identify the current life stages of John and Betty. (2 marks)
A: John is aged 31. He is in the early adulthood stage. Betty is 83. She is in the late adulthood stage.

Q: Give two examples of physical changes which occur in middle adulthood. (2 marks)
A: You could provide any of the following answers and you would receive one mark for each answer:

- Less testosterone
- Less oestrogen
- Live sperm production decreases
- Menstrual cycle stops
- Lower energy levels
- Skin loses elasticity
- Sight and hearing start to decline

Q: Explain how two different types of informal support could help Betty and Ray with their everyday living. (4 marks)
A: One type of informal support is family; their children could help Betty and Ray with everyday practical tasks such as housework, washing and bathing, and taking them to appointments, for example the opticians and doctors. They can also provide emotional support, such as reassurance that they are not being a burden, and including them in family decisions so they know they are loved and valued members of the family.

A second type of informal support is neighbours; they could help with practical tasks such as shopping and gardening, and also pop in to provide company so they don't feel isolated.

Q: Assess the possible impact attending the day centre may have for Betty and Ray's development. (8 marks)
A: Attending the day centre will have a positive impact on Betty and Ray's development by firstly providing company of their own age. By providing transport and a meeting place the day centre ensures that they do not have to stay at home every day due to their walking and mobility problems, so they will feel less lonely and less dependent on their family.

The day care centre will organise activities such as trips out, games, demonstrations, speakers and armchair exercise so they will continue to learn new skills and improve their knowledge, so keeping their brains active and their minds alert, as well as keep physically active so helping to maintain what mobility, strength and suppleness they still have. At the day centre Betty and Ray will have also access to other services, such as counsellors, so will have emotional support when needed, such as when a friend dies.

Attending the day centre may also have a negative impact on Betty and Ray, in that they may be upset and frustrated that they can no longer do such things on their own, or may not like some of the other older people who attend the centre, but overall the impact will be much more positive than negative.

Unit 9 answers

Q: Calculate Shaun's body mass index. (2 marks)
A: BMI = 122/(2 × 2) = 31.5kg/m²

Q: What does Shaun's BMI tell you about him? (1 mark)
A: Shaun's BMI shows that he is obese.

Q: Explain two ways in which drinking too much alcohol could affect Shaun's health and wellbeing. (4 marks)
A: Drinking too much alcohol means that Shaun is taking in extra calories and this will lead to more weight gain, so lead to problems such as joint problems, breathlessness and raised blood pressure.

Alcohol can also affect concentration, so Shaun may make mistakes at work due to lapses in attention.

Q: Assess how successful you think Shaun will be at losing weight, including discussing some strategies he could use to try to do this. (8 marks)
A: Shaun needs to go on a diet. He can find a suitable diet in several ways, such as consult his doctor who could refer him to a dietician, use the Internet or go to a Slimming Club. By setting himself some SMART targets, such as losing 2lbs a week, and changing his eating and drinking habits so the weight comes off gradually, any loss is more likely to stay off. He needs to ask his family to support him in this by all agreeing to eat more healthily. If there is no unhealthy food and lots of healthy snacks such as carrot sticks and fruit in the house he is less likely to be tempted to stray from his diet. Instead of going out for lunch in a pub or restaurant on Sundays he could take his family for a healthy family picnic so he can stick to his diet. This could be as part of some form of exercise, such as a bike ride or long walk, so the exercise helps burn off calories.

He could join a gym so instead of sitting watching television on a Saturday he can be getting some exercise to burn off more calories. He could set himself an exercise target of running a half marathon to raise money for charity by the end of the year, so he has something to aim at and keep himself motivated.

Shaun could also offer to be the designated driver for the pub quiz so he is not tempted to drink alcohol and ask his friends to discourage him from eating crisps or other nibbles at the quiz, explaining that he is on a diet and in training. Asking his work colleagues for support by telling them he is on a diet and asking them not to temp him with unhealthy lunches out or offering him their snacks, will help. If he is still struggling he could join a slimming club, for encouragement from others with the same problem and new strategies to help him stick to his diet from the club leader.

By adopting these strategies Shaun should be able to lose weight. The support of his family, friends and work colleagues, the setting of realistic targets, will help him be successful.

Disclaimer: These practice questions and sample answers are not actual exam questions and have been provided as a practice aide only. They should be used as practice material only and should not be assumed to reflect the format or coverage of the Edexcel external test.